CONTEMPORARY CASES IN RET
MANAGEMENT

WITHDRAWN

CONTEMPORARY CASES IN RETAIL OPERATIONS MANAGEMENT

Edited by

Brenda M. Oldfield, Ruth A. Schmidt, Ian Clarke, Cathy Hart and Malcolm H. Kirkup

MACMILLAN
Business

First published 2000 by
MACMILLAN PRESS LTD
Houndmills, Basingstoke, Hampshire RG21 6XS
and London
Companies and representatives
throughout the world

ISBN 0–333–76480–3 hardcover
ISBN 0–333–76481–1 paperback

A catalogue record for this book is available
from the British Library.

This book is printed on paper suitable for recycling and
made from fully managed and sustained forest sources.

10 9 8 7 6 5 4 3 2 1
09 08 07 06 05 04 03 02 01 00

Typeset by T&A Typesetting, Rochdale

Editing and origination by
Aardvark Editorial, Mendham, Suffolk

Printed and bound in Great Britain by
Antony Rowe Ltd, Chippenham, Wiltshire

CONTENTS

PART 1	OPERATIONS MANAGEMENT

CONTENTS

CONTENTS

LIST OF FIGURES

TEACHING NOTES

LIST OF TABLES

TEACHING NOTES

CASE EDITORS AND CONTRIBUTORS

Editors

Brenda M. Oldfield
Research Assistant
Department of Retailing and Marketing, Faculty of Management and Business, the Manchester Metropolitan University, Aytoun Building,
Aytoun Street, Manchester M1 3GH

Ruth A. Schmidt
Principal Lecturer
Department of Retailing and Marketing, the Manchester Metropolitan University, Faculty of Management and Business, Aytoun Street, Manchester M1 3GH

Ian Clarke
Booker Professor of Marketing
The Business School, Durham University, Old Hall Lane, Durham DH1 3LB

Cathy Hart
Sainsbury Retail Fellow
Loughborough University Business School, Ashby Road, Loughborough, Leicestershire LE11 3TU

Malcolm H. Kirkup
Senior Lecturer
Department of Commerce, Birmingham Business School,
University of Birmingham B15 2TT

Contributors

Nicholas Alexander
Professor of Retail Management
School of Service Industries, Bournemouth University, Talbot Campus, Poole BH12 5BB

Angela M. Arnold
Department of Consumer Studies, Glasgow Caledonian University,
1 Park Drive, Glasgow G3 6LP

John Austin
Department of Retailing and Marketing, the Manchester Metropolitan University, Aytoun Building, Aytoun Street, Manchester M1 3GH

Grete Birtwistle
Department of Consumer Studies, Glasgow Caledonian University, Park Campus,
1 Park Drive, Glasgow G3 6LP

Adelina Broadbridge
Institute for Retail Studies, University of Stirling, Stirling FK9 4LA

Richard Cuthbertson
OXIRM Templeton College, Oxford University, Kennington, Oxon OX1 5NY

Christopher J. Dutton
Department of Service Sector Management, Brighton University,
49 Darley Road, Eastbourne BN20 7UR

John Fernie
Professor of Retail Marketing
School of Management, Heriot-Watt University, Riccarton, Edinburgh EH14 4AS

Paul Gaffney
School of Business, Oxford Brookes University, Wheatley Campus,
Wheatley, Oxford OX33 1HX

Hanne Gardner
Department of Retailing and Marketing, the Manchester Metropolitan University,
Aytoun Building, Aytoun Street, Manchester M1 3GH

Helene Hill
Department of Retailing and Marketing, the Manchester Metropolitan University,
Aytoun Building, Aytoun Street, Manchester M1 3GH

Sandra Hogarth-Scott
Management Centre, University of Bradford, Emm Lane, Bradford BD9 4JL

Gaynor Lea-Greenwood
Department of Clothing Design and Technology, the Manchester Metropolitan University, Hollings Faculty, Old Hall Lane, Manchester M14 6HR

David Leaver
Department of Retailing and Marketing, the Manchester Metropolitan University,
Aytoun Building, Aytoun Street, Manchester M1 3GH

Morag M. McLean
Department of Consumer Studies, Glasgow Caledonian University,
1 Park Drive, Glasgow G3 6LP

Christopher M. Moore
Department of Consumer Studies, Glasgow Caledonian University, Park Campus,
1 Park Drive, Glasgow G3 6LP

David Muskett
Department of Retailing and Marketing, the Manchester Metropolitan University,
Aytoun Building, Aytoun Street, Manchester M1 3GH

CASE EDITORS AND CONTRIBUTORS

Mandi Partridge
Department of Retailing and Marketing, the Manchester Metropolitan University,
Aytoun Building, Aytoun Street, Manchester M1 3GH

Mike Pretious
School of Management, University of Abertay Dundee, Bell Street, Dundee DD1 1HG

John Temperley
Leeds Business Schoool, Leeds Metropolitan University,
Calverley Street, Leeds LS1 3HE

Rosemary Varley
School of Business, University of Huddersfield, Queensgate, Huddersfield HD1 3DH

Paul Walley
Warwick Business School, University of Warwick, Coventry CV4 7AL

Ian Walters
Bristol-Myers Co. Ltd, Swakeleys House, Milton Road, Uxbridge, Middx UB10 8NS

Gary Warnaby
Department of Retailing and Marketing, the Manchester Metropolitan University,
Aytoun Building, Aytoun Street, Manchester M1 3GH

Philippa Ward
Department of Business and Finance, Cheltenham and Gloucester College of Higher
Education, The Park, Cheltenham GL50 2QF

Helen Wright
Department of Retailing and Marketing, the Manchester Metropolitan University,
Aytoun Building, Aytoun Street, Manchester M1 3GH

FOREWORD

The retail industry is one of the largest, most dynamic and innovative in Britain, it is an industry that is central to communities but also plays a vital role in the national economy. Retailing is affected by people's developing tastes, by changing buying habits, by the nation's economic fortunes and the consumer spending that ensues.

Retailing provides employment for some 2.9 million people, around 11 per cent of the total UK workforce. It is important to remember that although the fortunes of individual businesses can move up and down as is to be expected in such a competitive environment, the sector as a whole continues to prosper. In the twelve months to December 1998 the retail sector created 57,400 new jobs according to the Office for National Statistics (ONS), thus retailing jobs accounted for one in six of the jobs created during this period.

Retail's position as a major player in the UK's economy is another defining characteristic of the industry. In 1996, retail turnover represented 24 per cent of GDP by expenditure and approximately 8 per cent by output. Internationalization is another emerging and important driver for the industry with many companies entering into strategic alliances and joint ventures.

The diversity of the sector combined with its everyday role in providing quality services are great strengths. Retailers are constantly redefining products to satisfy their markets – while balancing the need for mass appeal with the requirement to make sure every customer is treated as an individual. The provision of a wide range of goods, expanding opening hours and introducing innovative services are all responses to this fundamental business requirement. The breadth and variety of locations and formats retailers use to trade illustrates the complexity of the market they seek to serve. ONS Retailing Review (1998) found that 320,000 businesses make up the industry, ranging from the corner shop to the superstore. It is important not just to understand the size and composition of the industry, but also to appreciate how this impacts on the policies and behaviour of retail businesses.

Consumers are becoming more sophisticated and have higher expectations in terms of quality and choice. It is an exciting world where nothing stands still for long and retailers have to respond quickly and appropriately to new and changing demands. These requirements for business survival and success mean that many retail companies have become leading practitioners in managing change. Innovative supply change management using the developments in information systems like EDI provide another example of retail's ability to be flexible and adaptable. It is in the nature of retail businesses to take things and to make them work.

This large and successful industry is underpinned by investment in property, products and above all, people. Patterns of employment are continuing to change. People no longer stay in the same job for their entire working lives. People within retail develop highly transferable skills that can be used in various areas of the business. This flexibility is the envy of many other sectors.

Retail's emphasis on customer service means that retailers recognize they have to equip their people to deliver this. According to a recent British Retail Consortium survey of firms employing 400,000 staff and across all sectors, the industry spends £455m on training each year, which represents 2.4 per cent of the total retail wage bill. For 68 per cent of retailers the main reason for investing in training is the improvement in customer service that can result.

The individuals who will manage the future of the retail sector will need to have a real understanding of the operational issues that face the business. It is these that will ultimately inform the strategic debates about 'what business is this company in? What does this company do and how can it be achieved?' The case studies in the text provide an excellent opportunity to examine real life industry issues. As well as providing information about the business, readers of the case studies will also become aware of the exciting career opportunities within the sector. Understanding the kind of service and environment customers want and expect it is easy to see that success depends on having the right people. The diversity of the sector means there are rewarding careers for those who like to deal with people face to face but also many ways of making an impact behind the scenes, in finance and IT for example.

Retailing gets under the skin – hopefully these case studies will provide the first itch.

ANNETTE THOMAS
CORTCO

PREFACE

BRENDA M. OLDFIELD, RUTH A. SCHMIDT, IAN CLARKE, CATHY HART AND MALCOLM H. KIRKUP

BACKGROUND TO THE BOOK

The last two decades have seen significant changes in the role of the retail industry within the UK economy and in its relationship with higher education. Successive governments have worked to redefine the role of education, directing emphasis and financial backing towards initiatives which help develop lifelong learning, transferable skills or competencies of relevance to industry. Clearly, as both major drivers of economic change, and as powerful providers in the employment market, retail and service organizations play a critical part in the development of skills, as well as utilizing them in their own development.

Since the launch of the first full undergraduate degree in retailing in the UK, at the Manchester Metropolitan University in 1984, much has been done to underpin the academic base of retailing as a discipline of study. For example, there are now at least 23 UK higher education establishments offering under-graduate retail degree courses, numerous postgraduate and post-experience courses and retail electives on wider business-related programmes. The willing-ness and desire to collaborate with the retail industry is a feature which is common to many of these initiatives. Within this collaboration, however, it is arguably fair to say that the sector has found it difficult to establish itself as an attractive occupation for university graduates. Ironically, retailers have often found graduates lacking in the skills and knowledge base required early on in their careers to make them able to contribute more effectively to the business; skills which serve to underpin retail development in the longer term.

In parallel with these academic developments, a number of leading UK retailers assembled in 1986 to form a collaborative initiative, the Consortium of Retail Teaching Companies (CORTCO), with the aim of raising awareness of retailing as a graduate career, and as a means to enhance the image of the industry. This initiative was both popular and successful, resulting in the expansion of the group. In 1999 membership of CORTCO consisted of eleven companies:

Arcadia	Debenhams	J Sainsbury plc
B&Q	Kingfisher plc	Tesco plc
The Boots Company	John Lewis Partnership	Waitrose Ltd
C&A	Marks & Spencer plc	

Co-operation between CORTCO and the academic community was an important feature of the initiative from the beginning. Initially the collaboration between CORTCO and academia focused on a series of case conferences aimed at a relatively modest audience of practitioners and academics. Later, in 1997, a new vehicle was identified to develop a larger collection of cases for the benefit of a far wider audience of retail educators. A collaboration between Loughborough University and CORTCO led to the publication of a retail case text (Hart *et al.*, 1997) presenting 18 cases on operational aspects of retailing.

In 1996 funding was obtained from the Department for Education and Employment (DfEE) as part of their Discipline Network Programme to enable the creation of a retail education network – the Retail Education Group (REG) – the purpose of which was to develop co-operative links between retail education providers and enhance the employability of retail graduates. Additional match-funding was given by CORTCO to further support this initiative; to be achieved through the joint development of teaching materials between representatives of retail education institutions and individual retail companies. The project was co-ordinated by a partnership between three universities across the UK, all of them providers of graduates in retailing to the industry: the Manchester Metropolitan University, Loughborough University and Glasgow Caledonian University. The project resulted in a significant link-up between academic and industry networks, incorporating collaboration between a diverse range of institutions illustrated in Figure 1.

As a result of this underpinning, it has been possible for members of the REG network to produce case study teaching materials in co-operation with individual CORTCO companies aimed at enhancing the development of the personal transferable skills of graduates. This book represents a compilation of the outcomes of the REG project. It is intended to facilitate the wide dissemination of these outcomes to the broader community of retail educators, both in industry and academia, to support their work in developing graduates' work-related skills and knowledge base.

The cases presented in the text demonstrate typical day-to-day management problems. They have a significant practical, problem-solving flavour to give experience in the analysis and evaluation of retail business situations. They also have clear learning outcomes to help develop an awareness of the core competencies required by graduate employers. In developing the cases the focus was on operational rather than wider strategic issues so as to aid the development and transference of the core skills most likely to be needed by graduate entrants to retail management positions. The project outcomes collated here illustrate the fast-moving nature of the retail environment. Each case study evolved initially by inviting retail educators to submit abstracts for case study development. Such abstracts and ideas were subsequently considered by CORTCO member companies, thereby ensuring that retailer views on important current issues were addressed and facilitating close collaboration between an academic team and a retail partner. As a result, the issues presented are topical and offer a genuine insight into the duties of retail managers whose role the students are required to adopt in working with the case materials.

CORTCO COMPETENCIES AND LEARNING OBJECTIVES

Arguably, any meaningful kind of retail education must be responsive to the changing needs of retailers. In order to prepare students for a career in retail management, an awareness of the relevant competencies is crucial. However, in contrast to more established academic disciplines, such as financial or strategic management, the absence until very recently in retail education of retail-specific

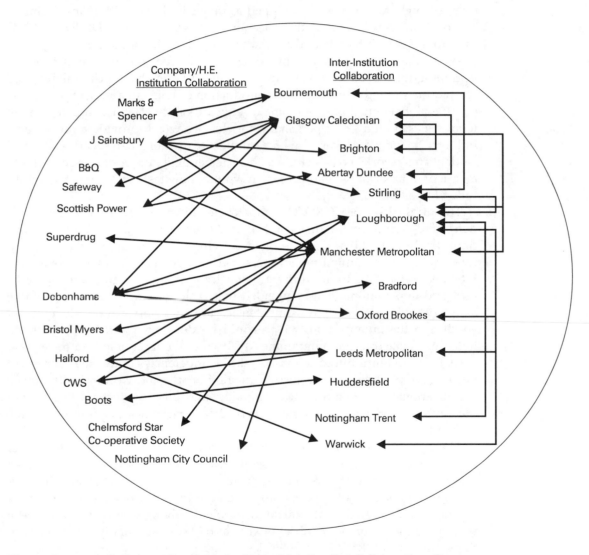

Figure 1   Collaborative links facilitated by the Retail Education Group

teaching material, particularly for operational issues, hindered curriculum and subsequently competence development.

Despite the efforts made by higher education providers to address the needs of retailers, recruitment officers in industry are still prone to question whether the retail specific programmes fully achieve what they set out to do. Despite the availability of retail management graduates, retailers continue to recruit graduates from any discipline. A key issue emerging is the extent to which retail degrees develop the competencies of prime importance to retailers. This broad recruitment strategy had suggested that the graduates from specialist retail degrees might not be as well equipped as they should be, with many failing to demonstrate these skills in the selection process. The REG/DfEE/CORTCO link-up therefore aimed to address and help resolve this situation.

While the means of dissemination have changed and evolved, from the beginning the means for achieving the CORTCO aims have primarily centred around the sharing of expertise and production of relevant and up-to-date case study material aimed at developing a range of jointly established core competencies. Based on a set of personal competencies which provide a broad retail industry standard towards which higher education, career advisors and students may work, a core feature is the transferability of these competencies to a variety of tasks and situations which would allow fast-track entry to a multitude of retail careers.

The original set of CORTCO competencies identified five areas: self-confidence and personal strength; leadership and teamwork; planning and organization; analytical skills and problem solving; and human relations and influencing. The foundation of personal competence in these areas was intended to form the framework from which the student or graduate would be recruited into retailing. It was intended that each individual retailer would be able to build on these base competencies and develop a more detailed set specific to the organization, which could be developed further through in-house graduate training programmes. In 1998, in the light of additional experience, CORTCO introduced a revised set of competencies under the four broad headings of personal effectiveness; managing people and working with others; organizational ability and creative thinking; and business focus. (A full set of the revised 1998 version of the CORTCO Competencies is provided in the Appendix.)

There are two key differences from the original list. First, the addition of business focus, an attribute of successful retail managers, emphasizing the need for commercial competence (such as customer focus, commercialism and business awareness, and job motivation). Second, a reduced role is assigned to the competence area analytical skills and problem solving, which has now been placed within the broader subset of critical thinking and analytical consideration within the CORTCO competencies.

The latter are skills traditionally emphasized in university work, and the diminished emphasis placed on this area by CORTCO points to the underlying emerging issue of how the responsibility for competence development can be better shared between the higher education provider and employer. In our view, the issue is not so much a conflict in expectations and objectives, but, who is best equipped to develop which specific competencies – retailers or academic institutions? Leadership and people skills may be best developed in the work environment whereas other skills such as communication, IT, achievement orientation, planning and organizing could have greater emphasis during academic study.

While the appropriate balance is likely to be the subject of debate for some time to come, there is a clear shared belief in the value of competence development. Thus the philosophical foundation of both CORTCO and the REG project lies in the belief that working with case studies enables students to develop the full range of competencies required both at university and in preparation for their future role in the retail environment. In this, a distinction can be made between those skills which will be largely developed through the unique process of working with the case study material in the teaching/learning context and those which are related to case content.

Table 1 serves as on overview of how, in this text, case content is related to the CORTCO competencies.

It should come as no surprise that, in terms of content, the great majority of cases places emphasis on the development of organizational ability and creative thinking, with special emphasis on the subcategory critical thinking and analytical consideration, thus reflecting the traditional role of universities. However, the categories managing people and working with others, as well as business focus, also receive a great deal of attention, illustrating the practical vocational outlook retail educators are taking in their teaching. The very wide range of competencies that can be developed through individual cases illustrates the value of case studies for communicating complexity and offering a realistic picture of the knowledge and skills needed in retailing. The cases should, therefore, help develop the skills required by young retail managers. With this objective in mind, it is envisaged that the cases can be used equally well with part-time students working in retail organizations as with full-time students, both on undergraduate and postgraduate courses. In point of fact, we are aware that some of the cases are already being used by trainers within retail companies to complement existing training materials.

Indeed, the development of retail management as an emerging management discipline, through its accessibility, provides many new opportunities for competence development in the form of role play, interactive retailer workshops, and problem solving 'live' management scenarios. While the complex nature of the generic CORTCO skills may suggest that the necessary foundation cannot be explicitly taught through focusing on case content alone, there is evidence that their development can be facilitated via a variety of teaching approaches.

In this text, competencies are developed in two ways. First the content of the cases helps develop specific competencies by enabling a student to try them out in a 'practice run', allowing them to mentally 'walk through' a situation they would be likely to encounter in the early days of their retail career. In this way students can realistically mirror the actions of their retail manager counterparts. Second, the teaching/learning situation can be set up in such a way that students are placed in a very real and challenging teamwork situation very

Table 1   Case study content mapped to CORTCO competencies

Competencies — *Case no.*

Competencies	1	2	3	4	5	6	7	8	9	10	11	12	13	14	15	16	17	18	19	20	21
(1) Personal effectiveness																					
Personal presence																					
Emotional resilience																					
Assertiveness				✓				✓													
Self-confidence								✓													
Task management							✓		✓					✓							
Flexibility/adaptability																					
Self-development																					
(2) Managing people and working with others																					
Team working and awareness					✓	✓	✓	✓	✓	✓			✓	✓		✓		✓	✓		
Team leading					✓	✓	✓	✓						✓				✓			
Communication skills			✓	✓	✓													✓			
Managing and coaching for performance									✓												
(3) Organizational ability and creative thinking																					
Planning and organizing	✓	✓	✓	✓		✓	✓		✓	✓	✓	✓	✓	✓	✓		✓	✓	✓		
Forward planning	✓	✓		✓			✓		✓		✓	✓	✓					✓	✓		
Critical thinking and analytical consideration	✓	✓	✓	✓			✓		✓	✓	✓	✓	✓	✓				✓			✓
Decisiveness			✓						✓		✓	✓		✓							✓
Innovation and strategic thinking									✓		✓									✓	✓
(4) Business focus																					
Customer focus										✓											
Commercialism and business awareness				✓			✓		✓				✓		✓	✓	✓	✓		✓	✓
Job motivation																	✓	✓	✓	✓	✓

similar to that encountered in retailing. Students can work on the cases in small teams to develop skills and gain new insights. Groups can be empowered and each team may be directed to investigate all or only some of the questions in the case. This process will enable students to demonstrate leadership skills consistent with the situation. Realism can be enhanced by introducing the additional pressures of role-play, presentations, deadlines and assessment on individual as well as team performance. However, while in-class application can greatly enhance competency development it is also hoped that distance learning students will be able to make use of the cases for self-tuition. This may be particularly relevant to part-time students who are already employed in retailing and therefore have ample opportunity to acquire the case application-driven competencies in their everyday working lives.

To aid both students and tutors, the text aims to provide a comprehensive resource, comprising the full cases complemented by detailed sets of application questions at the end of each case. The case questions, together with the respective degree of prior work experience, can be used to customize the application to undergraduate, postgraduate and post-experience courses. It is intended that the cases be applied in a highly flexible manner and readers are encouraged to experiment. The outline teaching notes provided in the second half of the text serve to offer guidance to tutors on how to make the best use of the material in the classroom context. They also set out the intended relationship between case content objectives and CORTCO core competency development, give outline answers and references to guide further reading.

THE STRUCTURE OF THE BOOK: THEMES AND COMPETENCIES

This text intentionally focuses on operational issues, rather than those of a strategic nature. The rationale for this was, and still is, the need for a counterbalance to the heavy concentration on strategic planning and management stressed by so many retail courses, textbooks and other case study books. The objective of the initiative is, therefore, to provide cases which highlight operational management issues, giving the opportunity for students to appreciate the importance of, and to provide real-life scenarios in which to develop, the skill-based competencies which are important in retail businesses and that are central to their ability to contribute to the success and development of companies in the first few years of their working life after graduation.

Unique Features of the Book

This text has two unique features. First, not only did we choose to classify the cases in terms of two business themes: operations management and marketing planning and management, but, perhaps most important, we have clearly shown the link between the cases and the groups of competencies developed by the case scenarios (see Table 1). In presenting the cases in this dual way we hope that the book will demonstrate the contribution the skills or competencies identified by the industry can make to the success of the retail business. This two-dimensional structure should also make it more accessible to teachers and students alike.

The second unique feature is the inclusion of outline teaching notes into the case book itself, rather than in a separate volume. We feel that such notes will not only be useful in helping the tutor to structure class discussions, but will also enable students themselves to get the most out of the cases, helping them prepare for class sessions and also to aid follow-up work. Specifically, the teaching notes identify the competencies developed by each case, outline the main business issues that they exemplify, and give references to pertinent materials for further wider reading. Such an overt dual focus, we believe, will better enable users of the cases to appreciate the influence of competencies on successful operational management – the principal objective of the Retail Education Group initiative.

REFERENCE

Hart, C., Kirkup, M., Preston, D., Rafiq, M., and Walley, P. (1997) *Cases in Retailing: Operational Perspectives*. Oxford: Blackwell.

ACKNOWLEDGEMENTS

This text would not have been possible without the support of CORTCO retailers; the editors would like to acknowledge the contributions of those CORTCO company representatives who facilitated the 'matching' of author teams with collaborating companies and, at a later stage, managers and employees of those companies who so freely gave of their time helping with data and interviews. Special thanks are due to Jay Snaith, the Chairman of CORTCO who has been a driving force behind the collaborative case study concept.

Particular thanks go the Department for Education and Employment and their foresight in setting up the Discipline Network initiative which funded the Retail Education Group Project and without whose help a major part of this work would not have been practicable.

The editors would also like to extend a thank you to a number of other people who have assisted in a variety of ways to bring this project to fruition: Professor Peter Jones and Professor Barry Davies, Anne-Marie Macdonald, Julie Ratcliffe and Philippa Ward.

PART 1

OPERATIONS MANAGEMENT

CASE 1

RETAILING IN TWO CURRENCIES

NICHOLAS ALEXANDER

The author would like to thank Paul A. Smith, Euro Project Manager, Marks & Spencer plc, for his invaluable help and support with this case study.

The information in this case study is based on real incidents, experiences, planning needs and objectives. However, in order to present a workable case, only some issues have been presented for consideration. Managing the introduction of the euro is a complex management issue which involves many aspects of a retailer's business.

INTRODUCTION

Seven committee members were present. Sir Thomas Arnold was in the Chair. Around the horseshoe table sat Clive Betts, Matthew Carrington, Quentin Davies, Nigel Forman, Barry Legg and Stephen Timms. The committee had been considering the issue of European Monetary Union (EMU) for some time, but today for the first time they were to consider it from an explicitly retail perspective.

It was Monday 13 May 1996. For a retailer such as Marks & Spencer, Monday is more usually concerned with the reports of trading activity from the previous week. However, on this particular day, three representatives had been called as witnesses before the Treasury Committee of the House of Commons. The three representatives were very senior personnel: Sir Richard Greenbury was Chairman of Marks & Spencer plc, and his two companions were Robert Colvill, Executive Director of Finance and Keith Bogg, the Divisional Director of Information Technology and Physical Distribution. The issue in question was worthy of such senior representation.

Establishing an Agenda

European Monetary Union is not a new concept. It is, in many respects, essential if a genuine single market is to be established within Europe. However, despite the legislation surrounding the establishment of the Single European Market in 1992, the European Union still laboured with a collection of national currencies and hence exchange rates, which ultimately restricted commercial integration and activity. This was changing, and the Maastricht Treaty had placed in motion a process of monetary union which was generating increasing attention by the summer of 1996. It was attracting increasing attention, not least because a surprising number of businesses in the EU had done very little thinking about it. What was more, a disproportionally large number of those businesses were based in the UK.

One of the reasons very little had been done in the UK was the political impasse. The UK had a government and an official opposition who would rather the whole issue went quietly away. The problem was that monetary union was no longer being talked about in the abstract in the rest of Europe but was definitely on the agenda. British business seemed less aware than its European counterparts of what EMU was and the type of benefits it might provide. When Andersen Consulting carried out a survey of leading European businesses in 1995, they found that, while 87 per cent of French businesses agreed that EMU would benefit business, only 61 per cent of UK businesses agreed (Andersen, 1996). Indeed, a sizeable number (26 per cent) of UK businesses were undecided, suggesting that the issue was still not high enough on the UK corporate agenda to have prompted the development of a considered opinion.

A MEMORANDUM FROM MARKS & SPENCER

Before the representatives from Marks & Spencer arrived at the House of Commons a memorandum, dated 1 April 1996, had been submitted by the company to the Treasury Committee (House of Commons, 1996). In it, the company outlined its major concerns. The document had a number of main headings: 'Our Assumptions', 'Transactions with the Customers', 'Transactions with Suppliers and Financial Intermediaries', 'Transactions with Ourselves', 'Practical Issues', and 'The Economic Consequences Relevant to Marks & Spencer'.

Working Assumptions

The company's assumptions were fourfold. They assumed that the 'core European' countries, as they described them – France, Belgium, Germany and the Netherlands – would engage in monetary union and that some international Marks & Spencer outlets would have to contend with the customer-associated issues of monetary union within the core market group. They assumed that the Republic of Ireland and Spain were also likely to join. Marks & Spencer assumed the UK would not be part of the founding group, but that economic policy would take the country to the point where its economic credentials would enable it to meet membership qualifications. At this time, the company had company-owned outlets in all of the core markets except Germany, a market in which it was to open a site later in the year, while the Republic of Ireland and

Spain were both markets in which Marks & Spencer had outlets. They assumed that their franchise operations in Portugal, Greece and Austria would also need to be considered in the light of monetary union. Since that time franchising operations have been established by Marks & Spencer in Finland.

The memorandum went on to consider the issues which the company would face in core markets in the EU and in the UK, because the company believed it would have to assume the UK might join EMU in 1999 or in a in a second wave thereafter.

The Point of Sale

The timetable for monetary union stipulated that from 1 January 2002 to 30 June 2002, both the national currency and the euro would be legal tender in participating countries (see Table 1.1). This meant that retailers would have to accept payment in both currencies during this period. Coping with this situation was going to put retailers under pressure.

Table 1.1   **Timetable for EMU as established by European Commission in 1995**

Phase A: 1 January 1998–31 December 1998

During the first six months, the European Council will name those countries who will be participating in EMU. The consequence of this will be the establishment of the European Central Bank (ECB) and the European System of Central Banks (ESCB). The ECB will replace the European Monetary Institute (EMI). Likewise, national governments will introduce legislation which gives the euro equal status with national currencies from 1 January 1999.

Phase B: 1 January 1999–31 December 2001

Exchange rates will be fixed from 1 January 1999. This will enable the euro to become a currency in its own right but it will not be available in notes and coins. Commercial banks will hold balances with central banks in euros. Governments will issue new public debt in euros. It is also anticipated that businesses and financial markets will move to denominating transactions in euros as they communicate with each other. It is anticipated that consumer transactions will occur in national currencies during this period.

Phase C: 1 January 2002–30 June 2002

This is the period of dual currency and the changeover from the use of national currency notes and coins to euro notes and coins. Euro notes and coins will be introduced and thereby coexist with national currency. In this period, prices and transactions will move to the euro. At the end of this period, national currencies will cease to be legal tender.

Source: Alexander and Hutchinson, 1997

Pricing

As far as transactions with customers were concerned, Marks & Spencer identified a number of areas where they envisaged problems would arise. These problems would come in the form of extra activities and disruption within the business and confusion among customers. Pricing was an important area where considerable confusion and disruption could occur.

As any student of retail management will tell you, prices are displayed at a number of points within the store. They may be found on the item which is offered for sale, on a shelf edge or on a display rack, at the point of sale and on till receipts. This meant that retailers would have to consider how they wished to display prices in both currencies and what legal requirements would be introduced to protect the public from unscrupulous retailers abusing the situation. In Marks & Spencer, pricing policy meant that clothing prices were displayed on the racks and shelves but not on the merchandise, while some food products, such as those in the cold chain, were priced on the product by item and by weight.

Marks & Spencer recommended that, while they recognized that both prices should be shown at the display and at the till, they did not support the idea that items should be priced in both currencies. Likewise, they believed that unit pricing by weight was an issue which needed particular consideration.

Payment Systems

While the idea of a cashless society has been around for some time, cash remains an important mechanism by which to purchase goods and services. In some retail outlets, such as convenience stores, cash is the most practical means of payment. In other outlets, where large ticket items are the norm, other payment methods will be favoured, but cash remains an important method of payment.

In their evidence to the Treasury Committee, Marks & Spencer noted the problems they envisaged with cash handling during the changeover period. They noted the need for two till drawers during the changeover period to handle two sets of coins and notes.

As far as cheques and plastic payment systems were concerned, the company considered this would be more of a problem for the banks than for the retailers. That is, it was the banks' responsibility to establish what systems were required and how credit and debit slips would be configured. For the retailer, at the point of sale, there would not be the same handling problems as there would be with cash. A cheque and the payment slips used with plastic cards could be suitably configured to deal with the issue of two currencies.

Marks & Spencer's memorandum noted that ATM (automatic teller machines) were often located in or near retail outlets. They assumed that these would be stocked with euros in the absence of good quality national currency notes during the period of the dual currency. Marks & Spencer's concern on this issue was the rapid replacement of old notes with new notes in order to accelerate the changeover period and reduce the time at which high volumes of both national and euro notes would be in circulation. While it was not a concern of Marks & Spencer, it is also worth noting, that there is the practical problem that ageing notes will only cause ATMs to breakdown. During the changeover period, new national currency notes would not be printed.

The company's main concern was with till software and hardware. The company estimated that the cost could be £100m for hardware, a further £10m for software and involve considerable management time. They noted the role of IT companies and the fact that they would be under considerable pressure to supply retailers with advice and other support during the changeover period.

Suppliers, Financial Intermediaries and Internal Marks & Spencer Considerations

For a company like Marks & Spencer, which operates in a number of markets throughout Europe, the introduction of the euro was going to demand changes at the point of sale irrespective of which countries did or did not join EMU. Somewhere in Europe, they would be dealing with the challenge. The question was how many markets would be affected? Likewise, with respect to the company's internal systems, and their relationship with other commercial organizations, the company would have to be euro-capable. The company would have to come to terms with dealing in euros whether the UK was in or not.

In April 1996, Marks & Spencer did not see considerable problems arising with their suppliers and financial intermediaries such as banks. Likewise, internally, they recognized the need to establish internal standards and move to the euro on a specific date, which would be affected by the timing of UK entry into monetary union.

Practical Issues

There were, nevertheless, practical issues which concerned the company. They were concerned about the education problems which would arise for both staff and customers. While they did not put a price on this, as they had for technology costs, they were interested to discover whether or not European and national government funds would be made available for educational purposes. In markets which introduce the new currency, retailers will play an important educational role as far as both customers and staff are concerned.

The official EU planning process envisaged that the transition from national currencies to the new currency of the euro would be spread over a period of six months. However, Marks & Spencer were keen to emphasize that the shorter the period the better. They believed that dual pricing could continue long after the dual currency period, that a short period for the financial changeover would establish the new currency in the public's mind faster.

The company was conscious of the need for industry to be aware of the lead times required to make the necessary changes to systems. This flagged up the need for timely guidance from government, although, the company was careful to tread a tactful path on this issue.

The company was concerned that the start date for the new currency, the first day of January, was a bad day for retailers; it favoured a date such as mid-February. The UK decimalized on 15 February 1971. The beginning of January is a busy time for retailers in the UK. The combination of post-Christmas sales and the introduction of new notes and coins looked like they would create considerable disruption and confusion for customers and retailers.

Economic Consequences for Marks & Spencer

Marks & Spencer summarized their memorandum by focusing on the broader picture. They were conscious that throughout the EU common pricing would be an issue. They noted that currently, the price of St Michael merchandise across Europe differed by some 20 per cent. This, they noted, was the result of different cost structures within different markets and that such factors as occupancy rates, be they freehold or rental, were markedly different in European markets as far as the company was concerned. Marks & Spencer, along with other retailers at this time, was concerned that common pricing might be imposed and that such a measure would make some markets uneconomic.

The different rates of VAT which exist within Europe were likewise seen as important when common pricing was considered. Marks & Spencer suggested, that because VAT rates were different in EU member states, the US system of quoting prices excluding local purchase taxes might be adopted in order to account for those differences.

The company finally returned to its concerns with the uncertainties which surrounded the UK's position on the euro, the uncertain political situation and the impact that this might have on exchange rates. They observed:

> Uncertainty about the UK's position (coupled with the political uncertainties of the next year) may lead to a weak Pound, thus helping our export prices, but conversely increasing domestic inflation and our prices here in the UK.

EXAMINATION OF WITNESSES

The Chairman of the Treasury Committee opened the questioning with a request for a general statement from Sir Richard Greenbury (House of Commons, 1996). He wanted to know if the retail sector, as opposed to other sectors, would face the greatest challenges during the changeover from one currency to another?

Greenbury agreed that the retail sector would face considerable problems as they dealt with millions of customers, and adopted new approaches to their EPOS (electronic point of sale) and information systems, pricing policies and money handling. Greenbury restated the written information that hardware and software costs would be over £100m. Robert Colvill supplemented this statement by noting that costs were, in great part, dependent on the timescale of the changeover: that 'the smoother the transition... the lesser the cost because it is likely to be masked by other changes which occur over a similar time span'. Keith Bogg developed this point further, after further questioning from Stephen Timms, when he noted that because technology required updating from time to time, the longer lead time retailers had to adjust to the euro, the less specifically euro-dependent those costs would be. This was particularly true as far as long-term planning was concerned at this time because of the year 2000 computer issue which was recognized by businesses generally. That is, costs were difficult to ascribe to any single business need; however, the less planning time there was, the more specific the costs were likely to be.

Immediately, therefore, the issue began to be established, within this very public forum, that retailers were placed at a disadvantage if they were not given time to prepare. However, when asked if Britain's opt-out was a problem that gave European retailers an advantage over Marks & Spencer, Greenbury answered an emphatic 'No'. Marks & Spencer was in Europe, the company already had 30 stores and was dedicated to doubling that figure within a decade. Here an important point was made. Whether their domestic market was in the system or outside the system, they would be in, because they had stores in the system. However, uncertainty was a concern. As Colvill noted, until some decisions were made, specific planning was difficult. Greenbury agreed, technological decisions were being held off as long as possible. Nevertheless, he was equally emphatic when questioned by Nigel Forman, stating that the company was committed to strategic development in Europe and decisions would have to be made as appropriate, irrespective of political or economic uncertainty.

The examination of the witnesses continued for some time, dealing with issues of the dual currency period, consumer education, the analogy of decimalization, pricing internationalization of retail operations and the other issues which the company had raised in its memorandum. The overall message, however, was one of uncertainty. In the summer of 1996, uncertainty was one of the biggest problems facing retailers in the UK preparing for the single currency.

Uncertainty Continues

Marks & Spencer continued its preparation for the euro, and continued to develop its operation in Europe by entering the German market for the first time in the autumn of 1996, but press monitoring showed that certainty was difficult to achieve as far as the single currency was concerned. In December 1996, for example Jan Kalff, speaking on behalf of ABN-Ambro in the Netherlands, while expressing general confidence in EMU, noted that no one in his bank could guarantee they would be ready in time and that there was always another aspect of the currency changeover that emerged as more was understood about it (*Financial Times*, 1996). This was in a sector which had been planning for EMU for some time. In the summer of 1994, the banks were calculating that EMU could cost them the equivalent of 2 per cent of annual operating cost for a period of three to four years during the change over period. That is, they saw EMU costing them Ecu 10b directly (*Financial Times*, 1996).

Even in Germany, doubt was thrown on the ability of the economy to conform to the convergence criteria required for membership of the single currency system. Not all countries would meet the convergence criteria and be eligible for membership of EMU. There had to be price stability, inflation had to be under control and not more than 1.5 per cent above the three best performing states. Government deficit had to be no more than 3 per cent of GDP, and government debt no higher than 60 per cent of GDP. Interest rates had to be no more than 2 per cent above the three best performing states. There must be participation in the exchange rate mechanism of the EMS for two years without devaluation. By the end of 1996, it appeared possible that only a few states would manage these requirements. Indeed, some of the euro's greatest supporters, such as the Italian government, looked less than certain to conform to the standards required. Germany, the Netherlands and Luxembourg had looked set to have figures which would conform to the necessary requirements; then, as 1997 progressed, Germany looked uncertain. In the middle of January 1997, the German Finance Minister Theo Waigel observed that 'the government's policy of budgetary consolidation would have to be applied more forcefully if Bonn were to achieve its goals of qualifying for EMU' (Norman, 1997). This was because Germany's budget deficit in 1996 was 3.9 per cent of GDP higher than the Maastricht limit of 3 per cent, and the 1995 figure of 3.5 per cent.

UK membership continued to be uncertain and increasingly unlikely as reports emerged that the Prime Minister (John Major) had united his cabinet around a position that it was 'very unlikely' the UK would be in the single currency from day one (Preston and Kampfner, 1997). However, some certainty, or at least confirmation of a given level of uncertainty, was introduced into the situation, when a few days later, the opposition party announced, for the consumption of European Union partners, that they did not envisage a New Labour Britain being part of the initial group of countries to introduce the euro (Kampfner and Mortimer, 1997).

Considerable doubts were expressed about the euro outside Europe. Reports suggested that Asian and US markets had little confidence in EMU. Indeed, some suggested that it would not only be of little relevance if it happened but that it was unlikely to happen at all (Baker, 1997). However, there was concern about the uncertainty itself. In the middle of March 1997, Mr Joseph Yam, Chief Executive of the Hong Kong Monetary Authority, observed: 'We are somewhat concerned about the uncertainties surrounding EMU and their impact on the performance of financial markets in Europe' (Ridding, 1997). This international doubt was hardly surprising, given the messages that the global community was receiving from Europe. There were persistent rumours of delay and continuing doubts as to the likelihood of EMU going ahead, despite Hans Tietmeyer (president of the Bundesbank) and Alexandre Lamfalussy (president of the

European Monetary Institute) insisting that the rumours of delay were just that; only rumours (Iksander *et al.*, 1997). However, the issue of the convergence criteria rumbled on and concern was expressed that the relaxation of EMU rules could lead to a soft rather than a hard currency. Concerns over the strength of the new currency were increased when Theo Waigel, Germany's finance minister, suggested that it might not be absolutely necessary for participating countries to achieve the public deficit target of 3 per cent of gross domestic product (Barber, 1997a).

Confusion was exacerbated by the fact that business opinion was divided. Some businesses, such as those in the travel industry, saw that the system could stimulate growth (Daneshkhu, 1997). This was not the case throughout industry. In late April 1997, the CBI (Confederation of British Industry) decided to launch a consultation exercise with its members as it sought to establish a position on the issue (Wagstyl, 1997).

POS 2000

In the meantime, Marks & Spencer had been pressing ahead with the development of its EPOS system. The existing system was already a decade old and was not going to meet the needs of the trading environment of the next few years, let alone offer a sophisticated platform on which to cope with the euro. The previous system had been introduced into Marks & Spencer stores in the UK in 1984 and it had been recognized as in need of replacement for three years. By the summer of 1997, ICL had provided a bespoke system for the company which would provide not only an improved EPOS provision for the normal trading environment but would be able to cope with a variety of currency issues. While ICL had put the package together, the new system drew on a variety of technology companies and skills. ICL provided computer software and computer hardware. Within the system, Microsoft operating systems used Compaq servers. The ICL hardware and software drove the EPOS systems and worked in conjunction with the till hardware, which was supplied by Siemens Nixdorf.

The new system allowed staff to accept payment in more than one currency. The laptop computer-style screen provided staff with considerable information and easy to use menu systems. The new system allowed till receipts to be printed with the details of the exchange rate and the price of the goods purchased in national currencies and the foreign tendered currency. Indeed, the system could cope with part payment in both the national and another currency. By the summer of 1997, the system was being trialled in a Marks & Spencer store in Reading town centre. Staff responded well to the new system, finding it user friendly.

Trials at the Reading store progressed through the summer and autumn as plans were laid to roll out the system involving over 11,000 tills within the UK, Ireland and continental Europe in late 1997, 1998 and 1999. The system had to be tested in-store to iron out point of sale problems as well as problems associated with the interface between the new 'tills' and existing information systems.

PLANNING REALITIES

Paul Smith took up the post of Euro Project Manager toward the end of 1997, and has been charged with overseeing the euro project. He has extensive experience of the Marks & Spencer operation.

Paul began by gathering further information on the euro issue and updating the information which the company had been gathering since the spring of 1996. The memorandum which had been submitted to the House of Commons Committee had highlighted the key issues but some factors had gained greater importance in the meantime.

Pricing

By the beginning of 1998, Marks & Spencer had decided that they would show prices in both currencies at the point of display but they had decided not to show both currencies on the till display at the point of sale. That is, at any one time, one currency would take precedence.

Thus, while dual pricing remained an issue with which retailers would have to cope at the point of sale, another pricing issue had gained greater significance in the minds of planners. Retailers use certain price points in their operation. For example, in Belgium it may be logical to price a shirt at BF 1.999, but it is not logical to price it at euro 48.82 (Warner, 1997). During the changeover period, retailers will have to use one price which does not 'look right'. However, retailers will come into the period of dual pricing with an appropriate national currency price and need to leave with an appropriate euro price. Retailers will, therefore, face the question when to switch from one to the other. This will have an impact on margins and on customers' perceptions. In the example given above, euro 49.99 would be a logical price point but would mean a 2.4 per cent rise in the price of the item. Certainly in the UK, this type of change in prices would draw on the popular beliefs prevalent at the time of decimalization that retailers profiteered from the confusion caused to the customer by the change in the coinage.

By the end of 1997, it looked increasingly likely that the dual pricing issue would have to be resolved in such a way as to avoid unnecessary system disruption. That is, for example, till receipts would only show the total cost of items in both currencies and that dual item pricing would not be feasible. The reason for this was simply mathematical. Because there is a legal requirement that conversion calculations will have to be carried out to six significant decimal digits, it was possible that item price rounding would mean that the total price conversion figure and the total item price conversion figure on a receipt would differ.

The switch from the national price point system to a euro price point system would also have implications for the type of coins held by a retailer. In the example above, if the retailer is using the price of BF 1.999 or euro 48.82 as a price point and is giving change in euros, the retailer will need a float of coins in the till which place an emphasis on 1 euro, 1, 2, 5 and ten cent (euro) coins: that is, when payment is offered in the form of euro notes to the value of euro 50.00. However, when the retailer moves to the euro price point of euro 49.99, the retailer will only have to give a 1 cent coin as change to customers. Thus, the retailer's coin stock requirements will alter during the currency changeover process as a result of price point considerations. The scenario described here is the simpler alternative. If retailers are obliged to give change in the national and euro currency throughout the change over period, then the problem would be doubled.

Cash Handling

To some extent, by the end of 1997, this issue looked less problematic than it once appeared to be. Retailers were beginning to assume they could accept both currencies during the changeover period but they would only be required to give change in euros. This would mean they did not have to use two till drawers but merely establish a secure system of collecting the national currency at the till. In some countries, where cross-border shopping is prevalent, retailers already cope with this issue.

However, in another respect, cash handling looked like it would become a greater problem. There had been hope among some retailers, particularly those based in the Republic of Ireland and the Netherlands, that the introduction of coins could be delayed until February or March 2002 when retailers, in a quieter business period, could introduce the new coins and collect the old. However, the EC seemed convinced that 1 January 2002 was the most appropriate day of introduction. This did not fit well with retailers' Christmas and New Year operations. Many retailers in Europe would be in the middle of their sales period. Likewise, notes brought into circulation to cope with Christmas spending would then have to be immediately withdrawn. Indeed, some retailers in the Republic of Ireland believed the introduction of notes and coins should be brought forward to September or October to pre-empt this problem (Croughan, 1997). However, the practicalities of producing the coins and notes on time did not appear to allow for this.

Education

Retailers will have an important role educating the public and their own staff. Retailers had initially expressed the hope that government and EU funds would be made available for this process. However, by the end of 1997, these hopes had faded. Retailers already planning for the introduction of the euro were therefore aware that they would need to integrate education on this subject into their training programmes and absorb associated costs. Some training would need to be early in the changeover process as customers would be able to use cheques and plastic cards to draw on accounts denominated in euros. However, it was also apparent that, in an industry where labour turnover is high, a considerable amount of training would need to be delivered near to the time of the introduction of coins and notes.

Suppliers

Initially, retailers had focused much of their attention on point of sale issues. However, as time progressed, retailers began to become aware of the considerable changes which would be required in their relationship with suppliers. While EU legislation guaranteed that contacts made in the national currency would be valid after the introduction of the euro, some businesses were sceptical and considered they would be wise to renegotiate contracts to ensure they were valid after the changeover.

Suppliers were also becoming aware that they would be subject to their retail customers' changeover from accounts kept in the national currency to accounts kept in the euro. Hence, it was clear that some retail customers, if they were large enough, would effectively dictate when their suppliers changed their systems. These changes could occur soon after 1 January 1999.

CONTINUING UNCERTAINTY

While businesses began to plan, or failed to plan, for the euro, the political situation in the UK seemed as confused as ever.

In their evidence to the Treasury Committee, senior personnel from Marks & Spencer had pointed out the need for business to know what was happening in order to evolve systems which would cope with the introduction of the euro and thereby reduce costs. By the end of 1997, as the media was increasingly pointing out, the cost of delay could also mean the cost of not influencing the decisions which would be made regarding the euro in the months ahead (Barber, 1997b). At the beginning of October 1977, the leader of the Liberal Democrats (Paddy Ashdown) called for a clear declaration on the government's position on the euro. Toward the end of October, the Chancellor (Gordon Brown) attempted to do that, but, while there were strong hints that the UK would join in 2002 or 2003, there was still a lot of wait and see in the statement. However, he did call on British business to prepare.

QUESTIONS

1. Assess the advantages and disadvantages to Marks & Spencer if the UK (a) enters EMU in the first wave of countries, (b) enters EMU in the second wave of countries, or (c) does not enter EMU in the foreseeable future. You should structure your answer around point of sale issues, channel relationship issues and the prospects for future international development by Marks & Spencer within the EU.

2. Draw up a planning chart for Paul Smith, indicating the areas which need consideration and at what point in time different tasks should be prioritized.

3. Assuming that the UK does not enter EMU in the first wave but will do so thereafter, Paul will be asked to identify a time at which the UK should introduce the euro currency. Identify the most acceptable period in the year for the introduction of notes and coins and justify your decision.

4. Marks & Spencer store managers in European countries introducing the euro in 2002 will need to receive operational guidelines. It is your task to draw up those guidelines. You should consider all aspects of the store manager's responsibilities, including in-store training.

5. The issues considered in this case study will be considerably affected by events subsequent to the date at which the case terminates. How have those events affected the issues which Paul Smith will need to address?

REFERENCES

Alexander, N. and Hutchinson, R. (1997) 'European Monetary Union: the need for a contingency strategy within the retail sector'. *International Journal of Retail and Distribution Management*, **25**: 146–58.

Andersen Consulting (1996) *Economic and Monetary Union – The Business View*. London: Andersen Consulting.

Anonymous (1996) 'Banks: Anxiety over EMU starts to creep in'. *Financial Times*, originally published 3 December, www.ft.com.

Baker, G. (1997) 'Single currency: EMU fails to excite US money men'. *Financial Times*, originally published 1 March, www.ft.com.

Barber, L. (1997a) 'Single currency: Bonn eases stance on EMU rules'. *Financial Times*, originally published 7 April, www.ft.com.

Barber, L. (1997b) 'The cost of dithering'. *Financial Times*, originally published 21 October, www.ft.com.

Croughan, D. (1997) 'Business preparations for EMU: Retailers message to governments' Paper presented at *Preparing for the Euro: Strategies for Retailers, Distributors and Manufacturers*. IBC UK Conferences Ltd, Glaziers Hall, London.

Daneshkhu, S. (1997) 'Travel industry looks for boost from the euro'. *Financial Times*, p. 3.

House of Commons (1996) *The Prognosis for Stage Three of Economic and Monetary Union*, Vol. 2. Minutes of Evidence and Appendices, Session 1995–96, London: House of Commons.

Iksander, S., Adams, R. and Studeman, F. (1997) 'Central banks: Rumours of EMU delay rejected'. *Financial Times*, originally published 4 March, www.ft.com.

Kampfner, J. and Mortimer, E. (1997) 'Single currency: Labour foresees delay in UK joining'. *Financial Times*, originally published 29 January 1, www.ft.com.

Norman, P. (1997) 'German budget: Deficit tops target'. *Financial Times*, originally published 16 January, www.ft.com.

Preston, R. and Kampfner, J. (1997) 'Euro: Major takes tougher line on EMU'. *Financial Times*, originally published 24 January, www.ft.com.

Ridding J (1997) 'Asia: Doubts over EMU start date surface'. *Financial Times*, originally published 14 March, www.ft.com.

Wagstyl, S. (1997) 'Europe: CBI seeks consensus on EMU'. *Financial Times*, originally published 24 April, www.ft.com.

Warner, P. (1997) 'The potential advantages of electronic payment systems'. Paper presented at *Preparing for the Euro: Strategies for Retailers, Distributors and Manufacturers*. IBC UK Conferences Ltd, Glaziers Hall, London.

CASE 2

B&Q ENFIELD: STAFFING A GREENFIELD OPERATION

JOHN AUSTIN AND MANDI PARTRIDGE

> The authors would like to thank B&Q for their unstinting support in developing this case study. This support came from many people both at head office and in the store.
>
> The case study is based on interviews with a sample of key people from various levels of the organization, both local and central, review of company documentation, survey of labour market data in the area and personal observation.
>
> The information was selected, interpreted and synthesized by us, but is essentially unchanged in spirit.

INTRODUCTION

The DIY market in the UK has been dominated since the 1980s by a small number of large scale operators including Homebase/Texas, Wickes, Do-it-All and B&Q. Together these account for around 40 per cent of a market worth over £10b. They have taken advantage of, and to an extent helped create, a market that has grown significantly and which is projected to grow further long term. Performance in the early and mid-1990s did suffer temporarily due to a combination of factors including a slowdown in the housing market, over capacity, and the difficulty of escaping long-term leases on older sites.

Faced with this the major operators responded with a mix of strategies including better control of costs and targeted improvement to key activities such as supply chain management and stock control.

B&Q, largest of the big operators with well over 15 per cent of the total market, is typical in adopting these types of response. However an additional key aspect of its strategy, short and long term, is its unique approach in offering two formats, designated respectively as Warehouse and Supercentre.

Warehouse and Supercentre formats differ in several major respects (head office briefing interview):

- Size of operation – Warehouses are typically larger both in terms of square footage (150,000 sq ft versus 60,000 sq ft) and turnover (£20m plus versus £5–10m)
- Large product range – (40,000 items versus 15–20,000 items)

16

■ Stock policy – Warehouses stock heavier products and in greater volume.
■ Culture – the Warehouse style was originally designed as consciously more energetic and radical version of the informal culture pioneered in the Supercentres.

As a category killer format, the Warehouse type operation is of key strategic importance to B&Q's future plans for the UK. The format is designed to appeal to the serious home DIY enthusiast and to trade customers, as well as to the more modest DIY individual, in a shopping atmosphere that is energizing and stimulating. The importance the company attributes to the development of this type of store is highlighted by the comparative number of store openings for Supercentres and Warehouse stores.

Table 2.1   **Comparative number of store openings**

	1994	1995	1996	1997	1998
Supercentre	270	265	264	260	253
Warehouse	10	14	18	22	27

Source: B&Q Head Office

The key role of the new format is also reflected by an internal restructuring which in January 1997 resulted in the creation of a new Warehouse senior management division consisting of a staff network headed by a general manager, and reporting relationships from store managers to management services team leader, all of whom took up position in January 1997 (see Figure 2.1).

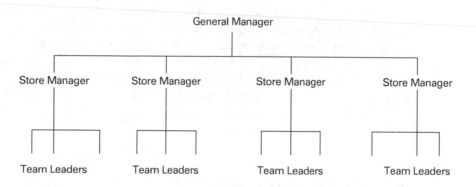

Figure 2.1   Warehouse management structure (B&Q internal documentation)

PLANNING THE ENFIELD STORE OPENING

In early 1996 B&Q obtained planning permission to open up a new Warehouse type store in Enfield, north-west London. The site chosen was a raised plot in a busy retail park next to a main arterial route into the city. Opening a new retail operation is a major project requiring a range of strategic activities, including building construction, merchandising, stock profiling and layout, as well as human resource planning.

Enfield Warehouse was planned to open in August of 1997, with access to the shell of the building anticipated in mid-1997. This gave an overall time frame of approval to opening of about 18 months. The planning and preparation process involved a complex range of issues: decisions on stock profile, layout, merchandising and marketing all had to be managed around the construction of the building. Furthermore, as a critical control mechanism, all activities had to be managed within a strict opening budget.

Central in this list of critical issues was the staffing of the new operation. As with any new store opening, the staffing process comprised several stages:

- Planning the preferred staff – in terms of the number and type of staff required
- Recruitment of appropriate staff – of the number and type specified
- Pre-opening training and development – to ensure full operational effectiveness from the first day of opening
- Post-opening monitoring, evaluation and fine-tuning.

These key stages are discussed in detail for the new Enfield B&Q Warehouse store below.

PLANNING THE STAFF PROFILE

The initial requirement of the staffing process was to decide the broad establishment – the profile and structure of personnel needed to prepare and run the operation. The main responsibility for this fell to the newly appointed senior management staff of the B&Q Warehouse division. It was this team, assisted by a human resources advisor from head office, who sat down in temporary premises to work out a preferred staff profile.

There were several basic considerations to take into account in informing these decisions, as outlined below.

The Size of the Operation

As a Warehouse the operation was designed to operate at high activity levels in all respects: a trading area of 135,000 sq ft, a weekly turnover of around £0.5m, a product range of 40,000 plus items, and an average stock level of £2m. It was envisaged that the store would be operating seven days a week, thirteen hours per day (six on Sunday), with ancillary operations such as stock replenishment taking place 'around the clock'.

Financial Constraints

Considerable discretion is given to recruitment teams to decide on the staff complement and profile. However this has to be done within a staff cost budget of 11 per cent of turnover, falling to 10 per cent after opening. In this case therefore the approximate cost of the staff establishment had to be no more than £2.2m per annum.

Previous Experience

Comparison Warehouse stores employ between 200 and 300 people depending on the mix of full- and part-timers.

The Main Areas of Work

The operation needed staff to cover the more obvious activities of any retail operation: departmental staff (decorative, hardware, lighting, showrooms), front end (checkouts, and greeters), administration, and warehouse. Specialist requirements included tradespeople (given the Warehouse strategy of selling to trade and offering specialist advice to the public on DIY projects), and garden centre staff (a 20,000 sq ft open-air garden area was part of the plan).

Pre- and Post-opening Phases

It is B&Q's policy that the people who prepare for store opening in terms of stock receipt and merchandising, would be the same people who will ultimately run the operation. There was no question, therefore, of employing different people for the two phases other than for highly specialized and temporary tasks such as shopfitting.

Culture

The clearly specified culture of the Warehouse operation is one of informality, energy, and enthusiastic customer service. This philosophy is articulated both in the mission statement and in the 'Purpose and Values' which staff carry with them on laminated cards (see Figure 2.2 below). Staffing plans had necessarily to recognize the demands and opportunities this overall approach placed on the recruitment process. It was considered essential to find processes of identifying and taking on staff who could work in the style required straight away or who could easily be acculturated to it.

We will be the best at giving people the inspiration, confidence and solutions to create homes to be proud of.

DOWN TO EARTH

Operating in a simple, consistent and cost effective way for the benefit of the customer. Keep it fun and friendly.

Simple
Consistent
Informal
Low cost

CAN DO

Staying ahead of the rest – take responsibility and focus on solutions. Be proud of our people and products and achievements.

Will do
Proud
Competitive

RESPECT FOR PEOPLE

Create the difference by having clear goals and trusting people to make decisions. Reward contribution, recognize potential and lead from the front.

Honest/Fair
Clear leadership
Team work
Respect for people

CUSTOMER DRIVEN

Meet and exceed customer needs by anticipating, listening and responding to them. If in doubt, favour the customer.

Driven by what is right for the customer

STRIVING TO BE BETTER

Beating the competition by learning from others, sharing experiences and mistakes and taking calculated risks.

Learning
Innovative

Figure 2.2   B&Q purpose and values (B&Q internal documentation)

Company and Legal Constraints

Staffing strategy had to recognize and conform to the normal requirements of employment legislation and also to company requirements. An illustration of this is B&Q's well-established, high-profile strategy of employing older workers and their firm policy not to employ on a temporary basis. This latter consideration meant that any planned staff establishment had to be rigorously thought through since temporary contracts could not be used to provide flexibility. This was particularly important given cost constraints.

In addition to these general considerations were others, more specifically related to the particular circumstances of Enfield. These included:

The Local Labour Market

Any staffing decisions would have to take into account the labour market in the area. In this case the key features of the market were:

- a relatively high unemployment rate
- a low skills base
- a relatively high ratio of ethnic minorities
- high competition for labour from adjacent operators including Homebase, Currys, Sainsburys and Toys 'R' Us.

Existing Operations

B&Q already had several Supercentre operations in the area, one of which was particularly near and therefore to be closed. Given B&Q's no redundancy policy it was intended to offer transfer to the new Warehouse or to other Supercentres in the area to all of the 90 existing Supercentre staff. This provided a possible source of recruits.

These were the main considerations the team had to take into account when planning the staff establishment. However there was still considerable scope for discretion on such issues as:

- The ratio of full-timers to part-timers employed
- The respective number of generalists moving flexibly across departments and specialists who would solely or primarily work in specified areas of the store
- Pay levels, within set company bands.

Since the latter were at the discretion of the recruitment team, some fine-tuning was possible between employing more experienced and therefore more expensive staff and less experienced and cheaper. However, since total costs had to remain within the budget, overall numbers would obviously be affected by whatever decision was made.

After detailed discussion it was decided to work to certain basic principles. Staff were to be taken on to work in specific sections, rather than as generalists working across several areas of the store. It was felt that the amount of training required to produce competent generalists was not feasible within the time frame and funds available. Applicants would therefore be invited to apply for specific sections, as set out in Figure 2.3 below.

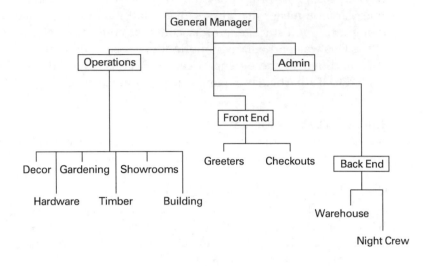

Figure 2.3   Warehouse structure (B&Q head ofice briefing)

Between one and four tradespeople were to be appointed within each section, depending on the size of the section and the cost implications of employing these more expensive specialists. A second major decision was to employ predominantly on a part-time basis with a significant core of 25 per cent to 30 per cent full-time staff. The dual aim here was to attract a wider range of applicants, not all of whom could work full-time hours, and to provide flexibility if trading activity varied from that anticipated. The number of hours offered to each part-time applicant was also to be flexible (ranging from 5 to 25 hours) in order to accommodate employee preferences and operational requirements.

The anticipated size of the workforce, given all the above, was estimated at around the equivalent of 200 full-time staff working a 39-hour week. However, the decision to employ significant numbers on a part-time basis meant that the actual head count could be anything between 250 and 350, depending on the profile actually chosen.

This staffing establishment was to be supported by a team of several store managers, each responsible for a major part of the store, and each supported in turn by two or three team leaders individually responsible for running particular sections.

RECRUITMENT

Having decided on the broad establishment the focus of attention switched to recruitment. By this time the date of the actual store opening was only six months away, and as the building took shape and staff were increasingly needed to stock and merchandise it, as well as prepare for opening. Recruitment was becoming more critical.

The basic tasks that needed to be addressed regarding recruitment were straightforward and followed the three key stages of generating applications, selecting from the applications and agreeing terms and conditions. However, given the varying times at which different parts of the store would become live, consideration also had to be given to the sequencing of the process. This was guided by the cost implications of taking on staff prematurely, thereby incurring unnecessary expense and endangering budgetary targets.

The task of generating applications required a two part strategy, covering transfers from the existing (but ultimately to be closed) Supercentre, and the recruitment of additional personnel required to cover the remaining gap between Supercentre transfers and the target establishment. There was some ambivalence among the recruitment team about the transfer of staff from the Supercentre. First, it was felt that they were likely to be more experienced and on relatively high pay levels within the B&Q band (with obvious implications for costs). Second, there was concern that staff brought up and trained in the Supercentre culture would find it difficult to adapt to the more extrovert and dynamic style required by the Warehouse approach. The existence of other B&Q Supercentres in the area who were seen as potentially talent spotting for their own operations, added a further twist.

Eventually, following a series of general presentations by the Warehouse management team, 70 Supercentre staff, from a variety of backgrounds and departments, applied for transfer, leaving a required gap of around 130 full-time equivalent vacancies against the planned establishment. Again depending on the part-time/full-time profile this represented a head count requirement of anything between 180 and 280 staff.

Having identified the external recruitment needs the team's next task was to decide how to meet it. It was normal in these circumstances to apply the documented recruitment process laid down in the general B&Q rule book, and this was largely followed.

Advertisements were placed in the local press inviting telephone enquiries. There was little attempt to screen calls at this stage other than through a broad description of job requirements in the advertisement. This, given local labour market conditions, resulted in a large number of calls: 2500 by the end of the first week, 3700 by week 2, tailing off thereafter to a final total of around 4000.

This volume of response in itself caused logistical problems in handling the calls and logging details onto the company software package, especially since at this stage the existing establishment still only comprised the general manager and the skeleton of a management team. The problem, and budget pressures, were eased somewhat by the secondment of 10 telephonists from the local job centre who took initial calls and passed details to the team on a daily basis. However the problem of inputting details onto the computer remained, the weight of the task falling on the small team of management services people in the store.

Screening took place at various stages. All telephone callers were sent application forms, plus information on the task and attitude requirements of the jobs on offer. Each resulting application form was then initially screened. Anyone unable to work within the hours required, or the pay bands offered, was rejected and informed. Team leaders, appointed from internal applicants the week after the advertisement went out, were then assigned to hold initial interviews and optional second interviews. They were supported in this by guidance from store managers, a well established and thoroughly documented interview procedure, pro-forma documents, and fast-track training in interviewing skills. Through this process the original 4000 telephone calls were reduced to 2000 written applications, and approximately 700 interviews.

The overall process was monitored by the general manager and the recruitment team. As each offer was made by the team leaders, details were entered on a wallplan of the planned staff complement.

The whole process, as well as being time consuming, threw up particular problems. Specialist tradespeople were particularly difficult to recruit. The plan was that each major area of the store would have a small team of specialist builders, electricians and plumbers and so on to advise customers and general staff and add to the ambience that was designed to attract trade custom. However the increasingly buoyant construction industry, the relative rates of pay compared to the going rate in the industry, and the shift of mindset required to move from a craft to a retailing operation, discouraged applications. Most of the people who did apply had particular personal reasons, including a need for job security, a workplace closer to home or a steadier position.

The sequencing of the whole process posed another problem. The pre-opening phase of the process carried its own staff budget (a total of £450,000, of which £30,000 was allocated to recruitment). This had to cover the cost of advertising and responding to 4000 enquiries, wages of staff needed to process enquiries and applications (eased in this case by support from the job centre), and the wages paid once staff were accepted onto the payroll.

Even at this stage, therefore, the costing had to be managed rigorously by the recruitment team, with continuing monitoring, phased recruitment on an as needed basis (warehouse staff obviously needed long before checkout staff) and careful judgement of the level of offers to be made within the set bands. The dilemma here was in achieving an optimum balance between paying rates high enough to attract good calibre people, without exceeding short or long-term staff budgets. The existence of a large number of retailers in the immediate area made this particularly difficult as the mid-range level of pay in B&Q, relative to other competitors, generated applications from people already in position as well as from the unemployed.

An early problem of labour turnover in particular parts of the store, well before opening, added another problem. In this case the existence on file of reserve applicants removed any need to re-advertise although not the need to interview.

Finally all of this – the contacting, screening, interviewing – had to be managed alongside all the other demands of store opening, before construction work on the building had been completed, and with the well-publicized opening deadline remorselessly approaching. The whole process was predictably complex and continually shifting, with adjustments, major and minor, made on the basis of financial recalculations, labour market shifts, application responses, and the involvement of a steadily growing management team who could increasingly take responsibility for the appointment of their own staff.

TRAINING AND DEVELOPMENT

As staff were recruited on a phased basis so the requirement to train and develop had to be similarly phased. By May the night crew were on board, by the end of June they had been joined by most of the departmental staff and by July by the front end.

The training and development requirements of these staff necessarily took different forms given their mixed backgrounds and roles. Ex-Supercentre staff could be expected to know the generic systems and procedures of the company and a significant proportion of the product range. Tradespeople were presumed to be conversant in their particular craft specialisms but not in company knowledge and were possibly unfamiliar with the demands of working in a large, structured retail operation and one, moreover, with a distinctive and less traditional style. New shop-floor staff had mixed retail experience, with a range of training needs that included general retailing skills as well as company specific ones, both of a procedural and attitudinal nature. The management team, largely recruited from other parts of the organization, could be expected to move quickly into an operational role but where they were from a Supercentre background, they did have to make adjustments to the Warehouse culture.

As ever, any decisions on training and development had to be made in the context of financial constraints, and mindful of the different phases of store opening, and the need for rapid staff training to enable them to take their places in the early stages of fitting out the building, receiving and merchandising stock, and setting up systems and procedures. All of this had to be co-ordinated towards and focused on the big day and the moment when the doors would finally open for the first time, to a buying public who would expect a business 100 per cent operationally effective, seven days a week, thirteen hours per day.

The main elements of the training and development strategy followed from these considerations. Induction days topped up with health and safety training were run for new recruits. The induction days in particular were seen as critical, designed not only to provide basic information about the Warehouse format and its aims, but also to reflect the culture at the heart of its approach.

They were, therefore, deliberately lively and informal with an emphasis on the style of behaviour expected from recruits. Physical exercises, songs and team games were included as well as the more traditional company videos and presentations.

Once completed, the induction training was then supplemented by skills training in product awareness, and operating procedures relevant to the particular sections in which the recruits would be working. Responsibility for all this was delegated to the newly appointed section team leaders. Training was carried out mainly on the shop floor, in the context of a store set-up that became more and more real as the months went by and the fixtures and fittings, and subsequently stock, were put in place. The essence of the approach was to incorporate learning into the real tasks of preparing for store opening. Much of the structured training occurred in the 30-minute team briefings held by each team leader at the start of the shift. The crucial issue of customer service was covered in a continuing series of informal role plays acted out between members of the team as they went about the numerous other tasks required as opening day approached.

Almost all training was on-site and internally administered. Formal and off-site initiatives were few and limited to specialist requirements. The night crew and receiving staff, whose ultimate role would be to restock and re-order the store, were sent for live experience to a parallel store where they had specialist training, such as fork-lift truck driving.

The final major consideration was the treatment of those staff transferred from Supercentre. They posed a particular challenge, first because the recruitment team had less choice over their selection and, second, because the possible development need was not skill or knowledge but attitude. How would these people feel about a move that was not of their making? How would they adapt to the different cultural approach used in Warehouse?

In the circumstances it was decided to induct these individuals by a process of informal familiarization while they were still in the Supercentre, followed by immediate incorporation into the respective teams once they had arrived at Enfield. The responsibility fell on the team leaders to deal with any issues that might arise.

The context of all these considerations continued to be a complex and fluid one with parallel demands on time from numerous other issues, such as stock management, merchandising, construction; a building that took shape as the workforce was taken on; a cost discipline that had to be continuously managed; and a deadline that was remorselessly approaching.

As the months became weeks, and weeks became days, so the final phases of staff training were put in place. On the Friday evening, a week before opening proper, the store held a family night that provided an opportunity for friends and relatives to visit in a party atmosphere of balloons, streamers, fizzy drinks, face painting and generally controlled mayhem. This also allowed for some real-life training as those same friends and relatives proceeded to buy £30,000 worth of goods.

On the Monday following, the store held a trade evening specifically to introduce the operation to local tradespeople and open accounts. For the remainder of the week a 'soft opening' policy was adopted whereby passing customers were allowed to shop and indirectly provide the expectant staff with last-minute opportunities to rehearse skills.

OPENING AND POST-OPENING

On 22 August 1997, 18 months after approval, eight months after the appointment of the general manager and four months after the first new recruits were taken on, the doors of B&Q's new Enfield Warehouse store officially opened.

The following weeks proved to be frenetic. Trading levels were significantly above those projected, with obvious effects on workload. A procession of visiting company executives added further distraction while the winding down and departure of the central support team reduced the help available. As this opening euphoria died down and life settled into a more predictable format, so the operating pressures changed. On the staff side the shift from a pre-opening to a post-opening style of operation caused its own problems.

Some people found it difficult to shift from the euphoric, less structured, deadline chasing, adrenalin pumping novelty of the pre-opening phase, to the somewhat more ordered and structured, though no less busy, life of an operational retail outlet. This was further complicated by unexpectedly high sales levels which led to pressures on staff workloads. In the short term these fell on existing staff, since adjustments in staff establishment had to be approved by head office. The general manager was consequently faced with dramatic and unexpected increases in workload with little short-term access to extra resources.

An issue too was the tension between some ex-Supercentre staff who saw themselves as experienced but undervalued in the Warehouse culture, and some of those newly recruited to B&Q who saw themselves as hand-picked for that format.

The tension followed no recognizable organizational boundaries. Both management and staff teams contained representatives of each camp. It was difficult to address the issue in a structured way, particularly given the pace of life following the successful opening. The matter was therefore left to line managers to resolve in whatever way they thought appropriate.

By the end of the first quarter of trading these issues were starting to surface. While trading continued very buoyant, labour turnover was worryingly high (rising to 20 per cent at one stage), and pressures on the staff budget grew (as overtime was used to cope with the high workload). These factors in turn put pressure on staff morale. For the general manager and his team, the issue now was not how to create a workforce but how to manage one.

QUESTIONS

1. Assume that you are the general manager of Enfield Warehouse. It is January 1997. The store is scheduled to open for trading August Bank Holiday. Design a time frame (critical path) for your key recruitment activities which will ensure that you are able to meet your opening deadline.

2. Given what you know of the local labour market, the culture of B&Q and the particular staffing requirements of your store, draft an appropriate recruitment advertisement for the local press, plus an accompanying job specification and person specification.

3. What would you see as the key information that needs to be imparted to new recruits? How does this differ in terms of ex-Supercentre staff and new recruits? Assume you are the team leader management services whose responsibility it is to co-ordinate induction. Design a programme and plan a schedule for its delivery.

4. How do you think B&Q's greenfield staffing process could be improved? What specific recommendations would you make? How could these be monitored?

5. In reality B&Q's Enfield Warehouse traded so successfully during its first months that the staffing ratio they implemented was inadequate. What could have been done to avoid this?

6. To what extent do you think B&Q's employment policies are beneficial or damaging to operational performance?

STRESS IN GROCERY RETAILING

ADELINA BROADBRIDGE

> The content of the case study is based on in-depth and group discussions with staff from various food retail companies. The author would like to thank those involved in developing this case study. The case, as presented, does not reflect an actual scenario at any one grocery retailer. This was in order to provide anonymity for the retailers involved. Thus although the company portrayed in the case, Clarkson's Supermarkets is fictional, the scenarios presented comprise an amalgamation of experiences from various grocery retailers.

INTRODUCTION

The 1980s saw rapid changes for British retailing and the 1990s has been no less turbulent. Over the past two decades, the structure and nature of retailing has undergone massive changes. Market concentration, new store formats, the introduction of new technologies, ever changing customer needs, locational and international issues are just some of the developments which have resulted in an increasingly competitive industry. Many of these developments have impacted on the retail workforce, staff and managers alike. Many companies have recognized that the people they employ represent a major asset in gaining significant competitive advantage, and the importance of delivering good customer service. At an operational level, there is increasing recognition of the importance of front line staff and the need to empower them. The whole operational role is geared towards a marketing approach of delivering high customer service levels and adding value to the retail experience. This is compounded in supermarket retailing, where the pace of change is immense owing to the highly competitive nature of the sector, and whereby up to 400 staff may be employed at any one superstore site. Customers have become accustomed to one stop shopping. Many expect to shop once a week and get everything in one trip. If anything is out of stock they can become very annoyed or show their displeasure because they do not want to come back again. So the emphasis on being able to fulfil customer expectations is very high. The introduction of new technologies makes this easier, but it has a tendency to keep raising expectations. Customers today expect to be able to get 99 per cent of their goods when they visit a store compared to perhaps 85 per cent ten years ago.

There is no denial that stress has become a disease of the 1990s. Coverage of stress in our daily lives and workplace is made by the media with regularity. Undoubtedly, the economic pressures of the 1990s have contributed towards the publicity of stress and its associated problems, as organizations become leaner and strive to maintain profit margins. All occupations have the capacity to be stressful, but some occupations and organizations are potentially more stressful than others. Cranwell-Ward (1987) identified organizations within the service industry, those with high technology and those undergoing structural job changes as potentially more stressful than others. The characteristics of the retail industry fit all these criteria. In another attempt to compare stress levels of different occupations, Cooper *et al.* (1988) devised a stress league table and ranked over a hundred jobs according to their degrees of stress. From it, sales and retailing and management jobs were identified as 'over average' stressful occupations. This exercise was repeated in 1997, and results showed these jobs are even more stressful than a decade ago (*Sunday Times*, 1997) and can now be classified as 'very stressful'.

Employers have a legal responsibility to manage stress at work, through the guidelines provided by the UK Health and Safety Executive. These state that employers have a legal duty to take reasonable care to ensure that health is not placed at risk through excessive and sustained levels of stress arising from the way work is organized, the way people deal with each other at their work or from the day to day demands placed on their workforce. In addition the threat of litigation, as well as reduced organizational performance, has encouraged many organizations to take stress management more seriously. They realize the need to be aware of the stressors people experience at work and be prepared to try to alleviate them.

WHAT IS STRESS?

The nature of stress is a complex issue to research because everyone experiences it at some stage in their lives, as it is a 'naturally occurring experience essential to our growth, development and performance both at home and at work' (Quick *et al.*, 1990, p. 22). We tend to associate it with words such as 'anxiety', 'tension' or 'panic'. Stress has come to mean the causes and the effects of feelings of pressure. But everyone has their own levels of resistance to stressors which makes research into the area difficult. Some people are better able to adapt their behaviour and hence cope with the pressures of life than others. Much of our response will be influenced by what else is going on at the time. So a particular incident may seem trivial to one person and they are more than able to deal with it. For another, however, it is seen as the 'final straw', that is although it may be a small issue or incident, nevertheless this slight addition makes the whole situation no longer bearable. Thus, the interplay of constraints, demands and supports is endlessly variable. Warren and Toll's (1997) definition of stress is a useful one to consider for this case. They define stress as 'a response to the perceived relationship between the demands on us and our ability to cope' (p. 9).

It is important to recognize, however, that all stressful outcomes are not negative. Although stressful events are inevitable they can lead to one of two outcomes: eustress or distress, depending on the individual's and organization's response to the stress (Quick and Quick, 1984). Eustress is a healthy, positive, constructive outcome of a stress agent, and leads to individual and organizational optimum health and well-being by stimulating productivity and supporting performance. Distress, however, is an unhealthy, negative and destructive outcome of a stress agent, and has adverse consequences for the individual and the organization. The factors which cause stress at work can be grouped into various categories: factors intrinsic to the job; role in the organization; relationships at work; career development; organizational structure and climate; extra-organizational sources of stress.

One of the reasons for the importance of examining occupational stress is its cost implications in terms of its impact on performance. In the UK, 360 million working days are lost each year through sickness, at a cost to organizations of £8m – at least half of these lost days relate to stress-related absence (Cooper and Cartwright, 1994). The direct costs are absenteeism and labour turnover which are easily quantifiable. What is more difficult to quantify are the indirect costs such as irrational thinking, faulty decision making, communication breakdowns, wasting time and so on, all of which may result in low morale, and high dissatisfaction from work. Clearly, both the direct and indirect costs of stress result in decreased productivity and poor quality performance not only from the individuals under stress, but potentially from those who have to work with them.

CLARKSON'S SUPERMARKETS

Clarkson's Supermarkets Ltd has 350 UK supermarkets with a total sales area of over 10 million sq ft. The company employs 85,000 people (33 per cent of whom are full-time and 67 per cent are part-time). Clarkson's Supermarkets generated an operating profit of £465.2m from £8.5b of sales (including taxes) in the year to 31 March 1998. A large store typically offers 8000 Clarkson brand lines and 11,500 manufacturers' lines. The own-brand produce is an expanding part of the company business. More display space is given over to fresh foods than previously, with fresh meat counters, fresh fish counters, fresh fruit and vegetables, delicatessen counters and fresh baked bread available in many of the stores. In response to customer demand, recent innovations have seen the introduction of a loyalty card, the use of self-scanning equipment and the trial of all-night shopping at weekends. The group currently invests £20m annually in staff training with the emphasis on personal development and serving the customer better.

Clarkson employ occupational health advisors (all of whom have nursing backgrounds), each of whom look after about 15 stores. A large part of their role is to advise on people's fitness to work or to make recommendations about reasonable adjustments if people have a disability. They offer advice on a range of health and safety issues and rehabilitation programmes after ill health, sickness and absence. About a third of their encounters are for stress-related types of problems.

Store-related Stress

Gerry Pritchard is 37 and has been with Clarkson's for ten years and a store manager for seven years. The store he currently manages is 35,000 sq ft, is located on the edge of town and deals with about 25,000 customers a week. In addition to the standard Clarkson's format it has a fresh meat and fish counter, delicatessen, in-store bakery and petrol forecourt. It employs 340 staff, although the majority of sales staff work part-time on four-hour shifts. His management team (most of whom work full-time) consists of three deputy managers, departmental managers and assistant departmental managers. The store generally performs well, and everybody is preparing for the run up to Christmas. However, last week's performance was down on last year's figures and shrinkage is currently running at 35 per cent above the company average. Therefore, the pressure is on everyone to build up store performance. It has not been helped with the opening of a new competitor store on the other side of town.

Gerry enjoys the fast, competitive nature of his job. He likes the speed of change in the grocery sector. Every day is different, with different issues to respond to, and he has to think on his feet a lot of the time. He tends to thrive on that kind of environment and does not tend to understand others who do not. As a manager, Gerry could be described as task-orientated. He runs a very complicated, labour intensive business and likes to see everything running to order. As a consequence he works long hours, especially now that seven-day trading operates in the store. As a key holder he has to be prepared to be called out even at nights or his day off which he tries to take on a Wednesday. The children are often in bed when he gets home, and he often falls asleep in the armchair but then he is paid a good salary for his job. And anyway if the store is under performing there is always the fear that he may be replaced, or not promoted.

Over the last few years, due to the competitive nature of the industry, pressure has been exerted throughout the company to maintain bottom line profit margins. One way of achieving this has been to reduce staffing levels to a minimum. As a consequence, when a member of staff leaves, they are often not replaced. This has resulted in increased workloads for those who remain and the pressure to accomplish a certain amount of work by a certain deadline. While many of the sales staff work four hour shifts, workloads build up during the day and can be passed on to workers coming onto shifts. Many of the part-timers are unable to work overtime (when it is available) because of their other commitments. Very often the junior and trainee managers bear the brunt and stay behind after their official leaving times to keep things ticking over, as well as trying to accomplish their own duties. Some think the general staff show no real interest in the company nor take any initiative but then again why should they? They are not paid to take decisions. Generally, however, most people have a pride in their job, and they try to do everything really well. In fact there are so many things to do that they cannot do everything really well, and that can be really frustrating. Gerry is able to delegate a lot of work to his deputy managers who, more often than not, delegate down to departmental and assistant managers. So sometimes this level of management feel they are getting it from both sides which, if it goes unrecognized, leads them to feel undervalued.

The store is always busy, but with the run up to Christmas it is particularly busy which places more pressure on the staff. Obviously at Christmas time there is a far bigger turnover of stock, which means more deliveries at the back door and more pressure to get the stock on to the shelves. Inevitably, there are bigger queues at the checkouts, and more customer service is required to cope with the extra demands. Some customers become irate when they have to wait at the checkouts, which Gerry doesn't like as the checkouts are the customers' last impression of the store and he wants them to leave happy. For a store his size, however, he normally gets three or four new members of staff to cover the seasonal period and relieve some of the additional pressures. He will let the new members work closely with Ellen, a general sales assistant, who at 22 has been working with the company for four years. She understands how the store operates, and is probably one of the best assistants to help integrate the new staff members quickly into the store. Ellen's job is quite varied. It comprises of stocking shelves, working on the customer service desk, and rotating around several departments. Because she's been there so long, she has a good knowledge of the products stocked in most departments. As Christmas approaches, however, she knows she'll spend more time on the checkouts. She finds that quite boring and customers are so fickle! Some can be really abusive, and although she knows the 'customer is king' and always tries to be polite and smile, for some customers no answer is good enough. Sometimes she'd like to tell them exactly what she thinks of them, but doesn't because of her loyalty to the company. Instead, she has a good moan to some of the other staff at tea break or to her boyfriend when she gets home. She's just heard she's to help the new members of staff settle in too. 'I suppose they'll be thrown in at the deep end with no induction, and it will be questions, questions, questions'. That really annoys Ellen as it slows her up with her own job. She gets frustrated at times. On the one hand, her managers are trusting her to integrate new members of staff into the store. On the other hand, however, she feels she has little opportunity to participate in the decision making process. The sales assistants' opinions never seem to be sought by the managers, even though they are those who are probably closest to customer views. So at times the job does not offer enough stimulation or job satisfaction for Ellen. She likes to go to swimming to unwind at the end of a shift, but hasn't had much time recently. At tea break she complains to Henry, one of the junior managers, about these new staff. 'Why do I always have to show new staff round?' 'Oh, you're good at it Ellen, and don't forget you were new once' he replies.

Henry, 24, junior manager in ambient foods, is career-orientated. He likes working for the company and wants to better himself. It is frustrating sometimes, however, as there are rules for everything. There doesn't appear to be any room for flair – the company doesn't seem to encourage you to express your initiative. All stores have to be merchandised the same and so on – all head office rules to abide to. To him, it appears head office are out of touch with reality at times. They sit in their offices devising this rule and that, which on paper may sound fine but in reality just doesn't work in the store. Some of these people need to come into store and see the impracticalities for themselves. Then they might understand the difficulties the store staff face. Sometimes Henry feels undervalued and resentful for the amount of work he does and the hours he puts in. Some jobs he is given are things the general assistants do. He is not paid for the overtime he does, but when he first arrived at the store he was told he had to work as long as he had to or until he was told he could go home. He wants to make a good impression with Gerry so he likes to be seen and doesn't go home before Gerry. This, he reckons, will help him in his next appraisal interview and enhance his career opportunities. He very often goes home exhausted, particularly when working shifts, and feels less able to deal with the stresses and strains of the job when he is tired.

Phil is one of the three deputy managers. The organization has undergone some new technological changes recently, for which he has control. Because the store is operating on a tight labour schedule, it is difficult for staff to be released for staff training. The departmental managers are telling him they can't afford to lose their staff for staff training, and so many staff have to pick up, as best they can, how to operate the new technology. His latest project is the introduction of self-scanning into the store which will come into operation in the spring. Staff will need training in this particularly as they have to help customers to use the scanners. He has to devise a way of ensuring staff do get the opportunity for training, which is not easy given all the shift patterns and people only working four hours at a time.

Phil often eats his lunch at his desk as this is a good opportunity to catch up on his post and e-mails or read a copy of *Retail Week*. He has to try to make his mark and get recognized. Opportunities to progress within a leaner organization are more difficult and there are not the same opportunities to move from one company to another as there were in the past. All information goes through the deputy managers and they have to sift and delegate the tasks to be carried out. Sometimes Phil feels as if he is hit from both sides – both senior management and the general staff. There is a constant demand from head office personnel for branch information and reports with short deadlines. Generally the demands are greater – staff have to be more versatile and more flexible especially with the long opening hours and the fact that some stores are now open 24 hours. While eating his sandwich one lunch time, he opens an e-mail from his colleague at head office who warns him that one of the directors, Malcolm Savage is travelling up to Scotland at the weekend. This means that every store around the M1 corridor has to be prepared for a store visit by Malcolm. Panic begins to set in. The pressure is on Phil to make a good impression as he is next in line for a store management promotion. Phil needs to ensure that everything in the store is A1, but they haven't got the staff to cope. Everyone will have to work doubly quickly and fit all the tasks in. Things come round the corner so rapidly in this business, you just have to react very very quickly.

Problems don't just happen on the shop floor. There are demands on warehouse staff too, particularly with new health and safety regulations to adhere to, and no extra resources. The amount of paperwork has increased for the receipt of goods, and there are now stringent regulations on the delivery of frozen foods with various rules having to be adhered to. Sandy, the warehouse manager, also has staffing problems. If his supervisor is off, that leaves him as the only person qualified to drive the yard truck. This means by 4pm all his paperwork is waiting for him in the office, so he has to settle down to another three or four hours work to catch up with it. If he leaves it, it will only be there to do the next day, so it's easier to stay behind and work beyond his normal hours.

Many of the store staff believe that the head office is to blame, and comments such as 'they don't seem to give much thought about how the procedures that they are putting in are going to affect the people at store level' are frequently heard throughout the store. The nature of communications between head office and the operational level seem to cause endless problems. For example, store staff often resent being told how to merchandise the stock from head office, or being sent stock to sell which is inappropriate for their region.

The company is aware of demands placed on people at work. To obtain a better picture of the most pressing demands, the occupational health unit wants to conduct a stress audit among the workforce. This will enable them to understand the range of factors which cause various levels of staff pressure at work. Once they have completed this they will be able to consider any strategies the company can adopt to help relieve the pressures placed upon their staff, which in turn, should help to reduce the costs of stress to the organization.

QUESTIONS

1. What are the potential stressors experienced by all staff working in the store?

2. Consider the implications of the issues you have identified in question 1 on:
   - the individuals involved
   - the performance of the store.

3. In what way might individuals try to relieve the stressors they experience?

4. What can the organization do to help alleviate stress in the store?

5. Gerry has a particular management style. Evaluate his management style and consider how may this affect the stressors experienced and solutions recommended?

REFERENCES

Cooper, C. and Cartwright, S. (1994) 'Healthy mind: healthy organisation. A proactive approach to occupational stress'. *Human Relations*, **47**(4): 455–71.

Cooper, C. L., Cooper, R. D. and Eaker, L. H. (1988) *Living with Stress*. London: Penguin.

Cranwell-Ward, J. (1987) *Managing Stress*. Aldershot: Gower.

Quick, J. C. and Quick, J. D. (1984) *Organisational Stress and Preventive Management*. New York: McGraw-Hill.

Quick, J. C., Nelson, D. J. and Quick, J. D. (1990) *Stress and Challenge at the Top: The Paradox of the Healthy Executive*. Chichester: Wiley.

Sunday Times (1997) 'Stress at work: how your job rates'. *Sunday Times*, 18 May, pp. 8–9.

Warren, E. and Toll, C. (1997) *The Stress Work Book*. London: Nicholas Brealey.

CASE 4

MANAGING THE IMPACT OF NEW STORE DEVELOPMENT: TRADING POTENTIAL AT SCOTTISH POWER RETAIL

IAN CLARKE AND MIKE PRETIOUS

The authors would like to thank the Scottish Power Retail division for their time and assistance in putting together this case study. Particular thanks go to Managing Director Alan Jefferson for enabling the research; Retail Estates Manager Iain McKenzie; and to managers Peter Fitzpatrick and Stephen Howie for the insights they provided into the management of their stores.

It is important to note that the information used on this case regarding the stores in Stirling represents *simulated* data and a pattern of events that *did not* occur in the company's outlet in the way it is described. The case has been significantly simplified so that the key learning objectives are highlighted. Consequently, while the issues raised can be viewed as realistic, readers should not regard the case content as factual.

INTRODUCTION

This case study focuses on the opening of a new store to draw out the management, personality and operational problems associated with such an event. The case, therefore, represents an excellent opportunity for the reader to appreciate the tensions that can exist (and why) between staff, store management, functional head office personnel and directors in the same company. By examining the opening of a single new superstore by the electrical retail chain Scottish Power in Stirling, Scotland, the case study draws attention to the operational issues stemming from strategic decisions. New store development is central to retailers increasing their share of local marketplaces, but to ensure that this is done profitably in order to prevent the effects of saturated markets (Guy, 1994), there is a critical need to determine trading potential. The difficulties associated with doing this are brought into the case study, since the management of 'variable' costs such as staff and management bare directly on the financial performance of a store.

In an increasingly competitive trading environment, most bulky goods retailers have sought to develop more efficient formats of retail delivery. The store format with the greatest impact on a range of retail sectors has been the 'superstore'. Like so many other bulky goods retailers, the UK electrical retailing sector – which in 1997 accounted for £8b or 3 per cent of disposable income – has been pressed to develop more accessible stores with greater capacity than is possible in the high street. These have tended to be located either on retail parks on the fringe of towns, or out of town. In these sites, occupancy rents are around one tenth of those in the high street, and the margin per sq ft of selling space makes the display of bulky electrical goods financially feasible (Brownlie and Lemond, 1992). Many retailers have sought, however, to maintain their niche presence in town centres with relatively small high street stores, but at the same time have exploited the growth in out-of-town shopping by positioning large stores in accessible locations away from city centres. Such dual and frequently multi-faceted strategies, involving different 'locational positions' (see Clarke *et al.*, 1997), introduce three related problems for the retailer. First, how to evaluate accurately the potential of new sites, including the possibility of future competitor outlets. Second, how to assess impact on existing outlets. Finally, how to determine and manage the impact of these changes in the operational decision-making of the stores.

This case study addresses these problems through the opening of a new Scottish Power superstore opening in Stirling. It uses a role-play scenario in which the reader is asked to assume the position of various store-based and head-office personnel in a meeting in the store two months prior to its opening. The task for the reader centres on the assimilation of information from a company document, its use in negotiations between these parties, and the making of critical decisions about store operations. The case provides a significant opportunity to develop and bring together analytical problem solving skills, with those of teamwork and negotiation, in a context where strategy has very real operational implications. In order to provide background to the issues and the sector, the first part of the case summarizes the key developments in electrical retailing. The case then moves on to provide specific insight into the company's new development in Stirling. The scenario is then presented through the eyes of the store manager, Joshua Gabriel, and in the ensuing role-play exercise the reader is asked to assume the role of various people in a meeting to discuss the new store opening.

ELECTRICAL RETAILING AND SCOTTISH POWER RETAIL DIVISION

Scottish Power's retail division was created within the organization prior to the privatization of this and other regional electricity companies (RECs) in 1990. At the time the company operated 73 high street shops, in south and central Scotland, and made a trading loss. These were the former electricity board 'showrooms', which sold products and provided a location in which customers could pay their electricity bills. Since privatization, substantial emphasis has been put on the expansion of the store network, especially in England and Wales. In part the retail division has expanded through acquisition: in 1992 the company acquired seventeen Rumbelows and Atlantis shops; in 1994 they took over fifty stores and a distribution depot from Clydesdale Electrical; and in 1995 they acquired five stores in the north west from Manweb. In the process of acquiring outlets Scottish Power endeavoured to reposition the stores through expansion and refocusing the product range, and now operate under three fascias. These are superstores (under the Scottish Power or Electricity Plus brand names); and small Sound & Vision outlets, which are located primarily in town centres and concentrate on sales of hi-fi, cameras and televisions. By 1996, turnover of the company had risen to £240m and an operating margin of 5.2 per cent as a result of the store portfolio expanding to 150 outlets. Three quarters of the total sales space is in the form of out-of-town superstores (Scottish Power, 1998).

The developments in Scottish Power must be set against the evolution of electricity retailing in the UK generally. Government statistics show that sales through large retailers of household goods expanded 63 per cent between 1990 and 1997, while sales through small businesses fell by 20 per cent. This shift in sales reflects the continued expansion of large retail superstores out of town. In the electrical retail sector independent retailers have been able to maintain a stronger presence through specialization – such that they still account for some 21 per cent of the market share. This compares with the share of the electrical multiple groups amounting to over 35 per cent, with sales through other formats such as department stores, catalogue shops, and mail order amounting to around 18 per cent. Sales through other formats such as variety stores, hypermarkets and freezer centres make up the remaining quarter of the market (Mintel, 1997). Within this distribution of trade, the Dixons Stores Group (DSG) occupies by far the strongest position, with a market share of almost 17 per cent in 1997; followed by the Kingfisher owned Comet chain (6 per cent) and Scottish Power (2.7 per cent). No other electrical multiple has a share greater than 1 per cent.

Despite the dominance of the DSG group in this description, research on the electrical retailing sector by Mintel (1997) shows that customers prefer to comparison shop. In this process of comparing, DSG store formats and Comet dominates the scene for major appliances and audio-visual equipment. Over two–thirds of the Mintel survey sample indicated that the DSG chain Currys is the most likely to be visited when deciding to make a purchase, much of which can be accounted for by their extensive network of stores (over 205 superstores and 173 high street stores). Two thirds of the sample also visited Comet. In this purchasing process, visits to the ex-RECs (see Note 1) account for 35 per cent of the comparison shops for large electrical appliances, 21 per cent for audio-visual equipment, and 17 per cent for small electrical items. Dominance of the DSG group in the sector has come about to a large extent from their ability to target market segments through individually positioned store formats – small Dixons stores and 'The Link' (a specialist telephone store) in town; Currys Superstores out of town; and PC World in the computer market. Growth in space out of town especially led to substantial sales growth and significant economies of scale in their operations (Mintel, 1997).

Growth of product ranges of the major electrical multiples collectively has come largely from expansion into the brown goods sector (televisions, video recorders and hi-fi), driven by technological innovations in these products (for example NICAM stereo), as well as the small office/home office market for personal computers. Sales in the more traditional white goods sector (refrigerators, freezers, washing machines, cookers and so on) tend to be limited by the high levels of market penetration. For example, Mintel note that this is as high as 98 per cent in the case of televisions, and 89 per cent in the case of washing machines. As a result, much of the white goods sector is largely a replacement market. The size and distribution of sales in the electrical sector is shown in more detail in Figure 4.1.

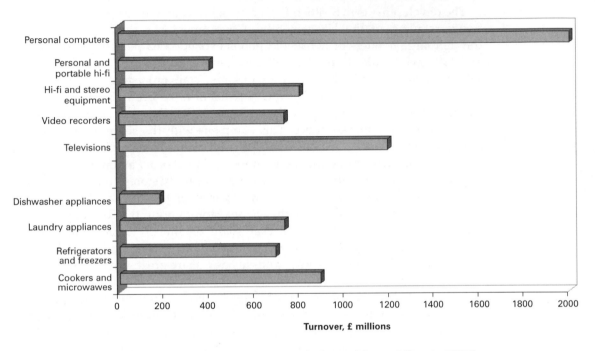

Figure 4.1   Electrical product market sizes (adapted from Mintel, 1997)

In summary, the electrical retailing sector within which Scottish Power trades in the UK is characterized by an increasingly wide distribution base in terms of the variety of formats from which products are purchased, and in which the traditional ex-RECs have undergone substantial rationalization. The strength of the Dixons Stores Group is particularly notable. Within the market, customers are principally looking for a combination of good aftersales service and low prices, but coupled with knowledgeable staff and wide ranges of well-known brands (Mintel, 1997). In the majority of markets in the UK, therefore, Scottish Power is likely to be trading principally against the market leaders in terms of out-of-town superstores, Currys and Comet, as well as Dixons town centre outlets. There is a considerable degree of comparison between these outlets in customer behaviour in search for the features mentioned above, making the market highly competitive. In this context, Scottish Power Retail Division Managing Director Alan Jefferson is realistic about the competitive position of the relatively new Scottish Power brand in general:

> It takes a long time to establish brand credibility... because we are a relatively new brand, it is best if they [the customers] come to the competitors which have been around a lot longer, and then come and see us. (personal interview, 1997)

In order to improve their market position, the strategy of the company has been focused on the development of out-of-town superstores, coupled with targeted Sound & Vision 'brown goods' stores in town and shopping centres. The discrete positioning of the two store brands makes the stores feel very different to the customer. Where appropriate, some of the Sound & Vision stores have been developed out of the old electricity board showrooms. In many cases, however, the locations of these outlets were inappropriate for effective retail trade, and the company disposed of them to move to more centrally located units. Opportunities for the opening of Sound & Vision outlets are inevitably more limited by the high rents and rates which tend to be commanded in town and city centres, where premium space is pressured for alternative retail uses. The principal strategy to open new out-of-town superstores has been driven by Alan Jefferson who, having been part of the growth of the Dixons group, understands the role of the superstore in obtaining market presence and achieving economies of scale. This same rationale is behind the continued drive to expand the superstore portfolio of the company from the current number of 205 at the time of writing in late 1998.

THE NEW STIRLING SUPERSTORE

Joshua Gabriel is the recently appointed manager of one such Scottish Power superstore, currently under construction on the Springkerse Retail Park located on the east of Stirling (see the site plan shown in Figure 4.2). He has worked in the electrical sector since he left school, starting first as a sales person with Currys before moving to their main competitor Comet, where he managed stores in Edinburgh, Falkirk and Aberdeen. While with Comet, he was promoted to a field management position, and worked in area management for about five years. In the shake-up and rationalization in the sector, he found himself the victim of redundancy, and moved to a small Scottish electrical retailer, Clydesdale. He managed stores in Perth and Uddingston until the company was eventually taken over by Scottish Power in 1992. His effectiveness in turning 'average' superstores around has not gone unnoticed in Scottish Power, and he has spent the last three years working as a relief manager to 'turn around' problem stores.

Joshua has been keen to obtain the position as manager of the new Stirling superstore. He first heard of the success of the company in obtaining a lease on unit 6 in the development last summer, 1997 (see Figure 4.3) and prior to his interview for the job, had thought hard about why he wanted it. First, there were personal reasons. Joshua had grown up on a family sheep farm in the Carse area 20 miles to the west of Stirling and was keen to come back and work nearer home, after having moved around so much over the last few years. When he was young, he had regularly visited the town with his father on market day and was always surprised how far some of the farmers were prepared to travel to Stirling to sell their stock – some came from over 50 miles to the north and west. There were no other market towns for miles. Ironically, he thought, some of that same Scottish meat sold at the Stirling market was now being sold at the Safeway superstore which had opened in the first phase of the Springkerse Retail Park twelve months earlier. When he had visited the town for his interview, he was surprised how both the older Tesco superstore and the new Safeway continued to trade strongly.

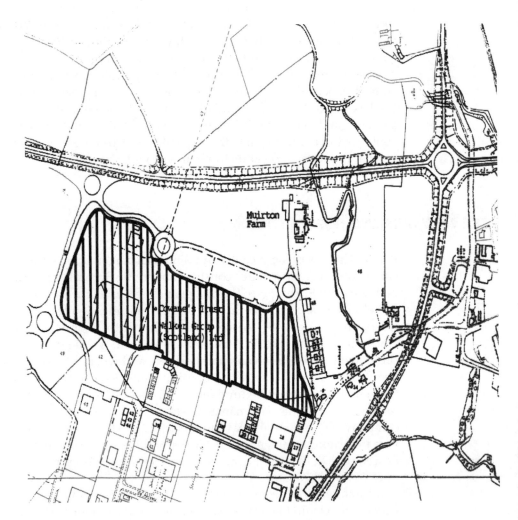

Figure 4.2   Stirling Springkerse site plan (Scottish Power)

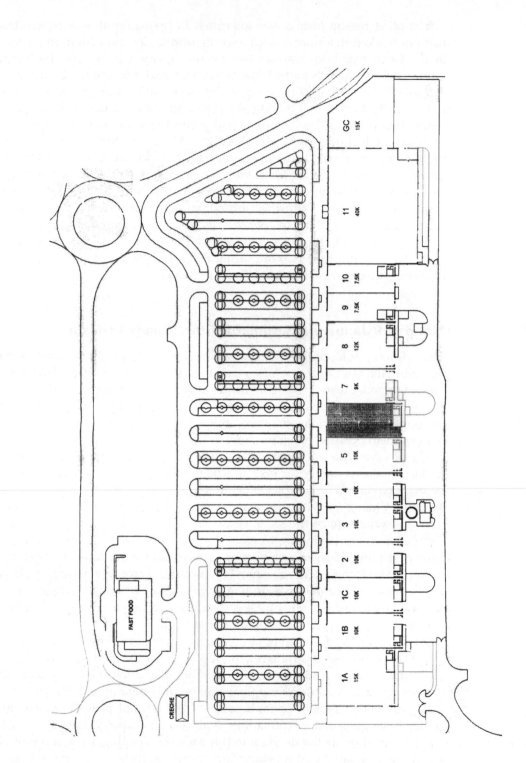
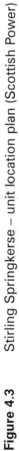

Figure 4.3   Stirling Springkerse – unit location plan (Scottish Power)

The other reason Joshua was interested in managing this store was that he had not worked in a store in such a strong trading location. Shopping provision in the town had been transformed by the opening of the Thistle Shopping Centre, to which BHS and Marks & Spencer had relocated. About that time, Scottish Power had acquired a small 1700 sq ft outlet near one of the entrances to the Thistle Centre that it had refitted as a specialist outlet under its Sound & Vision brand fascia. The company had given the store to a previous assistant manager of Joshua's, Amanda McKnight. Since she took over the store six months ago turnover had grown substantially. In the next year the second phase extension to the Thistle Centre was to open, with a new C&A as anchor store, a new Virgin superstore, and at least 30 other units in between. Moreover, there was going to be a further substantial injection of retail provision out of town at Springkerse. The first phase of the retail park, with Safeway and Burger King, had taken off. In addition to Scottish Power, several other operators were going to open in phase two, including B&Q, Halfords, Pets Mart, Reids furniture store, Carpetwise, Fads and Texstyle World.

Monday, 9 January – Getting the Store Ready to Trade

That Monday, 9 January, Joshua sat at his desk trying to think what he had to do before the new store opening meeting at the end of the week. It was 8.30am on a wet and blustery Scottish winter morning. Fitting-out of the store was proceeding at a furious pace. He was feeling racked with uncertainty because, although he had managed several other large superstores, this was his first management position in a new store.

He surveyed the work going on outside from his office window. The bitumen surface on the customer car park was being laid and parking spaces still had to be mapped out, to be completed before the arrival of the landscaping firm next Monday. Close by, a telescopic crane was slowly manoeuvring a heavy heating unit on to the roof of the store. Below his window, he could see the signage contractors were beginning to erect the Scottish Power sign and logo on the front of the unit. He had been waiting for this, because he knew just getting that up on the building would give him two months of free advertising by this busy new eastern relief road. In a trading environment where advertising spend of the company was substantially less than the two major competitors, DSG and Comet, little things like this were important.

At that same moment in the store, the key members of his team were already busy. This was their second week in the store after the contractors had 'handed over' the building ready for fitting-out. They had about eight weeks to fit out the store, recruit and train shop-floor staff before opening on 1 March 1999. This was early in the year to open, because of the normal post-Christmas 'lull' in trade, but construction difficulties had brought about the delay, and the company had made the decision to put back the opening a few more weeks to ensure a reasonable trading start. That morning, Joshua had met his assistant managers at seven o'clock for a 'walkabout'. The team of eight new 'core' full-time staff had spent an hour tweaking the suggested arrangements from head office for the first full week of training in their new store. They had to familiarize themselves with the 'space planning' layout diagrams and areas of merchandising, and ensure the fitting-out contractors had completed the installation of shelving and merchandising units within the overall layout plan by the end of Thursday of that week (Figure 4.4). Tomorrow, his deputy manager Graeme Stoddart, was to begin the process of planning recruitment of part-time staff for the store. Last week, the two of them had been in discussions with their regional manager, Peter Doyle and area personnel manager when they had heard the projected annual turnover was likely to be very strong for a new store – an annual turnover of around £12.3m by the second year. On that basis, it had been agreed in principle that they would be able to afford to recruit four part-time and weekend staff to complement the full-time management team. The staff budget appeared tight to Joshua, but the ratio of part-time to full-time staff was within the guidelines from head office (Table 4.1). That meant he could get a good blend of full and part-time staff and pay them reasonable rates. In a meeting with the area personnel manager, Joshua had been informed of his own salary and benefits package, which were also determined by store performance. The £12.3m turnover (an average weekly first year turnover of approximately £238,000) had put him into the salary 'Band B3' – unusual for a new store which was normally only achieved within established superstores after several years of trading. (Note: The reason for working on second year

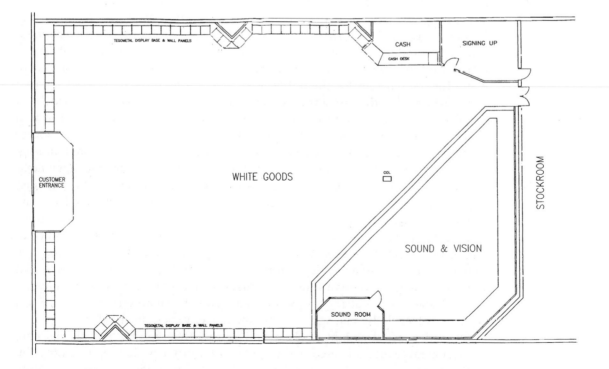

Figure 4.4   Stirling Sprinkerse – superstore layout plan (Scottish Power)

Table 4.1   **Suggested staffing ratios for new Scottish Power superstores, by turnover band**

Store band	Year 2 average weekly turnover (£000s)	Managers (store plus deputies)	Full-time staff	Part-time staff (full-time equivalents)	Indicative staffing budget (£000s)[1]
A	350–399	3	7	5	£170
B1	300–349	2	6	4	£130
B2	250–299	2	5	3	£115
B3	200–249	2	4	2	£100
C	150–199	1	3	1	£60

Current salary starting points (full-time equivalent):

Manager   £25,000
Full-time staff £10,000
Part-time   c.£5000

trading levels is that the company preferred to look at the situation once trade had stabilized.) Alongside a higher salary, this gave him a company car as part of his package, something that he had never enjoyed before.

Joshua knew that the expected performance of his new store was important in other respects. A turnover of this magnitude had produced an above average return on capital of 15 per cent, compared to the benchmark target of 12 per cent set by the company. This influenced some of his major fixed costs, especially the annual rent for the outlet. Rent was turnover-related, fixed for two years before the first review. Five checkouts on two desks had also been installed last week around the store. New stores received a minimum of two checkouts, up to an annual turnover of £10m, and then were entitled to another checkout when their predicted performance entered into a new store banding. Not all the checkouts are open all the time, but give the store manager flexibility to cope at busier periods of the week. Thus, a new superstore like Stirling, planned to take over £12m per annum, was allowed four checkouts. Even the number of stock deliveries per week were related to turnover, with stores trading between £250–300,000 receiving four lorries per week; the number of deliveries would have been three for a lower turnover £200–250,000, and five deliveries for a store achieving trading over £300,000 per week. He knew that with increasingly demanding consumers unwilling to wait for delivery, perhaps the most challenging job of management was to ensure no products went out of stock, by managing the timing of deliveries effectively.

Over the last fortnight, Joshua had found that getting the store's core management team motivated had been less of a problem than he had thought. Enthusiasm was helped by the salary points associated with working in a store in a high performance band. The management team had received substantial salary increases compared to their previous jobs in 'Band C' stores. All were working well together, buoyed by the busy atmosphere, the challenge and rewards of working in a large superstore expected to do well, and the excitement of the meeting with Alan Slimming – the commercial director responsible for new store openings – which was to take place that Friday. It was then that they were to meet to discuss more detailed up-to-date information regarding the research conducted by the company's specialist site evaluation unit, including details of the marketing campaign for the new outlet. This was the only real concern which had been voiced by the team, because the new store was opening in March, a relatively quiet period. In their eyes, a vigorous campaign was critical in helping to raise awareness of the new superstore by the public.

Thursday 12 January – Preparing for the New Store Opening Meeting

By 8am on the Thursday Joshua was at his desk dealing with his post. The first document he came to was impressively bound: it was the latest market research and trading evaluation for his new Stirling superstore received from the commercial planning division at head office. Joshua scanned the executive summary of the document for any changes. £12.3m projected second year turnover. Return on capital 15 per cent. Staffing budget £130,000 per annum. A table compared the new development to 'analogue' stores already trading within Scottish Power in different parts of the country (see Table 4.2). Of the stores with which it was compared, only the store in Perth achieved a higher turnover and sales density (indicated by the 'turnover/sq ft' statistic). His impression was that the levels of population in the area would readily support the high new store performance expected, and that effective competition was limited – the trading environment stepped up in competitiveness, he thought, on the fringes of his expected catchment. Closer by competition floor space was more limited than that of the analogue stores with which his store was being compared. Out of town, only Comet (who also traded at Springkerse) was of any significance. They were well established since phase 1 of the Springkerse Retail Park next to Safeway, but customer surveys conducted by Scottish Power had shown that their stores were a match for Comet in terms of most of the main attributes customers used to choose where to shop. In a town with a substantial population and only one out-of-town competitor, the chances were his store was going to perform well.

The big shock came when he flipped over onto the second page of the report, where he began to read the section headed 'Trading Potential'. He shifted uncomfortably as he read down the page, about the latest planning information unearthed only last week by the site evaluation unit. Apparently, a local press rumour that DSG had been negotiating a lease on unit 4 at Springkerse had been substantiated. Apparently, the unit had only become available when another retailer had withdrawn in the final stages of negotiating the lease on the property. In the enquiries made by the site evaluation unit, Stirling Council

Table 4.2   **Analogue store information for Stirling Sprinkerse**

Store	Annual turnover (£m in second year)	Size (sq ft)	£/ sq ft	Population by drive-time band (000s)*				Superstore competition by drive-time band* (000s sq ft)			
				5	10	15	30	5	10	15	30
(A) Stirling (site)	£12.3	7029	1750	35	45	50	93	7	7	7	25
(B) Perth	£12.9	6950	1856	25	35	46	50	5	10	17	52
(C) Shrewsbury	£12.7	9200	1380	28	37	56	90	6	17	21	30
(D) Yeovil	£11.1	8130	1365	33	40	60	80	14	22	25	52

Notes on composition of competition and size of population within 5, 10, 15 and 30-minutes drive of each Scottish Power store in each location
(A) Comet superstore; Sound & Vision; Argos; Dixons
(B) Currys superstore; Argos; Dixons
(C) Comet superstore; Argos; Dixons
(D) Currys superstore; Comet superstore; Sound & Vision; Argos; Dixons

had recently approved a change of use for the conversion of the unit to an electrical superstore, to be operated by the DSG chain as a Currys. He knew that, while Scottish Power might be able to hold their own against other operators, matching the brand strength of Currys would prove difficult. He wondered what the implications for his store would be.

Alan Slimming, the commercial director responsible for all aspects of new store openings, would be chairing the meeting the next day and would be bringing some of his specialist advisors with him. He was an extremely demanding if non-charismatic individual and he did not suffer fools gladly. Joshua had sat in on a new store opening meeting with Alan Slimming once before when he was a deputy manager in Aberdeen, and he knew that, while a lot of research went into producing the forecasts, they were still estimates and could be influenced. After all, Joshua thought, the trading situation had changed fundamentally since the opening forecast for the new store had been produced when the site was acquired nine months earlier. At the meeting there was bound to be debate about the projected turnover – so how should he play this? Should he try to protect his salary, and that of his team, and argue to maintain the opening forecast as it stood already? Or would it be better in the medium term to accept the 'hit' on the forecasts now, and work hard to develop the trade? The latter option had its attractions, but Joshua knew from his experience that the Currys store opening was surrounded by uncertainties over opening time. Just as his own store was due to open two months later than originally anticipated, so too might Currys. DSG had a formidable opening team who could well complete a store from starting on site within thirty weeks, and the shell for unit 4 was already virtually complete. So it was distinctly probable that the competing superstore would open half way through his own first year of trade. In the run-up to Christmas, trade on brown goods (televisions, hi-fi and cameras) could increase by as much as 75 per cent as people bought these as presents. This was, he thought, a critical period for establishing a strong franchise, and would be something DSG management would be keen to secure by opening as soon as possible. There was a chance to find out more too, because Slimming would be bringing with him Stuart Noble, associate director responsible for site evaluation. Why had they taken so long to find out this vital piece of information? Was Noble sure of the effect Currys might have on the potential of his new superstore? How certain was he of the original opening forecast in any event? If they judged the impact was going to be large, then surely there was a strong case for increasing local advertising?

Joshua had the day ahead of him to gather his thoughts. He picked up the phone and paged his deputy manager Graeme Stoddart. He took off his jacket and began to flick feverishly through the limited information he was able to secure from the report. Five minutes later, Graeme knocked at the door and as he sat down, Joshua poured him a coffee and began to break the bad news.

THE NEW STORE OPENING MEETING – A ROLE-PLAY EXERCISE

You are required to act as one of the participants in the new store opening meeting to be held at Springkerse Road. Your role will be allocated to you. Additional information is given for each role below. Those scheduled to attend the meeting are:

- Alan Slimming   Commercial Director for New Stores
- Peter Doyle   Regional Manager
- Stuart Noble   Associate Director, Site Evaluation Unit
- Joshua Gabriel   New Superstore Manager, Springkerse
- Graeme Stoddart   Deputy Manager, Springkerse
- Amanda McKnight   Sound & Vision Store Manager

Spend time getting ready for the meeting, by reading the case and your individual brief thoroughly, thinking about the points it raises, and particularly by considering the implications of the information. During the meeting, you will be expected to take a full part in the discussions.

Key Questions to Consider:

1. What will be the impact of the new DSG store development on the trading potential of both the Springkerse superstore *and* the existing Sound & Vision outlet?

2. What are the operational implications of your assessments of trading levels of the new superstore and potentially other out-of-town competi-

tors, both for the new superstore and the Sound & Vision? How might these effects be managed?

3.   Contrast the issues facing the managers of both Scottish Power stores.

Brief 1: Alan Slimming – Commercial Director for New Stores

Age 48. 30 years' experience in electrical retailing. Joined Scottish Power Retail Division as regional manager in 1995. Promoted to present position in 1996. He has had a busy schedule of meetings over the last few days – meetings in the company head office in Cumbernauld; attending a weekly board meeting to decide on new site acquisitions; on the road visiting new sites.

Before each new store opening, Slimming is fully briefed in a pre-meeting at which a representative from each of his commercial planning sections is present, normally the associate director for each function. New store meetings play a communicative role, ensuring the management team fully understands the rationale behind all decisions made by specialist departments at head office. To make efficient use of limited time, Slimming normally restricts discussion to a tight agenda.

His priorities for the Stirling meeting are:

1.   To discuss what a realistic turnover for the Springkerse store will be. He has asked Stuart to work out the most likely opening date of the new Currys, and to assess the potential effect on trading levels.

2.   To determine the relative effects of the Scottish Power superstore, the new Currys superstore, and the extension to the Thistle Centre in the central area, on the likely trade of the Sound & Vision store in the town centre.

3.   To assess the implications for the salary and benefits of the manager and his team, as well as for personnel in the town centre store. The new figures produced by Stuart will steer his thinking on this.

4.   To discuss the product ranging and merchandising plans developed for the new store (Figure 4.4).

5.   To reconsider the effects of the new trading environment on other aspects of the organization of the store which are not yet set in stone, especially the local marketing of the new store, and the provision of new checkouts (the number of which is turnover-related). His preference is for 'low key' openings since there is evidence from previous openings that the company can actually *benefit* from stronger competition by virtue of their brand strength 'pull' and magnitude of advertising.

Brief 2: Peter Doyle – Regional Manager

Over ten years with Scottish Power, first as a store manager, and over the last three years as a regional manager. He notified the site evaluation of the new Currys proposal, reported in *The Stirling Observer* last week. It included a statement from one of the directors of Dixons:

The Springkerse Currys superstore is an exciting development for the Dixons Stores Group. Stirling has long been on our development strategy. We believe there is substantial potential here for out-of-town retailing development. At the moment, only the Comet superstore is present and our evidence shows that it over trades chronically. This says to us that this is not a 'one-horse town'. The new store has gone straight to the top of our priority list for development – if Scottish Power think they are going to have this to themselves, they have another think coming. This is a race for local consumer patronage and we have the stronger brand format. We intend to use this to good effect.

He is inclined to think that there is room for both the new superstore and Sound & Vision outlets in such a significant shopping location. The effects of the Currys will not be as big as others think, so there is no reason to shift the budget sales figure for the next twelve months for either store.

His priority is to ensure the format of the store is appropriate. Currys advantage is its breadth of goods in the brown goods sector – particularly well-known brands such as Sony and Philips, coupled with its own-branded electrical (Matsui) for the more price-conscious consumer. He thinks space devoted to Sound & Vision brown goods in the superstore will need to be drastically expanded from the current layout (shown in Figure 4.4). To this end, he asked Peter Draper, controller in retail planning to provide an alternative layout for a similar sized store used in Trowbridge, where the company has been experimenting with expanding the brown goods space participation (Figure 4.5). In Trowbridge this led to a sales uplift of 30 per cent.

Brief 3: Dr Stuart Noble – Associate Director, Site Evaluation

32 years old. The most qualified of all the section heads in the commercial planning division of Scottish Power Retail. Undergraduate and MSc degrees in geography and PhD in store choice processes in grocery retailing. Several years in site location planning with Safeway. Took up his current post in Scottish Power two years ago. His ability to 'translate' objective findings into practical terms and knowing the limits of the data is critical to his success in the company. His reassessment of Stirling following Alan Slimming's request yesterday did not prove difficult. Trading potential is now likely to be substantially reduced, although there is some uncertainty over the strength of the company franchise in Scotland compared to other parts of the UK.

His team provided him with alternative forecasts that include the new Currys. He has a table to hand out in the meeting (Table 4.3) which illustrates these forecasts compared to the original estimate. The major unknown is whether the new stores will effectively saturate the market in Stirling. He has found out that while permission was granted for all the units in Springkerse Phase over six months ago, it was only last week that the site agent had released the identity of the occupant of unit 4 as Currys. They were under no obligation to release this earlier as the unit has permission for non-food retail, so strictly speaking did not represent a 'change of use' in planning terms.

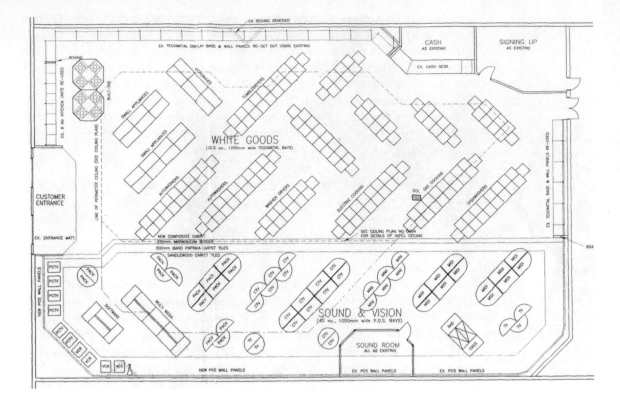

Figure 4.5   Alternative space plan for Stirling Springkerse as per 'new look' Sound &
Vision (Scottish Power)

In addition, a report on qualitative market research from the new Trowbridge
store, published only yesterday, involved in-depth focus group discussions
with selected customers and a pre- and post-conversion exit survey. The report
by the company market research department showed that perceptions of the SP
brand had changed substantially as a result of the 'new look' refit.

It has proven difficult to come to a firm conclusion on the town centre store,
since no Sound & Vision outlet currently traded against fully out-of-town
competition.

Brief 4: Joshua Gabriel – New Superstore Manager, Stirling Springkerse

Background as outlined in the case. His priority for the meeting is assessing the
effect of the change in trading circumstances for the morale of staff and the
running of the new Springkerse store. Stirling is no ordinary town but a
'gateway' to a much larger rural area, so there is room for both Scottish Power
and Currys to trade profitably – as a member of the Stirling Town Centre
Management Initiative, you have got to know the Safeway and Tesco managers,
and have been able to compare notes about the two retail sectors.

Table 4.3 **Alternative trading scenarios: Stirling Springkerse**

Scenario	Average weekly turnover (£000s)				Year-on-year growth, %		
	Year 1	Year 2	Year 3	Year 4	Year 1	Year 2	Year 3
(A) Opening forecast	190	238	261	274	25	19	5
(B) Currys open year 2	190	209	226	237	10	8	5
(C) Currys open year 1	166	174	183	192	5	5	5

Notes on trading scenarios assumptions:
(A) Assumes no competitor developments in years 1–4
(B) Expected Year 1 trade followed by 15 per cent impact of Currys new superstore in Year 2; growth rate in subsequent years reduced.
(C) First six months of trade in Year 1 as expected in (A); Currys opens earlier than expected at start of second half of year; growth on subsequent years reduced further as store has less time to establish trading franchise.

Brief 5: Graeme Stoddart – Deputy Manager, Stirling Springkerse

Fairly new to Scottish Power, his concern is the potential impact of Currys. He wants to ensure that this aspect is fully discussed in the meeting. There is a case for increasing the local advertising budget, since Comet's is typically five or six times larger, even in less competitive situations. DSG's budget can be as much as fifteen times larger. Joshua Gabriel delegates key areas of responsibility to Stoddart, particularly human resource management and motivation. He has a particular responsibility in the store for the Sound & Vision section, and has been liaising with Amanda McKnight in the town centre store to undertake staff training in product knowledge. He is keen to ensure training of any part-time staff he recruits is of the highest quality, and would like to pursue and resolve this in the meeting.

Brief 6: Amanda McKnight – Store Manager, Stirling Sound & Vision Store

One of few women managers in Scottish Power. She is concerned about the company's preoccupation with superstore management, since many of the personal sales skills that are required for managing town centre outlets are being lost. Town centre stores need to be much more sensitive to specific customer requirements. What is the company doing to develop these close selling and 'people' skills for small stores? She also wants to discuss the assessments of impact of the new Scottish Power superstore and the new Currys superstore on her branch. She believes that out-of-town and in-town trade are not totally discrete as the company seems to think. Potential threats to salaries and morale of staff are important and need to be given close consideration. If they are not, then she fears the problem of staff retention will only increase – she has herself recently been offered a position with a rival retailer.

Notes

1. Of the fourteen electricity boards originally privatised, only three now survive – Scottish Power, Northern Electric and Powerhouse.

REFERENCES

Brownlie, D. T. and Lemond, K. A. (1992) 'Electrical retailing in the 1990s: towards a new retail formula'. *International Journal of Retail and Distribution Management*, **20**(3): 3–9.

Clarke, I., Bennison, D. and Pal, J. (1997) 'Towards a contemporary perspective of retail location'. *The International Journal of Retail and Distribution Management*, **25**(2): 59–69.

Guy, C. (1994) *The Retail Development Process: Location, Property and Planning*. London: Routledge.

Scottish Power (1998) Web site at: http://www.scottishpower.plc.uk/corporate/news (May).

Mintel (1997) *Retail Intelligence: Electrical Retailing*. London.

CASE 5

SAINSBURY'S – THE TRIFLING CASE OF THE MISSING TRIFLE: LESSONS IN STOCK LOSS

RICHARD CUTHBERTSON AND CHRISTOPHER M. MOORE

This case study is the result of contributions from many people, particularly from Sainsbury's staff, and in particular Mike Goodman, Judy Kempshall, Martin Wilkinson and Jay Snaith. Thanks also to Ruth Schmidt for her comments and suggestions on final editing.

TRIFLE ARITHMETIC

Life was looking good for Peter and he knew it – a graduate trainee for Sainsbury's, on a good salary, on a good training programme. This would give him a good grounding in retailing.

'All those people who said that a marine biology graduate would never make it in retailing would have the smirk wiped from their faces.' As he daydreamed, walking on his way to the store, he thought about what his new job might bring. 'I could be involved in the launch of a new, top-secret product, conduct a customer focus group or even think about where the business ought to make its important investments in the next five years. Yes, this is where it's at; this is retailing; this is what matters.'

Peter got to the store and went to his department and looked around, as the staff were all busily going about their business of replenishing all the chilled products. Just then his manager, Ms Harvey, arrived and reminded him of a training session that he had to attend on health and safety. She agreed that she would meet with Peter again when it had finished. The course over, Peter returned to his boss.

'Right Peter, I need you to do a spot of investigating for me. The stock checks have identified a problem. We are continually showing a discrepancy between stock and sales in trifles. In a nutshell, there is something going wrong with the trifles.'

'Do you mean going off? Perhaps it is the refrigerators', suggested Peter.

'No, the trifles are going walkabouts or something. The amount that we get allocated from the distribution centre and the amount that we sell, and are left with, do not add up,' explained Ms Harvey.

'Oh', Peter said. The lack of interest on his face was plain for all to see.

'Not sexy enough for you?' said Ms Harvey, slightly irritated.

'Well, it is not really that important is it?' answered Peter, uneasily.

'Really? Well think on, Peter. Let's say that each of these trifles cost £2.25 and we were to lose three per day. Not much eh?… Well, that three per day are 21 a week. That is £6.75 per day, £47.25 per week. Over the year we are now talking about £2457 in total.'

Ms Harvey was clearly good at arithmetic.

'If someone were to pinch that amount out of the till or from your locker, you would soon think it important. If we let things like that happen on every product line, every day, then you would not really have much of a future, would you?'

Ms Harvey was getting quite red in the face.

'And if something similar was happening at each of the 350 or so stores, so that would be… £859,950 a year… quite an expense, even for Sainsbury's!'

Ms Harvey really was very good at arithmetic.

'Put like that, I see what you mean' said Peter and he listened to Ms Harvey's instructions which were to investigate the problem and give her a report by the end of the week detailing the possible reasons for the stock loss, as well as a list of possible solutions.

'Scooby do', thought Peter. 'What do I do? Where do I start? I wish it was lunchtime!'

It Has Got To Be Customers

Peter had never really spoken to the security people before. In a strange sort of way he was a bit afraid of them. They did look at you suspiciously at times, and Peter always felt that they thought he had a bottle of Beck's beer hidden under his paper when he left at night. However, on this occasion he felt that they might be able to help.

Peter spoke to one of the security guards, explaining the problem to him and suggested that it was probably down to someone with very sticky fingers.

'Internal or external?' enquired Alex, who was the senior security person.

Peter looked confused. 'Dumb graduate', thought Alex. 'Do you think that it is customers stealing the trifles or is it a member of staff?'

'Well I do doubt if it would be a member of staff. It is probably some professional shoplifter who knows exactly what they are after', Peter concluded.

'Oh, right', laughed Alex. 'Either we have some very fat shoplifters in here or we have a gang of trifles pushers in our midst. First and foremost, think about the product. How easy is it to conceal, and how attractive is it for someone to have or sell on?'

Peter explained that the plastic carton was about 60 mm x 100 mm, so it was not very easy to conceal and that although they did taste great, these trifles did not really have a 'street' value since they had to be consumed within 24 hours because they were made from fresh cream.

'Well that discounts the staff then, too. If it is that perishable they would virtually have to steal it and convert their locker into a mini-fridge, or else nick it on the way out from the store. Possible, but unlikely', Alex concluded.

In a style that would have made Inspector Morse proud, the security sleuth suggested that, while some of the missing trifles may be down to theft, the nature of the product, both in terms of size and storage requirements made it unlikely that they were the focus of pilfering. 'If I were you I would ask the staff who look after that product – you know, those that stock-up in that area. They will have as good an idea as any since they are constantly dealing with the product, day in, day out', he suggested helpfully.

Well Past the Sell-by Date

The idea of speaking to the people responsible for the area was not a bad one, for Peter knew that it was Julie, with the enormous false eyelashes who looked after that area. Peter had a thing about enormous false eyelashes.

In as debonair a fashion as he could muster, Peter explained the problem to Julie. He sounded professional, managerial even, he thought. She would be sure to be impressed. 'It's your packaging that is the problem', she snorted, not at all impressed by this spotty pup with the suit that was too big for him.

'I beg your pardon?'

'The packaging! The trays that they put the trifles in to get them from the lorries to the fridges. They are too flimsy. I drop at least one trifle a day because of them. The packaging just cannot take the weight and since they come in packs of six, you end up dropping one. Look, there is one there. You can hardly carry anything on that.'

'Oh, I see', said Peter. 'And have you told anyone about this problem?'

'Nobody has ever asked. Anyway, I have stopped putting it in the waste record book thing because no one ever seems to have a pen and I am sure no one reads it anyway.'

'Julie is certainly not acting like a typical Sainsbury's employee', thought Peter.

'Well, I am not blaming you. But that does account for some of the problem', said Peter, trying not to sound too judgmental.

'Yes, and we always end up with stuff that is out of date. I am not sure how it happens. I think sometimes we forget to bring the nearest date stuff to the front and because we have it in the fridge for such a short space of time, I often have to dump stuff in the waste bin.' Julie was on a roll with her experience of these trifles and Peter began to see why nobody had ever asked her about the trifles.

At that, Janet, who also looked after this area chipped in. She had a habit of listening in on every conversation in the store. 'Well, I think we get too many sent in here. I think that our allocation is too high, especially at the beginning of the week. Sometimes, I do not have enough space to put them out since the area gets so crammed with stuff. And I just leave it to put out for later once things have sold.'

'And do you go back and replenish?' asked Peter

'Replenish? Oh right... Well sometimes, if things do not really move during my shift, I have no space to put them out. And sometimes I forget to do it and I suppose the stuff must just get lost in the back somewhere', explained Janet with disarming honesty.

At that, a rather elegant lady picked up a trifle and went to place it in her shopping trolley.

'This lid is faulty. I have noticed that the packaging on this trifle is never right.'

Janet offered her apologies and immediately went to find the customer another trifle.

'Can I ask what the problem is with the packaging, madam?' asked Peter.

'Well, sometimes you get leaks, and other times it seems that the lid is too big for the base. I have often had to go through the whole compartment in order to find one that is not damaged. I keep meaning to write to your head office, but my sister said that if you do that, they take if off the shelves, and I love this trifle too much to give it up', she explained, rather sheepishly.

Goods in?

Going from the shop floor to the staff restaurant, Peter had to pass through the goods-receiving area. Just as he was passing through, he noticed that a number of the delivery trolleys with new deliveries were lined up against the side wall. 'What is going on here?' he wondered. At that, he met Geoff, a guy that had been in his class at high school. Geoff was in charge of the goods-receiving area and he looked harassed.

'What's up?' Peter asked.

'Staff, or the lack of them', explained Geoff 'I have all of this stock lined-up here and because of two vacancies, one guy off with the 'flu and another away on a training day, I just cannot get the stuff through.'

'So that means that the goods are locked in here, and because the store is now so busy and all hands are on the shop floor, this stuff is getting backed-up here?'

'I just said that', sighed Geoff, wearily. At that, one of the trolleys, which was packed full of merchandise, was pushed forward by a member of staff looking for a product for a customer. This trolley hit the one in front and a bottle of olive oil and a few vinegar bottles came crashing to the floor.

'I do not believe this', roared Geoff as he automatically reached for a brush. 'We lose so much stock because people are always rummaging through this back-log. I know that the customer has got to get the stock, but this just causes trouble.'

'And do you not get any help to shift the stuff and give you a clear path to get more stock through to the floor?' asked Peter.

At that Geoff rolled his eyes. 'Sometimes we are a low priority when it comes to staff because the customer is all important. If the store is busy everybody is called out to cover the cash-points. Anyway, who in their right mind would want to come in and work here? It is cold and windy and hard graft. Give me the lottery cash-point any day!'

'I had not really realized that stock could be lost in the back like this. Do you ever lose trifles in this way?' Peter asked.

'Sure we do. Especially because of the flimsy packaging that they come in', Geoff explained. 'You think that it is bad here. I have spoken to some of the delivery guys, and there can also be problems with stock elsewhere.'

'Do you mean further up the chain, before we get it in the store? What sorts of problems are there, then?'

'Look, I have enough to worry about here without going and asking them what their problems are. Why don't you speak to the other guys if you want know about this. Try the delivery guys and those at the distribution centre. I am sure they would tell you plenty if you asked them. And before you go for your tea break, will you shift some of this stuff for me?'

'One good turn, deserves another, Geoff. I will help you after I have had my tea', Peter promised.

'I knew you were going to say that, you may be clever but you're so lazy. You were the same at school', shouted Geoff, as he continued brushing up the broken vinegar bottles.

Trifle Distribution?

Two days later, Peter found himself in one of the regional distribution centres, where Clare, the depot Operations Manager, was dazzling the thoroughly over-whelmed Peter with her knowledge of the distribution operations.

'We move about 1.1m cases per week (around 2m at peak times, just before Christmas, for example). Just over half of the cases are perishable items. We hold about 1.5 week's stock of the non-perishable items and little or no stock of the perishable items. Main orders are placed by about 7.30am and are delivered to the branch by 7.30am the next day. So all are delivered within 24 hours but many are delivered long before then. We have about 60 to 70 vehicle deliveries during the day and 110 to 120 at night. This is a 24 hours a day, 7 days a week operation', she said with great satisfaction, before continuing. 'We run three shifts: 6am to 2pm, 1pm to 9pm and 10pm to 6am. You don't have to be an insomniac to work here but sometimes it helps,' she said cheerfully. She continued, hardly pausing for breath, 'we have about 160 deliveries from suppliers a day, which translates to about 1200 boards (pallets). These deliveries are scheduled in, so the supplier must turn up at the allotted time. One of our big problems is that suppliers use their own product codes, which are different from our own Sainsbury's codes. Now if this isn't input into our system correctly (and a lot of this is done manually at the moment), then we end up with the wrong information in the system to begin with, and therefore the wrong information all the way through the distribution chain – lots of problems, but it doesn't occur very often.'

'Now, that could be important', thought Peter.

Clare continued, 'each branch receives 3 or 4 deliveries a day and usually only one of those deliveries will be perishable items, including your trifle! Wednesday and Thursday orders are particularly high. Of course, we don't cover the whole country (we cover about 70 branches) nor do we cover the whole product range, but we do deliver your trifles. Well I've got to go now. You can contact me again if you need further advice.'

And with that Clare led Peter around to the reception area, shook his hand, said 'goodbye, nice to meet you', and was gone.

'How do you know how much stock to deliver?' Peter called after her.

'Talk to head office', came the reply from down the corridor.

TAKING STOCK OF HEAD OFFICE

So Peter decided to find out about the inventory management systems at Sainsbury's head office. He went to head office in Blackfriars in central London, where Anil, one of the stock managers, explained how the replenishment system worked.

■ 'The main element of the inventory management system is called SABRE, which is a **s**ales **b**ased **re**plenishment system, so that for every sale a replenishment order is made. At store level, this system consists of the two main sub-systems:

■ Forecasting and ordering;

■ Stock and receiving.'

'Could there be stock lost in either of these areas?' thought Peter.

Anil handed Peter a summary he had prepared prior to the meeting. It read:

Forecasting and Ordering

The forecasting and ordering system consists of the following key processes:

1. **Calculate the sales forecast** for the next 21 days – which is built up from: the underlying commodity sales using an exponential smoothing factor of about 0.4; any seasonal factors reflecting changes throughout the year; any head office recommendation due to an activity or event, such as a promotion; any event trade profile (ETP) which alters the spread of sales across the week, for example due to bank holidays; and finally any local trading factor, such as major roadworks temporarily affecting customers' ability to easily enter the store.

2. **Place an order** – which is calculated as follows:

   Target carryover – Predicted stock

   where:

   Target carryover is the quantity of stock that a store wishes to close with on a particular day

   and

   Predicted stock = Current inventory + Orders in transit – Sales forecast

   Calculate the order forecasts for the next 14 days – which is used as the basis from which to drive the supply chain.

'This looks complicated', thought Peter. 'Could there be stock loss in any of these areas?' he asked.

Anil replied that in each of these areas there may be problems resulting in stock loss.

Sales forecasts are always difficult to get right, and particularly with products such as food where a change in the weather may immediately change demand requirements. For example, a change to hot sunny weather creates increased demand for salad vegetables, barbecue meats, cold drinks and ice cream, whereas a change to cold weather creates increased demand for soups, winter vegetables, roast meat joints and hot drink powders.

Placing orders may also lead to stock loss. Place orders too high and products may pass by their sell-by date before being sold and so have to be thrown away. Of course, placing orders too low runs the risk of losing potential sales.

Finally, calculating the order forecasts incorrectly can have grave consequences since any error may have a knock-on effect throughout the supply chain, thus potentially compounding any initial error to an even greater magnitude.

Peter continued reading the summary sheet.

Stock and Receiving

The stock and receiving system consists of two main information requirements:

1. **Maintaining inventory information** – which is calculated as follows:

   Current stock + Confirmed receipts − (Sales + Reductions + Disposals)

2. **Goods receiving information** – where the orders-in-transit and actual inventory figures are updated.

Anil also confirmed to Peter that in each of these areas there may be problems with stock loss. In maintaining the inventory information there may be incorrect information, such as current stock figures not including any loss due to theft. If there is incorrect information then the calculation of inventory requirements will be incorrect and so processes are put in place which will help maintain the accuracy of this information, such as cyclical stock checks at stores. Similarly, if there are mistakes in deliveries that are not picked up on delivery then inaccurate information will find its way into the inventory management system. This not only results in inventory problems but may also cause disputes between the retailer and their suppliers.

Peter liked head office, the coffee machine was much better than in the store where he worked. Perhaps one day he would spend some time working here. Peter knew that many of the staff did at some stage in their careers.

WHAT TO DO?

Back at the store, Peter wondered what he should do now. He had spoken to many people, found out a lot of important information, but what was he to do with it? It seemed so complicated. There was potential stock loss all over the place. It almost seemed amazing that anything was ordered, delivered and put out onto the store shelves correctly, and yet Peter knew that Sainsbury's did this correctly nearly all of the time. Peter felt quite proud of what he had found out and now wanted to impress Ms Harvey. What should Peter do now? What should be in his report?

QUESTIONS

1. Identify potential reasons for stock loss.

2. Explain how issues in head office or the distribution centre have an impact on stock loss in the store and vice versa.

3. Recommend changes to reduce stock loss.

4. Identify and explain a realistic monitoring programme that could be implemented to help identify and reduce the major areas of stock loss.

CASE 6

CONCESSIONS MANAGEMENT IN DEPARTMENT STORES: THE DEBENHAMS LUGGAGE DEPARTMENT

PAUL GAFFNEY AND MALCOLM KIRKUP

The authors would like to thank Debenhams and Luggage Management International for their support in developing this case study. In particular we are grateful for the contributions provided by Bob Falconer, Jeff Davis and Darryl Carter.

The information in this case study, while believed to be accurate, is based on the memory of those involved and compiled from a variety of sources. It has also been simplified in order to focus on key learning objectives for students of management. For these reasons, the material should not be regarded as a totally factual account of events or views.

INTRODUCTION

Concession retailing has been defined as 'a means of trading whereby retail space is granted to a manufacturer or supplier of goods or services by the host organization which takes payment in the form of a fixed rent agreement, a percentage of turnover, or a mixture of both. The supplier or "concessionaire" may then set up a concession, the appearance of which is that of an individual trading unit within the host store' (Corporate Intelligence Group, 1996, p. 2). Concessions can be found in a wide variety of retail outlets including food superstores, DIY warehouses, garden centres and furnishing stores, but they are most commonly associated with department stores. Harvey Nichols, Beatties and House of Fraser are particularly heavy users of concessions, and popular product areas include china and glass (for example Wedgwood and Royal Doulton) and fashion (for example Jaeger and Windsmoor).

This case study considers the strategic and operational issues involved in concessions management within department stores, and examines the activities of Debenhams and their concessionaire Luggage Management International (LMI). The case presents perspectives from the three main parties involved in the concession – the supplier, the concessions director for Debenhams, and the local host store. The case illustrates the strategic rationale for concessions, but focuses primarily on a recent proposal to expand LMI's involvement in the

Debenhams business through the trialling of a new premium leather department. The main tasks proposed at the end of the case study centre around the operational challenges presented by the new concession and the likely contractual arrangements involved. The case provides an opportunity to apply and develop analytical, problem-solving, negotiation and creativity skills.

CONCESSIONS AT DEBENHAMS

Debenhams operate 88 department stores in the UK and Ireland, with a total sales turnover approaching £1b. Prior to its acquisition by the Burton Group in 1985, Debenhams' concession business was high volume and low margin, and had grown to some 45 per cent of total sales. In fact the Burton Group focused on Debenhams' excessive use of concessions in promoting their hostile take-over bid – 'the company had forgotten retailing, becoming instead landlords and credit card operators dependent on the retailing skills of others' (McGoldrick, 1990, p. 107). Concessions have since been cut back to around 20 per cent of sales, partly through the closure of departments previously heavily dependent on concessions (for example electricals and carpets), but also through the development of stronger own-bought ranges. Debenhams' concession business is now highly profitable, and focuses on high margin products such as women's wear, accessories, men's formal wear, housewares, home furnishings and luggage. Debenhams works with around 125 concession operators, although the number of concessions varies greatly between stores depending on selling space and the profile of each store's catchment.

The Debenhams concession business has its own directorate, headed by Bob Falconer. This directorate is virtually unique within the retail sector – it provides focused board-level authority to control the strategic and operational aspects of this substantial part of the Debenhams' business. Bob Falconer explains Debenhams' approach to concessions.

> We want concessionaires that can develop a unique range, and bring in recognized national and international brands which are well advertised and supported. Ideally we want exclusivity – brands and/or ranges that no other department stores can get their hands on. This is not to say we will pay for exclusivity at any price – we can and do turn them away if the deal is not right. Appropriate product areas for concessions tend to be those that are high value, slow stock turn, high stock investment and require selling. Concessions have expert staff who are trained in the product and good at selling it.

Debenhams will only work with concessions that are profitable and flexible. Concessions have to pay their way, and Debenhams require minimum sales and profit densities from any given space. Commission rates vary between 15 per cent and 32 per cent, depending largely on product, profits achievable and location in store. Debenhams have a unique system for calculating the true productivity of each individual concession and own-buy department, taking into account central costs and even the position of each department in each store. The performance of concessions and own-buy can then be directly compared, to ensure the most profitable use of space in each store. As Bob Falconer points out, 'We drive hard bargains, but we are fair – we won't screw concessionaires down because it isn't in our interests if they go out of business.'

Bob Falconer stresses that concessions have to be on board with the Debenhams strategy.

> They must be willing to co-operate on aspects such as product selection, marketing initiatives, point of sale promotions, customer returns policies, credit facilities for customers and staff discount. We want a 'seamless join' with no distinction apparent to the customer between a concession and an own-bought department. We want to be able to move concessions around the store to fit in with our space management plans, and we want them to refurbish when we refurbish. Although we don't pay towards a concessionaire's shopfit, we will want to approve their proposed shopfit design in terms of aesthetics and health and safety. We also want to see concession managers integrating well into stores – our store managers will make sure they are as closely involved in what goes on in-store as any own-bought department manager. I also want concessions linked into our IT and price look-up systems, and in the long term I'd like to see them linked in more with our logistics – delivering to our distribution centres rather than to individual stores.

Debenhams exercise tight control over concession ranges. Bob explains:

> We will not allow the development of a particular product category if we think it is inappropriate in relation to quality or our strategy. We occasionally get the big concessionaires wanting us to take their whole range rather than cherry-pick, but we will only agree if they then carry all the options – which we wouldn't do if it was own-buy. Some concessionaires are good at helping us keep up with market trends. Newness and uniqueness count in the fashion market and we want to see new lines constantly coming on stream. Some fashion concessions can respond very rapidly to trends, particularly if they hold cloth to make up at short notice, and some are manufacturing almost on a weekly basis.

Bob Falconer believes Debenhams offer good opportunities for concessionaires:

> The key benefit to them is access to our footfall which gives them their business. We can sometimes vary the terms and contracts to accommodate their needs, and as commitment increases we can extend contracts. If they are capital intensive businesses we might be able to offer write-downs on shopfitting equipment. We can also provide concessionaire staff with regular sales data to enable store-by-store performance comparisons. Concessionaires pay a small sum for this, but the information can help them become more profitable.

The Debenhams Luggage Department

Originally the luggage department in Debenhams was mainly own-bought, but the Debenhams board believed there was an opportunity to increase the department's profitability significantly. They felt a luggage concessionaire could offer much-needed specialist selling skills and experience and could possibly exploit the luggage market potential more effectively. Debenhams already had dealings with a company supplying the Equator luggage brand, and this company was approached to develop and manage a concession-based department. Initially the operation was limited to 50 stores, and de-risked to guarantee minimum income for Debenhams, but the new department has since proved immensely successful.

The company behind the Debenhams luggage department is Luggage Management International (LMI). They provide a department with 70 per cent Equator brand (exclusive to Debenhams) supported by manufacturer brands such as Delsey, Samsonite and Hedgren. Debenhams do not have complete exclusivity on these latter brands but LMI have negotiated some exclusive sub-ranges, colours and styles. The department is split into three areas – formal (traditional square luggage and bags associated with travel), casual (luggage geared to particular occasions, lifestyle or image), and business (for example briefcases and computer cases). Under LMI's management the Debenhams luggage department has extended its penetration of the UK market to 10 per cent. Competitors include high street multiples, independents, department stores and variety stores, but Debenhams now have the highest market share of any retailer in the luggage sector.

Bob Falconer believes Debenhams work well with LMI. 'They can develop a unique and exclusive range for us, they can deal with the national and international brands, they have good knowledge of the market and they have the ability to deliver. They adapt the ranges to fit our requirements and they are always looking to innovate. They follow-up new ideas rapidly and they have worked extremely effectively, for example, in moving the department towards upright luggage ranges and bringing the Hedgren brand to Debenhams.'

LUGGAGE MANAGEMENT INTERNATIONAL

LMI is the retail trading division of the Greenwich Group which has substantial interests in luggage, travel goods and associated products. In addition to concessions in Debenhams, the group retails through a number of factory outlets, manufactures 60 per cent of the Equator product they sell, and wholesales luggage to other retailers. LMI focuses particularly on running the Debenhams luggage department – supplying mostly the Equator brand but also sourcing other national and international brands. Jeff Davis, Retail Director for LMI points out, 'It is important to note that Equator is effectively a Debenhams brand – we run it and manage it, but at the end of the day we can't sell it to anyone else.'

The focus on concessions has been a conscious decision for LMI. Jeff Davis explains:

> The luggage industry is small (around £180m p.a.) and it is difficult to operate profitably from high street stores – you don't get enough customers to cover the rental costs for the good locations. Companies like the Baggage Centre can only survive because they focus on the lower end of the market where volumes are much higher. From our point of view, concessions are a lower cost, more profitable, and safer route to market, and we can gain access to the guaranteed footfall from Debenhams. We believe we are good at delivering what Debenhams want and we can achieve a good business for ourselves at the same time. The concessions route is appropriate for Debenhams in luggage, because luggage is a small proportion of their income but a product that customers expect to see. An own-buy operation would require disproportionate resources to make it work well. For us, however, luggage is our LIFE. We live and breathe this category, and Debenhams benefit from this expertise without the grief. So long as they are happy with the commission they receive, and we can be profitable, then it works for both of us.

> The alignment of strategies is critical to success. There is not a Debenhams strategy and an LMI strategy. Our strategy is a Debenhams strategy. At a strategic level if they wish to change their market positioning we would need to fit in with it, and at an operational level if they change, for example, their photographic approach then we will also change ours. Our department must fit in with the Debenhams environment from the customer's perspective. Of course we expect certain things from the relationship (that is, a profit) and we talk to Debenhams about what we expect, but in terms of our strategy we are clearly a part of Debenhams.

> Before we can know what products to put on the shelf we have to fully understand the Debenhams marketing approach. We monitor their overall customer profile and we can respond to differences in local customer profiles by selecting different combinations of products for each store. We are also interested in increasing our market share beyond the normal Debenhams shopper – so we will try to draw customers away from other department stores through local advertising. We invest a lot of time in driving innovation. Innovation adds value and allows us to achieve higher margins. Of course we have to justify any new ideas we have, and Debenhams will ask to see the research to support our proposals, but we spend more on market information than anyone in our industry – we want to know all there is to know to ensure we are marketing the best offer.

> Relationships are important if you want to be successful with concessions. A close relationship ensures we get the right information which then allows us to make the right decisions, which in turn enables us to maximize sales and profit. We are different to many other concessionaires in that we don't concession for anyone else – we are not a brand that picks and chooses which department stores we want to be in. We are working with Debenhams against other retailers, we are not competing against other commodities within the store. We link with Deben-

hams at various levels in our organizational structure, and we have regular communication strategically, operationally and socially. I link with Bob Falconer and his concession managers. My marketing, merchandising and personnel managers link in with equivalent managers at Debenhams. On the 'field management' side the regional directors at Debenhams link with our operations controllers and our area managers link with Debenhams store managers. Close contact allows us to keep informed of any Debenhams' initiatives we might be able to respond to, and ensures that any problems are sorted immediately.

We have two clear objectives. First, we aim to maximize our sales within Debenhams to generate a profit density that compares well with other departments and therefore doesn't put us under pressure. Debenhams have a clear system – the higher the profit you return per square foot the more square footage you can have (if you want it) and the better the site you can have within the stores. This is very important to us, because the penalty of poor performance is a worse site, smaller space or, ultimately, removal. Our second objective is to use our space within Debenhams to grow our own marketplace – by meeting consumer needs and educating the customer to appreciate the value of the Debenhams' luggage department.

There are some disadvantages of a concessions-based strategy for us. We can't gain access to 100 per cent of our potential market – we are limited to the customer profile and numbers generated by Debenhams. A disadvantage of being strategically led by another company is also the need occasionally to compromise on your own preferred approach to marketing – for example, we can't always offer products that might compete with Debenhams' own-bought departments, and we might not be able to fully exploit promotional discounting in our departments if Debenhams decide they wish to portray a more premium image. A big downside of concessions is that we are given our space in the stores – we are a destination department and often seen as a 'space-filler' to go almost anywhere. We therefore have to argue our case (on performance measures) to get the space and floor-levels we want in each town. Although by working with Debenhams we limit our market potential, it's important to have focus in business. At least this way we have one main customer, one clear strategy and there is actually quite a lot of scope for business from the opportunities they provide.

I believe there is a *formula* to trading well as a concessionaire. In a way it doesn't matter what the product is – we could probably also perform well offering china and glass. Okay, you have to build a team with the relevant product knowledge and expertise, but you can buy these people in. The key challenge is the *connection* – providing the management expertise, the communication, the research, the innovation, and then linking and aligning the commodity with the Debenhams strategy. Bringing the two together for maximum effect is the challenge. Maybe it's not really concessions management – maybe it is a form of 'out-sourcing'.

THE OXFORD PROPOSAL

Debenhams are currently considering the trial of an additional and new concession with LMI. The fashion accessories department at head office has identified a space in the Oxford store that can be released for next year's autumn/winter season without reducing its profit potential. The location of the space restricts its use to fashion accessories (see Figure 6.1), but it is felt there is scope to introduce a new concession. Given the relationship with LMI and their particular location within the Oxford store, LMI have been invited to develop proposals for the space.

LMI's idea is to introduce a new 'Fine Leather Goods' department. Debenhams have expressed interest in principle, and LMI are now working on detailed proposals for a possible trial. The following sections outline the views of the two parties as they approach negotiations.

The LMI View

We're always looking for ways to grow our market within Debenhams, so when we heard about the space available in Oxford, right next to our existing department, we jumped at the opportunity to develop a proposal. We've always been successful in Oxford with higher priced and special merchandise, so we feel there is a good market for a department that we've already been thinking about – premium leather products. The ranges will be new for us but they'll have a neat association with travel and luggage. The concept will be consistent with Debenhams' desire to bring in new merchandise and brands to enhance their appeal to consumers, and it will give them a competitive edge in the leather market. We may have our work cut out persuading some of the premium brands to consider Debenhams as an outlet for their product, but we will exploit our connections, educate suppliers and hopefully negotiate some exclusive ranges.

Our eventual proposal won't just be confined to Oxford. A one-store trial won't make economic sense from our point of view – if we're going to commit huge resource to buying, fixturing, stock and staffing, we'll want to trial in at least two or three stores. After the trial I'd like to roll-out to at least 15 stores. In an ideal world I'd like to roll-out across the chain, but I realize not all Debenhams stores will have the catchment profile to make it work. For the trial I'll want to reduce the commission rate to make it profitable. I'm not interested in doing it unless I can do it properly – with proper fixturing and image – but that will cost money. It might be a drop in the ocean to Debenhams, but it's a lot for us. We usually pay for the stock, fixtures and staff, and Debenhams get their commission from sales. For a trial, however, that's all open to negotiation – it could be a joint arrangement and they might underwrite it. If we can get the financial arrangements right there should be enough profit in it for both of us.

Our proposed concept is a 'fine leather goods' department, selling premium brands at premium prices. In the Oxford store we will have 380 sq ft. Prices will range between £100 and £500. Premium quality products need to be sold in the right environment and so we will create a 'quality' statement – possibly with a shop-fit like a drawing room with a Chesterfield suite set among glass displays. The department will be organized by brand (maybe four to six) with each brand offering a full range – wallets, handbags, holdalls, umbrellas, suiters, briefcases and so on. Brands might include Mulberry, Brics, Bridge and Burberry. There will be a high service element – staff with expert knowledge of leathers to educate customers as to why each product is worth the price. We will be promotionally active, not in terms of discounting but in terms of special offers and possibly free gifts, and we will invest heavily in graphics, external advertising and mailings.

I'm concerned about a few things. For starters I want to know we are protected financially – I can't afford to throw massive resource at it without some confidence that we'll make a return. A particular concern in Oxford is the state of the shopfit – it's an old store. The lighting is poor, the decor is dated and the approach to the new area from our existing department is through an archway and up some steps (see Figure 6.1). The location of the department is not that brilliant either, although we can attract footfall through advertising. I want stockroom space and I'll want to know how the logistics will work – we're talking about high value merchandise so we need to be careful about how the product will be stored, transported, delivered and handled. We'll also have to think about security – if we get the same percentage stock-loss as a normal department we'll lose a fortune. The displays could be lockable and display-stock will be minimized anyway. We'll need expert staff who also match the profile of the product. I don't usually like tills in our departments because when the store gets busy you lose a lot of salesforce time serving customers from all the other departments. However, for the new concept a dedicated till would help us build a comfortable care package around the customer. I will also want strong marketing support from Debenhams – a forceful window promotion, in-store signage, features in their magazine, and a mailshot to account holders. (Jeff Davis, Retail Director, LMI)

The Debenhams Concessions Director's View

I'm quite keen on the idea. LMI's proposal fits in with our strategy because we're always looking for something new. I like the concept, and I'm happy for them to have a go, but the trial will have to be funded entirely by them and we'll need to check the proposed shopfit and the final ranging. I'm looking for the same margin from them in the trial as they achieve in their existing operation. If the trial is successful we can get round the table and consider whether, and how far, we wish to roll it out. Given the nature of the market I'm not sure whether a roll-out could be applied to more than a dozen stores. (Bob Falconer, Director of Concessions)

The Store Manager's View

I'm looking forward to the trial. It's a shame we can't get it in for spring/summer. I hope it can be agreed fairly soon because there are proposals to rebuild our store in a few years time and I'd like to see it trialled before then. The new concession will have quite a few implications for me. It will be a stand-alone department in the business, to be supported as we would any other new department. I'll be looking to support LMI throughout the trial, to make sure they deliver good service, visual impact and planned sales. I want to see a really impressive department – something really different and new for our customers. Although our store is difficult environmentally, this can be used to create strong identities within areas and so this department should have clear definition.

A lot of pre-launch work will be needed. I'll need to liaise with shopfitting contractors to confirm their programme of work, ensure they are briefed on health and safety, and I'll need to get the space prepared. I'm not sure whether we'll be involved in recruiting staff, but we will be involved with induction and training and this needs to be co-ordinated within the store training programme. I'll need to consider stockroom and delivery arrangements, because in that part of the store there's a stockroom access point which I might have to change. I'll want to make sure LMI get window promotion support so customers know the new department has arrived. Security/stockloss for concessions is their responsibility and cost. However, we can provide support with camera cover and some equipment such as security mirrors. Till arrangements could be an issue, because LMI may have to use the adjacent Vivaldi or cosmetics till. If there's anything special that needs to be done at the till for their merchandise (for example retaining a ticket off the product), then I'll need to brief all the other departments. In terms of lead-time I'll probably only get a month's notice of the date for the shopfit so there won't be long to get things organized. (Darryl Carter, Oxford Store Manager)

Debenhams and LMI now need to decide whether and how the proposal should be progressed. There are strategic and operational implications for both parties. They have shared goals in relation to the success of the project, but the two companies also have their own specific objectives and concerns. As decision time approaches they will both want to be clear on their requirements, their respective responsibilities, the reassurances they need, and the terms on which any trial is to be based.

QUESTIONS

1. Bob Falconer does not believe there are many disadvantages to operating concessions. To what extent do you agree with this, and what potential disadvantages might concessions present for other department stores?

2. Jeff Davis has mentioned a number of disadvantages of concessions from LMI's point of view. What other drawbacks might there be for LMI, and for concessionaires generally when dealing with department stores?

3. Assume the role of Darryl Carter who will shortly be receiving a presentation by LMI on the proposed new concession trial in his store. What concerns will he have about the new project from an operational point of view, and what reassurances will he want to secure from LMI?

4. From the perspective of (a) LMI and (b) Debenhams, draw up a list of requirements that each party might wish to secure from the trial programme. Identify the *shared* goals of both parties, their *individual* goals and concerns, and identify the requirements that might need to be negotiated. Using the case study as the basis of a negotiation exercise, discuss, develop and agree the terms of an outline contract between the two parties for a trial programme.

5. On the basis of the information provided, discuss whether Debenhams should proceed with the trial in Oxford, and justify your answer. Suggest alternative uses for the space in question, and justify your recommendations.

6. Develop more detailed proposals for the merchandising of the proposed 'Fine Leather Goods' department. Your proposals should include more detailed range recommendations, a floor plan and consideration of materials, displays, furniture, brand adjacencies and promotional support.

REFERENCES

Corporate Intelligence Group (1996) *Concession Retailing in the UK*. London: CIG.

McGoldrick, P. (1990) *Retail Marketing*. London: McGraw-Hill.

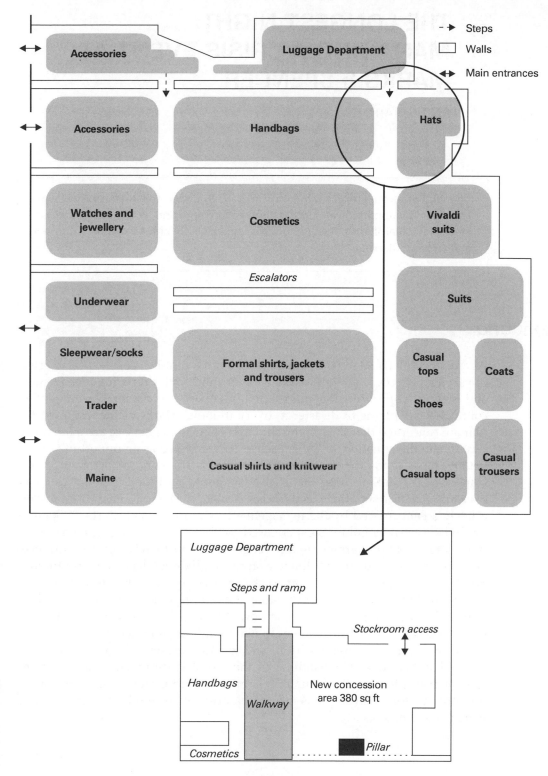

Figure 6.1   Schematic of ground floor layout – Debenhams Oxford

CASE 7

THE LONGEST NIGHT: MANAGING A CRISIS EVENT AT MARKS & SPENCER

CATHY HART

The author would like to thank Marks & Spencer for their enthusiasm, advice and support given during the researching and writing of this case study. Particular thanks must go to Chris Larkin, Debbie Moodie, Kelly Thrussell and Andrew Clarke.

INTRODUCTION

At any one time, a retail store can be faced with a number of unexpected crises of varying degrees of danger to its customers and staff. Preparing management and staff to cope with the unexpected involves a considerable amount of contingency planning or disaster recovery training. Marks & Spencer in particular are concerned that their high standards of customer service are maintained throughout the situation, and that each event is viewed as an opportunity to be better prepared for the next. Central to this is the concept of management competencies, and ensuring that each manager is equipped to adapt to whatever role is required of them as the crisis develops. The following case presents a likely scenario faced by the management team in a small Marks & Spencer unit where a power failure is experienced. Such an event can occur for a variety of reasons, without warning, in any retail store. Fortunately, these occurrences are relatively infrequent, but due to a store's high dependence on a continuous power supply, most large retailers install a back-up generator to run systems and maintain the operations of the store at a minimum level. However, various issues may arise following a simple power failure that cause an escalation of events requiring clear management thinking and decision making.

The characters, store, location and events presented in the case are completely fictitious. The handling of this event is designed to illustrate the type of issues that might occur in a similar scenario, and to offer maximum opportunity for analysis. It is not necessarily an example of good or bad management practice.

THE CASE

The basic principles of retail management are the same as any other kind of business management. The difference lies in the pace at which circumstances change and decisions must be made. (*The Whole Story*, Marks & Spencer Management Careers booklet)

Diane Webster was busy checking off the Christmas stock figures in anticipation of the busiest three trading weeks of the retail year. It was the first late night trading for the small town centre unit, and also Diane's first appointment as a regional manager since she graduated just over three years ago. She had successfully achieved a fast track promotion in her previous appointment to assistant manager in a large out-of-town store, when she heard about the internal vacancy for a regional manager in the 'child' store co-managed by her current management team. Having been advised to wait and let someone more experienced take the position, Diane had fought hard to convince her divisional manager that she was capable of managing the store during the forthcoming peak trading period. Now that she was in the position, Diane was determined to prove her effectiveness and needed to learn as much as she could about the store, its staff and local customers. The late night would provide a valuable opportunity for this and also to ensure that the stock systems were providing maximum availability – hence the early stock check.

The daytime staff and management had just left the store at 5.40pm when the first indication that this was going to be a challenging evening manifested itself. The lights on the first floor briefly flickered, and then went out. Various shouts, and exclamations of surprise, were followed by a few distant screams. After a second, the lighting returned to a dimmer level, the emergency power having switched on automatically. Then another second and the lights returned to about half strength. Diane was initially irritated by the interruption to her planned workload for the next 30 minutes but this quickly changed to apprehension as she realized the wider impact of the power cut and her sole responsibility for resolving and managing it. Adjusting to the half light, Diane instinctively hurried towards the till points on the ground floor. The escalators were not working so she walked towards the stairs trying not to bump into the textile fixtures that appeared more bulky than in the usual brightly-lit store. Diane almost collided with an old gentleman customer who was looking for his wife – last seen stepping on to the escalator. Reassuring him that they would probably find her downstairs, Diane ushered him, together with a few other confused customers, down the stairs towards the front of the building on the ground floor. The scene that greeted her was slightly chaotic. A huddle of people were gathered at the base of the escalator. One or two, she couldn't work out if they were staff or not, were bent over two others lying on the ground. Small crowds of agitated shoppers buzzed around the till points, while other groups of shoppers stood motionless in the food hall waiting for something to happen. Small pin points of bright red lights appeared to be flashing, from the direction of the freezers and the till alarms were ringing almost in unison. As Diane made her way towards the food section, the reality of the situation became apparent. Lynne, the textile supervisor came running up, 'Looks like the power is down – possibly in the whole street but we can't make it out yet.' Diane asked for a quick summary of the customer situation. The escalators had halted immediately the power failed, causing customers to tumble abruptly forwards knocking an old lady to the floor. A slight panic had spread, resulting in one or two other customers suffering slight injuries. Diane responded, 'Lynne, check that the first aider on this shift sees to the injured and get someone to call an ambulance.'

Operating Procedures

Diane was racking her brains to remember the standard procedure from her last Disaster Recovery training course. Despite gaining top marks in the course assessment, her mind had gone blank except for 'protect customers, staff and stock'. The trainers had been right that instinct was the best motivator in a crisis situation. Another problem was Diane's lack of familiarity with the store and staff; she had only been in place for two weeks and ideally could have done with at least another month before being thrown into this kind of situation. But then the reason why Diane had first chosen store management was its unpredictability, not knowing what could happen at a moment's notice. This was, she felt, the true test for an effective manager – an ability to resolve problems, while also organizing and planning ahead for the next week, month or year. She had tried working in an office environment during her placement year but missed the risk-taking, thinking on her feet, the pressure and buzz of the sales floor and most of all, the people and customer contact. There could be times at the end of a busy day when she was so tired, it was even an effort to drive home. But then the satisfaction of seeing the increased sales figures for her department, and knowing it was, to a large extent, due to her initiatives and management skill, made it worthwhile. Diane was convinced that her only route through this crisis was to utilize her managers' experience of the store, while she provided the leadership, support and decision making. She also sensed that the staff were watching for signs that she was in control of the situation.

The till assistants were coping well under the pressure, by reassuring the waiting customers that the power would soon be returned, but they would need management guidance if this wasn't the case in the next few minutes. Jim Cross, the deputy foods supervisor, was clearly agitated when he joined Diane, 'One of the generators hasn't started up, and only half of the freezers and fridges are working on the shop floor. The cold room and the main storage freezer won't be powered either but can hold their temperature if we don't open the doors. We'll have at most about 15 minutes on some of the chilled foods, then we'll have to start emptying fridges. Oh and we've got a delivery expected after 6.15pm.' Diane's immediate concern was to look after the customers, but recognized the need for more information, and to provide direction for the staff. She called a quick meeting on the shop floor to summarize the situation. 'Bob, can you get onto the electricity board and find out how long the power is likely to be off? Also, can someone ask Mike to have a look at the generator to see if it can be restarted?' Jim hesitated, 'If you ask me, the best plan is to close the store, and then we can concentrate on the stock.' This suggestion had already crossed Diane's mind but she was reluctant to make that decision yet. The power could be back on in minutes, and they could still have a full two hours trading. Furthermore, the pedestrianized street outside was full of shoppers who had arrived to see the Christmas lights switched on followed by two hours of entertainers in the town centre. 'Lets get more information before we make any decisions. It might be worth finding out what Woolworths, BHS and the new Tesco store, are doing. If they stay open, we might have to.' Diane then quickly discussed priorities with her management team and delegated roles. Most of the customer activity was in the food department so most of the textile staff would be moved over to help on tills and then with any stock movement if required. Two new Christmas temporary staff had only started last week so they might need more supervision and were assigned to Jim. Bob the warehouse assistant would cover on the operations side, linking with Mike, the in-store technician regarding generators, systems and any maintenance problems.

Diane's next move was to inform various internal contacts of the current situation. She started with Safewatch, the contracted security company who would then make the necessary phone calls on her behalf to head office store operations and the generator company, leaving Diane free to manage the situation. She next phoned her line manager, Alex Jones, the commercial manager of the parent store. The small Middletown store was managed with four other similar sized town-centre stores on a regional basis by a large parent store. Key functions such as finance, personnel and administration were controlled by the parent store, with a small management team *in situ* running the day-to-day operations. The small management team was headed up by a regional store manager who would then report to the parent store on a weekly basis. The situation concerned Alex, mainly due to Diane's unfamiliarity with the store, and he offered to send an experienced manager over immediately to lend support to the situation. Diane declined with the excuse that the parent store's needs were greater, and by the time the support manager arrived (the parent store was at least 60 minutes drive away at this time in the evening) the power would probably be restored. Secretly, Diane wanted to prove to Alex that she could cope perfectly well by herself.

The till operators were starting to feel the strain. Normally only three of the six tills would be manned on a late Monday afternoon before closing at 5.30pm. Now there were four sales assistants on the tills, two were temporary food staff, with an additional relief manager trying to help placate the customers as the queues slowly edged towards the till point. The sixth member of the food staff was trained in first aid and was looking after the injured people until the ambulance arrived. Instead of getting shorter, the queues appeared to be growing longer as customers cut short their food shopping to pay for the essentials and get out of the store. The problem was aggravated by the tills being off-line from the latest price file and as a result, as each item's bar code was scanned the till bleeped to alert the operator to confirm or manually key in the correct price.

Diane had a quick word with the waiting customers who appeared to be in good spirits despite the delay. However, one customer had cornered Jenny, the relief manager and was clearly getting agitated. Diane enquired if she could lend some support, 'this lady had been waiting at the customer ordering desk, but the assistant was called away to help with first aid', Jenny explained. The customer ordering facility was very popular in smaller stores that couldn't stock the full range. However, the power cut would also affect the online stock checking and ordering facility. Diane took the customer's details and product request, promising to raise the order the next day. The customer left but Jenny hesitated, 'Diane, I'm worried that the system might have lost its connection with the central processor. We're okay for the next three hours as all transactions should be captured in the memory bubble. But we may have problems with the "end of day" procedure in trying to process these back to head office.' Diane knew that this could have major implications for trading in the morning if the system was not back online to process the data both to and from head office. 'Don't worry, we'll get back up from the systems people at head office', Diane reassured.

Escalating Problems

The textiles department was split over the two floors with ladies fashion on the ground floor with food. There appeared to be some activity developing next to the front doors so Diane went to investigate. Lynne, the textile supervisor and a textile sales assistant were trying to free a lady in a wheelchair who had somehow been caught between the automatic doors as the power went off. 'This is very unusual,' Lynne began to explain, 'normally the doors would spring back on contact with anything but they appear to be caught behind one of the wheels.' Crowds of shoppers were also gathering around outside, curious to see what was happening. Just as Diane suggested they get more help, another problem emerged. Dave, the relief food manager came running up and gestured for a private word with Diane. 'I've just been down to check the cold store and could hear some noises coming from the lift. It sounds like a woman and a child, – but they shouldn't be in there.' The lift was not intended for customer use and was mainly used to transport stock between the floors down to the basement loading bay and cold store. However, due to the small store only having stairs or escalators, occasionally mothers with prams or pushchairs were allowed to use the lift, provided a member of staff supervised. Dave succeeded in freeing the wheelchair as Bob Mason, the warehouse assistant, joined Diane on her way to the back of the foods section.

'The electricity board are trying to find the cause of the failure, so can't say for sure, but estimate that it could be at least 20 minutes before it comes back on', Bob reported. Diane was trying to work out how long the frozen food would have before it started to lose temperature. 'What's the status on the other generator? How far has Mike got in restarting it?', she enquired. Bob would keep her updated on this as soon as he had any more information. Diane's immediate concern was, How would they get the people out of the lift? The lift alarm was ringing when they reached it but it was still possible to hear some noises from the lift shaft – a child was crying. It was an older style lift and had few options for releasing it. 'It will have to be hand-wound down', said Jim.

Two people were needed for this so Jim enlisted the help of Bob, who was trained in this operation. Diane soon began to wish that she had accepted the offer of more help from the parent store – her staff were being rapidly occupied in other departments. A growing worry was whether the electricity would come back on soon enough, or if the generator could be started up in the meantime to cover some of the fridges and cold store.

The time was now 5.55pm, almost 15 minutes since the power failed. One of Jim's food staff, Julie, was checking temperatures in the freezers and refrigerators. 'Jim says I've got to start moving stock over into the refrigerators that are still working – depending on how fast the temperature rises. It'll be tight on space. Then we'll probably have to move it all back again when the power's on, and after that put away the new delivery… ' Julie's words trailed off as Diane remembered that a delivery was on its way to the store with tomorrow's stock replenishment. How long before it arrived and needed to be unloaded and put into the cold room? The first problem would be where to store the stock. The cold room would only retain its current temperature if the doors remained shut. It couldn't go into the shop-floor refrigerators as half weren't working and would soon be over loaded. The second problem was how to unload the lorry – the loading bay had an electric lift which would also be out of action, meaning that all crates would have to be physically lifted from the lorry – a long slow process. Diane reached the conclusion that the lorry would have to be turned back to the depot, unless the power was on by then. She went back to Jim to confirm this. Jim disagreed 'If we send it back, we'll not have enough stock for the morning. We'll only get a smaller delivery in the morning and we'll not catch up until the afternoon. Anyway, even if the electricity isn't back on we might persuade the driver to hang on a little longer. The lorries are refrigerated and will save us having to put it in the chiller or freezer.' Diane thought this was a logical solution. The lift, however, wasn't proving so easy to resolve. The winding mechanism was too tight and proving difficult to release. The only alternative was to call in the fire brigade, who would have the right type of equipment. Bob managed to shout to the trapped customer and reassure her that help was on its way. Mike, the in-store technician returned from inspecting the generator on the roof of the building. 'I can't get the second generator to start, there appears to be some mechanical failure. Safewatch have called out the generator company and I've contacted Gerry Preston, but it's unlikely any one will get through for at least another hour.' Gerry was the maintenance manager for the region and also Bob's line manager. Both were contracted from a maintenance company to offer in-store technical support.

Pete Field was also having a tedious evening. Instead of gaining the choice coverage of the spectacular band on ice event in the next town, his boss, the editor of the *Middletown Mercury*, had sent him on a mission to cover the start of late night Christmas shopping. Hardly the peak of his journalistic career, Pete grudgingly made his way to the town centre. As he walked out of the car park, he thought that it seemed a very dark night and then realized that the street lights were off. The scene was far more active than he had imagined. Crowds of shoppers were lingering around the street in anticipation of the Christmas lights but were also gathering around the entrances to some of the stores. The largest seemed to be outside the Marks & Spencer store. Pete got his notepad out and started moving through the crowd. Things were looking up, he thought to himself, this might not be such a bad job after all.

Diane went to check how things were looking on the shop floor. If the power didn't come on soon, she would have to cease the evening trading as the conditions would start to impact on Marks & Spencer's high standards and image of quality service. The first floor was empty, the subdued lighting and the still escalators were deterring customers from venturing up to the other departments. The ground floor still appeared busy with last minute food shoppers. Over by the freezer cabinets, Jim and a temporary assistant were busy loading up a trolley with frozen chickens, prawns and frozen fish, in the process of transferring them to the freezer store. In the middle, Julie was moving the yoghurts, puddings and selective dairy products over into the adjacent fridges. The hard cheeses were left intact, including some expensive Stilton gift packs, yet the Camembert, Bries and soft cheeses were being moved. Visually, it looked confusing to customers trying to complete their shopping. Diane was about to check Julie's priorities when she was interrupted by Anna, the textile sales assistant, requesting her urgent presence in the ladies blouse department. When Diane arrived, Lynne was talking to another assistant, 'Debbie thinks that a rail of silk blouses might have been stolen.' This was unwelcome news for Diane. Various clues suggested shoplifting was likely; an empty arm on the blouse fixture with one or two blouses crumpled on their hangers had fallen on the floor. The blouse display was near to the street windows in the far corner away from the main doors. The security guard would have usually been in attendance until 6.00pm, but had been taken ill and had gone home at 5.30pm. Normally, at least one or two textile assistants would be keeping a watchful eye on vulnerable areas, while stocking up the shelves, but the last 15 minutes had diverted them on to other more urgent duties. The police would have to be alerted, the shoplifters could still be in the vicinity – trying to make the most of an opportunity. As the relief manager for textiles, Lynne had other concerns, 'The red light on the CCTV has gone out and might not be working. This means we won't have a record of the incident. Also, with the system down, we can't account for how many blouses have gone or whether that's all that has been taken.'

Pete Field was making the most of an opportunity. As customers came through the front entrance of the store, he promptly questioned any who hesitated outside. He had collected a nice set of quotes from people who'd been kept waiting in till queues; a witness who had seen another customer fall down an escalator; and another who had just heard rumours of shoplifting and children being trapped in a lift. What he really needed was a good quote from the inside and so he managed to push his way through to the shop floor. Pete turned to a clean page in his notebook and looked around for any suitable member of staff. Anna refused to comment, and referred him to Diane. Pete was becoming impatient, the sooner he could wrap this story up, the sooner he could get to the pub. Diane was irritated by this latest interruption but avoided being drawn into any contentious statements. She emphasized that this problem was affecting *all* of the town centre and as yet there was no further information regarding its cause or when it might be resolved. She gave the minimum facts of the situation, carefully choosing her words to protect Marks & Spencer's position and image within the local community. While talking, Diane was escorting Pete towards the exit. When he looked up from his scribbling, Pete was next to the front door. Despite protestations, Diane managed to extricate herself on the promise of a more detailed interview the following afternoon. As he left, Pete turned his attention to the new Tesco Metro across the street. There were still a few lights on but it looked like they were starting to lock the doors. If he hurried, he might catch the manager who was just visible talking to customers in a doorway.

Damage Limitation

Diane now considered how best to deploy her staff. Jim and his five staff were all actively occupied in the food department either on the shop floor serving customers or behind the scenes moving stock. One of the textile staff was the first aid person and was assisting the injured customers into the ambulance. Two textile staff were needed on the doors to stop new customers coming in, but also to let the remaining customers out. Ideally, another assistant was needed to keep an eye on the ground floor textiles until all of the customers had left the store. Two of the other textile assistants were still operating the food checkouts. That left only one to help the food staff move any remaining frozen food into the freezer store. This was enough to force Diane into a decision – the store would have to be closed and the customers politely asked to leave. As Diane began to put this decision into action, Dave sought her out at the front of the store. Diane was beginning to wonder how she ever managed without a pager and the use of department phones – with only one external phone line still working and a mobile phone, any communication had to be relayed by word of mouth. 'The delivery has arrived and Bob is talking with the driver at the moment. He doesn't seem too keen to wait for long. Bob thinks you should try and talk him round.' While Bob could be counted on to help out in a crisis or emergency, he was not officially supervisory or management team as he often reminded them when too many responsibilities were being thrust upon him. Diane went back to the other end of the store – feeling like she had covered every inch of the store's 8000 sq ft of ground floor in the past 30 minutes. On the way she was updated with the lift situation. The fire engine was delayed but in the meantime, Gerry Preston, the maintenance manager, had arrived and seemed to be making good progress in starting the hand winding. The trapped customers could be out within about five minutes. The loading bay was on a lower basement level, and by the time Diane reached the back door, she was feeling ready to go home and put her feet up. There would be little chance of any tea break here until the situation was resolved.

Bob was relieved to see Diane and was glad for an excuse to avoid any confrontation 'Diane this is Steve', he introduced her to the driver. 'Sorry but I've got to go and help with the lift.' Diane wondered whether she could appeal to the driver's better nature to avoid the prospect of empty shelves the next morning. He pre-empted Diane's thoughts. 'I'm sorry Miss Webster, I'd gladly help but I've been stuck in traffic for 30 minutes across town and I'm running out of hours. I need to be back at the depot by eight tonight.' Legally, Steve was restricted to nine hours driving time excluding breaks, and given the time of year with additional deliveries he would be using up all of his allocation. Diane ran through the options; sending the delivery back would mean that the store would open with only part of its replenishment until later in the next morning. Stock would probably be depleted as a result of the power cut, thus aggravating the low stock situation. One option was if the driver could leave the refrigerated trailer behind and then it could be unloaded later. Diane was about to phone the depot to discuss the latter suggestion when she realized that unless the power was on before 8.00pm, many of the staff would need to go, leaving too few to clear up, unload the trailer and put the stock away. It was now 6.50pm and she decided to have one last try with the electricity board. The cause had been traced to the town centre Christmas lights, but there was still no definite time of reconnection except that it 'could be in the next hour'. By that time, Diane could count on about half of her team and staff being able to stay behind but the others would need to get back to their families. By then, they might also have more clearing up to do as the shop-floor freezers were beginning to warm up and water was somehow leaking on to the floor. There might also be difficulties rebooting the system and getting the data connected with the central processor, occupying another member of staff. The systems central support service were on standby to help but until full power was returned it would be difficult to know what was possible and how much stock had already been automatically re-ordered. There was little choice but to send the lorry back. Diane phoned the depot to negotiate a return delivery as early as possible in the morning.

Diane wandered back towards the lift. By now, Gerry and Bob had succeeded in winding down the lift and the door was opened. A weary but relieved and unscathed young mother emerged pushing a buggy containing a sleeping toddler. Bob arranged for a cup of tea while Dave used the mobile phone to call her home number, and then a taxi. Hopefully, they would be the last customers to leave the store tonight.

With the last customer gone Diane's priorities could be more focused on the stock and staff. She went on a floor walk to survey the situation. The doors were now being locked and a quick tidying up of wire baskets and various fixtures. The textile stock would be filled up – stock permitting, in the morning. Most activity was still in the food department. Sales assistants were sorting out the tills and cashing up. Julie and Dave were moving more stock to the cooler backstage area – this time the longer life food. Jim was starting to note down some of the food stock that had already come out of the cold chain. 'How does it look?' enquired Diane. 'Difficult to say until we know when the power is definitely on.' Jim continued, 'We salvaged most of the frozen stock by consolidating it and getting it into the freezer store. It holds the temperature in there for eight hours if we don't open the door too often. The chilled food is more of a problem as the cold store loses temperature more quickly. It will only last for two hours with the door shut. We tried to pile up the fridges still operating on the shop floor, but couldn't fit in that much because of the risk of contamination. The fresh chickens were most affected because of their bulk and weight. They had to be segregated from other foods and that would have meant taking them off the shelves in the first ten minutes while we were still trading. We didn't have enough manpower. Perhaps with more staff we could have prioritized better.' Jim then added 'It could be worse, next week we get the delivery of the Christmas turkeys.' Diane was about to follow up Jim's previous comment when she noticed a group of people approaching from the front door. Lynne led two police officers and an anxious-looking suited man. The latter was looking for his wife and child who were due to meet him from work an hour earlier. Realizing that this was the husband of the family trapped in the lift, Diane brought Dave into the conversation to explain what had happened, leaving her free to deal with the police, who were responding to the reported shoplifting. A statement was required and Debbie escorted the officers to the nearest and lightest office.

Wrapping Up

It was now 7.20pm and time for Diane to report back to Safewatch. The security department would also need informing that the store had closed earlier than planned. Store operations were also concerned about rebooting the system when the power came back on. Diane needed to keep two or three staff behind to help with this, but after the food stock was secured, there was little more to be done than wait. Diane instructed the supervisors to release staff as soon as their departments were secure.

Diane rang Alex Jones to update him of the situation and for advice. Diane's systems knowledge was good but not being familiar with this older store, there were one or two aspects she may need to be aware of. Alex advised that she ask Mike to stay to reboot the system, with Jenny on hand to help with the 'end of day' procedure. Bob would need to be there to close up and secure the premises. Jim was also reluctant to leave and offered to stay on.

The store was feeling quite cold and empty. The heating had been off for an hour and a half although Diane hadn't noticed in the rush of the first hour. She put on her coat and tried to keep moving although there was little she could do apart from wait. The ring of the loading bay bell broke her concentration, the man from the generator company had arrived to repair it. Mike escorted him to the roof. Diane started to plan her tasks for the next day. It was too cold to sit in her office, so she made a mental note as she walked around the store. The textile supervisor would need to check how many items were missing – involving a manual stock count. Then the central system would need to be updated. Other stores would need to be alerted about the stolen stock to be prepared for possible refund claims. After the stock count the displays would need filling up and tidying but this depended on the delivery. All food wastage would need recording before disposal. Then there would be the task of filling out the insurance claims. More immediately, the food section would need a good clean out of all the non-functioning fridges and freezers. More cleaners would need drafting in – possibly an hour earlier before opening. She needed to check her labour allowance with the regional personnel manager as this would come out of the store's budget and not insurance. Only then could the shelves be restocked – that was hoping that there was sufficient stock in the morning's delivery. Diane decided to phone the depot to see if she could bring forward the 6.00am delivery to 5.00am. They would certainly lose sales in the morning and it might take a few days to recover the stock situation. Lost sales were not covered by the insurance. The generator would probably need repairing – hopefully not replacing, which was another unexpected cost to the maintenance budget. The Christmas period would have to generate some good turnover to ensure her profit figures were achieved. Over and above all of this, Diane would need to debrief her team about the way the incident was managed and handled, in readiness for any future crisis event.

Jim joined Diane on her store walk and suggested that she go home. There was little more she could do until the morning. Everything was under control and Jim would call her at home as soon as the power returned. Diane felt too tired to protest and had to agree. Particularly as she would need to be in early the next morning to progress the insurance forms and check the stock situation. As she made her way to her office to gather up some papers, the lights flickered again. This time they returned to full strength. A quick look outside confirmed that the town centre was back on power at 8.20pm. She went back to the team with a last burst of energy to help support them with the systems, but also for her own peace of mind that everything was functioning. She also needed to make a few vital phone calls to let people know that the store was operational again.

When finally walked out of the store at 9.00pm, Diane reflected back over the evening and thought that she had coped pretty well with everything that had been thrown at her. She knew that one or two other stores in the street had managed to continue trading but they had fully operating generators providing more back-up power. Then she started to wonder how the evening's events would be interpreted by Alex Jones as he would require a full review tomorrow morning.

QUESTIONS

1. You have been asked to provide a report to Alex Jones, commercial manager, analysing the way that the event was managed. Examine Diane's approach and suggest recommendations to improve the situation in the event of another power failure.

2. Discuss the type of competency profile required to manage an Marks & Spencer store. How might this differ to other retailer competency profiles? Note: you may wish to refer to the generic CORTCO competences. Which competences are most important to managers in a crisis situation?

3. As part of the store operations department in head office, you need to prepare a chapter for the staff training manual on guidelines for operating procedures in the event of a power cut. Identify and discuss the key store operations areas on which to focus. What other issues and subjects should be covered?

4. Assuming the role of Diane, prepare a de-brief of the staff and management team involved in the previous evening's event. Consider how you would approach the staff and feedback on the way *they* were involved and behaved in the event.

CASE 8
EUROPEAN AND UK PACKAGING WASTE LEGISLATION: THE MARKS & SPENCER RESPONSE

CATHY HART AND JOHN FERNIE

The authors would particularly like to thank Rowland Hill and Roy Dixon of Marks & Spencer, who provided valuable contributions and support during the researching and writing of this case.

INTRODUCTION

In March 1997 the Producer Responsibility Obligations (Packaging Waste) Regulations came into force. The legislation was derived from the European Directive, 94/62/EC, which aimed to reduce the amount of packaging waste going to landfill sites, with a long-term aim to reduce the volume of packaging waste generated across the supply chain. From January 1998, various members of UK supply chains were obliged to recover and recycle specific amounts of packaging waste. Criticized as 'Bureaucratic, ill-conceived and confusing' (Castle, 1997), the legislation threatened major disruption to many retailers, at an estimated cost of £300–£600m to manufacturing and retail industry. Twelve months down the line, different retailers had responded in different ways. This case study examines the background to the legislation and the approach adopted by one retailer, Marks & Spencer.

THE LEGISLATION

The UK legislation stipulated that by 1998 a minimum of 38 per cent of all packaging waste must be recovered, rising to 52 per cent by 2001. The term 'recovery' refers to the collection of waste packaging, and includes recycling, reprocessing and incineration. Three different types of packaging were included in the legislation:

- **Primary** or sales packaging containing the core product, for example glass bottle, toothpaste tube as used and disposed of by the consumer.
- **Secondary** packaging included additional sales packaging for example a carton around the toothpaste tube, or a container holding a number of indi-

vidual units for example a card box of 10 tubes. This packaging would normally be disposed of by either the retailer or consumer.

■ **Transit** packaging referred to packs used to transport the smaller units between sites. If used more than three times it became exempt.

Within these figures, the overall recycling target had been set at 7 per cent by 1998 and 26 per cent by 2001. The responsibility for recovery had been 'shared' across the different members of the supply chain.

Table 8.1 **Share of recovery targets**

6%	Raw material producers
11%	Packaging manufacturers
36%	Packer/fillers
47%	Retailers

As seen in Table 8.1, the greater responsibility has fallen on the retailers as the last member of the supply chain. However, only retailers with a turnover in excess of £5m, or handling over fifty tonnes of packaging waste must comply. This threshold dropped to £1m in 1999. From this date, any retailer falling below these limits has their recovery responsibility passed up the distribution chain to the wholesaler who supplied them. Initially, some retailers mistakenly assumed that only secondary and transit packaging were affected, only to discover that all primary/sales packaging were included in these recovery targets.

The method of waste recovery required that each company must either join a collective compliance scheme, or register with the Environment Agency (by 31 August 1997) and then make their own collection arrangements. Within the recovery targets, each company must recycle specific percentages of different types of materials for example aluminium, glass, cardboard, plastic, steel. This may also include reprocessing into new material, composting and incineration with energy recovery. Furthermore, companies had to provide data on all packaging they have generated, recovered and recycled over the previous year. All companies must reach their recycling and recovery targets by the end of each calendar year (starting December 1998), or face prosecution. A Certificate of Compliance provided evidence that this had been achieved and had to be sent to the Environment Agency by 31 January 1999 and annually thereafter.

RETAILER IMPACT

In comparing different product sectors, it appeared that most packaging was generated through the food supply chain, particularly given the growing trend for convenience and prepared foods. Three operational issues emerged from the legislation. First, how much weight of plastic, glass and tin, had been sold to customers during the past year? A detailed audit of the packaging waste stream would be required. Second, data collection systems would have to be set up to monitor and update this data. Third, who should assume management responsibility for this task: a central head office function, or another level, and if so in which department? The final decision concerned the physical collection of the waste. While many retailers had arrangements for returning transit packaging, that is, materials used to protect products during transportation to the store, the legislation also applied to the primary packaging sold on to and disposed of by the consumers. The government envisaged that most retailers would not actually recycle packaging themselves but would join an exemption scheme who would then take over the legal responsibility for meeting that company's recovery targets. These schemes act as agents on behalf of the retailers, using their expertise and economy of scale to negotiate with reprocessors. The schemes use membership funds to purchase certificates, known as packaging recovery notes (PRNs) from the reprocessors to meet members' recovery targets. The system suggested a growing market for PRNs, which due to the undercapacity of reprocessing in the UK, could drive up costs to the retailer, which may then be passed on to the consumer. At the current stage in the legislation there was little information regarding the long-term costs involved, which could be evaluated against setting up a retailer's own recovery system.

THE GERMAN APPROACH

Marks & Spencer had been developing an active European expansion policy in the 1980s and in 1990 began targeting the German market. In particular, the Marks & Spencer food offer held a prime 'quality' differentiation factor compared with local German supermarkets. However, the German retailers held a prior advantage by already complying with local environmental legislation. In June 1991, less than a year after reunification, Germany introduced the Packaging Ordinance, the first packaging waste policy of all EU countries. Their target was to reduce household waste by 25–30 per cent by 1995.

The obligation for recovery, recycling, and disposal of packaging was shared between manufacturers, retailers and consumers. The German approach was based on the 'closed loop' philosophy that industry and trade should be responsible for taking back and recycling the products they have introduced on to the market. The aim was 'to prevent and reduce waste, to recycle the packaging materials and return them to the manufacturing process' (Duales System Deutschland, 1998). The concept involved reversing the flow of packaging waste back up the supply chain; retailers were responsible for taking back sales packaging from consumers, manufacturers to retrieve it from the retailers and the packaging companies to take it back from manufacturers. One of the main difficulties in reverse flow of any product or waste material is in organizing the physical collection, sorting and handling. Initially, consumers were encouraged to leave secondary packaging behind in the shops for the retailer to then organize its re-processing or recycling. This caused considerable logistical problems and an alternative route was sought, with a key objective being to relieve the local authorities of the burden of disposal.

German trade and industry were given the option to organize their own collection system, independent of but alongside the municipal waste disposal. The scheme known as Duales System Deutschland (DSD) was established with over 600 companies in its membership. The DSD collection system was a private enterprise which enabled retailers to avoid actually handling the waste. The joint nationwide, household collection system collected, sorted and arranged the recycling of post-consumer sales packaging, thus exempting industry from their individual 'takeback' obligation. It operated two forms of collection; the kerbside system whereby plastics, composites, tins and paper were picked up from households, and the 'bring' system, in which consumers take collected packaging to recycling stations or containers that have been set up locally. The scheme was funded by licence fees according to the kind of material and the weight, plus an additional fee per piece. The fees were based on the different collection, sorting and recycling costs; for example, plastic is much higher than glass on account of the more expensive sorting process and the additional payment made for recycling. The packaging participating in the scheme was identified by a green dot. The German Ministry of Environment granted licences to use the green dot, providing the companies achieved the minimum recycling levels. Failure to do so meant the licence was revoked and the retailer reverted to individually organizing collection of post-sales packaging.

In 1993 the German legislation was further tightened when product containers were subjected to a deposit to encourage consumer recycling of bottles and so on In 1995 the quotas increased significantly; at least 64 per cent of all sales packaging had to be recycled (including cardboard, plastics and compound materials). More specifically a minimum of 72 per cent of glass, tin plate and aluminium had to be recycled.

Critics of the DSD system claimed that it was expensive and politically 'cherry picking' as it dealt only with sales packaging which is, to the electorate, the most visible form of waste. Furthermore, the DSD membership only covered approximately 75 per cent of German companies, with the remainder organizing their own collection schemes. A fundamental weakness from the early implementation of the ordinance, was the lack of German reprocessing capacity causing a missing link in the recycling chain. Often the huge amounts of collected recyclables had no end market domestically or no method for cost effective reuse. This resulted in domestic and overseas markets being flooded with surplus stocks which, for example resulted in price collapses and damage to the recovered paper market. From 1991–96, 20 million tonnes of used bags, boxes, cans and bottles were forwarded for recycling by the Dual System.

The DSD is collecting high percentages of waste at enormous cost, the availability of sorting, recycling and end-use capacity has led to the export of outsourced mixed plastic to the Far East in sufficient quantities to become a health hazard in China. (Stenning, 1998)

Success Factors of DSD

In spite of key weaknesses in the system, some successes could be claimed. Manufacturers had been forced to change their packaging habits by developing more efficient production techniques to reduce waste. Some branded companies exploited this further through competitive advertising by claiming environmental advantages. Packaging design had improved, becoming lighter and smaller as a result of the differential fees for different materials. The higher fees on plastics and glass meant that many containers had been replaced with lower fee cardboard. Any useless packaging not fulfilling a function had virtually disappeared. The actual packaging use had also been drastically reduced. In 1995 there were 1.3 million tonnes less packaging generated than in 1991 when it was first introduced. Consumer awareness of recycling also increased as the green dot and household collection systems came into national circulation.

In setting up the environmental packaging waste standards for retailing in Germany, Marks & Spencer liaised closely with the DSD to develop a working relationship. At the outset, the main activity was the forward planning involved in meeting the regulations. It soon became evident that there were also key operational issues to resolve: Marks & Spencer entered the German market by opening their first store in Cologne, October 1996. Being the first EU country to develop packaging legislation, Germany had established very clear if stringent, requirements. The German Packaging Ordinance dictated that individual material weights of all components had to be specified. Also, the external pack volume as occupying the landfill had to identified. Marks & Spencer thus had to isolate all of the detailed packaging data relevant to one store across the individual materials generated, for example labels, material composition, components, and volumes. Although Marks & Spencer could provide rough estimates of the quantities used by that one store, they were not allowed to do so and had to calculate the data from each product line specification and then multiply by the EPOS (electronic point of sale) sales data. The DSD provided the software to help set up the systems to calculate the data.

A major issue to consider was that approximately one third of the Marks & Spencer food range changes each year. This may involve different designs of packaging and thus different weights and specifications. In operationalizing the process, two teams were set up centrally, one for textiles and one for foods, who were responsible for gathering the data. These teams were linked with an administrator in the Cologne store who was responsible for co-ordinating the sales figures and submitting the forms to the DSD. The IT department was the other key player, who had to set up and enter the data on the system. The whole system then had to be audited by Coopers and Lybrand in order to verify the figures for the DSD.

PACKAGING WASTE AND THE UK

The UK was somewhat slower than its European counterparts in developing a waste policy. Following the German Packaging Ordinance adopted in 1991, the Dutch Covenant was signed in the same year. France and Austria adopted their Packaging Decree and Ordinance in 1992. Sweden followed suit in 1994 and Italy in 1996. In 1997 Belgium introduced its Decree, and the UK and Spain joined the group by introducing their own derivatives of the EC Directive in the same year. The original directive gives member states a duty to set a packaging recycling target between 25 per cent and 45 per cent with a minimum recycling rate of 15 per cent for each material. The UK government set the lowest recycling target.

Currently, Switzerland claim to have the highest recycling rates for specific materials in Europe with figures ranging from 55 per cent of steel cans up to 89 per cent of glass. The total waste generation per person in Switzerland has fallen 17 per cent from 1989 to 1995. The high rates are attributed to a well-informed public and good recycling infrastructure, particularly in source separation by householders.

Compared with the German Ordinance, the UK legislation was relatively relaxed. The data were required at an aggregate level for each company that is, the total weight of the various materials such as glass, plastic and so on rather than individual components. These figures were also rounded to the nearest tonne. Furthermore, estimates could be initially provided if actual data were not available. This offered considerable savings in terms of management time and resources.

MARKS & SPENCER, LEADER OF THE PACK?

Having previously gained experience in adopting the more rigorous German packaging waste legislation, when the UK legislation was introduced in 1997, Marks & Spencer found that its implementation would be more of a formality. In 1992, the environmental projects department carried out a waste management review to assess the current situation and identify their future environment needs in Europe. The Marks & Spencer stores appeared to be the focus for most of waste handling. The majority of waste activity was generated by used transit packaging, which the stores then had to remove from merchandise, segregate, bale and return it where possible to their local distribution centre. The vagaries of equipment, storage space and vehicle schedules dictated that barely 40 per cent was recovered. The remainder was destined for landfill. The first priority was to reduce the amount of waste created and alleviate pressure in stores. Reusable transit packaging systems such as plastic containers, were introduced. The next stage was to manage the remaining waste more effectively. The distribution centres were better equipped and more efficient at managing waste than the stores, so Marks & Spencer altered the way in which the merchandise was delivered to the stores. All remaining transit packaging was removed, segregated, baled, and recycled at the distribution centre prior to the merchandise being despatched in reusable delivery systems to stores. 'The benefits have been enormous. Stores receive merchandise "ready for display", have minimal packaging waste to handle and our distribution centres are able to recycle over 95 per cent of it' (Hill, 1997). The amount of packaging going to landfill from these products was also reduced by over 95 per cent, from 18,000 tonnes to 4000. Current initiatives plan to reduce it further to 1000 tonnes.

In deciding on an approach for recycling sales packaging in the UK, Marks & Spencer wanted to develop a system that would reflect their partnership ethos and values. They also needed an effective system that would prevent Marks & Spencer from having to diversify into the business of measuring, recycling and certifying their own waste. Conversely, they also wanted to avoid setting up additional contractual arrangements that required more management effort. As a result, they opted to form a joint compliance scheme, with UK Waste Management Ltd who currently managed their waste collection and disposal. 'Recycle UK' (a subsidiary of Waste Management Ltd) was set up in June 1997. Its key role was to physically handle the packaging waste and to liaise with the reprocessors on behalf of Marks & Spencer. The advantage of Recycle UK was that one company could handle all of the environment services including recovery and recycling. Furthermore, the partnership was based on a proactive approach, whereby Recycle UK used their prior expertise and access to existing facilities to minimize packaging waste and labour costs, and maximize waste recovery and recycling. The membership of Recycle UK included other organizations and Marks & Spencer suppliers, who could then share recycling 'best practice'.

Having already implemented the data collection systems for aggregating the packaging information for the DSD and Germany, Marks & Spencer needed to adapt the system to the UK and Europe. Their international expansion policy meant that Marks & Spencer were or would soon be trading in every major European country. Despite the general dictate from the European Directive, each country had adapted the legislation to suit their cultural, environmental differences. Denmark imposed a total ban on drink cans, claiming that returnable bottles were the most environmentally friendly form of packaging. As a result, they demanded data on different types and colours of glass used. Due to the national preferences for beer in Germany and wine in France, these countries have also introduced more complex recycling and reusable systems for glass bottles. The Eco-Emballages system in France also required detail of the type and content of material within each sales container. Ironically, each European member country's idiosyncratic interpretation of the legislation has created new trade barriers that the EU claimed to have originally removed.

The challenge faced by Marks & Spencer was to design a pan-European solution to comply with each set of legislation, while also meeting the UK requirements. Marks & Spencer chose a centralized approach of building a database for the whole of Europe. This was achieved by combining the most demanding packaging requirements from each country into one central system. It had to be an evolving database which would be continually refined to include new legislation and also a changing product range. The next stage encompassed devolving operational responsibility to individual buying teams who could then manage the process of integrating and updating new packaging specifications. The food and packaging suppliers form an important part of the process in that they are responsible for supplying accurate packaging data, and ultimately they could identify and share best practice in improving the systems.

In November 1997, revision 005 of the UK Producer Responsibility Regulations included a protocol for data exchange between suppliers and customers. While packaging suppliers normally dealt in tonnage, further down the packaging chain the items were transferred as numbers of packs. Clearly, all suppliers had records of their sales to customers and therefore it was vital that these data were also communicated across the different members of the supply chain. The legislation had also opened up reverse communication links between members in the supply chain which was a step towards improving efficiencies across the chain.

CONFLICT OF ISSUES

Although the packaging legislation has been devised to reduce the packaging generated across the supply chain, there are a number of issues likely to conflict with this objective. Social and demographic research (MAFF, 1993/94) indicated that the average household is reducing in size, more people are eating alone, and the continued increase in the consumption of convenience foods suggested that there will need to be a 4 per cent increase in the quantity of packaging used by the year 2000. From a marketing viewpoint, the packaging is often the only form of promotion, particularly in own-label products, therefore there may be constraints on reducing the size or impact of the package. Furthermore, the consumer is familiar with certain types of product packaging and may need 're-educating' to purchase and use different designs. UK consumers are generally less environmentally aware and proactive compared with their continental cousins.

At current levels, there is also debate regarding the UK capacity for reprocessing the packaging quotas. Although glass recycling is well developed, far more green glass bottles are imported into this country than can be recycled by the container manufacturers. As a result this could drive up the costs of green glass PRNs (packaging recovery notes) by 400 per cent. Plastic bottle recycling levels have a huge shortfall and will need to grow by ten times in the next four years in order to meet the targets. In the past, other countries have responded by exporting excess waste to under developed countries for sorting and processing. These solutions all incur additional financial and environmental costs to various players in the supply chain.

THE FUTURE: WHAT WASTE CRISIS?

Critics of the UK legislation believed that it was 'too little too late' and would not achieve the minimum targets without additional incentives;

> The government will fail to reach its 25 per cent recycling rate unless it acts tough on waste now. It must increase the landfill tax substantially and extend it to cover incineration, and it must come down hard on the wasteful packaging industry. If the government doesn't do these things then we will continue to waste valuable resources by sending them up in smoke or throwing them into holes in the ground. (Thomas, 1997)

It has been estimated that the government plans for recycling packaging waste may only increase rates by about 3 per cent by the year 2000. This would result in an overall recycling rate of less than 10 per cent, falling short of the government's target for recycling 25 per cent of domestic waste by 2000 (a rate that is already being achieved in the United States).

While Marks & Spencer and other UK retailers strive to reduce the amount of packaging going to landfill, there are other lobbying groups who feel that their resources could be better utilized. Packaging is less than a third of household waste in weight, and in volume terms, contributes approximately 6 per cent of total land-filled waste, the major culprit (50 per cent) being other commercial and industrial waste. Furthermore, households dispose of approximately the same quantities of food waste as packaging waste. The Industry Council for Packaging and the Environment analysed the extent of waste and losses along the complete food chain and concluded that packaged foods generate less waste than fresh foods (INCPEN, 1997). Waste food is also a far greater waste of resources in terms of energy. The energy used for packaging is 11 per cent of that used in the whole food supply system. Energy used by consumers for shopping, storing and cooking food is over three times the energy consumed for packaging.

Despite the predicted growth in the quantity of packaging used, there is also evidence to suggest that the weight of packaging waste is static. More packaged goods may be available now, approximately 15,000 product lines compared with 2000 in the 1960s. But 'the packaging used for each pack and the total weight of material used for all packaging is probably no more than it was 20 years ago' (Bickerstaff, 1997).

It should also be remembered that additional energy is consumed in actually collecting, sorting and recycling the packaging waste. The current EC law has set a minimum of 15 per cent recycling for all packaging materials. It is not known if this is a sensible level and due to the lack of recycling awareness, it is likely that materials will be collected and sorted for recycling even when there is no environmental gain.

THE FUTURE: ENVIRONMENTAL LOGISTICS

The legislation has identified a new set of players in the supply chain. The environmental waste management industry could be considered the new logistics partner for the new millennium, much in the same way that third party logistics operators developed during the 1980s. While many retailers perceived the new packaging legislation as a 'waste of space', it clearly indicates that recycling and packaging waste reduction is here to stay. The management of that process will be the key challenge for retailers during the next five years. One outcome may involve trading off the costs across the whole supply chain, versus the benefits for the environment. Ultimately, the Marks & Spencer response illustrates how one company has managed to cut their waste disposal costs by 50 per cent as a result of their efforts to minimize packaging and maximize recycling.

QUESTIONS

1. Compare and contrast the German and the UK legislative approach to reducing packaging waste. Evaluate which is the more effective route and why?

2. What are the key barriers to facilitating the packaging waste legislation in the UK? How might these be resolved?

3. What alternative approaches could be taken to further spread the responsibility for packaging waste?

4. What lessons could be learnt from Germany and other countries' approach?

5. Suggest future strategies which could be developed to reduce the overall quantity of packaging generated and used across the whole supply chain

6. You have been asked to provide a briefing note for recommended revisions to the UK legislation in 2001. Predict the likely direction in which the legislation could move and outline your recommendations.

REFERENCES

Bickerstaff, J. (1997) 'Packaging and the environment'. Paper presented at the *Packaging and the Environment Conference*. London, 19 February.

Castle, D. (1997) 'Paper shuffling exercise'. *The Grocer*, 26 July, pp. 32–5.

Duales System Deutschland (1998) http://www.gruener-punkt.de/e/index.htm.

Ministry of Agriculture, Fisheries and Food (1993/94) *The National Food Survey*. Annual Report on household food consumption and expenditure. London: HMSO.

Hill, R. (1997) Extract from talk given by the Environmental Projects Manager, Marks & Spencer.

INCPEN (1997) 'A working partnership tipping the scales in favour of the environment'. Consultation Document, *The Industry Council for Packaging and the Environment*.

Stenning, K. (1998) Vice Chairman of the Packaging and Industrial Films Association, *Packaging News*, January, http://www.tecweb.com.

Thomas, A. (1997) Waste Campaigner, Friends of the Earth, 30 September webmaster@foe.co.uk.

CASE 9

SHRINK BUSTERS!
A DIY CASE IN FINANCIAL
MANAGEMENT AND CONTROL

RUTH A. SCHMIDT, BRENDA M. OLDFIELD AND DAVID LEAVER

The authors would like to thank staff from a UK retailer, who wishes to remain unnamed, for their support in developing this case study. Paintworld is a fictitious company and so are all names used in the case study. The content of this case study has been simplified to enable students to focus on key learning objectives, and therefore is not a complete picture of the management of shrinkage at store level.

INTRODUCTION

DIY store-level management play a critical role in the control of shrinkage, an area where in-store operational measures link into aggregate corporate financial performance in a direct manner. The impact of store managers is twofold; through their own actions in making use of the correct processes and procedures and also as trainers of other staff. This case was developed with the aim of illustrating the key issues surrounding the management of shrinkage as a tool for teaching students in retail education as well as for practical in-company management training. The twin focus of the case is the process of developing and implementation of the 'Shrink Busters' initiative and an evaluation of the impact of this initiative on overall business performance. A general understanding of key financial statements and the principles of ratio analysis is a useful prerequisite for a full attempt at the first two of the case questions. It is therefore intended that the case should be used in conjunction with further teaching material relating to financial techniques, such as ratio analysis, as indicated in the further reading references.

BACKGROUND

In 1996 the UK DIY market was valued at £10.9b (Verdict, 1997). For the leading retailers, gaining additional market share, expanding the store portfolio and influencing the development of out-of-town DIY retailing, as well as the creation of a unique selling proposition in a mass market pose challenging tasks. In the wake of the price war of the early 1990s average industry margins remain low, price matching and guarantees the norm, with a number of operators emphasizing the importance of discounting. Most multiple DIY retailers, including Paintworld, continue to focus on maintaining their margins through tight and innovative cost control measures while at the same time striving to increase the level of customer service. Much of the future success of Paintworld's strategy hinges on the continuous improvement of cost effectiveness in the management of space and stock, especially as increases in suppliers' costs may well be passed on to the DIY retail chains, further squeezing already tight margins.

At store level, the tight management of stock is a key area for enhancing operational controls and thereby profitability. A major threat to this is shrinkage – the loss of stock due to customer and staff theft or administrative error. Shrinkage can be calculated as the difference between the EPOS (electronic point of sale) cost of sales based on manufacturer prices related to till records and the actual cost of sales based on the manually updated stock database. Thus shrinkage is the measured amount of total avoidable money losses attributable to poor stock management. An estimate by UK Retail Crime Statistics (1997) indicates that overall shrinkage costs retailers 24 per cent of net profit. The causal breakdown attributes responsibility as: 43 per cent to customer theft; 30 per cent to staff theft; 10 per cent to supplier theft; 17 per cent to administrative errors. In addition, The British Retail Consortium estimated the cost of crime for the UK DIY sector in 1997 at £208m (UK Retail Crime Statistics, 1997).

JIM'S STORY: DEVISING AND IMPLEMENTING A WORKABLE SHRINKAGE CONTROL STRATEGY

The War on Shrink: Financial Objectives

Jim Doors has been responsible for loss prevention at Paintworld for the past eighteen months. For Jim, designing and implementing a company-wide loss prevention strategy has been the culmination of his career to date. Jim says about his background, 'The point I would make is that all my retail and operations management experience has been invaluable; without that experience I could not be doing the job I'm doing now because the figures and all the detailed things I do now would just not make sense, and it would not give me the focus, in terms of what are the big levers to push to get the results we want.'

Initially, a key challenge for Jim was to evaluate the different factors which cause shrinkage and to identify the full range of measures available to combat them. Clearly, nothing comes free of charge, and Jim was aware that in order to win the war on shrinkage, he would most probably have to invest in fixed assets in the form of security devices and sophisticated technology as well as incurring further spending on security staff and general staff training. The real challenge was to find the optimum mix of measures! In order to devise a comprehensive business plan for the whole initiative, Jim then had to evaluate the costs and benefits of the different measures and project the likely impact on overall financial performance.

Unlike many retail organizations, within Paintworld shrinkage is measured at cost (excluding mark-up and VAT) and expressed as a percentage of sales (excluding VAT). This means that the cost of shrinkage adds to the cost of goods sold and, therefore, depresses gross margins.

Generally speaking, managing shrinkage is about controlling preventable stock losses; however, an initial full analysis has revealed that a lot of detail needs to be considered when determining what should be included in an operating definition. Shrinkage is especially pronounced for lines of merchandise where customers expect to be able to take away samples, or where theft is relatively easily accomplished. Clearly, customer and staff theft, as well as stock losses occasioned through customer sampling and store own use, are part of shrinkage. Less obviously, there are also unknown losses, for example, due to failure of recording own use (in-store), damage or spillage of products, and last but not least, the whole area of shrinkage which appears only as paper figures and is due completely to poorly devised administrative procedures.

Historically the company has managed shrinkage by focusing on in-store security with an emphasis on the capture of potential thieves. This was quite successful and Jim soon realized that in comparison to competitors, 'The actual theft that is created by members of the public is relatively small on average. You'll have some stores which will be "hit" by professional thieves more frequently than others and therefore, in a few stores, it is a very big problem, but across the board it's not a big problem.' He is sure, however, that it is largely due to the traditionally strong focus on security that customer theft has been contained. He argues against complacency: 'If we stop spending the money that we do on deterrents to detect theft by the public, then it could become a big problem. For example, at the moment we spend something in the region of £2.2m per year for guards and store detectives. We have video cameras recording in most of our stores, and we continue to improve that further. We are just about to implement electronic article surveillance into all of our stores.'

Information collated from store detectives and security guards is used to ensure that all known incidents are logged onto database and the information recorded is analysed in a very detailed way. This facilitates profiling by age, gender, preferred days of the week and times of the day, as well as key product areas prone to theft.

Jim noted: 'What we do is put together the crimes profile and feed it out to our store detectives to say that, typically, in this particular store, or this particular geographical area, these are the sort of trends that we are noticing.' This can be particularly useful in apprehending professional thieves, who, on occasion, 'do the rounds' and carry out refund fraud in a loop of stores. Linking the company database to a CD autoroute planner together with a CCTV record of the car registration number, and visual data on the people involved, can act as an early warning system. Thus police can be alerted and brought in to arrest would-be thieves for conspiracy, which (due to the element of intent and planning involved) carries a higher penalty than theft.

In addition to customer theft at store level, 'careless' staff use can also be a large contributing factor, as illustrated by the following tale Jim recounted. 'A store manager would find discarded packaging in the store where clearly somebody – we don't know who – had taken things out of the package and stolen or used it. Typically, for example, in a store somebody would take a Stanley knife from the shelf to do a job. It may just be to open cartons and boxes or things like that, and you may say well it's only one item worth £1, but of course if you've ten of those every week and every store in the company is doing that, it's obviously going to become big numbers.'

In the effective control of shrinkage the store very often is only the 'tip of the iceberg'. It is, therefore, very important to have a comprehensive company-wide system and to communicate to store management that they are not expected to do everything and that their commitment to shrinkage control will be backed and complemented by wider measures. Jim is very clear that shrinkage is a company-wide challenge. He stated: 'I think one of the biggest challenges we have as a business, is to get the mind set right; to treat it as actually a company problem and not just a store problem. Within most businesses when you talk about shrinkage, everybody looks at the store manager and says, "well he's no bloody good, he's a useless manager".' While this may occasionally be the case, it is not always a very helpful point of view since some of the most important contributing elements are located outside the control of store management. Consequently systems must be firmly in place to control these aspects in a comprehensive and visible manner if store management are to be fully committed to controlling their own share of the shrinkage problem.

One such area partly outside the control of store management concerns the design and implementation of systems for dealing with products which are particularly vulnerable to theft. Jim continued, 'We're going to identify what those sensitive products are, assembling them separately, putting them into sealed containers within a sealed vehicle, so when they get to the store they're checked off as a matter of priority 100 per cent, and put straight into a service area on the shop floor. Customers can only buy them by taking a card off a display and going to the checkout. Now that means that high value products are not on open display. By high value, it doesn't necessarily mean that the value of the individual item is high, there are some products where the value per item is fairly low, but, when they are stolen, they are stolen in volume and therefore the loss that year is fairly high. Examples of such items are taps, electric showers, drills, certain lighting, certain types of rechargeable battery and even torches, especially some of the more expensive ones.'

A further major issue with system-wide impact within Paintworld centres on controlling shrinkage, in the context of the central distribution function. Jim explains: 'Physical security of distribution centres is vital: fences, cameras, lighting, methods of checking, which cover the fundamentals of physical security so we can then step back and say "OK we know it's not leaking out through those channels". But then we're going to say, "right let's start to look at what other losses go on in the large distribution centres". For example, when the loads leave the depot, how accurate are they? Now a percentage of the lorries that leave the depots are pulled over to one side and they have their loads checked to see how accurate they are. We are putting in a new system for sealing vehicles so that when the load leaves, if the seal is tampered with we can see it: it's all retail detail, basic stuff. Then we're starting to look at the damages and the pick accuracy. Sometimes the distribution centre could send one product, which is very similar to another, but it may only have half the retail value, and therefore when the stores check it off, if they don't check it properly, they miss it.' Measures like these are designed to prevent what can amount to relatively large-scale losses in the earlier stages of the supply chain.

However, possibly one of the greatest challenges for the company lies in the fact that shrinkage can quite simply be the outcome of poor administrative procedures. Jim gave an example of how, on paper, shrinkage can inadvertently be created simply by ill-thought out procedures: 'Recently a buyer carried out a promotion of pressure washers where a free rack was included with every washer bought, with a view to generating add-on sales of further accessories. A good idea in principle, but as it happened, this resulted in shrinkage, as the rack was still charged into the store at cost value, but passed through the tills at zero value. Naturally the supplier of the racks knew about the promotional tie-in and credited the cost to Paintworld as a central credit, however this was not passed on to the stores – thus creating "paper shrinkage" simply due to poor data integrity!'

The above example illustrates why the company is scrutinizing and stream-lining its administrative processes, making the paperwork more user friendly and easier to check and using technology wherever possible. Jim adds, 'We have a vision which says that in five years time we will have enhanced our use of new technology to the extent that we will be routinely using "intelligent text", so when a vehicle or a pallet comes in, the bar code on the pallet is scanned. The transfer of the receipt for that pallet is transferred to the store's inventory automatically and then by exception the check-in will take up items that were missing or which were damaged. Again, it's pretty simple stuff really. The key lies in just giving all of your time to think through where the problems can occur, what can be done about them, and most of the time you can address things in very simple ways – in very simple low cost ways as well.' By looking at all of those factors, Jim and his team intend to impact on shrinkage affected by factors outside of the store manager's control.

IMPLEMENTING A COMPANY SHRINKAGE CONTROL PLAN

Having identified the key contributing factors, it was the task of Jim and his team to devise and implement a plan for dealing with the problem on a company-wide basis. As a result of their deliberations over an 18-month period, Paintworld now operate a full business plan which breaks down shrinkage control into six very clear subject areas: shrinkage prevention programmes; activities for new and closure stores; management information; resources; external factors; communications. For each area, the plan indicates what action needs to be taken to develop, maintain or improve current processes. It also indicates responsibilities and timeframes and thus acts as a control document. Retail operation meetings take place against the backdrop of the longer term business plan and its six focal areas. The plan remains flexible and as new issues arise, their importance is assessed. If necessary, they are incorporated into a revised business plan.

Within the overall framework, the company categorizes its stores, thus identifying the highest risk stores in terms of their shrinkage record, which are, therefore, the stores to focus on in more detail. This is a clearly prescribed system, with measurable operationalization of what happens in response to a combination of shrinkage history, percentage and trend information. The cost of proposed security measures, such as new fencing, is evaluated against the history of the store, bearing in mind that stores vulnerable in one form are often also seen as targets in other ways.

The plan also recognizes that stores are particularly at risk of increased shrinkage when, for example, they are first opened, handed over to a new manager or finally closed. Monitoring these critical events separately and putting adequate procedures in place has succeeded in cutting shrinkage levels at those times in a store's life to around 10 per cent of previous levels.

In the implementation of the shrinkage strategy, the training of people in procedures has been identified as the key success factor. Jim sees the potential problem clearly: 'Management often complain about not having enough staff – but this can also be a self-perpetuating myth. The greater the volume of work the more pressure on managers and the lower their administrative and time management skill, the less likely they are to give priority to this area. However, the less effective the individual is, the more time gets wasted and the less work gets done. Slack discipline and administrative mistakes creates even greater work pressure. As a result, there will be even less time to get it right, and this just carries on. A well-managed store typically has well-motivated staff and low staff turnover with a good level of camaraderie and mutual help. While formal appraisals can be rushed at times, the key to controlling shrinkage is to get staff to identify with the measures and to take pride in getting it right. This can only be achieved by establishing a clear link to individual benefits in the form of recognition, bonuses and eventual promotion.'

In general terms, every store has a shrinkage bonus which is awarded as targets are achieved. This has a proven motivating effect, as it can add up to a very substantial amount of money even for part-time staff who may be able to pay for half a holiday with this bonus alone. There are also prizes for the best store in every region. In total the company has spent nearly £30,000 p.a. on prizes which compares very favourably to the amount of money saved.

Part of the implementation strategy therefore, rests on excellent and easy to remember communication devices designed to capture staff attention. Under Jim's leadership, an HQ-based loss prevention team of fourteen people worked on the development and operationalization of the business plan. Coming up with catchy names such as 'Shrink War', 'Shrink Line', and the famous in-store team of 'Shrink Busters' often took several weeks of formal and informal brainstorming work, but brought about rich dividends by capturing staff imagination and generating enthusiasm and commitment to the initiative.

Jim underlines the importance of ongoing communication: 'We have briefing sessions that go on, which to start with, I rolled out to area managers and they in turn had meetings that go on, plus, they went to the store managers. In addition, what we're going to do is to launch a communication document called *Shrink Rap*. This newsletter will be sent out on a monthly basis and will talk about the things that we've done, good ideas, best practices. We'll try to make it as interesting as possible. Headings like, "Did you know this?", "This store did this well", "Have you tried this?" So really, trying to get people on board and motivated and stimulated to do all these things.'

Developing a modular training scheme was also central to implementation. This scheme now takes the form of folders which set out the overall structure and are then filled up by modules which are sent out one by one. At store level, the momentum created through training is kept going through regular meetings of the designated team of 'Shrink Busters'. These are intended to identify, discuss and give feedback on areas of best practice in controlling shrinkage, possibly to be communicated more widely via the *Shrink Rap* newsletter.

Another communications success story has been the launch of the 'Shrink Line', a particularly useful telephone 'hotline' device in the apprehension of internal staff theft and fraud. Jim explains, 'There's no nice way of saying this, this is a "snitch line" so that if people in the business are aware of colleagues or of people who are stealing from us then they can just phone that number. When we launched this, every store got a couple of posters and then every single employee in the business received a card. In the first six months after it was launched we had about 63 phone calls, and of the 63 we've now got seven people who've actually been dismissed from the business following investigation. I would guess that its about 10 per cent or 12 per cent of the calls that we have had come through actually lead to something which would be substantiated, including one involving £10,000 worth of goods.'

CONCLUSION

True to the focus on detail and numbers implied by Jim Doors' retail operations and work study background, the Paintworld shrinkage control strategy is based on the principles of cost/benefit analysis. Here, alternative courses of action are compared and evaluated in the light of where the biggest returns would be expected. At present, Paintworld are in the process of assembling the total cost of the business plan which is estimated at approximately £1.5m as compared to benefits in the region of £7–£10m. Traditionally the company's emphasis had been on security rather than loss prevention. The challenge is therefore, to change the focus of attention and to bring about a shift in the company's culture and the mindset of management.

Many opportunities remain to extend current measures in imaginative ways which could enhance the operationalization of the in-store marketing mix at the same time. Taking the area of wallpaper samples as an example; it costs the company around £3m a year in shrinkage, a loss which might make it well worth employing an additional sales assistant. This could result in improved sales levels, enhanced control and have the additional benefit of improved customer service – an area of the marketing mix not yet full exploited by the leading UK DIY retailers.

Looking back on his very successful time in charge of the Paintworld loss prevention programme, Jim says in summary: 'The opportunities at Paintworld are huge. Because the company has grown very rapidly over a short period of time, lots of our systems were archaic and our computer systems didn't talk to each other. Management information was just non-existent. There was lots of data, but there was not a lot of management information. The shrinkage history of this business had been erratic at best. Looking to the future, we've got a target; we want to get our shrinkage down to about 1.5 per cent of sales. I've got it down to 2.1 per cent; the money that has been put back on the bottom line is just huge, it's out of this world. As sales increase with the growth of the business, even if we keep shrinkage fixed at 3 per cent, that's pretty good. If we can start to drive it down more than 1 per cent it's going to be even better. That's where we're coming from.'

QUESTIONS

1. Evaluate the key sources of shrinkage and their relative weighting within the overall shrinkage figures. Make a comprehensive list of the control measures implemented as part of the Shrink Busters campaign and critically assess the extent to which the different sources of shrinkage can be controlled.

2. When Jim was first put in charge of devising a company wide shrinkage control scheme for Paintworld, one of the key challenges he faced was to find ways of evaluating the likely profile of costs and benefits of the measures he proposed in order to convince the board of directors that the planned Shrink Busters campaign would be worthwhile and enhance performance overall.

   For the control measures you have listed in response to Question 1, discuss which areas of the profit and loss account and balance sheet would be affected and the likely trade-offs which would need to be evaluated in order to come to a balanced view of the overall financial benefits of the measures.

3. Assess the likely impact of the proposed shrinkage control measures on merchandising and customer service. What criteria would you use to achieve optimum balance between customer service and attractively merchandised stores, with the need to control shrinkage within a store?

4. Working in a small group, and making use of the criteria established as part of Question 3, generate ideas for different ways in which shrinkage can be tackled within a store, paying particular attention to the implications for

service and merchandising. For each idea, devise a plan for how it might be implemented in-store.

5. What information would be useful from a store perspective to forward to head office so that they can control shrinkage within the supply chain?

REFERENCES

UK Retail Crime Statistics (1997) http://www.emnet.co.uk/retailresearch.
Verdict (1997) *Verdict on DIY Retailers*. Verdict Executive Retail Summary, July. London: Verdict.

BUYING OPERATIONS AT BOOTS THE CHEMIST: THE CASE OF A PRODUCT RANGE UPDATE

ROSEMARY VARLEY

The author would like to extend her thanks to the lunchtime and snacks merchandise and marketing team at Boots the Chemist for their very helpful input in the preparation of this case.

INTRODUCTION

Managing the product range of a retail business is a surprisingly complex task. Product concepts have to be developed in line with rapidly changing market opportunities; the product and its packaging have to be designed; suppliers need to be found who can produce an item to the required quality standard; marketing communication support must be organized for the product launch; and once on sale, the performance of the product must be monitored, and its position in the range has to be under constant review. In today's fast moving and competitive industry, retailers like Boots have to ensure that every product in the store is earning its place within the total product offer.

COMPANY BACKGROUND

Boots the Chemist is a highly successful retail company. In 1997 it generated a sales turnover of just over £3300m from its 1258 outlets (see Table 10.1). Originally a specialist retailer in the pharmacy sector trading in toiletries, cosmetics, healthcare and pharmaceuticals, Boots now have an extensive product range including gifts, music, photographic supplies and processing, and electrical appliances; the range is so diverse that they are now classified as a variety store in the mixed retailer sector. During the early 1990s, Boots was faced with increased competition from discount retailers in the sector, whose price-orientated offer seemed appealing to consumers in the economic recession; however, since 1993, sales have grown by 24 per cent, and the company continues to have a very high customer flow, with one in three people visiting a Boots store every week. This enables Boots to maintain a healthy profit performance (see Table 10.1).

Table 10.1   **Boots the Chemist – sales and profit performance (£m)**

	1995	1996	1997
Sales	2943.8	3107.6	3313.5
Operating profit	349.7	384.8	426.5

Store Profile

Boots have a wide range of store formats. Traditionally situated on high streets of large and small towns, with the size of the store roughly in line with the size of the town, recent store investment has included EOT (edge of town) locations and Boots now have eight large EOT stores. They are also opening stores in airport terminals, motorway stations and hospital sites. Internationally, Boots are not yet a major player, but a chain of stores (currently six) is being developed in the Republic of Ireland and test stores have been opened in Thailand and the Netherlands.

Boots' Product Offer

The business is split into three main divisions for sales reporting:

- Healthcare, dispensing, baby consumables and dietary food
- Beauty (includes toiletries)
- Leisure (includes gifts, clothing, photographic processing/supply and food)

The leisure division accounts for around 20 per cent of Boots' sales, while the other two divisions account for around half of the balance each. The traditional emphasis on high quality pharmaceutical and healthcare products has earned Boots the reputation of being a trustworthy retailer, with a high ethical standing. This does, however, have implications for the introduction of other products, with a risk of being criticized as hypocritical by selling chocolate, sugary soft drinks and so on.

Boots have a wide range of own-label products which is constantly being updated and developed in response to market opportunities, aided by its vertical integration with Boots Contract Manufacturing and close relationships with other major suppliers. In addition, Boots branded ranges, such as the well known and trusted No 7 (cosmetics), Soltan (suncream) and Shapers (slimming foods) are market leaders in their respective product sectors. Like many other leading UK retailers Boots have recently launched a customer loyalty scheme – the Advantage Card, which will enable the company to build a customer database and refine its marketing activities.

MERCHANDISE AND MARKETING

Located at company headquarters in Nottingham, the merchandise and marketing (M/M) operation of Boots is centralized, as are the other operational areas: store development, information systems, finance and logistics. The organizational structure of M/M is led by product area, with teams headed up by a director of merchandise and marketing. The leisure product area includes the following merchandise categories: gifts, kitchen and home, children's clothing, 'photo', and 'lunchtime food'. These are lead by a category general manager (CGM) who is responsible for strategic merchandise planning, including buying, supply chain management and marketing. The CGMs are supported by a team of category managers who in turn lead a team of product managers, who are concerned with the finer detail of a concise product range. Within the general merchandise area of 'lunchtime food', for example, there are three category managers responsible for coffee shop (in 20 stores), lunchtime (sandwiches and so on) and snacks. Product managers then support the category managers, for example in the snacking category there is a product manager for drinks/savoury snacks and one for sweet snacks. The merchandise and marketing teams are given technical support by the product quality and development department who work on a project basis for them. The corporate brand is managed by a separate marketing department, who liaise with the category management teams to ensure all products and their presentation conform to the corporate brand image and standard.

Product reviews occur between one and three times a year depending on the seasonality of the product. These are accompanied by a distribution review, when decisions are made on which product ranges will go to each store, depending on the store format. Product category business reviews, which involve the whole of the category team, take place formally on an annual basis, although supplier approaches may prompt an informal review more frequently. Likewise, product market strategy is formally reviewed annually, but may be instigated on an 'as need' basis.

Sales are reported to the product managers at different levels, as shown in the matrix below:

Table 10.2   Levels of sales reporting within a Boots product category

Level	Example(s) of sales report
Concept group	All lunchtime and snack products
Product group	All sandwiches
Merchandise group	Boots sandwiches, Shapers sandwiches

For each product item, or stock keeping unit, Boots' information system is able to output an 'economic profitability figure', which is a DPP (direct product profit) calculation incorporating a charge for capital employed.

THE LUNCHTIME AND SNACKS DEPARTMENT

The following table shows the different product groups within the lunchtime category, or concept group. The department does not include any dietary food products, although slimming options (for example Shapers sandwiches, desserts and so on) are included.

Table 10.3   **Breakdown of product groups within lunchtime/snacks department**

Sub-category	Product group
Lunchtime	Sandwiches
	Rolls/pastries
	Salads
	Desserts
Snacks	Drinks
	Sweet snacks
	Savoury snacks

Source: Boots Departmental Data, 1997

The location of the department in a 'typical' Boots store can be seen in Figure 10.1 at the end of the chapter.

The Sweet Snack Product Market

The majority of products sold under the heading 'sweet snack' can be classified as 'countlines'. Originating from the term 'counter line' which was an item traditionally served on the counter in a retail store (a presentation method still found in many CTNs and independents), a countline is considered to be a confectionery product which is consumed 'all in one go' and therefore includes the vast array of chocolate bars (Mars, Twix, Lion Bar and so on) and small ready-packed sugar confectionery (Opal Fruits, Polos and Chewits for example). The product market is dominated by major brands like Cadburys, Mars and Nestlé, whose products are sold through an extensive and fragmented distribution network of approximately 200,000 outlets, which includes larger players like Woolworths and the CTN (confectionery, tobacco and newspaper) multiples, as well as the many convenience stores and small independent retailers. Some retailers have managed to gain market share by producing own-label countlines, notably Marks & Spencers, and some of the supermarket chains have produced their own versions of some popular lines such as KitKat.

Purchasing motivations for the product are impulse driven, with an estimated 80 per cent of purchases made for snacking (Boots' commissioned market research), and consequently advertising and on pack promotional activity are important for driving sales. New product development is also required to maintain consumer interest, for example some caramel variants of existing products (for example Wispa Gold) are selling faster than the original product. Consumers expect countline products to be of high quality, tasty and satisfying, and consider them to be an indulgence or a treat. Countlines have wide appeal, with consumers of all ages and socio-economic groupings. They benefit from the trend towards 'grazing' or snacking, to replace the formal mealtime, and countlines are frequently bought as a 'dessert' in the sandwich lunch.

Although something of a contradiction in terms, there has been an attempt to produce healthy, or diet countline confectionery in response to the growing awareness of health issues (dental care, cholesterol levels, weight gain and so on). These products tend to appeal to young, female consumers from the higher social grades. While there is a proportion of the population who are committed to calorie counting products, many consumers doubt the feasibility of 'healthy' confectionery in terms of delivering sufficient taste satisfaction compared to the 'unhealthy' countline product.

Boots Sweet Snack Offering

Boots confectionery offer includes boxed chocolates, seasonal items, family bags and countlines. The countline offer can be broken down into three sections, as shown in Table 10.4.

Table 10.4   **Boots sweet snack products**

Product range	Sales%
Boots own label	8
Shapers range	19
Proprietary brand range	73

Source: Boots Departmental Data, 1997

Within the own-label section there are essentially two types of confectionery. The first is a small range of premium bars; luxury products with an emphasis on self-indulgence. The second type is the reduced fat and reduced sugar range, which are not positioned as diet products for the calorie counter, more a 'less unhealthy' version of traditional confectionery. In contrast the confectionery products sold under Boots own-brand name Shapers are directly positioned as diet products for the serious slimmer, with a tape measure incorporated into the packaging design and the calorific value emphasized on the packaging to aid the conscientious calorie counter. Shapers branded products make a significant contribution to the lunchtime food offer at Boots; the range includes sandwiches, drinks, desserts, and savoury snacks as well as the sweet snacks. The proprietary brand range includes representations from all the leading confectioners, as well as the well-established branded 'slimming' bars Lo and Halo.

The Boots Light Range

Boots launched the Light range in the early 1990s in response to the increasingly health-concerned consumer. The range consisted of seven confectionery products, listed below in order of GMROI (gross margin return on investment) performance.

Table 10.5   **Products in Boots Light range**

Product name
Light Mild Mints
Light Nougat Crisp bar
Light Soft Mints
Light Praline Bar
Light Peanut Bar
Light Lemon Sweets
Light Fudge Caramel

Source: Boots Departmental Data, 1996

The Light range launch was initially successful. The point of sale support to encourage trial worked well and public relations activity resulted in considerable interest from various magazines. After a while however, sales levelled out and it began to emerge that trial of the products was not followed by repeat purchase. After two years of trading, Boots decided to conduct a market research survey, both inside and outside Boots stores to establish the reason for the poor take up of the products, the findings of which are summarized below:

1. Half of Boots customers and a third of consumers interviewed on the street were aware of the brand Boots Light, although many had no idea what was in the range. The main association was with chocolate bars.

2. Boots Light products were not bought for a second time because:

    The product failed to deliver on taste, substantiality and satisfaction.

    The size of the bar was considered small compared to equivalent countline products.

    Product quality was considered to be poor. The products did not evoke the kind of emotions generated by conventional confectionery products.

3. Healthy/diet snacks and confectionery are generally bought on a regular basis, are primarily for self-consumption, and are bought as alternatives to other healthy/diet products, rather than as an alternative to standard snacks and confectionery.

4. Motives for buying healthy snacks and confectionery include general health concerns and sugar/dental concerns, as well as calorie counting and weight considerations.

5. Low calorie was considered a main specific benefit of healthy/diet confectionery products, but the word 'light' tended to have a specific meaning for certain product categories:

   – For crisps and snacks – low fat;

   – For chocolate bars – low sugar or low fat;

   – For sweets – low sugar.

   Men tended to associate *light* with low fat, whereas women interpreted *light* more often as low calorie.

6. Light brand customers do not differentiate between low fat and low calorie, therefore a low fat message is likely to be interpreted as low calorie.

7. The majority of customers who buy Light products also buy Shapers products, but less than one in three Shapers buyers have tried the Boots Light range, indicating that there could be a market for 'light' confectionery products beyond the Shapers customer. The research finding also highlighted the brand loyalty of Shapers customers.

THE SITUATION

In February 1996, Linda Kingston, a graduate in retail marketing, who had recently been promoted from assistant product manager for haircare to product manager for sweets and bakery, was asked to attend a briefing by the category general manager for the lunchtime area, Stephen Panns. Also attending the meeting was Rowena Smith, category manager for snacks.

Stephen began the briefing by stating concerns that the Boots Light range had not been performing very well for some time. In fact, the snack range as a whole did not generate the volume of sales that might be expected from a busy retailer such as Boots.

Linda sighed inwardly; she had spoken before to Stephen about improving the space allocation of snacks in the past, and in particular about placing countline products at the CPU (cash point unit), but the 'ethical problems', as he put it, prevented any contemplation of change in that direction. The problem was that pharmacy guidelines state that ordinary confectionery must not be displayed around the till area, so as not to encourage tooth decay. The guidelines do not specify what *ordinary* is, but it would certainly include the bulk of proprietary brand confectionery.

The Light range, Stephen continued, has never really been a strong performer. Sales peaked 18 months after launch at £4m per annum, and the most recent figures show the whole range only turning over £1m p.a. This can be contrasted with Halo and Lo which generate a combined turnover of £16m! Again, Linda felt despondent. The taste seemed to be the major concern; she had been briefed about the various difficulties involved with the development of reduced-fat confectionery. Chocolate itself is particularly difficult, so anything based on 100 per cent chocolate, whether solid (like Yorkie) or textured (like Aero) had to be ruled out. Wafer also is a high fat component, so a reduced-fat version of something like KitKat or Time Out would not be possible, and likewise caramel is tricky. The easiest ingredients in which the fat or sugar content could be reduced seemed to be biscuit, crispies or fudge-type centres.

Another significant weakness was the packaging. Linda felt it was outdated, and gave the impression that the items in the Light range were niche products, solely aimed at the slimmers' market. Figure 10.2 shows an example of a Light countline product. The prices were relatively high, being about five pence above a comparable 'unhealthy' product, but this was necessary because of the higher raw material costs, and Linda did not see the prices as a problem. Boots' market research had indicated that customers were prepared to pay a premium for a specific product benefit such as low fat.

At a recent business review with Mars, Stephen continued, there seemed to be a lot of excitement about a new low-fat chocolate covered bar that was being developed, not specifically formulated as a low-calorie bar, but having half the fat content of comparable countline products. Stephen, Rowena and Linda were all convinced that there was an opportunity to sell reduced-fat and low-sugar confectionery within Boots, beyond the calorie-counting market. The challenge, however, was to come up with a serious and attractive product proposition. Linda was asked to reconsider the Light range and report back to Stephen and Rowena in two weeks time. While she felt that this seemed a hefty challenge, Linda felt encouraged by the motivation of her colleagues to address the situation in an open-minded and flexible manner. She also began to think about the success that her previous department had experienced with a range of own-label versions of leading-brand shampoos.

Back at her desk, Linda made a mental list of the suppliers who might be useful in any product development work that might be required should the range be updated, or even replaced by something new. It would be her decision who would be used to develop prototypes and it was likely that it would be her decision which supplier would get the business. Rowena would help if it was a difficult choice. Stephen would want to do a taste test on the final perfected sample before it went into production, but he invariably accepts the findings of the taste panel. In general, he only gets really involved if the consideration is of strategic importance to Boots.

There were a number of key issues which would influence the choice of supplier. Price was obviously an important issue, but getting the product right in the first place was the overriding factor. Some suppliers were so difficult to deal with; they seem to find it impossible to understand, or perhaps more accurately to react to the feedback she gave on samples produced. Some of the suppliers she knew were somewhat restricted in their machinery, so that they could not get the appearance, or shape of the product she required, while other suppliers simply would not meet Boots' quality standard requirements, for example that all machinery should have metal detectors to identify any harmful foreign bodies. Mars, of course, would be the first choice as a supply partner, but they would not entertain making confectionery under a retailer's brand name. The one thing Linda was quite sure of was that none of her own-label suppliers were making reduced fat and low sugar confectionery at the moment, so few of them were any good at product innovation, but at least that meant that Boots had the opportunity to establish themselves in what was believed to be an important emerging market. At least she would not be relying on the suppliers for any packaging re-design input. If that was necessary it would all be handled by Boots own design agencies, working to a design brief that she would write. Linda picked up the phone and dialled the first supplier on her list.

QUESTIONS

?

1. Discuss why you think the product team are convinced that there is a market for reduced-fat and low-sugar confectionery, beyond the calorie counters. Identify trends and situational factors which will influence the sales estimate of this product range.

2. Identify the product criteria which will be important in the redevelopment and selection of this range. Present a list of criteria upon which suppliers in the sweet snack product area are assessed. (It may help to distinguish between own-label and proprietary brand suppliers.)

3. Outline the organizational structure of the 'buying centre' at Boots the Chemist, and describe how the performance of product ranges are monitored. Use organizational charts and diagrams to aid your discussion.

4. Present a product proposal, which includes marketing and store support for the reconsidered range. Each product within the range should be detailed and justified.

5. Develop a customer profile for the reduced-fat/low-sugar range, and suggest how the product should be positioned to appeal to this customer. Devise an advertising campaign which would reflect this positioning. This should include: definition of advertising objectives, development of the media plan and creation of the advertising message.

6. Develop a design brief for the packaging of this product. This should address the design objectives and the design constraints and include creative ideas (colours, images, words and lettering and so on) that you feel are appropriate.

FURTHER READING

Collier, R. A. (1995) *Profitable Product Management*. Oxford: Butterworth-Heinemann.

Davies, G. (1993) *Trade Marketing Strategy*. London: Paul Chapman.

Levy, M. and Weitz, B. A. (1996) *Essentials of Retailing*. Chicago: Irwin.

McDonald, M. and Tideman, C. (1993) *Retail Marketing Plans*. Oxford: Butterworth-Heinemann.

McGoldrick, P. J. (1990) *Retail Marketing*. Maidenhead: McGraw-Hill.

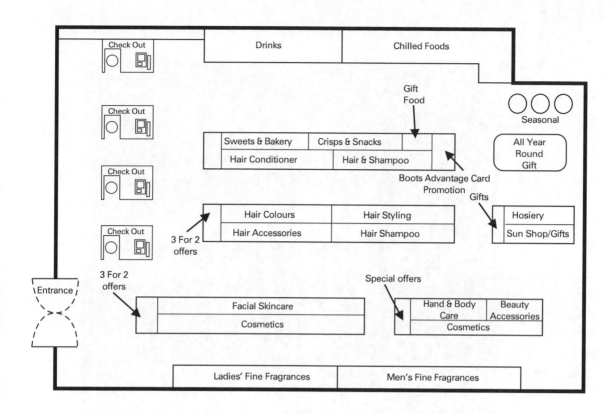

Figure 10.1   Boots the Chemists – store layout

Figure 10.2   Chocolate bars

PART 2

MARKETING PLANNING AND MANAGEMENT

CASE 11

THE ROAD TO EMPOWERMENT AT SAINSBURY'S

ANGELA M. ARNOLD, MORAG M. MCLEAN AND
CHRISTOPHER J. DUTTON

The authors would like to thank Sainsbury's for their support in developing this case study. In particular, we are grateful for the contributions of Howard Bentley, Elliot Pilcher, Mick Lightfoot, store managers, department managers and the many employees who took part in focus group sessions.

In writing this case study we have endeavoured to bring together stories related to the impact of empowerment in Sainsbury's. The issues identified in this case represent a synthesis of the personal perceptions of individuals and are in no way attributed to either any one store nor to any individual. We are aware that since writing the case study (which is one snapshot in time, 1997/98) the company has responded positively to change and that of the issues arising, may now have been addressed. However, we hope the case study provides a learning opportunity, even though things may well be very different today.

INTRODUCTION

Food retailers in the mature stage of the life cycle are facing numerous challenges. Most have sought to meet these challenges by incorporating new technology where appropriate and by focusing on customer needs and service quality. The drive for leaner organizations and the need for speed of response requires confident, quick decision-making based on a high degree of employee competence. To achieve this, some organizations have introduced varying degrees of empowerment for staff at all levels within the organization. Sainsbury's is an example of one such organization and this case considers the implementation process and perceptions of the impact within stores.

THE SAINSBURY'S CONTEXT

Sainsbury's is one of the world's most successful food retailers with annual sales in 1998 of £11.6b and an operating profit of £734.6m (Annual Report, 1998). Under the chairmanship of John Sainsbury and subsequently David Sainsbury, the great-grandsons of the founders, the company has grown significantly and employs around 127,000 people, retailing through some 391 stores (Annual Report, 1998). Rapid change in the grocery market in the mid-1990s saw Sainsbury's slow to adjust to the variety of new formats and marketing initiatives set in motion by a rejuvenated Tesco, who took over the premier slot in the mid 1990s.

Change became inevitable, and in 1993, the company set out to implement a new quality driven, continuous improvement programme that met with some success. However any initiative is not without its difficulties, and three years later Sainsbury's sought to review its strategic direction led by a new super-market executive committee (SEC). In 1996, the Board launched internally a fresh strategic direction designed to enhance customer loyalty. It recognized that in order to achieve its objectives, there was a need to release the potential and talent of all its colleagues, to motivate and enable them to meet the needs of customers ahead of the competition. The SEC group reformulated the organization's mission and developed a business strategy based on a detailed market analysis tool, the so-called 'Web'. This tool encourages Sainsbury's to evaluate its position with customers and competitors against eight key levers, which influence long-term customer loyalty and performance. A tight strategic frame-work of business plans and measures were cascaded and inherent to this was the aim of developing 'the people and the organization' such that everyone could 'own' their part of the business. In this structure, empowerment was centrally controlled, enabling people to make local improvements and actions for the benefit of customers, without jeopardizing the overall company strategy or consistency of offer. The effective implementation of the new strategy would entail considerable changes in organizational culture and processes. It has been said by inside observers that the organization's culture, at the outset of the change programme, could be described as directive, centrally controlled with very little free exchange of information, with few decisions or initiatives taken because of fear of retribution. Openness and trust became the new watchwords as Sainsbury's sought to communicate its new direction to all of its stakeholders.

At the same time, Sainsbury's moved away from the sole use of traditional financial indicators when evaluating effective performance. To achieve this, they introduced a balanced scorecard approach for managing the business, which required a broadening of the criteria on which management information is gathered and utilized for measuring performance. Kaplan and Norton (1996) recommend that 'an organization's long-term strategic objectives are better able to be achieved by supplementing short-term financial measures and targets, with three additional perspectives: those of customers, internal business processes and learning and growth'. Thus, as well as reporting on the tradi-tional 'hard' measures, such as turnover and stock loss, Sainsbury's adopted a broader perspective, seeking to measure and report on 'soft' factors such as customer retention and satisfaction, and employee satisfaction.

Recent activities, appointments and approaches to the measurement of performance have sought to challenge and break assumptions regarding the effectiveness of the former culture.

IMPLEMENTATION PROCESS

The road to the effective implementation of quality-orientated strategic change processes is littered with failures. These are often attributed to a lack of top management commitment and an unrealistic focus on short-term gains. Failures are seen to be most glaring in circumstances where employees are required to change not only their behaviours but, significantly, their attitudes.

Against this backdrop, Sainsbury's took the decision that the message of change would be most effectively communicated using a cascading approach reaching the local level with full and open support from head office (Blackfriars). This support was clearly visible in the investment by the company in its own satellite television station, used to communicate regularly with all its business locations. Key appointments to new positions of business improvement advisers were made, and these individuals were charged with the responsibility of facilitating the change process in individual stores within their region or in head office departments. Advisers became a critical part of the communication and change process, and interestingly, were seconded laterally from applicants who were largely experienced store managers and strongly people orientated. These appointments would come to an end when the required culture change was sufficiently embedded.

Given the detailed corporate framework of the 'Web', the business improvement advisers set about the task of working with the individual managers who are ultimately responsible for what happens in their store. Communication and information systems were extended both horizontally and vertically. A series of workshops introduced the 'Web' and the business planning process, which focused on objectives, goals, strategies and measures at all levels of the organization. A range of implementation tools were developed and helped managers work with their own team in translating the details of the Sainsbury's mission into tangible and balanced objectives for both the store and for individuals within the unit. Once clarified, a personal management agenda was created, whereby individual performance would regularly be reviewed in light of the negotiated, clearly defined personal objectives and performance measures, ultimately leading to individual rewards. In this way, employees at all levels were encouraged to take responsibility for the achievement of outcomes and thus experience ownership and accountability for their part of the business. The rationale for adopting this considered approach was firmly rooted in the belief that, while organizations could improve profitability significantly and quickly through autocratic processes, the long-term sustainability of such an approach was felt to be inappropriate in this people-orientated business. Empowerment was important. At the same time, it was crucial for Sainsbury's to maintain or improve standardized practices and the corporate image with which the customer was familiar.

IMPACT IN STORES

The business planning process was thus cascaded to stores with the support of business improvement advisers who operated to help individual managers translate the strategy into action. It was rolled out over an extended period of time and continuously reviewed, affecting particular parts and levels of the organization at different times. This case focuses on a single 'snapshot in time' while the change process was occurring, and it seeks to explore the impact and reality of empowerment from a number of different perspectives and levels within Sainsbury's. It is interesting to record how change was perceived by employees in stores, and the following personalized stories are testimony both to the value, and to the inherent tensions of empowerment.

A Store Manager's Story

To me, empowerment is about letting people take the responsibility to get the job done but it's also about encouraging them to air their ideas in a positive way. By that I mean that you give people as much rein as you can within the framework laid down by the company. You can't have anarchy, but it is my job to resolve issues with the district, or even Blackfriars, if I feel that things could be done in a better way. I try to give my deputies and department managers every opportunity to get on and do the job in the most effective way. Sometimes things go wrong and it is very hard not to lose your cool but I really try to talk about why things went wrong and what we can learn from that for the future. I'm not perfect and I must admit that sometimes it is easier to just tell people what to do or even do things myself, but I'm learning and it really helps when people from district or Blackfriars adopt the same approach. I know things have got to be done properly and that customers deserve to have the full catalogue on the shelves and excellent service when they come in to do their shopping. I suppose its human nature to have a go at someone if your neck is on the line when things go wrong. But sometimes it's hard to have the confidence to help others learn from their mistakes, even though our performance management system looks at all dimensions of my work.

We are working very hard in this store to try to give department managers as much control over their area as possible. We all meet to discuss how best to use our hours allocation each week. We have all the information up on a white board and then discuss the priorities and needs of each area for the coming week. Then we try to come to a fair decision about how to carve up the cake available to us. That's teamwork! Of course we have to be flexible at the end of the day because we do not always have much notice of things that we are required to action at once. Sometimes it seems that people at Blackfriars don't talk to each other and we can be inundated with initiatives from several product groups and departments all at the same time. When that sort of thing happens you just have to get your department managers together and move staff around to cover the most needy priorities. People sometimes find it hard to swallow when all their plans are thrown up in the air. But, that's retailing I suppose!

When it comes to how we use our hours, we have to try to work smarter. You see, it is cheaper in the long run to get part-time staff to work extra hours rather than to get full-timers to work overtime because then you have to pay premium rates. At the moment it's the number of hours used that appear on your performance indicators but I understand that in some stores they are testing out a new way of measuring, which looks at the cost in financial terms rather than just the number of hours. It seems to me that that kind of practice is much more effective in the longer term and I would certainly feel empowered to make better staffing decisions on that basis.

Store managers do have more autonomy to make their own decisions on some issues. For example, I can now develop my people and promote them to assistant manager level without having to go to district. I negotiate with a local taxi firm to provide transport for our customers who use the taxi telephone. I also have a small pot of money called the 'value fund', which I can use to reward staff when they have done something that is special. I might use it to buy someone a bouquet of flowers or I've even been known to get one lad a ticket for an important football match. So if an employee really adds value to the business, I can reward that person which is great and the staff say that they really appreciate it. I feel that the trust involved here is really important. I also have direct access to performance indicators for other stores in my district, which allows me to benchmark performance in my store against that of my colleagues.

A Department Manager's Story

My role within the store has changed completely. Department managers used to work on the shop floor alongside their staff. Now, I still have to do my job but I am also responsible for recruitment, training, absence, discipline, performance and coaching of my staff. So, if you like, my job has been enlarged. But there is still only me to do it all and only so many hours in the day. Don't get me wrong, that's how I think things should be, but when the pressure is on, it can be really tough. If you have time, you can coach your staff to enable them to take on new roles. That's the ideal because, if you train staff and enable them to make decisions and show their initiative, they can be empowered. That way they feel more involved and you can get on with managing the department. But retailing is a 'now' business. You cannot tell a customer to wait for a couple of hours while you teach someone to do the ordering. She wants her bacon now, not later! You see, what an 'E' grade (senior sales) is doing now, an assistant manager used to do and what an assistant manager is doing now, a department manager used to do. The end result is that the 'new' empowered department manager is more accountable, and in many ways more focused, because he may take a wider overview of the whole department.

I suppose you could say that what's happening is delegation, but it needs to be more than that if it is really going to help us achieve our objectives. But, to me, the difference between delegation and empowerment is very much related to your management style. If you have free access to the information and resources needed to really do the job properly, and you talk with your staff about what has to be achieved, they can use the tools to get on and complete the task. Next time, they might just do it on their own initiative. Information about your store, other stores and the company generally is much more widely available now which is great. After all, the store is open for in excess of 100 hours a week and we all need to be able to deal with situations as they arise.

To an extent you can work within your own area in a way that helps your staff to take on more responsibility and also achieves your targets. But sometimes all your plans fall apart. The company used to expect all managers to behave in the same way – like Sainsbury's clones I suppose. Now, I think they want you to discover your own style and then develop it. They are always saying that they want more communication coming up from the bottom of the organization as well as down from the top. I really believe that that is what they want but there always seems to be a blockage somewhere between us and Blackfriars. If I speak to the 'Boss', (a term of endearment used to identify some store managers) I know he will listen and take the issue up at district level who should then go through the region to Blackfriars. Somewhere up there, people just are not prepared to take the issues on board. If your boss or district manager is the command and control type, big issues and great ideas just wither, never to be seen again. Of course, it's all about relationships, but maybe, they need to try practising what they preach. At the end of the day, you can only hit your head against a brick wall so often. I know that for many people they have decided to 'put up and shut up' because they think that's the best way to promotion but that's not the answer either. There's a general feeling that if you get results it doesn't matter how you achieve it. Yet, you can be in here 50 or 60 hours a week coaching your staff but, if you don't hit your targets or fill your shelves, or have a bad visit, it's all forgotten. My boss is great, others are not so lucky, but district dictates at the end of the day.

A Sales Assistant's Story

I get to hear more information generally now, but there used to be lots of secret meetings and we had no idea what was going on. You see, the company has got this new strategy to help us achieve our targets as a company and as individual stores. Before all this came out, there were an awful lot of things I didn't know about. Now, I feel that I want to go looking for the information about how things are going. At the end of the week the manager wants to know what you've taken and what your losses were. I think they're trying to spread the work so that it takes the pressures off the management because they have more to do now. I help to gather the information for our department and I suppose it makes me more interested in the job. But, some people just aren't interested though. They don't want to do the ordering because they know they'll get it in the neck if something goes wrong especially if the manager or, worse still, someone from district notices. (We call them 'suits'!) You see, the 'suits' hardly ever speak to you directly, they speak to the manager who speaks to the department manager who then deals with you. There's no second chances here.

We do have 'communicators' on each area who go to meetings with the boss and then spread the word to the rest of the staff. Sometimes it works really well but, with our long opening hours and people working different shifts, the message doesn't always get through. But, you know, we can make some decisions for ourselves. If I need a certain day off I can arrange to swap with someone else as long as everyone knows what is happening. We can organize our own breaks as long as the floor is properly covered and we tell someone when we are going for lunch. It's not so easy for the people on checkouts because there are so many of them. So, where we can, we work things out between us. If I've got a new layout to do, I can talk it through with my department manager and get on with it. We have to stick to the layouts most of the time, but sometimes we can use our own initiative if there is an availability problem or something like that. But, for example, why can't we have tea and sugar next to each other – I think the customers would like that. That's empowerment isn't it? You know, I think people would be able to make bigger decisions for themselves if they had the right training first and if they weren't scared of getting grief if they made one mistake. It seems to me that if you know what the company policy is you know how far you can go. A lot seems to depend on how things are in your department. In some departments you are trusted and respected, in others you're not.

QUESTIONS

1. You are department managers working for Sainsbury's. You have been asked to prepare a presentation to your store manager and the district team identifying the following:

   ■ The potential role of empowerment as a strategic lever;

   ■ The tasks in retailing that could be carried out by empowered staff;

   ■ The difficulties and benefits that the organization and individuals might experience.

2. Identify what eight key levers Sainsbury might use to evaluate its position with customers and competitors.

3. Evaluate the approach Sainsbury's has taken to communicate/implement change.

4. Identify the structural and labour market barriers to empowerment within retailing.

5. Appraise the concept of the balanced scorecard as a strategic performance management system. Identify the differences between hard and soft measures of performance. List examples of both types which would be appropriate for:

   ■ A store manager/department manager;

   ■ A sales assistant who can help at the checkouts.

6. What role does organizational culture play in empowerment?

7. Discuss the impact of the changing role of line managers at Sainsbury's.

REFERENCES

Kaplan, R. S. and Norton, D. P. (1996) 'Using the balanced scorecard as a strategic management system'. *Harvard Business Review*, **74**(1): 75–85.

STORE MERCHANDISING AND EFFECTIVE USE OF SPACE: THE SAFEWAY EXPERIENCE OF IN-STORE PHARMACIES

GRETE BIRTWISTLE

The author would like to thank Safeway plc for their support in developing this case study. In particular I would like to thank Andrew Reston and Jill Bell for their contributions. The content of this case study has been simplified to enable students to focus on key learning objectives, and therefore this is not a complete picture of store merchandising and space planning at Safeway plc.

INTRODUCTION

During the 1980s and 90s food retailing has experienced several major changes, the most important of which was the move to 'out-of-town' superstores. This trend has influenced the five largest supermarket multiples – Tesco, Sainsbury's, Safeway, Asda and Somerfield to increase their salesfloor area and concentrate new developments in larger stores. Furthermore, the growth in car ownership has provided consumers with greater choice of where to purchase their weekly groceries and in turn, led to increased competition between the main multiples. At the same time these supermarket chains have come under increased pressure from the grocery discounters: Kwik Save, Netto, Lidl and Aldi.

Today's shoppers have high expectations of retailing. These include the availability of products, competitive prices, provisions of additional services, the availability of in-store facilities and the general ambience of the environment. New stores are designed with wider aisles, lower gondolas and larger salesfloor areas to display an increasing range of products (approximately 15,000 lines in an average superstore), a trend which has resulted in food retailers coming under increasing pressure to manage their space more efficiently (McGoldrick, 1990; Levy and Weitz, 1995; Berman and Evans, 1997).

Safeway's aim is 'to be the first choice retailer for the everyday food and household needs for today's family and the most dynamic and innovative retailer in meeting those needs' (Safeway, 1997). The company has identified that its customers want consistency in product, value and availability. Its main proposition is to provide as many ancillary facilities as possible and to make the store layout and the shopping environment more comfortable, thereby reducing the stress of shopping. The company uses customer surveys for feed-back, and data confirm that the in-store pharmacy is a facility highly favoured by customers. Increasing numbers are expecting to find this service in super-stores and perceive it to be of high quality and with the added benefits of having long opening hours. Typically the pharmacy in a superstore would be open at the same time as the main store. Tesco, for example, have four in-store pharmacies which are open 24-hours per day (McLoughlin, 1997). This case study, consequently, deals with the way Safeway introduced pharmacies in their large stores thus increasing the service provision to customers.

DEVELOPMENT OF IN-STORE PHARMACIES AT SAFEWAY

In 1981, the Lothian Health Board suggested to Safeway that they should open a pharmacy in Livingston to provide the dispensing service for a new health centre. By 1993 Safeway managed 56 pharmacy outlets and by 1996 these had increased to 94. This meant that nearly one in five Safeway stores now had in-store pharmacies, a trend which is also evident in the other large supermarket groups (Table 12.1). These data also suggest that there is a general move towards company owned pharmacies and a move away from concessions. The pharmacies in general are situated near the entrance of the supermarkets and are designed on the 'shop within a shop' principle. Recently there has been a tendency to place company owned pharmacies into the main store next to the toiletries and healthcare departments (Mintel, 1997a).

Although the main food retailers are increasing the number of dispensing chemists in their stores, their competitors are still the traditional multiple chemist such as Boots the Chemist, Lloyds Chemists, Moss Chemists and the independent sector. The grocery retailers are extending their sales, year on year, of over-the-counter (OTC) products and are estimated to have 26 per cent share of the market compared with the dedicated chemists which still take the largest share with 67 per cent (Mintel, 1997b).

Table 12.1 **In-store pharmacies, company owned and concessions, 1993–97**

	1993			1995			1997		
	Co. owned	Conces.	Total	Co. owned	Conces.	Total	Co. owned	Conces.	Total
Tesco	25	27	52	107	34	141	169	19	188
J Sainsbury	–	44	44	–	57	57	13	43	56
Safeway	56	–	56	69	–	69	94	–	94
Asda	–	30	30	–	65	65	6	62	68

Source: Mintel (1997b)

Safeway, and the other food retailers, need to obtain dispensing licences from local health boards before they are able to open pharmacy outlets. This is normally achieved by trying to procure a new contract or by purchasing an existing pharmacy. Thus, if a new superstore is to be opened, local chemists could be approached to investigate the possibility of an agreed sale. All pharmacies have to be registered with the local health board to obtain a dispensing licence. Furthermore, they also have to be registered with the Royal Pharmaceutical Society and the premises have to be registered with them as a pharmacy.

The income from a pharmacy comes from four sources: OTC (over-the-counter) sales (Figure 12.1); dispensing sales; a practice allowance paid by the health board for providing the service; and fees paid by pharmaceutical companies for promoting their products. Different stores have different sales profiles depending how near they are situated to a health centre or general practice. Dispensing sales can vary from 25 per cent to 80 per cent of total sales and balance is made up of OTC sales. The GSL (general sales list) of medicines have the highest profit margin, and in this group, own brands are more profitable than manufacturers brands. UK sales of OTC medicines grew by 4.7 per cent last year to £1241m of which a sixth was spent on oral analgesics (Church, 1996).

Pharmacy lines are divided into three categories:

POM: Prescription only medicines dispensed by a pharmacist from a doctor's prescription.

P: Pharmacy medicines or potent medicines which do not need a prescription but can only be sold under pharmacist supervision. These are often larger packs of medicines such as aspirins or ibuprofen.

GSL: General sales list lines can normally be sold without a prescription and without pharmacist supervision. These lines can, therefore, be sold by self-service from open displays.

Furthermore, some medicines are referred to as 'over-the-counter' (OTC) lines. These are medicines in the P or GSL categories that are either available for self-service or kept behind the pharmacy counter.

Figure 12.1   Drug categories (adapted from *The Grocer*, 1994)

Some pharmacies have a consulting room that can be used for health checks or for special promotions. For example, the pharmacist can demonstrate to asthma sufferers how inhalers work, give advice about asthma and check patients understanding about the subject. Health checks such as cholesterol checks, blood pressure measurements and height and weight measurements are provided as an extra service to customers. Safeway also offer a number of community services. For example, the pharmacy will, free of charge, dispense weekly medicines and pre-pack them, in hourly or daily doses, for patients in residential nursing care, instead of dispensing them in separate bottles. The service can also be used by people in the community who may find it difficult to read the medication instructions due to poor eye sight, or have problems with the top of security bottles. Approximately 5 per cent of prescriptions are dispensed in this way.

Furthermore, the in-store pharmacy supports the local health board in new promotions, for example by providing methadone to registered addicts under supervision. This is a method of trying to prevent addicts either selling their prescription or drinking a weekly dose in one go. It means that registered addicts have to consume methadone, under supervision, in the consulting room. The pharmacy is paid an extra fee for this service.

Space Management at Safeway

Safeway was the third largest grocery retailer in the UK, when compared on turnover and trading area based on trade in the financial year 1996 (Table 12.2). Sales growth in recent years is partly a result of investments in areas such as new space, refurbishment, service initiatives and new departments. Like-for-like growth, during the latest trading period, shows 8 per cent for Tesco, 4.5 per cent for Safeway and 4 per cent for Sainsbury, but some analysts believe that this pace of growth cannot be sustained (Gilbert, 1997).

Table 12.2   Performance data for the major grocery multiples (financial year to 1996)

	Store numbers	Turnover excl. VAT £m	Trading area 000 sq ft	Annual sales in £ per sq ft	Market share %
Tesco (UK only)	545	11,560	13,397	862.9	15.1
J Sainsbury	363	10,148	9767	966.7	13.4
Safeway	479	6069	9264	655.0	7.9
Asda	206	6010	8436	712.4	7.9

Source: Mintel (1997a)

Supermarkets use self-service as the primary method of selling products, and optimize sales by making shelf displays as attractive as possible. The individual retailer has to decide which products and brands to stock and then allocate appropriate shelf area to ensure maximization of sales and profit while minimizing costs. As shelf space is limited, a natural choice for the retailer might be to stock the products which provide the highest gross margin, but this may fail to match local customer requirements. Furthermore, space allocation must also take stock replenishment into consideration, since stores cannot afford to run out of products and lose sales or have to replenish shelves during peak trading hours.

Due to the increasingly complex nature of space management, more and more retailers now use computerized packages to help in-store merchandising. The systems provide efficient category management solutions based on sales information generated via EPOS (electronic point of sale) systems (Nielsen, 1997). The data is analysed at head office and merchandisers can, on simulated plans, reset sections, change facings, move products, calculate sales ratios and produce accurate planograms very quickly. By using space management programmes it is possible to perform cross-category analysis to identify where space may be made available for sections requiring additional shelf space. Category management will analyse sales turnover and is the process which enables merchandisers to make decisions to optimize space allocation and provide higher profits. Replacing a few products of low turnover with better selling lines can have dramatic effects on sales. However, due to the high cost of stock management programmes, some of these systems may omit factors, such as local requirements, space elasticity and distribution and handling costs. They tend to be based on aggregated sales or profit optimization. For example, research by McGoldrick (1990) established that there is a positive relationship between space allocated and unit sales, especially for impulse purchases such as vitamins, mineral supplements and alternative medicines. It is essential, therefore, for staff within the store to understand the space plan, its limitations and the consequences of not adhering to it. Untidy displays, 'out of stocks' and wrong allocation all decrease sales; whereas, good displays stimulate consumer purchasing behaviour, store image and long-term customer loyalty.

Own-brand developments have increased their proportion of Safeway's sales to 46 per cent in 1996, a trend aided by the Safeway Savers range that comprised 110 lines. Safeway commenced a range review programme in 1994, with the purpose of achieving that balance of economy, standard and premium products which the targeted customers had indicated they wished to buy. Over 3200 own range products, including OTC pharmacy lines, were launched or upgraded during the year ending April 1997 (Safeway, 1997).

Store Layout and Stock Management

The merchandise layout for the pharmacy is decided by the business unit at head office and is varied by store size but follows a set standard. Planograms are issued twice a year with major layout changes and every two months with minor variations. These must be implemented as closely as possible. Space planning is based on a number of different categories:

- analgesics (high stock turnover, average profit margin)
- antacids and laxatives (medium stock turnover, average profit margin)
- vitamins and supplements (high stock turnover, high profit margin)
- cold remedies and decongestants (seasonal high turnover, medium profit margin)
- cough and throat remedies (seasonal high turnover, medium profit margin)

- alternative medicines including herbal medicines, homeopathic remedies and aromatherapy oils (medium turnover, high profit margin)
- contact lens products (high stock turnover, average profit margin)
- first aid (low stock turnover, average profit margin)
- dietary lines (seasonal stock turnover, low profit margin)
- medicine cabinet products includes remedies for irritation and itching as well as insect repellents, pregnancy testing kits and miscellaneous product (medium stock turnover, some seasonal like hay fever products, others like gynaecological products have increasing stock turnover, high profit margin)
- veterinary lines (low stock turnover, high-profit margin).

The basic layout consists of a display sale counter and four gondola shelving units for GSL products which customers can access. Two of the sections are stocked with 'general medicines' such as vitamins, supplements, alternative medicines and dietary lines. The vitamin section has to be quite condensed, although vitamins have to be prominent due to their high-profit margin, and dietary lines are on the bottom shelf due to their lower margins. A third gondola is stocked with the contact lens products at the top and first aid lines at the bottom. The final section is stocked with cold cures and pain killers, in smaller packs. Staff also have a designated area for dispensing prescriptions and counter space for pharmacy medicines. These are kept behind a glass divider on the sales counter so that they can only be accessed by pharmacy staff. The pharmacy manager has to order prescription and pharmacy medicines directly from the drug companies who will generally deliver the ordered stock the following day.

On the sales floor, the pharmacy is also responsible for a further number of gondolas containing self-service lines (OTC medicines). The night staff fill these shelves from the deliveries. All self-service lines are automatically replaced via the EPOS sales records and the Stock Management 3 Programme. The night crew checks the sales floor sections for 'out of stocks'. Pharmacy staff do not spend time on the shop floor and it is not their responsibility, although the sales from those gondolas are allocated to the pharmacy department. All merchandising is based on the planograms but minor changes in layout to optimize sales can be taken by the area manager in conjunction with the regional office. The pharmacy manager has little influence over merchandise plans, but can offer suggestions to the area manager when the store is visited every six to eight weeks.

Generic lines are unbranded products sold without trademarks. For example, this could be a product similar to Benylin or Calpol, but sold at a lower price. If a customer asks for something by name, then they will be given the product by staff, but if a customer asks for advice, they will be questioned about the patient's symptoms and advised about the most appropriate product. Products offered to them might be Safeway's own-brand or a generic medicine, which is cheaper than the brand leader. The company policy is to recommend the most cost-effective solution for the patient. The pharmacy manager is not provided with details about profit margins on the different lines. This protects the quality of advice given to the customer but staff generally assume that the Safeway brand would be more profitable than the brand leader.

As part of their agreement with the health board, the pharmacy has to distribute leaflets to improve general health care and information. In addition, drug company promotions are displayed on top of the sales counter, because manufacturers pay Safeway to have them prominently publicized. These companies generally pay for lines being promoted for four week periods and these often coincide with or follow TV advertising promotions.

Staffing

The pharmacy manager is contracted to work 39 hours and is aided by a support pharmacist who normally works part time. A number of locums cover the additional hours required. The next layer in the pharmacy structure is the pharmacy dispenser, a technician who packs the medicine into bottles. In addition, there are a number of pharmacy counter staff working full and part-time. It is the pharmacy manager's responsibility to employ and manage those pharmacy staff who are dedicated to the pharmacy and do not work elsewhere in the store. All staff are required to work toward the attainment of pharmacy NVQs. The company policy is to have a minimum of one pharmacist and one counter (dispenser) assistant on duty at any one time.

THE PROJECT

In the scenario provided here, you are the newly appointed pharmacy manager of a major new Safeway store located on the outskirts of a large city with a catchment population of 500,000. The surrounding area of the store is made up of apartment housing, consisting largely of rented properties, and a suburban area of owner occupier housing. Local competition within the area comes from a new Sainsbury store, Tesco and Asda. The store is situated near a number of hospitals, including a homeopathic hospital. Some of these hold GP clinics out-of-hours. The store has 40,000 sq ft of sales area and the pharmacy is allocated 500 sq ft opposite the checkouts and next to the customer service desk, in-store restaurant and crèche (Figure 12.2). The pharmacy has the standard layout described above (Figure 12.3) and has, in addition, three sections of shelving within the toiletry department on the main sales floor, where self-service lines are displayed.

You are responsible for merchandising the pharmacy area and the three gondola sections on the main salesfloor (marked X on the store layout plan). Sales targets are high and wage budgets are tight so you have to control staffing hours closely. Furthermore, overstocks are expensive and some lines have short sell by dates so you have to ensure that there is enough stock available to optimize sales. New planograms have just arrived from Safeway's head office in Hayes and you need to plan the tasks required to maximize profitability.

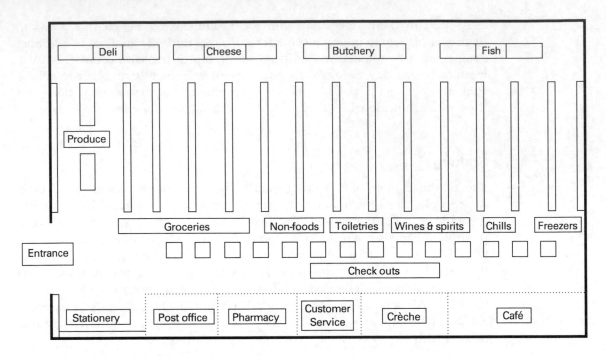

Figure 12.2   Store layout

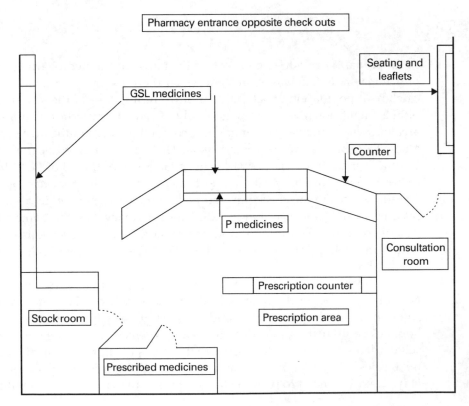

Figure 12.3   Pharmacy layout

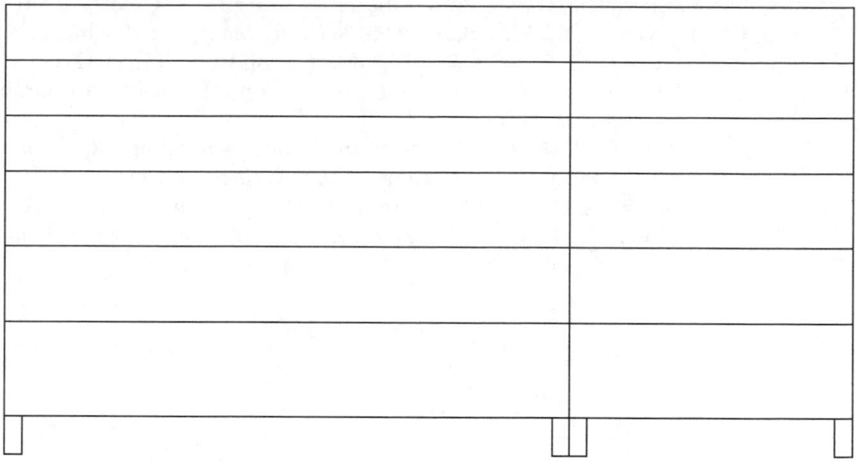

Figure 12.4   Shelf layout for one full gondola and a half section

QUESTIONS

1. Consider what factors affect stock levels, and highlight how they will affect the daily stock management routine.

2. Plan the sequence of tasks that need to be completed when new planograms are issued and explain why these have to be undertaken.

3. This store has the benefit of having an extra half section over and above the issued planograms, which can be merchandised at the manager's discretion. What factors would you take into consideration before planning the layout for this section? Indicate product categories on the layout plan in Figure 12.4.

4. The store has a homeopathic hospital in the vicinity. How would this influence the way that you merchandise the stock?

5. Due to the high costs of operating the pharmacy it has proved to be less profitable per sq ft than some of the other departments within the store such as wines and spirits, baby foods and kidswear. How could profitability be improved? What factors do you think the regional sales manager would take into consideration when planning new shopfits?

6. What are the benefits to customers and the company of having an in-store pharmacy? What plans may food retailers have for increasing their market share of prescription and OTC medicines?

REFERENCES

Berman, B. and Evans, J. (1997) *Retail Management: A Strategic Approach* 7th edn. Upper Saddle River, NJ: Prentice Hall.

Church, C. (1996) 'Counter measures'. *The Grocer*, 2 Nov., p. 45.

Gilbert, M. (1997) 'Toppling Tesco will not be easy'. *The Grocer*, 15 March, p. 18.

Grocer (The) (1994) 'Prescription for success?' *The Grocer*, 19 Nov., 19: 45–6.

Levy, M. and Weitz, B. A. (1995) *Retailing Management*. Chicago: Irwin.

McGoldrick, P. (1990) *Retail Marketing*. London: McGraw-Hill.

McLoughlin, L. (1997) 'The Grocer focus on OTC healthcare: Grab a 36-pack please dear.' *The Grocer*, 28 June, pp. 39–40.

Mintel (1997a) 'OTC/Prescription medicines retailing'. *Retail Intelligence*, September.

Mintel (1997b) 'Food Retailing'. *Retail Intelligence*, March.

Nielsen, A. C. (1997) Merchandising Management. http://www.acnielsen.com.

Safeway plc (1997) *Building our Brand, Annual Report and Accounts*.

'MAINE NEW ENGLAND' AT DEBENHAMS: DEVELOPING A NEW RANGE

GAYNOR LEA-GREENWOOD, CHRISTOPHER M. MOORE AND BRENDA M. OLDFIELD

The authors would like to thank Debenhams buyers (London) and store management (Manchester) for their support in developing this case study. In particular we are grateful for the contributions provided by Claire Christie and Sarah Scott of the buying department.

The information in this case study, while believed to be accurate, is based on the memory of those involved. It has been simplified in order to focus on key learning objectives for students of management.

INTRODUCTION AND BACKGROUND

Debenhams was acquired by The Burton Group in 1985 and by 1997 there were 96 stand-alone Debenhams stores in the UK. In the first half of the trading period 1996–97 these stores enjoyed a turnover of £610.4m, an increase of almost 10 per cent on the same period in 1995–96, with a trading profit of £72.3m, an increase of 23.8 per cent on 1995–96. The full year turnover for the 1995–96 period was £998.3m, with an operating profit of £102.8m.

While predominantly targeting the 25–55 year age group, Debenhams sold a complete range of clothing for the whole family and had a greater share of the clothing market than any other department store group within the UK (Corporate Intelligence on Retailing, 1997). The company clothing offer was a mix of own-bought merchandise (which included a large proportion of own-label and exclusive lines) and concessions, the latter being of particular importance within the womenswear market. As was the case for other department store groups, womenswear was a very important product category and the Debenhams offer included some of the most successful department store concession operators such as Eastex, Alexon and Windsmoor. Mindful of the need to develop concessions for the younger female market, Debenhams' buyers successfully negotiated the introduction of fashion-forward brands with the establishment of Oasis and Kaliko concessions.

During the period immediately following The Burton Group acquisition of Debenhams, in-store units featuring other Burton Group fascias such as Principles, Top Shop and Dorothy Perkins were much in evidence. However, with a subsequent lessening of emphasis placed upon these fascia, Debenhams successfully developed a range of exclusive own-brand ranges; 'Anne Brooks', a range for the petite woman; 'J. Taylor', a range of co-ordinated fashion for the career woman; 'Trader', operating within the Casual Club section of the business focusing upon denim and casual clothing.

With the de-merger of Debenhams from The Burton Group in January 1998, (the remainder of The Burton Group being renamed Arcadia), Debenhams management were intent upon creating and maintaining a positioning for the department store group which was not only distinct from that of the Arcadia offer but distinct from other department store retailers in the UK.

In order to achieve such differentiation, a key dimension of the Debenhams' merchandise management strategy was the development of own-brand ranges, targeted to precise customer segments, many of which were inadequately served by other 'high street' fashion retailers. For example, the company identified and categorized 10 per cent of their customers as 'contemporary' in their approach to fashion. These consumers being, typically, attracted to the innovation and exclusivity of fashion designers but being unable to afford the high prices of exclusive fashion brands. In response to this customer need Debenhams collaborated with designers such as Ben de Lise, Jasper Conran and Pierce Fionda to produce ranges, marketed under the designer's name, but designed for and sold exclusively by Debenhams.

By ensuring a competent balance of fashionability, affordabilty and good quality, the buying teams at Debenhams recognized that their company could achieve significant market advantage, particularly within the British middle fashion market. One of the most successful initiatives undertaken by Debenhams and targeted at the middle fashion market has been the introduction of the 'Maine New England' own-brand range, and the process of launching, developing and extending the 'Maine New England' range is presented in this case study.

THE ORIGINS OF THE NEW OWN-BRAND – 'MAINE NEW ENGLAND'

In recognition of the general movement towards a more casual approach to dressing within the British fashion market, Debenhams launched the 'Casual Club' range in the early 1990s. This range sought to offer both men and women an own-brand option that was competitively priced, comfortable and designed to complement the 'leisure lifestyle' of customers. As part of the Casual Club offer Debenhams developed sub-brands, one of which was 'Maine New England', which was composed of sailing and outdoor performance wear targeted at men in the mid-20s to early-40s age group.

The inspiration for 'Maine New England' came from the American retail brand 'Nautica', a relatively expensive brand that draws heavily in its marketing communications imagery upon sophisticated leisure and sporting pursuits. From this came the idea that 'Maine New England' might also represent similar lifestyle values but at a more affordable price. Through the introduction of a range with a clear and individual identity, achieved largely through on-garment labelling, Debenhams soon found that they had developed a distinct own-brand that was popular among their male customers. By virtue of the strength of the name, the buying team also recognized that higher prices could be charged for this range, particularly when compared to other parts of the Casual Club offer.

Demand for the 'Maine New England' range was not confined to male customers. The buying team identified that female customers were buying the range for themselves in the smaller sizes. This led the team to commission a leading fashion marketing research company, TMS, to investigate the potential of developing 'Maine New England' for the womenswear market, the results of the research, given in Table 13.1, were presented to the board in December 1996 in an effort to convince them of the wisdom of the proposed womenswear range.

Table 13.1   **Results of the TMS research**

The 'Maine New England' concept

The concept of 'Maine Womenswear' could be developed to take advantage of the growing opportunity for a better end, own-buy women's casualwear brand.

This opportunity is supported by:

- The fact that the outdoor clothing/waterproof market has grown by 50 per cent over the past five years, while the percentage of adults participating in outdoor activities such as walking and hiking has increased threefold over the same period
- The increasing popularity of non-performance sportswear and better end casualwear such as that offered by The Gap, Next, Racing Green, Marks & Spencer and River Island

Casualwear market size

- Overall size of the Casualwear Market in the UK was £3.2b in 1995
- Of this £1.2b is in the female age range of 25–44, which is the target age group for the 'Maine Womenswear' range

Source: TMS

This research, coupled with market information relating to general trends in the female fashion market, given in Table 13.2, led Debenhams to the realization that there was significant demand for fashionable, but affordable, female casualwear and that this demand was not being addressed adequately by the competition. There was an obvious opening for the extension of 'Maine New England' into the female market and Debenhams were determined to take advantage of such an opportunity.

Table 13.2 **Casualwear market size**

Casualwear Market Size: Age Group 25–44 (by product type at February 1996)

	Mkt Size	% Mix	Product Mix
Casual woven trousers	101.2	8.2	32.5
Leggings/jersey bottoms	101.3	8.3	52.1
Shirts/overshirts	135.9	11.1	35.3
Shorts	64.9	5.3	51.3
Knitwear	382.4	31.2	36.6
Casual tee shirts	120.9	9.9	42.2
Casual sweatshirts	45.9	3.7	40.8
Casual polo shirts	4.6	0.4	25.1
Bodies	79.7	6.5	52.1
Casual knitted tops	53.3	4.3	39.8
Formal knitted tops	9.3	0.8	34.8
Outerwear (excl. raincoats/leather)	127.6	10.4	32.7
Total casualwear	1227.0	100.0	38.6

Source: TMS

Encouraged by the results of the TMS research, as well as the fact that the 'Maine New England' sub-brand was consistently out-selling all other ranges in the Casual Club category, and was doing so often at twice the price of similar Casual Club products, the decision was made to establish 'Maine New England' as a brand in its own right available to both men and women. The customer profile for the 'Maine New England' female is shown in Table 13.3 below.

Table 13.3 **'Maine New England' female customer profile**

- Age group 25–45
- She is aware of mainstream fashion trends
- She is familiar with active fabric and clothing brands. She aspires to designer sportswear brands for example DKNY and Ralph Lauren
- She aspires to a lifestyle that incorporates outdoor pursuits (for example the great outdoors/skiing/walking and so on)
- She recognizes the benefits of good quality and is prepared to pay for it
- Comfort and fit are very important to her, particularly in her casual wardrobe
- She shops at M&S, Next, Gap, Racing Green and speciality outdoor clothing shops (for example Berghaus)
- The range includes time performance elements as well as fashion performance looks
- The Maine range is a co-ordinated range of weekend wear smart casual clothing (better/best garments)
- She is always looking for something new
- She is looking for flexibility from her purchases and may choose to wear some pieces in any situation, for example work/leisure

Source: TMS

DEVELOPING THE STAND-ALONE BRAND

Debenhams' buying managers recognized that for 'Maine New England' to exist and succeed as a separate own-brand two things had to happen. First a dedicated buying team had to be established. Second, the choice of types and styles of products had to be increased.

While there are many advantages to be gained from own-brand development, not least those associated with controlling the image of the brand and exercising exclusive rights over its distribution, the development of an own-brand places a high degree of risk and responsibility upon the retailer. Debenhams did not have a group of designers to co-ordinate a look for 'Maine New England' men's and women's ranges. Nor did the company have the raw material sourcing, manufacturing and testing capacity needed to support a new brand. In an effort to overcome some of these problems, the buying team went to New York and, spending only £5000, they bought sample pieces which would serve as an inspiration and provide design direction for the first stand-alone collection.

With some ideas in place with regard to how the new collection might look, the Maine buying team sought expertise from a company called Unimix. At that time Unimix functioned as a dedicated supplier to The Burton Group having formed a strategic alliance in order to supply merchandise for a range of own-brands within the group. As part of their service Unimix not only designed garments but took care of fabric sourcing and laboratory testing. Additionally Unimix organized and managed the production of garments from their dedicated manufacturing capacity in China (transported to the UK via Hong Kong), and from production sites in Dubai. Unimix also took responsibility for quality control monitoring throughout the production process and ensured timely distribution of the garments into the UK. In effect, Unimix acted as a highly co-operative supplier but, while being a very expensive service, the Maine buying team saw collaboration with Unimix as the perfect solution, since this gave them direct control over the image and design characteristics of the Maine range, but released them from the problems associated with sourcing, manufacturing and distributing an own-brand range.

Given the increasingly dynamic nature of fashion, particularly in relation to style, colour and fabric trends, retailers must interpret the latest trends and have them available in stores as part of their own-brand ranges as soon as possible. Unimix were able to convert the samples that the Maine buyers brought from New York into a product suited to Maine customer requirements within a 45 day period. This quick turnaround provided 'Maine New England' with a tremendous advantage. The brand could be positioned as an accessible high street interpretation of the latest fashion looks.

INTRODUCING THE 'MAINE NEW ENGLAND' BRAND IN-STORE

Previously, when 'Maine New England' had been a sub-brand within the men's Casual Club offer, the range was merchandised using dark wooden fixtures, differentiating it from other own-brands, such as Trader and Casual Club. With the launch of 'Maine New England' as a brand in its own right, no attempt was made to change the character of these fixtures; after all, these had worked in the past, as the high sales attested, and there was a commitment to manage costs to ensure that the new range provided as high a return on investment as was possible.

With the move into womenswear however, it was felt that the fixtures used for the men's Maine range would have to be adapted in order to better fit in with other fixtures used within the womenswear departments. It should be noted that since Debenhams department stores are merchandised by floor level (that is, womenswear on one floor, menswear on another) the 'Maine New England' range for men and women could not be merchandised as a single unit on the same floor. Therefore, to integrate with the fixtures used within womenswear departments, the style and shape of the fixture remained the same but they were made-up using a lighter coloured wood with white inlays to the base of the fixtures. In adopting this approach, the company sought to retain some of the original identity of the Maine look, which had not previously put women off buying, while at the same time integrating and harmonizing this new range with existing fixtures on the shop floor. As is typically the case with Debenhams own-brand merchandise, the company produced a brand installation guide for each store, the purpose of which was to provide staff with guidance on merchandise layout and presentation standards for the new brand. No additional staff at store level were recruited specifically to look after the Maine brand.

It was further determined that similar styles of signage, product packaging and labelling were used in the new womenswear range. In addition, the style of logo-script for the on-product branding of menswear be used for comparable styles within the womenswear ranges.

Promotion of the 'Maine New England' Brand

When Debenhams launched their exclusive 'J' brand designed by Jasper Conran the range was given significant promotional support in the form of in-store fashion shows, specially designed packaging, in-store photography and point-of-sale flyers and brochures. In addition, the 'J' brand was supported by a highly creative advertising campaign featured within the quality press, key fashion journals and Sunday supplements and the company PR department ensured that the range enjoyed significant editorial coverage in many of these publications. 'J' was also advertised on billboards and on public transport.

When 'Maine New England' was launched, Debenhams did not provide a national launch advertising and promotional budget and apart from a four-page pullout in *Just 17* magazine the range was not advertised. This lack of advertising spend came as no surprise to the Maine buying team since own-brands did not typically enjoy promotional support at launch within the company, a situation which could be re-considered if an own-brand became better established and successful.

Initial Customer Response

Despite the fact that the repositioning of the men's Maine range and the launch of 'Maine New England' for women did not receive dedicated advertising support, initial reaction to the development of the brand was well received with initial sales being strong and above budget. *Ad hoc* research of customers undertaken by the Maine buying team found that customer attitudes were very positive towards the new own-brand; customers felt that the merchandise was of good quality, was well designed and offered value for money. Female customers said that they were pleased that the range had been extended into womenswear and suggested that the Maine brand filled a gap within the market.

Much to the surprise of the buying team, customers had not recognized this to be a Debenhams' own-brand. Instead, many customers thought that 'Maine New England' was an American brand that was sold exclusively through Debenhams stores. One reason why they had not seen it to be a Debenhams' own-brand was because it had a very definite identity, as evidenced in the colours used, the branding devices and the way in which the brand was coherently merchandised.

Further Extensions of the 'Maine New England' Brand

With the continued success of 'Maine New England' throughout 1996, the Maine buying team recognized that there was the potential to extend the brand into other product categories. Consequently, in early 1997 a fashion accessories and men's and women's underwear range was launched. As the Maine brand enjoyed customer recognition, it was decided that rather than sell these ranges within the Maine fashion areas they should be sold within the underwear/lingerie and fashion accessories departments of Debenhams. This decision was based upon the recognition that customers prefer to choose these products within dedicated departments, allowing them the opportunity to view the full range on offer and thereby make product comparisons. By placing these Maine products within 'home' departments it was expected that sales would be greater, a strategy that appears to have been the right one since the Maine brand has achieved good sales penetration levels within both the underwear and fashion accessories categories.

Encouraged by this success a decision was made to launch a Maine boyswear range for introduction in August 1997. Somewhat later, it was decided that a girlswear range should also be launched at the same time. In September 1997 department store managers were informed that a Maine childrenswear range was to be launched and that adequate space had to be made available on the shop floor in order to accommodate the new launch. However, due to the short timescale between the decision to introduce the girlswear range and the time of the proposed launch, exacerbated by other technical difficulties, (such as the need to introduce pink into the girlswear range which was not part of the Maine colour palette for the season), the full childrenswear range was not delivered on time. The floor space identified for Maine was allocated to a new concession, Joe Bloggs for children. The full Maine childrenswear range was not available in-store until Christmas 1997.

TAKING A BRAND MANAGEMENT APPROACH

In an effort to take a more strategic approach to the control, management and development of the brand, a 'Maine New England' brand manager was appointed in late autumn 1997. As part of the remit the new brand manager was given responsibility for overseeing the existing Maine ranges and ensuring that these had a consistency of approach in terms of image, design, quality and positioning. This role was felt to be particularly important since the brand had grown into so many product areas that is was becoming impossible for the buyers to focus attention upon the development of their own product ranges, while at the same time ensuring overall coherence of the ranges within the brand.

As well as overseeing the existing ranges marketed under the Maine brand it was the responsibility of the brand manager to identify new areas in which the Maine brand could be developed. In recognition of the growth in the market for 'lifestyle' products within the business, the brand manager and the buying team identified an opportunity for the introduction of a 'Maine New England' bed and bath range. This range, covering bed linens, bath towels, ceramics and ornaments was successfully launched in February 1998. These household ranges clearly followed the 'design handwriting' of the 'Maine New England' clothing ranges, shared similar product branding devices, (such as packaging, ticketing and on-product logos) and were merchandised using fixtures and methods in keeping with those used for other product categories. The 'Main New England' bed and bath ranges are integrated within the household accessories departments.

It is interesting to note that the extension of the 'Maine New England' brand into new product categories has been achieved with minimal advertising spend. And while these ranges have enjoyed editorial coverage within the fashion and home lifestyle press, the impetus for such coverage has been as much from the publications themselves as from the PR department at Debenhams.

While the management of Debenhams were delighted with the success that the 'Maine New England' brand had enjoyed over a range of product categories, they were also aware of the need to consolidate the identity and standards of the brand. The company continue to be committed to improving the quality and design of all 'Maine New England' products and are intent upon ensuring that the range maintains its competitive advantage, achieved through the delivery of products which are contemporary and which deliver value for money.

At the time of writing this case study the brand manager and buying team had no immediate plans for further development of 'Maine New England'. However, industry commentators have suggested that the range could be extended into such areas as sportswear, kitchen goods and giftware.

QUESTIONS

1. What do you consider to be the key features of a successful fashion own-brand?

2. Within the context of your response to question 1, evaluate the extent to which you consider 'Maine New England' to be a successful fashion own-brand.

3. Outline the main stages that a buying team may follow as part of the creation and launch of a fashion own-brand. To what extent did the 'Maine New England' buying team follow the pattern of development that you have proposed?

4. Identify and evaluate the advantages and disadvantages of the sourcing method that the 'Maine New England' buying team adopted as part of the move to create a stand-alone own-brand.

5. Comment on Debenhams recruitment of a brand manager for 'Maine New England'. Write a short description of that person's role and responsibilities.

6. 'Maine New England' has become the focus for fairly extensive brand-extension within Debenhams. Identify the key characteristics of a successful brand extension strategy.

7. Identify the issues which may arise in the future with regards to the management of the 'Maine New England' brand portfolio. Suggest ways in which these issues could be 'successfully managed'.

REFERENCE

Corporate Intelligence on Retailing (1997). Corporate Intelligence Group: London.

SUPERDRUG: THE ROUTE TO BECOMING MORE INNOVATIVE

HELENE HILL

The author would like to thank Superdrug and Kingfisher for their active support in developing this case study. Particular thanks go to Peter Raine (Head of Total Quality, Superdrug), Tony Mann (Category General Manager, Superdrug), Peter Geddes (Head of Marketing, Superdrug), John Phipps (Regional Manager, Superdrug) and all staff in the Sheffield Meadowhall and Manchester Piccadilly stores.

The information presented in this case is based on interviews with staff from a number of perspectives: strategic management, regional management, and store at both shop floor and management level. The information presented, believed to be largely accurate, is based on the memory of the author and her synthesis and simplification of key facts to facilitate the achievement of the key learning outcomes for students.

INTRODUCTION

Back in 1966 on Putney High Street, Ronald and Peter Goldstein opened the first of what was to become a key force in personal care retailing: Superdrug. By 1983 it had become a public limited company, and in 1987 it was integrated into the Kingfisher group, with (at that time) 339 stores to its tally.

Along its history to the current day, new formats have been developed as a response to trends in consumer markets, and as a vision of future opportunities for business operations: 1991 saw the introduction of fragrance counters, with pharmacy counters soon to follow in 1992. However, apart from changes to the format, a new concept store was trialled in 1995 that incorporated a clearly defined vision for the future and a mission statement. This concept is now being developed across the company with an anticipated deliverable benefit of £8.75m per annum.

The Kingfisher Group

The Kingfisher Group is one of a number of well-known retail groups, and is based around its well recognized subsidiary operations that span a wide range of shopping experiences and offers. These include B&Q in the DIY/gardening sector, Comet in the home appliance/electrical goods sector, Woolworths with their variety sector presence, Superdrug in the health and beauty sector, and finally, the less recognized names of Chartwell (property development) and Darty (French electrical retailer).

Their strategy to be one of Europe's most profitable volume retailers is to be achieved by concentrating on markets centred on the home and family, ones which they feel they know and understand, and developing strong retail brands with leading positions in their markets. Their focus is to build on existing businesses using opportunities for internationalization of their operations where appropriate.

Superdrug Fact File

Superdrug is firmly established as the number two UK health and beauty retailer, behind Boots with 10.3 per cent share of the health and beauty market in 1997.

The portfolio was made up of 705 stores. These were mainly in high street locations with average turnover per store of £971,348 and an average of 2992 square footage.

The consumer offer is perceived to consist of a combination of quality with good value for money, with both branded and own-brand products. The own-brand component within Superdrug has accelerated by 30 per cent over the past year, introducing over 1400 own-brand products in 1997.

Inherent within this vision are a number of factors: understanding consumer needs, the integral role of brand development, the importance of distribution networks, the increasing significance of store format and presentation, the pivotal role of innovation and new product development, and finally, the company culture which must tie all of these facets together with systems, procedures and personnel that can effectively move towards a common goal or mission.

THE MODEL FOR CHANGE: *LIVING THE MISSION*

As part of the company's move towards becoming more competitive, an extensive strategic change programme has been undertaken. This programme is designed to move Superdrug towards its future vision, and has been named *Living The Mission*. The programme was devised using feedback from all staff within the company: a competition asking for ideas for a mission statement based on the key principles that Superdrug exemplify. These became the stands. This strategy ensured staff 'buy in' to a mission statement that they could associate with and feel part of. This programme was underpinned by the principles of TQM (total quality management): it involves everyone in the company; in terms of quality it has defined requirements; and it is a managed and controlled process. All areas of the company have been affected and involved and the focus for action was placed upon three factors, deemed to be pivotal for gaining a competitive advantage via a customer focus: improving core processes that would deliver a competitive edge, focusing on customers, and the people/staff.

The *Living The Mission* programme or 'journey' facilitates the achievement of the company vision in three ways.

First, the destination of the programme is centred around the company mission and stands. The company mission, 'to be the customer's favourite, up-to-the-minute health and beauty shop, 'loved' for its value, choice, friendliness and fun', translates into 'stands' (Superdrug *Living The Mission* Store Team Workshop booklet). These seven stands are:

1. Our primary market focus will be on health and beauty
2. Superdrug offers superior value
3. Superdrug offers superior choice
4. Superdrug has its finger on the pulse
5. Superdrug goes the last mile for the customer
6. Superdrug is friendly and fun
7. Superdrug creates winning teams

The second aspect, facilitating the journey towards the company vision, is the vehicle by which this will be achieved. This is via the Superdrug brand. The essence of the Superdrug brand is 'accessible value and choice in a shopping experience that makes me feel good about me' (Superdrug *Living The Mission* Store Team Workshop booklet). This brand essence is a central feature in the new concept stores under development currently, and it is this new store concept which epitomises the future for Superdrug. This is reflected in the current training programme of store staff. The training which all staff undergo before commencing work in these new concept stores is similar in outcome to that of the *Living The Mission* programme for existing stores. Both strategies reflect this move towards a united approach to retailing: including both old style community stores (secondary pitch sites) and transit stores (expressway sites stores), and concept store format (primary pitch sites). Therefore, the additional burden that existing stores must overcome is how to move from the old style to the new way of 'living the mission'.

The third component of the *Living The Mission* vision consists of the values which the people in the company must believe in and share. These result in the way in which all personnel conduct themselves as representatives of the organization. The highlighted values are:

- Delighting the customer
- Winning
- Generosity of spirit
- Constructive rigour
- Being straightforward
- Diversity
- **I**nvolvement, **O**wnership, **P**ride, **E**xcellence of execution (IOPE).

In summary, the stated overall aims of this programme are to:

- Continuously improve the way we meet our paying customers' requirements consistent with our mission and brand
- Harnessing everyone's commitment and potential through involvement, ownership, pride, and excellence of execution (IOPE)
- Getting things right, on time, first time, every time at the lowest cost. (Superdrug *Living The Mission* Store Team Workshop booklet).

While this programme gives broad aims and strategies, it must be recognized that this strategic framework is heavily dependent upon the operationalization of this plan at the regional and store level. The mission statement was seen as a mechanism to facilitate an improvement in store standards. To this end, these broad outlines were operationalized into the following issues for store management:

- Understand and focus on our paying customers
- Live IOPE: train everyone in TQM values and TQM management/ improvement tools and techniques
- Teams win
- Plan up-front with clear, measurable, owned, time-dated objectives
- Continuously improve – plan, do, measure, improve, share
- Recognize and celebrate successful involvement
- Management lead by example.

At this level, a number of key issues begin to emerge: a customer focus; the role of teams; *Living The Mission* at all levels; having a framework for action that aids continuous improvement; and recognition of success.

COMPANY STRUCTURE

With 705 stores and 12,355 employees within the total organization, a key issue for Superdrug was how this programme was going to translate into a plan of action across the various functions and levels of the company that would ensure a consistency of experience across all existing stores: in terms of training, process, and measurement of outcomes.

The roll-out of *Living The Mission* was segmented into three core areas of the company: distribution, head office and stores. While the focus of this case will be at the store level, the roll-out programmes of the other two core personnel areas are illustrated to provide an overall picture of the *Living The Mission* programme design and implementation throughout the entire organization.

Distribution

The following roll-out programme was followed within the distribution function in Superdrug.

Management	2 days	20 senior managers
Supervisors	2 days	40 supervisors
Improvement groups	2 days	30 staff

Head Office

Within the head-office functions within Superdrug the following structure was used to roll out the *Living The Mission* programme training.

Champions	2 days	20 senior managers
Functional	1 day	380 head office staff
Internal customer	3 x ½ day	380 head office staff service standards

Stores

Across the 705 stores, personnel needed to be given a consistent presentation of the *Living The Mission* programme. Serious consideration had to be given therefore as to how this would be rolled out at store level. The structure at the operational store level is more complicated, and resulted in the segmentation of personnel for training according to varying management levels, down to store staff, and also for the presenters who would, unequivocally, be responsible for the training sessions given to all stores. This led to five separate phases:

1. Regional
2. Area
3. Presenters
4. Stores
5. Follow-up team time sessions

All personnel within this overall store structure would need to understand and behave in a manner that reflected the principles underlying *Living The Mission*. This was especially important in relation to personnel who operated outside individual stores. For example, visiting area and regional managers would be expected to 'live the mission' on store visits; otherwise this strategy would be perceived by staff in-store as not being important. Therefore, potentially, there are many breaking points in this chain: any person failing to 'live the mission' is signalling its lack of importance to their junior staff who may, as a consequence, be less likely themselves to 'live the mission' and value its significance.

All 60 regional and area staff received two days training and the 800 area and store management staff were given a one day session. At the store level the 12,000 staff had a half day (four hour) workshop session, which was followed up approximately four weeks later with another four hour session. All remaining issues would be covered in regular monthly team time sessions in-store.

The presenters, 120 store management, were all given a three day training session before they then themselves rolled out this programme to stores. The selected store managers then presented the sessions within the region from which they originated. It was therefore not necessarily the store manager who would present *Living The Mission* to his or her own staff. The time required to present to other stores was included alongside their normal working hours within their own stores. The training session consisted of all personnel being given their prepared training programme material: a large number of overhead slides, set exercises, video material. The presenters' training session involved the designer of the material, an individual external to Superdrug who was consulted on the design of the *Living The Mission* programme, discussing its contents, and giving the trainers the opportunity to look through this material and test present small sections of the total package. The second component of the training session, facilitated by an internal person, consisted of training for the skills as a presenter.

This programme was rolled out moving north over the length of the project. The project in total took six months to complete.

THE INITIAL *LIVING THE MISSION* SESSION WITHIN STORES

Each store had an initial four hour training session which all staff, whether full-time or part-time, attended wherever possible. This initial training session introduced *Living The Mission*, its aims and objectives, why it was important, and the role that each individual and team played in the achievement of the objectives. Every member of staff was given a *Living The Mission* booklet to be used both as a tool for conducting the reflective and practical exercises, and as a tool to facilitate every individual having a personal record of the training session, its contents, and key learning points.

The Starfish

The key issues at store level, which were introduced and explored within the workshop session, have been exemplified visually by the starfish framework for customer service standards. This represents both the brand identity, but importantly, is used as an outline for plotting and measuring the attainment of key customer service goals within all stores.

The five legs of the starfish translate into five aspects of service standards within each store from the consumers' perspective. All of these standards can be seen to relate directly to issues of managing service-based operations. Here the emphasis requires additional consideration beyond that of product, price, promotion and place, into that of physical surroundings, process (what the shopping experience consists of) and personnel. The aim of the company is to position themselves in this market with the fun, friendly and helpful image, and to move away from the 'white coat' style commonly associated with Boots. The five aspects considered from the *consumers'* perspective are:

1. *When I look around the shop.* This issue covers cleanliness, signage and layout of the store.

2. *When I see you.* This aspect tackles personal appearance and the manner of all store personnel when interacting with customers.

3. *When I'm deciding what I want.* When consumers are in the store this area gives consideration to product knowledge, clarity of pricing and special offer displays, and availability of products when requested.

4. *When I pay.* This aspect of service focuses upon both cleanliness and speed of till areas, but also the manner in which staff involve themselves when customers pay for their purchases, for example offering to giftwrap perfume, and packing of goods.

5. *When I need extra help.* The focus of this aspect is upon the manner in which staff make consumers feel at ease with their shopping experience, and that they are aided where possible to make it as positive an experience as possible.

The Measurement of Service Standards

As stated, the starfish is also used as a tool for measuring these service standards.

All stores are provided with a large starfish which allows the achieved standards on the five axes to be plotted. This is used both to highlight areas for improvement, and to action progress within the store on all of these aspects. While the starfish focuses on customer service standards, alongside service, the other main components of measurement are productivity and people; for example shrinkage levels, takings, what individual staff have highlighted as areas for improvement in the store.

Central to this measurement of standards is the process by which these store measures are decided and agreed upon.

The second, follow-up session on the *Living The Mission* training programme involves store team members discussing and deciding upon a rating for their store on all axes at that particular point in time. It also requires the store team to devise action plans which will allow them to improve on all aspects of their service standards, productivity and people issues. This process includes part-time, full-time, shop floor and management levels in each store. These decisions form the basis of their *Living The Mission* contract: how these targets will be achieved, and who will be responsible for ensuring they are achieved. There is no fixed formula as to how the store should implement this measurement, and it becomes part of the store team's decision prior to its commencement.

All of these service standards then provide for an overall view of store standards and integrate into the store visit framework, whether at area or regional level.

THE ROLE OF INNOVATION IN *LIVING THE MISSION*

As highlighted earlier in the case, over 1400 own-brand products were introduced in 1997 alone. The importance of new product development and innovation is apparent in a number of ways. 'Innovation and learning' is one of the five elements within the Superdrug balanced scorecard: a new but well recognized business strategy mechanism which indicates the key areas for managing within the company, and then highlights what aspects in particular must be actioned under each area of the scorecard. The importance of innovation and new product development is also implicitly reflected within the *Living The Mission* stands. For example, the 'need for continuous improvement' requires innovation, 'offering superior choice' involves developing new products and services, 'has its finger on the pulse' is reflected by appropriate product ranges and service levels, and 'goes the last mile for the customer' also implies up-to-date product ranges and service provision which require new product development activity.

So it is evident that all levels and types of change or innovation are incumbent within *Living The Mission*. This continuum, that reflects the degree of innovation, ranges from 'new product development' as a more major change at the strategic level, to 'steady improvements in-store' at the operational level of the company.

Facilitating and Organizing Different Levels of Innovation

At the strategic level, major changes are initiated via appointed strategic project teams which focus upon approximately seven or eight key initiatives within Superdrug. While these groups operate at a strategic level, the original ideas behind these projects may have been suggested and developed at any level in the organization. The tendency is for them to have been initiated at a strategic level in the organization. This is partly a consequence of store staff confidence and motivation to suggest potential projects: there is some disbelief that their ideas would be taken seriously; that this development role in the store is in fact not part of their remit; or simply they do not have sufficient time to undertake additional roles. All of these concerns are a consequence of the change in company culture which *Living The Mission* is attempting to develop further, and the relative cost-driven structures that exist in all retail operations. The existing procedures within Superdrug do state that all ideas will be given consideration. It is only to be expected that not every idea suggested will automatically be accepted: similar ideas may already be in the system, or ideas may not be in line with the overall corporate mission and aims. The existing procedures do specify that any individual whose idea has been rejected will be told of this and reasons for rejection justified. The existing systems are also being developed in an attempt to ensure that staff, when proposing ideas, do think of all the implications of the idea and assess whether it does complement the brand essence and is a cost-effective use of resources. This is facilitated by assessments of project proposals which require specific consideration on:

- Fit within the balanced scorecard/key growth areas of company
- Resources required (staff levels and numbers)
- Success criteria for the proposed project
- Any assumptions/risks implicit within the project
- Key obstacles to the success of the proposal.

Such measurement ensures that the associated risks and value of each project is consistently considered and extensively evaluated.

At the operational store level the focus of innovation is placed more on steady improvement. This is facilitated by a number of mechanisms.

First, improvement groups are in existence which are formed to look at a particular issue that has arisen. Such groups may consist of regional managers, area managers, store managers, and occasionally store staff. The choice of group members is based around the necessary skills for the task to be performed, and also the types of team members that will ensure more effective teamwork. To this end Belbin (1981) group member roles are selected for a more complete team grouping.

The second way in which steady improvement is advanced is by the use of the customer service standards starfish framework and the *Living The Mission* contracts which are an integral part of this programme. This operates at the store level, and has been described above. All of these issues are discussed in the monthly team meetings held in each store. As part of a drive to reward and recognize successful innovation at store level regarding the main areas of measurement, the current 'premier crew' store competition has been undertaken to select and reward the most successful stores throughout the UK. This also feeds into best practice.

The final aspect of steady improvement is at the individual level in-store. One of the key constructs in *Living The Mission* revolves around what is termed 'the empowerment cycle'. This cycle is a model of operating which encourages all staff to suggest ideas for improvement, and which will then go through a series of stages to focus the idea further, and to ensure that all implications have been considered. This would be done with the store manager.

All of these action plans and store strategies need to be incorporated into the broader strategic business framework. For example, an outcome of this empowerment cycle may be an improved way of operating which can then be fed into the area's model of best practice. It was indicated that the importance of shouting about the successes is central to this process of being successful: it both gives positive reinforcement to such behaviour and it also enhances the likelihood that these improvements will be spread through the organization. Communication of best practice is pivotal for overall corporate improvement throughout all stores. As indicated previously, while staff are willing in theory to suggest ideas, the extent to which they have been thought through, or their ability to complement the brand are sometimes limited. It was also highlighted that time was a major factor that would inhibit the ability to consider these issues in any depth. The implications of these issues were at the time being suitably rectified. Apart from measuring for best practice, measures are also taken at store level, for example number of ideas per store, number of ideas implemented per store. Overall, measurement is a major tool used by Superdrug at all levels in the organization as a form of assessment on progress to date on the *Living The Mission* programme, and as an indicator of future actions.

QUESTIONS

1. Identify the manner in which the *Living The Mission* programme was devised, and the role this programme plays within the corporate strategy.

2. How was the *Living The Mission* programme structured? What are the key reasons behind this structure, and what potential difficulties did this design have to take account of?

3. To what extent do you think this programme will enhance the development of a more innovative culture? What key problems must management recognize to ensure this programme works effectively?

4. What are the main lessons to be learnt from this programme? Are these only specific to this company, and if not, in what other circumstances may these lessons prove valuable?

5. How, if at all, have the company circumstances of providing a branded offer, and in a service context, affected the design and implementation of this programme?

6. Taking into account the major learning points to date, what key things does this company need to do to ensure the success and effectiveness of this programme in the future?

7. The case indicates that each store decides upon the details of how this programme will be implemented. Asking students to take on the role of store manager, what are the key issues they must manage, how could/should they prioritize them, and how do these fit alongside the other store team member roles? How would they facilitate this programme being proactively accepted by all staff and valued within store practice? What would they want to be included in the first training session for store staff on *Living The Mission* and why?

REFERENCES

Belbin, M. (1981) *Management Teams – Why They Succeed or Fail*. London: Heinemann.
Kingfisher Internet Website.
Superdrug *Living The Mission* Store Team Workshop booklet.

CASE

THE ROLE OF CATEGORY MANAGEMENT IN HAIR COLOURANTS: BRISTOL-MYERS

SANDRA HOGARTH-SCOTT AND IAN WALTERS

> This case study is based on taped interviews with one of the authors, Ian Walters of Bristol-Myers, and a variety of sources. The material is not fully comprehensive, nor should it be regarded as totally factual. Parts have been simplified in order to focus on the key learning objectives.

Putting out the stall and waiting for passing shoppers to stop and buy used to form the basic philosophy of retailing. Today, it has more to do with identifying the individual shoppers and concentrating on the demand chain, rather than the traditional supply pipeline… Not only will customers expect goods and services to be available at time, anywhere, retailers will reap the rewards of the information age… any networked world will not only link buyers and sellers but every part of the organization to every other. (*Retail: The Way Forward*, IBM 1997, p. 12)

INTRODUCTION

Bristol-Myers Squibb is an American company, whose core business is pharmaceuticals, but they also have significant businesses in consumer medicines, beauty care and nutritional products. World-wide turnover is in excess of $16b.

Clairol, another American company specializing in haircare products, was acquired by Bristol-Myers back in the 1950s. Today, Clairol has a portfolio of hair colourants developed to meet consumers specific needs, depending on the colour effect they wish to achieve as well as the level of permanence they require. During the late 1990s Clairol started to expand its business into other markets, these include central and eastern Europe, south America and the Far East. The flagship brand in hair colour is Nice 'N' Easy, sold alongside other brands such as Loving Care, Lasting Colour, Natural Instincts. In 1996, Clairol developed the first permanent, water-based hair colour product – Hydrience, which was launched first in the USA, followed by the UK, Europe, Australia and Asia.

Clairol has also moved into other haircare categories, notably shampoo and conditioner with a new brand – Herbal Essences. As part of the development of the brand, other hair related products have also been launched, these include styling products. The brand has its own unique identity, supported by an advertising campaign described as 'disruptive' in comparison to the major brands in the market. Herbal Essences has been launched in over 50 countries around the world. However, Bristol-Myers current strength is in the hair colourant subcategory.

Bristol-Myers was seeking to maintain and build market share in with all its major retailers. The general trade marketing manager, Ian Walters, had recently moved from Nestlé to Bristol-Myers. Bristol-Myers were hoping to use his expertise to build relationships with their key accounts and extend their dominance in the hair colourant subcategory to dominance in the overall haircare category. They faced some tough opposition.

THE TRADE MARKETING FUNCTION AT BRISTOL-MYERS

Figure 15.1 shows the trade marketing team made up of three trade marketing managers, one for each channel of distribution, as well as a range and a space planning manager. Creative services are also part of trade marketing. (N.B. Creative services are responsible for preparing artwork for point of sale material, UK and Europe, press advertising, sourcing consumer promotions and consumer promotion tracking.) Each trade marketing manager is a member of both a category team and a trade channel team. Teams are made up from managers from sales, trade marketing, marketing, finance and logistics. The team marketing process, allows functional experts to focus on areas of the busi-

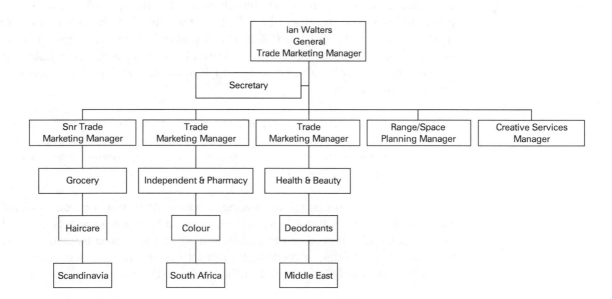

Figure 15.1   Trade marketing department – Bristol-Myers UK

ness, developing and implementing strategies by channel and by category, but retaining the overall business objectives in mind.

The major competitive strengths are the diverse backgrounds of the team members who come from both commercial and academic areas. Their main functions are: efficient consumer response (ECR) and implementation in the business; category management; specific retailer projects; management of market data; promotion evaluation; functional contact within accounts (beyond the buying function); and co-ordinating the range review process with the retailer, sales and marketing.

THE RETAILERS

Developments in the retail marketplace in the 1980s and 1990s had important implications for how Bristol-Myers might formulate their short and medium term marketing strategies. Most important among these changes were: concentration of retailers; the continuing trend towards own-brand with its implications for mainstream brands, and the development of the retailer as a brand; and the blurring of product demarcation lines between types of retailers. Both major health and beauty retailers, such as Boots and Superdrug, were expanding their lines. The major grocers were also beginning to perceive total haircare as a major growth area, albeit one outside their traditional area of expertise. It was being perceived not only as a growth area, but as one with high margin potential. New business would come primarily from existing health and beauty retailers, especially Boots and Superdrug.

Whether to develop own or private brands (for retailers) has been an issue confronting manufacturers for two decades. Until the 1980s retailers were primarily 'stores' of producer brands, they were weak as brands in their own right. But concentration of retailers was a major factor in the growth of own-brands. The greater the penetration of own-brand the more the retailer could develop brands with value, quality and innovation. This is illustrated by the following quotation:

> At around 50 private labels (e.g. Sainsbury's, Boots) the retail brand has probably become the dominant brand in the consumer's mind. At complete penetration (e.g. M&S), the retailer brand is the producer brand and owns consumer loyalty. (*Retail Week*, 11 July 1997, p. 12)

Retailers have a potential for making markets their own, for example chilled foods where retailer own brands are strong and branded products weak. The major retailers are investing in building strong retailer brand franchise through investing in marketing, advertising, product quality and service. Sainsbury's, Boots, Safeways and Tesco are all in the top ten advertised grocery brands.

Channels of Distribution for Bristol-Myers Products

The distribution market for haircare products segments into three:

- the grocery multiples
- the health and beauty area retailers, notably Boots and Superdrug
- the independents.

Within the grocery trade, retail concentration has increased over the past two decades, at the expense of the Co-operatives and the small independents. This has resulted in the top four retailers – Tesco, Sainsbury, Asda and Safeway – gaining 59.3 per cent of share of trade in 1997 (*The Food Pocket Book*, 1997). Although there has been some concentration among pharmacy outlets it is not as significant – 29.2 per cent share of trade went through multiple and co-operative pharmacies, with 58.8 per cent through independent pharmacies. (Multiples/co-operative pharmacies include all chemists and others belonging to groups of 10 or more retail shops. Pharmacies have 20 per cent or more of total turnover in drugs, toiletries and cosmetics with a qualified pharmacist in attendance, *Retail Pocket Book*, 1998.)

However, the health and beauty multiples are the most important outlet for hair colourants. Boots has grown market share. It has supported new brand introductions, and attempted to simplify consumer choice at point of sale. The independent chemist's market share has declined, even though it has a tradition of offering advice. The main problem area is lack of wide choice in brands and shades. In contrast multiple grocers have increased market share of hair colourants by providing increased shelf space to a wider range. Table 15.1 shows retail sales of colourants by outlet in 1997.

Table 15.1 **Retail sales of colourants, by type of outlet**

	1997		1995–97
	£m	%	% change
Chemists	69	55	+21
Discounters/drugstores	35	28	+21
Grocers (multiples)	14	11	+56
Other*	8	6	+14
Total	125	100	+23

Source: Mintel, 1998

* includes hairdressing salons and department stores

The Grocery Multiples

The multiples are attempting to expand in toiletries by offering added service and value in categories where they are not traditionally strong. Their strength in the toiletries market is with core grocery associated lines: bar soaps, deodorants, shampoos and toothpaste. They are picking up sales in these areas, where brands are well known and choices are easy. Where they are not doing so well is in areas where they do not have traditional strengths, in product areas which require a more personal touch and an in-store environment that creates a health and beauty ambience where shoppers can browse. The importance of this is underlined in the following quotation:

> there are two types of consumer, those who want time to browse and feel pampered, and those who are happy to whizz the aisles, quickly picking up the brand they know they want. The retail sector share winners will be whoever caters for this larger group. (*Checkout*, February 1998, p. 30)

Ian Walters of Bristol-Myers also felt that, for the consumer, hair colour in a grocery store is very much a replenishment category:

> I'm in the store every Friday, haven't got much time, they stock my shade, I can pick that up along with the cotton wool, shampoo and all my other needs as well as food and fresh food.

The Health and Beauty Retailers

These retailers emphasize products that require sales assistants, advice and/or time to browse and to be able to test and sample. They also stock a wide range as part of the service. These two points are illustrated by the following quotations:

> The pharmacy environment conveys a sense of reassurance, which cascades down. For example, if you've got sensitive teeth, the pharmacist is on hand to talk about oral health as well as general health.

and

> One difficulty is identifying halo products, which although not shifting volume, give the range a comprehensive look. Boots takes in extra lines because it believes this offers a service'. (*Checkout*, April 1997, p. 32)

Confirming this Ian Walters observed that:

> The mindset of people like Superdrug and Boots is different because of the nature of the products and the in-store environment they have created. They wish to be seen by consumers as experts, the first place that you would go to find out more about health and beauty products before making a purchase, especially

a first purchase in a category. The high street is still a very competitive environment, the grocery retailers have recognized the size of the opportunity and developed strategies accordingly – witness the growth of in-store pharmacies among Tesco, Sainsburys, ASDA and Safeway.

CATEGORY MANAGEMENT

Category management is part of an overall marketing strategy:

> One part of the whole effort to identify the role of the category within each trade channel and then working with the grocers and the health and beauty retailers to make the most of that product. It is not just about altering and tinkering the range at fixture level. It's starting at the fixture and working all the way back through the supply chain. (Ian Walters, Trade Marketing Manager, Bristol-Myers)

Definition of the category is critical to the category management process. From a consumer perspective a category should consider all the related items that might be considered when making a particular purchasing decision. Single categories will include own-label and branded goods. For example, the haircare category includes shampoo, conditioner, hairspray, colorants and styling aids. Hair colourants is a subcategory of haircare.

Although category management enables categories to be managed more efficiently on the retailer's behalf, it also affects suppliers' businesses. Suppliers may have to take a different view of net margins. Some of their products may be delisted as part of information technology driven range reviews; listing charges may go; retailers may choose only one supplier in the category to work with in partnership; and, the focus will be on efficiency throughout the supply chain (IGD, 1995).

The emphasis of these teams is cross functional and multi-level. Retailers and manufacturers work together in business teams with joint business goals. Instead of one buyer negotiating with one salesperson, teams from both parties involve contribution from distribution, merchandising, marketing and sales, information technology, finance and operations. Expertise is called on where and when required. The teams are usually led by the retailer, and one or more suppliers in each category are selected to lead the category on the supply side and is referred to as category captain or preferred supplier.

Measurements and targets used by category management teams go well beyond the traditional sales and margins measures. They may include measures of sales, volume, gross margin, profit contribution, reduced cost of selling, direct product costs, financial returns, market share in product category, trading objectives (for example product quality, customer satisfaction, and measures of competitive advantage). Table 15.2 summarizes the potential role of category management teams and shows extensive range of data collection and co-operation. Relationship management and resource is key.

Table 15.2   **The role of category management teams**

Analysis	Understanding	Project work	Strategy/action
Sales	All trade customers	Assess possible projects	Competitive
DPP			Supply chain
Profit gross/ margin	Retailer's consumer profiles	Prioritize objectives	In-store trading
Market research	Space allocation within retailers	Set objectives	NPD
Fair share of trade		Allocate resources	Ranging
Lost expenditure	Products within category	Complete projects	
Promotions		Assess results	
SWOT analysis by category supplier/retailer		Draw up plans	
Demographics			
Loyalty/ propensity			

Source: Institute of Grocery Distribution, 1995, p. 61

If one of the objectives of category management is to better satisfy consumer needs then the retailer and supplier can work together to understand the consumer as a means to understanding the category. Consumer information is central to category management and some of the information required is shown in Table 15.3.

Consumers shop different categories in different ways. Some are functional and the shopper sees the process as a chore. Others are emotional. Both needs should be explored and acknowledged.

The fact that category management is being driven in UK by retailers, and in particular by food retailers is a reflection of the changing power in the channel of distribution. A few retailers control access to the consumers. Through factors such as concentration and saturation among retailers, changing consumers and shopping habits, and a recognition by both retailers and suppliers that there are mutual benefits for both parties, retailers and suppliers are working together in a way that might have been unimaginable 15 years ago.

THE HAIRCARE CATEGORY

Natural, healthy, glossy looking hair is what everyone wants and value appears to be the key (*The Grocer*, 1997).

This has combined with technically innovative products and a growing market. The £940m haircare category includes shampoo, conditioner, hairspray,

Table 15.3   **What category managers need to know about consumers**

Macro research	Micro research
Why a particular retailer?	What motivates a product purchase?
What draws a consumer to a store?	How are products seen on shelf?
How do purchasers shop outlets?	How do consumers react to promotional activity?
What identifies a category?	Where are the category hotspots?
Are all aisles shopped?	How do actual purchases compare to intended purchases?
	What products are key to consumers within categories?
	What are the consumer demographics?
	How can the consumers be classified?

Source: IGD, 1995, p. 114

colourants and styling aids. The market is intensely competitive with a constant stream of new entrants, resulting in a fragmented market. Major mass market shampoo brands have introduced high performance products. The shampoo market has a yearly growth of 11 per cent. The colourant market has also grown – 34 per cent between 1992 and 1996, with continual product improvement and ease of application and is the fastest growing market. Growth is expected to continue (*Checkout*, April 1997).

Technology is the driving force in the category and brand loyalty low in some areas. While the grocery trade is benefiting from the shampoo and conditioner sales, colourant sales are dominated by chemists.

Table 15.4 shows the subcategories in the total haircare category.

Table 15.4   **Retail sales of women's haircare products 1997**

	1997 £m	1997 %	1995–97 % change
Shampoos	268	35	+6
Styling products	230	30	+7
Conditioners	133	17	+10
Hair colourants	125	16	+23
Home perms	9	1	−25
Total	765	100	+9

Source: Mintel, 1998

It can be seen from Table 15.4 that haircare is dominated by Procter and Gamble, Elida Fabergé and own-label. Bristol-Myers' Clairol brand is number 10, but with significant per cent change.

Table 15.5   Top ten haircare brands by value sales (year ending November 1997)

Product/brand	Manufacturer	Value (£m)	Change %
1. Pantene Pro-V unisex shampoo	Procter and Gamble	50.25	+10
2. Unisex shampoo	Own-label	40.60	−3
3. Organic unisex shampoo	Elida Fabergé	25.05	−10
4. Pantene Pro-V unisex conditioner	Procter and Gamble	24.22	+6
5. Head and Shoulders unisex shampoo	Procter and Gamble	24.11	+4
6. Unisex conditioner	Own-label	21.47	−1
7. Pantene Pro-V unisex hairspray	Procter and Gamble	19.14	+60
8. Unisex hairspray	Own-label	16.68	0
9. Elnett unisex hairspray	L'Oréal	16.47	−1
10. Clairol Nice 'N' Easy	Bristol-Myers	15.81	+12

Source: IRI InfoScan in *Checkout* February 1998, p. 28

From dominance in the hair colourant subcategory, Bristol-Myers are now starting to move into the total haircare market, one dominated by major market players, such as Procter and Gamble, Elida Fabergé (Unilever) and L'Oréal. This move has been facilitated by successful NPD, consumer understanding and the building of trust in relationships with retailers.

In the subcategory of hair colourants the leading players are Clairol (Bristol-Myers Squibb), L'Oréal (including Garnier), Wella and Alberto Culver. The companies have a portfolio of brands targeted at different haircare sectors. (Mintel, 1998). The manufacturers' shares are shown in Table 15.6.

Table 15.6   Hair colourants: manufacturers' shares 1995 and 1997

	1995		1997 (est)		1995–97
	£m	%	£m	%	% change
Clairol	35	34	41	33	+17
L'Oréal	27	26	34	27	+26
Garnier	8	8	13	10	+63
Wella	8	8	10	8	+25
Alberto Culver	4	4	5	4	+25
Elida Fabergé	4	4	4	3	–
Other brands	8	8	9	7	+13
Own-label	8	8	10	8	+25
Total	102	100	125	100	+23

Source: Mintel, 1998

Data may not equal totals due to rounding

Recent media attention on couture fashion shows has influenced the hair colourant market in the return to a more glamorous look with increased emphasis on colour. Home care colouring has been a beneficiary of this trend, with hair colourant manufacturers positioning wash-out colourants as a fashion accessory to be used in much the same way as a cosmetic. For example, Wella's Shaders and Toners target the young fashion conscious teenager who wants to change the colour of her hair without the commitment to a longer lasting product. Women aged 35–54 also represent a key target group for products aimed at covering grey. These are predicted to increase in numbers by 16 per cent between 1991 and 2001 (Mintel, 1998).

Permanents are the largest sector within the total colourants market, accounting for an estimated half of value sales in 1997, and buoyed by increasing numbers of women seeking a solution to greying hair. NPD has provided growth. The emphasis is on products which give a 'natural' look. Tone-on-tone colourants are taking share from semi-permanents, and, although a small sector, temporary colourants market is also growing. Research shows that consumers feel there is a risk attached to home colouring – that the product might go wrong (Mintel, 1998).

COMPETITORS IN HAIR COLOURANT SUBCATEGORY

The leading players in the subcategory of hair colourants are Clairol (Bristol-Myers-Squibb), L'Oréal (including Garnier), Wella and Alberto Culver. The companies have a portfolio of brands targeted at different haircare sectors. (Mintel, 1998). The manufacturers' shares are shown in Table 15.6.

Bristol-Myers (owners of Clairol) are hair colourant (33 per cent value share in 1997) market share leaders. In 1997 they introduced a simplified colour choice system which groups colourants according to how long they last. This is designed to help the consumer understand exactly how each colourant works and move away from manufacturer driven definitions such as permanents and semi-permanents Clairol has a portfolio of brands aimed at the different markets, and includes Nice 'N' Easy, the brand leader in permanent colourants. In 1997 they launched Hydrience, the first water-based permanent colourant.

L'Oréal competes under L'Oréal and Laboratoires Garnier house names. Recital is L'Oréal's largest brand and is the second largest permanent in the market. L'Oréal has also launched new brands in 1995 to 1997. Earlier, in 1993 they were one of the first companies to launch the tone-on-tone concept which claims long-lasting deep shine for up to 24 washes.

Wella replaced its long standing Colour Confidence permanent colourant from the market in 1997, replacing it with a longer lasting and fade resistant brand – Viva Colour. Viva Colour emphasis youthfulness and vitality rather than the benefit of covering grey. They also (1996) relaunched temporary hair colourant (Shaders and Toners) to appeal to the first time young fashion conscious consumer.

Alberto Culver developed its colourants business on the back of its VO5 haircare range, and in 1996 launched the first semi-permanent range to include both fashion shades and natural shades that cover grey. Alberto Culver has also developed a way to simplify colour choice.

Elida Fabergé's Harmony semi-permanent colourants have lost market share in recent years. The company has concentrated on other areas of haircare, notably the Organics range (Mintel, 1998).

The hair colourants market, believed to be worth £110m, is the second fastest growing sector among the top twenty health and beauty categories, and grew by 9.4 per cent in 1996. The multiples are not considered to have reached their full potential in this sector. Although the biggest sector is still the semi-permanents (41 per cent of total spend), it is in decline with consumers moving to demi-permanents. The growth is driven by young consumers who are independent, often bored with their appearance, and who like to experiment. Clairol leads all three sectors and is heavily supported with TV and women's press advertising. The two main players, Wella and Bristol-Myers are extending into the total haircare market with ranges of new products, and there is a constant stream of entrants into the market (*Checkout*, April, 1997; *Checkout Ireland*, June, 1997).

The level of advertising expenditure on haircare products has increased significantly in the past two years, including colourants which increased by +36 per cent change between 1995 and 1996. Overall the category increased by 23 per cent. Colourants was the second most advertised haircare category and accounted for 17.6 per cent of total advertising expenditure in 1996. L'Oréal and Clairol dominate advertising expenditure of hair colourants. They had a combined spend in 1996 of £10.7m (Mintel, 1998).

BRISTOL-MYERS AND CATEGORY MANAGEMENT

Like most other manufacturers, Bristol-Myers have embraced category management as a way of working more closely with trade customers in developing product categories, but focused on meeting consumer requirements. As part of this process, great emphasis is placed on understanding the consumer better. Influences on consumer making decision are shown in Figure 15.2.

With the help of the major retailers, a shopper research programme within each of the primary categories has been undertaken. This has given both the company and their retail partners a further insight into understanding how consumers perceive each category at the point of purchase and how they segment different products with each subcategory.

Bristol-Myers have a strong record of consumer research, and they use that understanding of the consumer to adopt a merchandising system to manage the category, and to define clear strategies for hair colourant category for each of the channels. The category is the total hair category, but of that hair colour is the largest percentage of their business. This strategy needs to address the issues of replenishment versus discovery or experimentation; the different

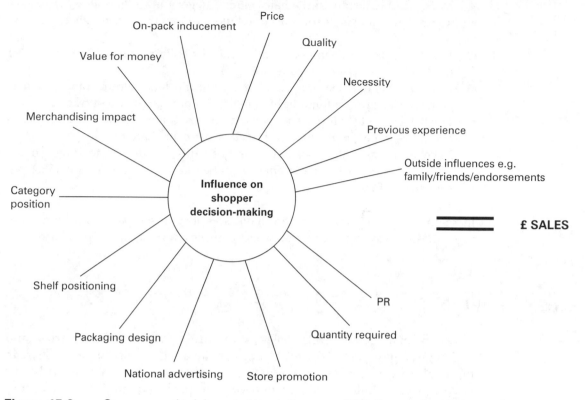

Figure 15.2 Consumer decision-making influences (IGD Research, 1995, p. 115)

goals of the different channel customers; the different ways consumers shop for haircare products, and in particular, given the risk and emotional elements attached to the use of hair colourants, the information needs at point of sale.

The use of other information, such as AGB panel data, retailer EPOS data and IRI market information and loyalty card data, augments the amount of knowledge available within the company and is put to use in developing strategies across each category within each trade channel.

The company has also had a global investment of the latest computerized space planning software and decision support tools in each market, which not only speeds the preparation of shelf layouts but also gives an added dimension to any proposed layouts as there is far greater depth of data behind each decision to stock selected products appropriate to the size of the store.

As a result of extensive consumer research, Clairol have developed an in-store merchandising system called the colour choice system (CCS). The rationale behind this initiative is to make the purchase of hair colour products less confusing, using a combination of on pack product information as well as point of sale material, it guides the consumer through the decision making process surrounding the colour effect she wants to achieve (that is, cover grey or enhance existing colour) and how long she wants it to last.

The system breaks down the hair colour category in to the following 'levels' and their merchandising proposals to retailers follow these criteria:

- **Level 0:** lasts 1–5 shampoos, adds tones of colour, will not cover grey or lighten hair (9.2 per cent share of trade).
- **Level 1:** lasts 6/8 shampoos, enhances natural hair colour, some products gently cover grey, will not lighten hair (13.5 per cent share of trade).
- **Level 2:** lasts 24 shampoos approximately, gradually washes away, enriches and adds shine, gently covers grey (18.1 per cent share of trade).
- **Level 3:** permanent – does not wash out, adds condition and shine, covers all grey, subtle or dramatic effects, can darken and lighten hair (53.4 per cent share of trade).

In many cases the major retailers have accepted this type of merchandising principle as a way of making things less complex at the point of purchase.

THE TASK AHEAD

Category management relationships require commitment and trust and exchange of information. Bristol-Myers, despite not having a dominant share in the total haircare category, have discovered that they do not have to be the largest player within a category, to become a 'preferred supplier' or category captain (that is, jointly lead the category with the retailer). However, they still need to establish firm relationships. This is illustrated by the following quotation from Ian Walters:

> The usual thing facing most manufacturers is getting trust and credibility with the retailer or wholesaler. It's not just about working with retailers. Getting retailers to share data with you is the usual problem, but you have to show credibility and that you are adding value to the total relationship. It's not just about the buyer-seller relationship. We see it as part of our job to develop contact beyond the buyer. We have a lot of influence with accounts where two years ago we did not. I guess it's sharing with the retailer our strategy and their sharing theirs with us. We are on the verge of developing what I would call true strategic alliances.

Expansion into the total haircare market brings Bristol-Myers up against market leaders as Proctor and Gamble, Elida Fabergé and L'Oréal. These companies are well entrenched and dominant in the shampoo and conditioner markets and in related markets where they are household names. Bristol-Myers are launching shampoo products, but because they are not market leaders in the overall category, there are issues of credibility with the trade.

We have clearly differentiated the product offering. We have developed a model of pre-, during-, and post-launch activities that we need to undertake and so we are now being taken seriously by the trade in both colour and haircare. The trade are receptive to our product launches. We are starting to have influence within the major accounts, especially health and beauty. They want our advice and to share our knowledge. We share our findings with our trade customer. (Ian Walters, Trade Marketing Manager, Bristol-Myers)

In early 1998 Ian Walters considered the 50 pages of Shopper Research data on his desk, and how it might help him in his meeting the following week with his boss, the director of trade marketing. The data had been expensive to acquire and was only part of the story he had to tell. Ian had come from Nestlé just over a year ago. In the space of a year he had had to adapt from a company that had dominant market share and brand leadership in the category he managed, to another global player like Bristol-Myers, but in a very different marketplace. It was sometimes difficult for him to remember that Bristol-Myers had some way to go before achieving dominance in the overall haircare category. The rules were different to those he had been used to at Nestlé, and the decisions he now made would determine the part he would play in shaping the colour and haircare category over the short and medium term.

Ian's research had confirmed other research including greater interest in toiletry shopping than food shopping. It also confirmed the consumer behaviour evidence that within the toiletry categories functional products such as soap and toothpaste were seen as functional, boring family shopping. At the other end of the continuum was perfumes and make-up. Hair colourants were in the middle, along with shampoos. It also confirmed the general perception that supermarket shopping for toiletries was all about convenience and speed, and limited choice, whereas health and beauty retailer shopping for toiletries was perceived as a special trip with a relaxed, browsing mindset, emotional rather than functional, with range, expertise and value.

Consumers felt that hair colouring was important, with emotional needs paramount, notably self-expression. However, functional needs could not be ignored, including the process and the affect on the hair. Consumers used different hair colourants depending on their needs, for example to completely change their colour (permanent colour), to enhance natural colour (semi-permanents) and greys (semi to permanent). Hair colourants were an emotional/high level purchase for all groups.

When replenishing the same product the multiples were used (along with health and beauty retailers). However, for first timers, discovery purchasers, health and beauty outlets were most likely. Here the relaxed, browsing element was important.

One issue that Ian had to address was the perception that consumers saw displays as confusing, difficult to engage with, and failing to deliver to emotional needs. This applied to all channels. Sales could only be maximized if information needs were addressed to reduce risk and fulfil emotional needs. Ian had the information technology, and good category management teams.

Ian considered the latest penetration figures for the hair colourant subcategory that had just landed on his desk that morning (opportune, given the importance of the meeting next week). They showed Boots in the lead with penetration of 30 per cent, closely followed by Superdrug with 25 per cent. The four major grocers between them accounted for 20 per cent penetration, with Asda leading them, primarily due to their everyday low pricing policy (and with expectations of dramatic growth in the subcategory), but closely followed by Tesco and Sainsbury. The total penetration for Bristol-Myers was 33 per cent with the number of buyers increasing and average expenditure increasing. So, the prognosis was good for the subcategory.

In the less certain area of total toiletries the evidence showed that the multiples were continuing to take share; their customer shopping frequency was growing; and, loyalty was up in all multiples except Asda. Perhaps the most interesting piece of news was that Boots appeared to have lost a million customers to Tesco and Sainsbury but the customers they were retaining were spending more. The battle ahead, for all, was for more buyers and for increasing loyalty.

Like all category managers Ian knew that relationships with the retailers was at the heart of his task, but, in his marketplace he had three different groups of customers to manage: the independent pharmacists, the grocers such as Tesco, Sainsbury, Asda, Safeway and Waitrose, and the real drivers of the category – Boots and Superdrug. Bristol-Myers had developed a strategy for each of the trade channels, based on shopper research and relationship building with the retailers. Ian felt that he had good relationships with key players, especially in the multiple grocer and health and beauty channels. But he also had to decide where the real growth lay. He had to make sense between the blurring line between the grocers and the health and beauty retailers. Nor could he afford to write off the independent pharmacists. The three channels required different skills and relationships and, of course, budget allocations. He and his team had to manage and optimize these relationships. Where, he wondered, did his priorities lie. He had meetings schedules with Boots and Superdrug and the four grocers in the coming weeks. He would have to be clear before meeting them.

Bristol-Myers were making an aggressive bid for leadership of the total haircare category. They were launching new products across the total category. The goal was to reinforce their position in the market with new and relevant products, and to utilize the strong R&D from their parent company in the USA. Thirty-five per cent of Bristol-Myers haircare turnover in the UK was from products that did not exist two years ago. But they were facing fierce competition, and a threat from a new international entrant.

Ian had now to decide where to start and how to put the case to his boss.

QUESTIONS

1. Consider the overall marketplace for haircare products. What are the trends? Where is the growth likely to come from, which retailer(s), which consumers?

2. Analyse the competition in the haircare market? How do you think they would react to aggressive moves from Bristol-Myers?

3. Given their dominance in the hair colourant sub-category what do you think are the chances of Bristol-Myers gaining a major role in the total haircare category?

4. Within the hair colourant category what are the three major retail segments? How do they differ? Which do you consider to be the most important segment for Bristol-Myers? How would Bristol-Myer's trade marketing strategies differ for each segment?

5. What is the role of category management in relationships between Bristol-Myers and the retailers? How important do you think it is in the relationship building process? Why?

6. What implications does the shopper research have for how the category should be managed?

7. How might Ian Walters use his expertise in category management and the results of the shopper survey to further his ambitions to become 'preferred supplier' for the total haircare category?

8. Propose an outline plan for the next 12 months that Ian Walters might present to the director of trade marketing.

REFERENCES

Checkout (1997) Health and Beauty Category Report. April, p. 34.
Checkout (1998) Toiletries Category Report. February, p. 30.
Checkout Ireland (1997) Special Report: Body Care. June, p. 48.
Food Pocket Book (The) (1997). NTC Publications, p. 96.
Grocer (The) (1997) 'The Grocer focus on haircare'. 15 Nov, p. 40.
IBM (1997) 'Retail: the way forward', *Retail Week*, London.
IGD (1995) *The Category Management Revolution*. Watford: IGD Publication.
Mintel (1998) Hair Colourants and Home Perms, *Market Intelligence*. February.
Retail Week (1997) 11 July, p. 12.
Retail Pocket Book (The) (1998) A. C. Nielsen/NTC Publications, p. 66.

HALFORDS MOTOR OILS (A): A CASE OF SUCCESS BY DESIGN

MALCOLM KIRKUP, PAUL WALLEY AND JOHN TEMPERLEY

The authors would like to thank Halfords, Pentagram and Plysu Containers UK for their support in developing this case study. In particular we are grateful for the contributions provided by Chris Forman, Peter Foskett and John Tofts.

The information in this case study, while believed to be largely accurate, is based on the memory of those involved and compiled from a variety of sources. It has also been simplified in order to focus on key learning objectives for students of management. For these reasons, the material should not be regarded as a totally factual account of events or views.

INTRODUCTION

In 1996 and 1997 Halfords won widespread praise and top awards for the launch of their new range of own-label motor oils. In the 1997 Retail Week Awards, Halfords was judged winner of the category 'New Product Launch of the Year':

> In a sector dominated by brand names and aggressive price competition, the judges were overwhelming in their admiration for the way that a retailer had taken the initiative and demonstrated real innovation. The judges commended the way that Halfords had really brought something to the consumer experience from packaging to merchandising. Here was a retailer actually teaching brands something. (*Retail Week*, 1997)

The redesign and repositioning resulted in a range that offered high technical quality, clear range segmentation, unique and customer-friendly packaging, competitive pricing and effective marketing communication. The financial results underline the commercial success of the range. One year after launch Halfords were reporting average product prices across the range up 12 per cent, a 19 per cent increase in sales volume, 44 per cent increase in sales value and 54 per cent increase in margin. Halfords own-brand increased its share of total oil sales in-store from 22 per cent to 30 per cent. Halfords Premium saw a 60 per cent increase in sales value and 90 per cent in profitability. Halfords brand share in the UK motor oil market increased from 6 per cent in 1996 to 12 per cent in 1997.

This case study is the first of two cases which consider the development of the Halfords new oil range. This case considers the background to the project, the company's objectives and the process of research and concept design. The second case focuses on aspects of the design and manufacture of the oil containers. Both cases draw on a series of interviews with managers from Halfords, the Pentagram design agency and Plysu Containers UK, and documentation provided by these companies.

HALFORDS

Halfords is part of The Boots Company. Halfords has been established for over 90 years, and is the largest UK retailer of car parts and accessories, cycles and cycle accessories, with 411 stores in 1997. Halfords is also the largest garage servicing organization in the country – 135 of its outlets offer a maintenance service including full diagnostics and repair. Since 1995 the company has also developed an alliance with Daewoo – an innovative concept involving the promotion, servicing and repair of Daewoo cars in Halfords garages (Boots, 1995).

The majority of Halfords outlets (66 per cent) are superstores located out of town. In 1996/97 28 new superstores were opened and 20 high street stores closed. The company's strategy at this time was:

> to expand aggressively, repositioning itself from high streets to superstores to meet consumers' preference for wide choice and their view of Halfords as a destination store. (Boots, 1997)

Turnover in 1996/97 rose to £412.8m, an increase of £22.3m on 1995/96. Sales growth of 2.4 per cent in existing stores plus sales through new outlets produced the overall increase of 5.7 per cent. In 1996/97 the highest proportion of sales turnover came from auto accessories, tools and audio (47 per cent), with cycles and cycle accessories accounting for 27 per cent, car parts 16 per cent, and garage servicing 10 per cent. Margins increased strongly, notably through a substantial increase in own-brand sales, and operating profit in 1996/97 reached £26.8m (21.3 per cent up on the previous year).

The business is exploiting the significant potential for own-brand products. Own-brand accounted for 42 per cent of sales in 1996/97, up from 35 per cent in 1995/96. This strong growth was driven by the continuing expansion of the Halfords car parts range and the new range of own-brand motor oils – the aim always being 'to achieve an equivalent quality to original equipment or leading brands, at value for money prices'. The Halfords own-brand is a key strategic cornerstone for the business, and further development and innovation is planned to build the brand credentials and leverage performance.

Motor Oil

Motor oil is sold in a wide variety of retail outlets – car accessory stores, garage forecourts, supermarkets and DIY stores. Halfords is the country's leading retailer of motor oil with a 20 per cent market share, three times more than its nearest competitor. The most popular oil brand sold is Castrol (with over 30 per cent brand share) followed by Duckhams. In 1996 the Halfords own-label range had around 6 per cent brand share.

Motor oil is sold in standard five-litre and one-litre containers, and each manufacturer usually offers a range of different grades of oil to suit different types of engine, ages of engine, or different driving conditions. Castrol for example offer GTX Improved Formula, GTX Protection Plus, GTX Magnatec, RS Synthetic, GTD Diesel and RX Super Diesel. Different grades of oil differ in the quantity and performance of the 'additives' they contain (for example detergents, neutralizing agents, dispersents). Different additives and quality lead to differences in oil consumption, engine wear, fuel efficiency and cold start protection.

Grades of oil differ particularly in their 'viscosity' and the viscosity value is featured prominently on packaging to guide consumers on the correct oil for their car. Viscosity is a measure of an oil's thickness or thinness and its ability to be pumped around an engine under both cold start and hot running conditions. A grade of 15W/50, for example, specifies the viscosity of 15 in cold winter (W) and 50 at running temperature. Higher viscosity oils like this are suitable for older cars or cars with high mileage, but newer cars are designed to run on thinner oils.

TIME TO CHANGE THE OIL

In 1995 Halfords offered a range of oils that included proprietary brands (Duckhams, Castrol and Mobil) alongside Halfords own-brand offer – Multigrade, XP7 and XP7i (see Figures 16.1 and 16.2). The range was merchandised into five groups of oil – standard old, standard new, premium, diesel and synthetic. In addition, but merchandised separately, Halfords offered a non-branded 'Power Oil' as a price-defender to compete with the low price ranges sold by supermarkets and DIY stores. Halfords did not offer an own-brand version of diesel or synthetic oil.

All product ranges within Halfords are reviewed annually. In early 1995 a product range review was undertaken for motor oils, chiefly involving Chris Forman, Buying Controller for the Auto Business Centre, and Simon Price, Buyer/Product Manager for motor oils. Chris observed:

> In terms of the performance of the range there were no real problems – we were in line with general market performance and we had 6 per cent brand share. However, we felt there were actually significant opportunities to increase sales

Merchandise Category	Halfords Own-brand	Retail Price	Castrol Brand	Retail Price*	Duckhams Brand	Retail Price*
Value	Power Oil 20W/50	£3.99	–	–	–	–
Standard Old	Multigrade 20W/50	£5.99	GTX 15W/50	£9.99	Hypergrade 15W/50	£9.99
Standard New	XP7 15W/40	£8.99	GTX2 15W/40	£12.99	Hypergrade Plus 15W/40	£12.99
Premium	XP7i 10W/40	£13.99	GTX3 10W/40	£17.99	QXR 10W/40	£18.99
Diesel	–	–	GTD 15W/40	£12.99	Diesel 15W/40	£10.99
Synthetic	–	–	RS 10W/60	£24.99	QS 5W/40	£22.99

Figure 16.1   Main brands in Halfords oil range in 1995

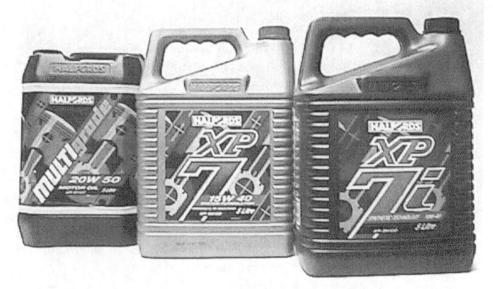

Figure 16.2   The starting point – Halfords existing oil container

and profit growth by improving the own-brand range. Profit growth for Halfords was being constrained by a powerful brand leader.

Their review of market characteristics and trends included a number of significant observations:

■ The UK motor oil market is highly competitive and price aggressive. Volumes have been declining over the past 15 years due to better engines, longer service intervals, cleaner fuels and more sophisticated lubricants, despite an increase in the number of cars sold.

■ The decline in volume sales has been compensated by an increase in the total value of oil sold, due to new product development, improved oil technology and market segmentation introducing specialist lubricants to meet the needs of modern cars. The premium end of the market has therefore become more important and offers new opportunities.

■ The Halfords brand of oil in 1995 was perceived by consumers as offering value for money in terms of price and quality but was not regarded in the same quality league as the main proprietary brands (for example Castrol and Duckhams).

■ The market is characterized by confused customers with limited understanding of motor oil technology. Few consumers can explain the difference between oil grades, or terms such as viscosity, and many make their choice on the basis of habit or price. Despite attempts by the main brand manufacturers to raise the importance of oil and to emphasize the importance of the right grade of oil for each car, an imbalance still exists between the amount of 'standard' oil purchased by customers (75 per cent) and the number of cars on the road that need it (50 per cent). The implication is that a quarter of cars, at least, are receiving the wrong oil.

■ The consumer has low involvement with the oil 'product'. The consumer cannot immediately 'feel' the benefit of new oil in a car, and the only direct contact with oil is when pouring takes place. From the marketer's point of view this stage therefore has to be right for the consumer. Factors such as handling, pouring, spillage, reuse of the container, and instructions can become critical to creating the feel of a quality product.

The buying team felt significant benefits could be gained by redesigning and repositioning the Halfords own-brand range. There was scope to improve Halfords own market position by upgrading the Halfords brand as a serious alternative to the brand leaders. This would add value to the business and establish a competitive advantage.

The buying team submitted their proposals for redesign and repositioning to the Halfords design management group. This group of directors, including an external design consultant, oversees all new Halfords-brand design work across the business, protects the integrity of the brand, and advises on the recruitment of design agencies. The project was swiftly approved and underway by March 1995.

OBJECTIVES AND STRATEGIES

The marketing objectives focused on the need both to increase sales and achieve a more profitable mix. Specifically, the company sought to increase the perceived value of the Halfords brand and the sales of the new Halfords range of oils. The company also wanted to change the mix of oil sales (of both Halfords and proprietary brands) towards premium (higher margin) products by improving customer understanding of the segmentation, and to increase the overall share of their profitable Halfords own-brand oils against lower margin proprietary brands. The launch was planned for spring 1996.

There were a number of elements to the new product range being developed:

- Halfords brand offer was to be extended to include diesel and, eventually, synthetic oil. The initial range would be Standard, Standard Plus, Premium and Diesel. Synthetic oil would be launched one year later. Synthetic oil sales represented a relatively small proportion of Halfords oil sales mix. Furthermore, the Halfords oil brand had traditionally been a price-led alternative. Synthetic oil was a more specialist and high premium offer, and the team felt it more appropriate to launch synthetic oil once consumer confidence and perceptions had been uplifted in the new repositioned brand.

- The oil quality was to be upgraded. Halfords recognized from the outset that it would be very difficult for them to improve on the quality of oil marketed by the leading proprietary brands, and so their commercial objective was to sell a new range that was 'as good as' the market leaders. This required upgrading the formulation quality of their oil to match the API (American Petroleum Institute) ratings of leading brands. This was a straightforward part of the product relaunch. Halfords invited the major oil producers to tender for the contract to supply the new oil, chose two different companies to supply the different grades, and negotiated to secure the right oil specification at the best cost price.

- Given the difficulty of differentiating on product quality, Halfords' main energies focused instead on designing a container that provided significant added value benefits to consumers. The old style packaging had to be changed if consumer perceptions and understanding of the product were to be improved. Halfords decided to deploy creative design to develop innovative product benefits that would exceed industry standards and differentiate the brand.

- An effective communication strategy would be required to help consumers make an informed choice of oil grade and understand the benefits of Halfords oil. The team felt they could remove some of the confusion felt by consumers, through better communication. They had already taken some steps to categorize their oil range to help consumers (see Figure 16.1), but it had not noticeably changed buying patterns. More effective communication would be in the interests of consumers and their cars, but would also benefit Halfords as customers traded up.

PROJECT PLANNING AND ORGANIZATION

The buying team had around 12 months to complete the project and deliver the new range to stores. Chris Forman, as Buying Controller for the Auto Business Centre, was overall project manager.

Chris explained the organization behind the project:

The whole project involved a major team effort. Within the company we had a team of managers involved, and externally we needed a large team of suppliers to help us achieve our objectives. At Halfords I was closely supported by Simon Price, the buyer, who had particular responsibility for negotiations with the oil and packaging suppliers. The marketing team in the Auto Business Centre looked after advertising, PR, and in-store merchandising. We had to work together to ensure consistency between the packaging and the other marketing communication elements. We had technical support from our quality manager who guided us on issues such as manufacturing processes when we were dealing with suppliers. Later in the project we also worked closely with our logistics department in forecasting and planning stock requirements and deliveries to stores.

In terms of external organizations, a critical role was played by the Pentagram design agency. Pentagram were chosen to take on the role of overall 'concept creators' – to design the main structure and form of the new containers. In addition, however, they also contributed significantly to project management. Chris Forman explained:

Pentagram, through Peter Foskett, acted as project advisor, developing and revising the project schedules and helping keep the timing of the project on track. Pentagram also brought their extensive experience of other design and engineering projects from other industries. Their knowledge and problem-solving skills helped us push harder for what we wanted to achieve with the suppliers, and they were particularly involved on our behalf in the technical discussions with the cap manufacturers and the bottle moulder.

A second design agency, Lippa Pearce, took on responsibility for the packaging graphics (labelling and colour). Consumer research to test the new concept was commissioned from Baughman Associates. A patent agent was required, initially to search existing patents to ensure Halfords were not infringing on any other designs on the market, and later to register design aspects of the new Halfords container. Two suppliers were contracted to produce the oil and to fill the containers. The containers themselves were to be manufactured by a blow-moulder Blowmocan Ltd (the industrial division of which was acquired by Plysu Containers UK in 1996), who had been supplying Halfords' own-brand oil containers since the late 1980s. A tool-maker was required to design and produce the blowmoulding machinery to be used by Blowmocan. Cap makers were required to supply closures for the containers.

Masterbatch manufacturers were required to supply the plastic and colour pigment for the containers. Other suppliers were required to print labels and to produce cartons for palletizing the containers for transit. As the products arrived in-store, further specialist agencies were planned to support internal and external marketing.

Chris planned to hold regular meetings with all the key suppliers present. He planned to keep key suppliers fully exposed to the marketing and research issues as the project progressed, to keep everyone informed and focused. Given the timescale and number of organizations involved, and the strategic importance of the project, sound management and control of the process was vital.

CONCEPT DESIGN

The Halfords buying team developed a detailed design brief for Pentagram. Peter Foskett noted that:

> It was the most detailed brief we had ever seen and showed that Halfords really knew their customer. It was extremely helpful in focusing our mind on the key consumer and commercial requirements. It was also gratifying to see that Halfords understood the value of design. We didn't have to sell what design could do for them – they came with an enthusiastic expectation.

The design had to stick to market convention and focus on a five-litre and one-litre container. The cost of the new containers had to be kept in the same proportion to the cost of product as the existing Halfords containers. However, the design objectives required that the new packaging should equal or exceed proprietary brands. The design had to produce real visual impact when on display, communicate effectively, and demonstrate design flair and aesthetic appeal. The container and graphics had to work in harmony. Halfords wanted distinctive added value benefits in the packaging to differentiate Halfords new 'added value' range – for example, to address consumer requirements for improved pouring and less leakage and spillage. The new range also had to reflect the brand values of quality, value for money, trust and confidence consistent with Halfords' reputation.

Peter Foskett outlines the design process:

> We divided the process into four stages – concept design, design development, detailed design and implementation. It helps structure the work and the client can appreciate more clearly what is involved.

> Concept design began with an 'exploration' phase – researching the oil market and competition, and brainstorming to explore the issues in oil packaging and the benefits sought by consumers – for example in handling, pouring and reducing spillage. We also examined numerous existing competing oil containers. The whole design team threw in ideas and we explored as many

conceptual routes as possible to seek a novel solution. Our emphasis throughout was on the five-litre container given the number of these sold by Halfords, but we had to ensure there could be a family resemblance to spring off to the one-litre container. In generating ideas, consideration was given to style and aesthetics, handling and ergonomics, ease of filling for the oil company, ease of manufacture, ease of transporting, plus uniqueness and shelf-impact. We generated hundreds of ideas and drawings – t-bar grips to help with pouring, hexagonal containers to enable tessellating in bulk storage and shelf-presentation, churn-like containers to mimic the old fashioned oil jugs, and even a shape that resembled a car wheel (see Figure 16.3). We constructed basic models of containers to test different positions for handles and spouts and eventually moved to foam card models to assess container volume and mass' (see Figure 16.4).

We generated 12 designs, and we utilized the quality function deployment technique to help evaluate the designs against 15 criteria covering aspects of handling, production, distribution, style and aesthetics. Our designers scored each design on each concept and from this evaluation we were able to guide Halfords on how the concepts compared and identify the preferred designs. To help Halfords make their choice we presented solid models of the three leading concepts (see Figure 16.5) and incorporated the preliminary graphic designs prepared by Lippa Pearce.

Chris Forman reflected on the first Pentagram presentation:

I understand it was rare for them to show a client so many designs. They clearly felt there were some unique elements in all of them, and they wanted to show us the process they followed. I was impressed. We hadn't worked with Pentagram before and they convinced us they had taken a systematic approach. They didn't just design 'creative' concepts – they designed things that worked. Interestingly we didn't go for the solution that scored the highest on Pentagram's analysis. We went for the most 'unique' design of the three they recommended. It was a bold decision but it was absolutely right – a unique design is more difficult to copy and offered us some clear differentiation in the market.

Design Development

This next stage for Pentagram was to refine the chosen concept, and looked at issues such as comfort, the detail of the handle profile and the development of the cap. Hollow models were developed to more realistically test pouring and handling. These models also allowed the oil producers to see how they would run on a filling-line. The deliverable from this stage was working drawings of the containers and the production of coloured and labelled mock-ups for the planned consumer research.

The chosen design can be seen in Figure 16.6. The handle was on the front face of the can, with a relatively deep undercut behind for ease of grip. The user could lower the spout considerably nearer to the engine before the oil begins to pour – making pouring easier and reducing spillage. The concept design also featured a 'visi-strip' down the centre to indicate the oil level. There was debate over the choice of cap for the container. Two alternative ideas were developed – a flip-cap and a screw-cap – both to be tamper- and leak-proof. The flip-cap was unique and would offer major differentiation. The screw-cap was conventional but had the benefit of established reliability.

Pentagram liaised closely with Lippa Pearce in refining the graphics. Lippa Pearce were seeking to enhance the form and shape of the container, and provide labelling that would help consumers make an informed choice about

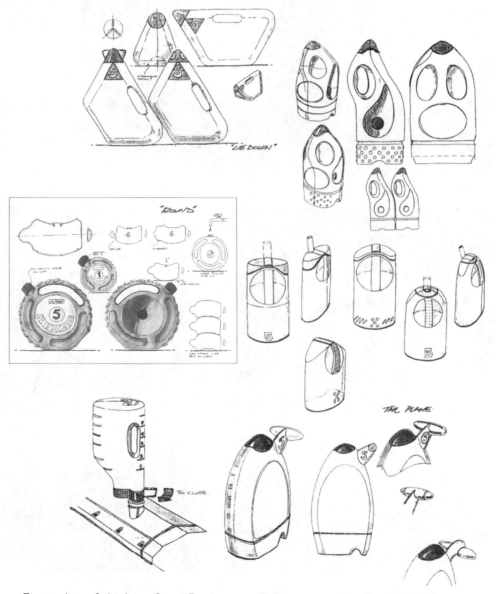

Figure 16.3   Examples of designs from Pentagram © Pentagram Design 1995/96

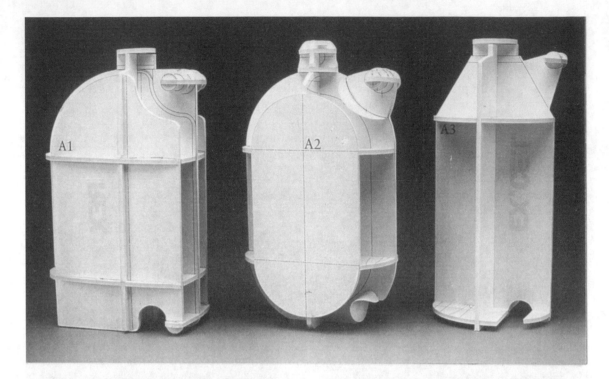

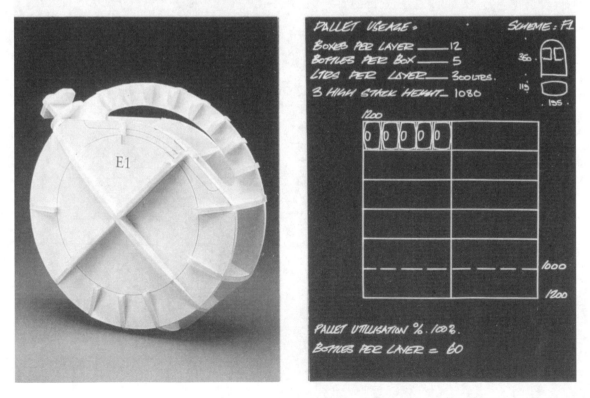

Figure 16.4   Early modelling during the design process © Pentagram Design 1995

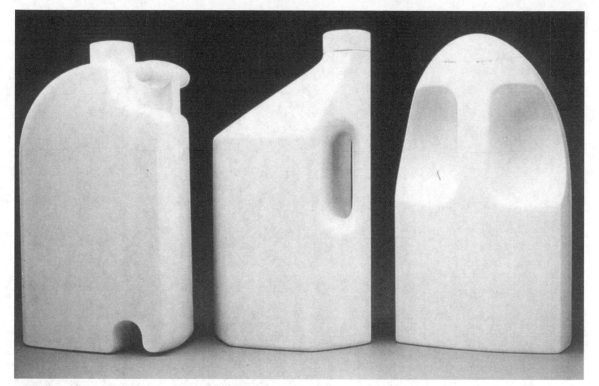

Figure 16.5   Solid models of the leading concepts presented by Pentagram to Halfords
© Pentagram Design 1995

the oil grade most appropriate for their car. Different coloured containers were proposed for each grade of oil. The graphics adopted an information-led approach, taking a visual direction from the type of information panels found in cars to give a feeling of technology and quality. Information on the front of the container was to be simple and limited – viscosity, grade of oil, a description of cars for which that grade is suitable, and a brief statement noting the special formulations suited to particular cars and mileages. Information of secondary importance was to be on the reverse of the pack – an explanation to help consumers interpret the technical grade, oil change tips, safety and environ- mental warnings, list of the Halfords range, instructions on how to use the cap, the API rating, company address and bar code.

Research

Consumer research was commissioned in May 1995 to explore consumer purchasing behaviour in the sector and, in particular, to further improve the design proposals by probing consumer reactions, needs and opportunities. Baughman Associates were asked to conduct seven extended focus groups. From previous research Halfords had identified that their auto business

Figure 16.6   The design concept for the new containers

attracted three main customer types – 'car enthusiasts' (the grease monkey), 'driver-dabblers' and 'light users'. Two separate focus groups were therefore held with each segment. Three groups were held in the north and three in the south, all with male consumers. One all-female focus group was also held to consider whether female attitudes varied from male.

The research confirmed perceptions of the main oil brands. In the north, Halfords were placed in the 'middle quality' band, below brands like Castrol and Duckhams but alongside own-brand oils sold by car accessory retailers such as Charlie Brown and Motor World. In the south, Halfords were placed alongside the lower quality supermarket and DIY brands.

The research confirmed confusion and lack of understanding among consumers when purchasing motor oils (see Figure 16.7). Factors influencing the choice of brand and grade included the degree of assurance the consumer needs, perceived quality (created by brand or retailer reputation), price and convenience. Premium oil users might be motivated by the age of their vehicle, a sense of responsibility to maintain a new or more expensive car, or through affection for their car. Middle quality oil users might be seeking adequate protection and reassurance but at a lower price. Lower quality oil users might select on price or convenience. The research suggested limited brand loyalty, and many of those few who do regularly buy a similar brand appear to do it out of habit rather than a belief that their choice is superior or ideal for their car. However, the research observed that consumers are often loyal to a particular grade of oil – to ensure consistency in the type used – and will switch between brands depending on convenience and price on a given occasion.

The research evaluated various product segmentation systems used by oil manufacturer brands and their communication messages. These included the use of colour-coding for different oils, segmentation of oils into 'type of car' categories, and also the use of chart-based engine-specific guides. The Halfords classification proposals (see Table 16.1) were presented anonymously to the consumer groups and were welcomed as 'short, sweet and to the point'. The proposed colour-coding scheme was seen as helpful to distinguish clearly between oil grades.

Consumers were presented with two block-models of the container – one with a flip-cap and one with a screw-cap. The container shape was described variously as *modern, sculptured, expensive, different, impressive, eye catching*, and *quality*. Some consumers instantly appreciated the advantage of the shape for ease of pouring – even before handling the container. The flip-cap was well-received – some consumers suggested it would pour better, although they sought reassurances on leakage, spillage and how it could be re-used for old oil. The consumers spontaneously noticed the visi-strip on the handle and noted it was in an ideal place. They liked the proposed green (premium) and silver (synthetic) colours for the container, and the metallic treatment was seen as enhancing the impression of quality. The proposed yellow for the Standard Plus Oil, however, was viewed as looking 'cheap'. One group of consumers in the south of England favoured a more traditional choice of colourway (white) for the main types of oil. The consumers welcomed the proposed label content on

What type of oil do you usually buy?

- 'Usually the cheapest.'

- 'The guy who services my car tells me to use 20/50 – I don't know much about oil apart from that.'

- 'I buy one of those synthetic oils – I probably pay more than I have to.'

- 'I've always bought Duckhams. I don't know which one – it costs about a tenner.'

- 'I use Esso. I wouldn't buy the one for £20 – the one in the middle is good enough for me.'

- 'I suppose the more expensive ones are purer.'

- 'I don't know much about oil so I use Castrol. It's been around for years so it must be good.'

Figure 16.7   Examples of consumer attitudes to purchasing motor oils

the container, but felt there was also a need for a strong 'quality' statement to emphasize the comparability with leading brands.

The focus groups showed that the new packaging successfully moved Halfords Motor Oil up the hierarchy of brands. The consumers saw the new design moving Halfords to the top of the middle quality brands and superior (in the north) to Charlie Brown and Motor World.

Following the focus groups, the buying team commissioned further research to identify a powerful quality statement, particularly as comparability was a key element in the Halfords brand positioning. Chris Forman explains:

Table 16.1   **Halfords classification system for own-brand oils**

Standard of oil	Final colour of packaging	Use
Standard	Red	For older cars with high mileage (over 78,000 miles)
Standard Plus	Blue	For all modern cars with average mileage up to 12,000 miles p.a.
Premium	Green	For fuel injected, multi-valve and turbo charged engines and modern cars averaging more than 12,000 miles p.a. including diesel
Fully Synthetic	Silver	For high performance cars and for demanding driving conditions
Diesel	Black	For all diesel and turbo diesel cars and vans averaging up to 12,000 miles p.a.

Six alternative statements were developed for testing, and consumer interviews were held in a Halfords store to identify the most powerful phrases. The choice of statement also had to take into account legal requirements, and we also consulted with our oil suppliers who market their own oil ranges – clearly we didn't want to upset the very suppliers we were trying to build relationships with. A clear and effective quality statement was important to us because it was part of generating 'confidence' – we were trying to maximize impact, minimize conflict and maximize consumer understanding.

DETAIL DESIGN AND IMPLEMENTATION

Pentagram's involvement continued with their final two stages of the design process. The detail design stage involved incorporating the results of the research and refining the design for manufacture. Colours could be adjusted in conjunction with the masterbatch suppliers, the metallic finishes could be perfected, and the labelling artwork finalized (Figure 16.8). During June and July of 1995 Pentagram worked with the manufacturers to refine technical details and produce engineering drawings.

Pentagram's final involvement was to be during the 'implementation' stage as the manufacturers and suppliers prepared for production. As Peter Foskett noted:

> Our job doesn't finish with the drawings. We want to ensure that what comes out at the other end is faithful to our original design. We want to help the manufacturers and suppliers to ensure the production specifications are accurately translated, and to help overcome any difficulties. We knew the implementation phase wouldn't be easy – by choosing the most radical design solution, Halfords had posed significant challenges to the manufacturers.

CONSIDERING A LAUNCH STRATEGY

In the summer of 1995 as technical discussions continued over how to manufacture the new containers, the Halfords buying and marketing teams also began considering the launch strategy.

In terms of pricing the team were hoping to lift price points as a result of the 'added value' injected through improved product quality and container design. Econometric modelling was to be used to optimize the profitability of the category, taking account of data from previous years to see how the sales and profit of different brands had responded to different pricing and promotional strategies.

In terms of customer communication, Chris Forman wanted the display and communications team to improve the impact of oil displays in-store, promote additional sales opportunities through increased authority, communicate

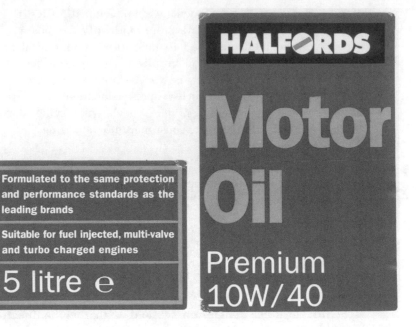

front face

rear face

Figure 16.8   Five-litre container labelling

segmentation and encourage trading up, and convey the unique product benefits of the new Halfords range. Chris wanted customers to appreciate that with a Halfords oil they could trade-up to a higher grade but also save money. Acknowledging the research findings, the primary communication message was to be:

Halfords oil is just as good as the best on the market but offers better value for money than other leading brands

The secondary messages were that Halfords oil:

comes in unique bottles which make pouring easier and minimize spillage,

and

it is easier to select the right oil for my car from the Halfords range.

The marketing team had to consider how to merchandise the five-litre oil containers. They could utilize the existing free-standing display units available in-store (see Figure 16.9) which had only recently been introduced. New graphics boards could perhaps be used to help communicate key messages. It was suggested that the colour-coded segmentation system they had developed for the packaging could somehow be utilized in the display. They had to decide which brands would be located next to which and, critically, which brand should feature on the top eye-level shelf. The existing Halfords Value Oil, in simple plain packaging, was not to be merchandised alongside the new range.

The team had to consider the external communications strategy – when and how to launch any advertising and PR to support the POS (point of sale) strategy. The marketing team pointed out the important role that individual store staff would play in communicating to customers, and there would be a need to inform, educate, train and motivate staff to put their full effort behind the new range. A video was suggested, although this would be very costly, and some form of training pack and launch document.

Forecasting stock requirements was going to be difficult – complicated by the planned communication strategy to encourage consumers to trade-up through the range. Chris Forman pointed out that:

Simply using 'historical rates of sale' would not provide an accurate projection of stock requirements, and wouldn't be a logical basis anyway if the visual merchandising strategy sought to display any particular oil grades more prominently.

The launch was planned for spring 1996. The team did not consider 'test marketing' would be appropriate. They opted for a national launch on a set date. As Chris Forman observed:

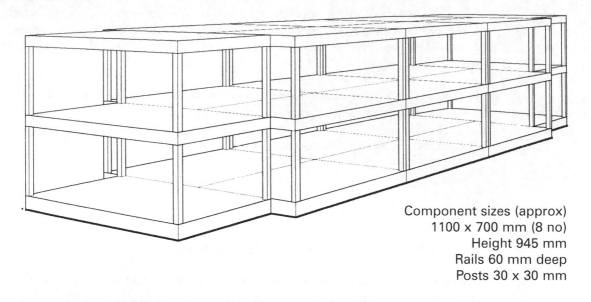

Component sizes (approx)
1100 x 700 mm (8 no)
Height 945 mm
Rails 60 mm deep
Posts 30 x 30 mm

Figure 16.9   Existing floor display units

We feel we understand the customer extremely well from the research we have undertaken, and personally I am very confident about the product. Test marketing also poses the danger, of course, of competitor retaliation!

QUESTIONS

1. Draw up a list of the main activities involved in the development process for the new range, including the remaining activities yet to be completed prior to launch. Develop a bar chart to show the timing of each of the activities, and estimate when each of the remaining tasks need to completed in order to ensure a launch, say, in May 1996? Discuss the role and activities of the buying team during the project period.

2. Assume the role of Chris Forman or a member of the marketing team and develop recommendations for a launch strategy for the new range. Your proposals could consider the following:

    ■ A summary of the most important market characteristics and consumer requirements that Halfords should be looking to take advantage of with their new range.

    ■ A pricing strategy for the new range, including specific proposals for each grade of oil and justify your recommendations.

    ■ A strategy for in-store merchandising.

    ■ A strategy for external communications – considering media, message, timing and consumer targets.

    ■ A strategy for communicating to store management and sales staff.

3. What additional and/or alternative forms of research could Halfords have undertaken to support the relaunch strategy?

4. Halfords will need to advise their suppliers of specific order quantities for each grade of oil, as well as forecast specific stock requirements for stores. What approach and techniques would you recommend?

REFERENCES

Retail Week (1997) 'Retail Week Awards in association with KPMG. *Retail Week Annual Supplement.*

The Boots Company (1995) *Report and Accounts*, 31 March.

The Boots Company (1997) *Report and Accounts*, 31 March.

HALFORDS MOTOR OILS (B): TRANSLATING CONSUMER NEEDS INTO PRODUCTS

PAUL WALLEY, MALCOLM KIRKUP AND JOHN TEMPERLEY

The authors would like to thank Halfords, Pentagram and Plysu Containers UK for their support in developing this case study. In particular we are grateful for the contributions provided by Chris Forman, Peter Foskett and John Tofts.

The information in this case study, while believed to be largely accurate, is based on the memory of those involved and compiled from a variety of sources. It has also been simplified in order to focus on key learning objectives for students of management. For these reasons, the material should not be regarded as a totally factual account of events or views.

INTRODUCTION

In 1996 and 1997 Halfords won widespread praise and top awards for the launch of a new range of own-brand motor oils. The redesign and repositioning resulted in a range that offered high technical quality, clear range segmentation, unique and customer-friendly packaging, competitive pricing and effective marketing communication. Halfords achieved considerable commercial success with the new range – increases in price points, sales value, volume, margin and market share.

This case study is the second of two cases which examine the development of the Halfords new oil range. The first case – Halfords Motor Oils (A) – considers the background to the product relaunch, the company's objectives and the process of research and concept design. This second case study focuses on aspects of the design and manufacture of the oil containers. Both cases draw on a series of interviews with managers from Halfords, the Pentagram design agency and Plysu Containers UK, and documentation provided by these companies.

DESIGN MEETS MANUFACTURING

The relaunch project began in March 1995 but we join the project in June. Pentagram had submitted their alternative design proposals, and Halfords had chosen their preferred concept. The task of translating the design into a manufactured product had now begun.

Peter Foskett, project manager for the Pentagram design agency, made the final preparations for his presentation. He was fully prepared for the first important meeting with the other companies involved in the oil container design project. Since Halfords had commissioned the new design, Peter had been very busy. To see how large plastic containers were manufactured he had made trips to the blowmoulders, Blowmocan (the industrial division of Blowmocan Ltd was acquired by Plysu Containers UK in 1996). He had also liaised with the oil companies to understand existing filling processes.

The Halfords design brief had been quite precise and reflected a detailed understanding of market characteristics and consumer requirements. Peter remembered his early conversations with Chris Forman (buying controller for Halfords) when Chris had explained some of the findings from the Halfords oil range review:

> The motor oil market is very competitive and price aggressive. Volumes have been declining because of better engines, longer service intervals, cleaner fuels and more sophisticated lubricants, despite an increase in the number of cars sold. However, there has been an increase in the total value of oil sold, due to new product development, improved oil technology and market segmentation. The premium end of the market has therefore become more important and offers new opportunities.

> The Halfords brand is seen as offering value for money in terms of price and quality but isn't seen in the same quality league as brands such as Castrol and Duckhams. Many consumers are confused – they don't understand much about oil technology. Few know the difference between oil grades, or terms such as viscosity – quite often they buy on the basis of habit or price. Around 25 per cent of cars are receiving the wrong oil. Consumers also have low involvement with the oil 'product' – they don't 'feel' the benefit of new oil in their car – the only direct contact with oil is when pouring takes place. So we have to get this stage right for the consumer. Handling, pouring, spillage, re-use of the container, and instructions therefore help create the feel of a quality product.

Chris had confirmed with Peter that the Halfords brand offer was to be extended to include diesel and, eventually, synthetic oil. The initial range would be Standard, Standard Plus, Premium and Diesel. Synthetic would be launched a year later, mainly because it was a more specialist and premium product and Halfords' first priority was to uplift consumer confidence and perceptions in the repositioned brand.

Chris had pointed out that he would not be trying to differentiate based on the product itself. The packaging, itself, had to be a means of differentiating the product from the competition and had to add value to a greater extent than the existing XP7 range. Peter and his team had taken a lot of time to develop 12 different bottle shapes. In each case they had studied the design by building cardboard models. By a simple ranking process, they had managed to reduce this to three concept ideas, to present to the Halfords design management group. The board chose the most unusual design put in front of them, in a bold attempt to secure an extra degree of differentiation. However, even with the limited time Peter had spent with the container manufacturers, he knew there was a lot of work now to be done to convert his product concept into a practicable design. He also needed close co-operation from all parties involved in the project.

The launch was planned for spring 1996. Even with the amount of time they had, there was little contingency with the project. The timetable was planned carefully:

Research and concept design	May/June 1995
Detailed design	June-October 1995
Bottle tooling	November 1995
First off bottle samples	December 1995
Bottle production	January 1996
Bottle filling	March 1996
Cap production	February 1996
Label production	December 1995
Carton/packaging cutting	February 1996
Distribution to stores	April 1996

The First Meeting

The meeting, in June 1995, took place in the conference room at Pentagram's offices in London. Ten people were seated round the table, including Chris Forman (the overall project manager from Halfords), Simon Price (Halfords Oil buyer/product manager), Peter Foskett from Pentagram, Chris Chick – sales manager from Blowmocan, the two oil producers, and the bottle cap manufacturers. The main objective of the meeting was to discuss the state of play on the design of the new containers and to agree a process to move forward, establishing clear guidelines for all to work to.

Peter explained Pentagram's thought processes to the assembled group, and he outlined the main tasks he envisaged in the remaining product development process. He stressed the limited time they all had to deliver the new range – to provide bottle samples by December 1995.

Peter reiterated the general aims of the design brief. He then added:

Of course, one of our main constraints is that we have to keep the cost of the package down to about the same as the existing containers. This perhaps limits our scope a little, with expensive pigments and so on, but hopefully that shouldn't stop us from introducing new features which customers should find appealing. Our main objective has been to design a container which allows the oil to pour from it without too much spillage onto the engine compartment and with minimal 'glugging'. Our mock-up trials have shown that the relative positions of the handle and spout make a big difference. The volume of oil in the can is another parameter. Our tests reveal that the concept design reduces the pouring distance by about two-thirds, to 10 centimetres.

Peter went on to explain the other characteristics which both Pentagram and Halfords had considered important:

The product's features have been specified using a tool known as quality function deployment. This has allowed us to refine the product so that it is closely tailored to the customer's needs. The concept is a unique shape and we believe a graduated, tinted, translucent strip down the middle of one side of the container (which is the upper-most side, when pouring oil), acting as an oil level indicator, is another useful feature. A finger-grip is also featured on the bottom of the container. The containers will be in bright colours, with a pearlescent finish to enhance the 'quality' appearance. A cap is needed that is tamper and leak-proof with a built-in spout. Our concept design includes a novel flip-top cap. We are not sure how consumers will react to this, but the reason some of you are here is to investigate the idea of developing this as one of the key features. Halfords would also like a draining facility to enable used engine oil to be stored, ready for disposal. For the overall concept, what are your first reactions?

Chris Chick from Blowmocan was the first to respond:

The concept is certainly very different from existing containers, and I can't say that I've seen anything comparable in the factory. It will take a lot of development work, and I will definitely have to consult the technical people back at the plant to identify the key process and tool design issues. The smaller one-litre version will be much more straightforward.

The cap manufacturer raised a specific point:

I am concerned about the feasibility of the flip-top cap. I suspect that we will have to work to very tight tolerances, and probably develop a completely new sealing system, if we are to stop the container from leaking. If we fill the containers with some of the more advanced oils, we could run into difficulties because they find gaps in any seals.

The oil companies expressed concern about transportation, before filling and after filling. Pentagram discovered that Blowmocan and the oil fillers used pallets of different size. Unless they carefully planned the number per pallet, the oil companies would receive product in the wrong 'multiple' quantities. The discussion then moved on to timescale. The target date for completion was December, which would give Halfords time to launch the new range in the spring selling season.

Deliberations by Blowmocan

Blow moulding is a commonly used method of making large, thin-walled plastic containers, such as oil and bleach containers. The plastic used in the process is HDPE, which is naturally translucent, but can be pigmented as required. The HDPE is put through an extruder, to form a 'tube' of molten plastic, which hangs vertically in mid-air as it is being formed. The moulding tool is closed around the tube and air is blown in – expanding it until it meets the sides of the mould. Once the tube has fully expanded, the mould is cooled to let the plastic set, and then the mould is opened, leaving the formed product. Where the tooling is joined together, the plastic flows slightly into the gaps, leaving small raised areas or 'witness lines' in the surface of the plastic. A trimming operation takes place, before the plastic is fully cooled, to remove excess material – for example from within the gap between container body and handle, and from above and below the container. After a short while longer, the plastic is cool enough to allow the labels to be applied in an adjacent process. Blowmoulding is part art and part science. It is not a closed tool like injection moulding where you can control every dimension. With blowmoulding you are only controlling the 'exterior' dimensions, so the testing and trialling process for unusual shapes can take some time. With complex new designs it is often very difficult to predict what might happen in the mould trialling process.

Following the meeting at Pentagram, Blowmocan managers considered the technical issues raised by the concept design. The technical director commented:

> Of all the 12 designs developed by Pentagram, Halfords have chosen the one that presents the greatest technical challenge. If this was more of a speculative request from an unknown client, we would think twice before taking such a project on. We want to take on the challenge because our relationship with Halfords is a valuable one.

Blowmocan had a number of specific concerns:

> The size and shape of the finger-grip underneath will add to the complexity of the tooling. The position of the handle will unusually require us to blow the plastic into a deep mould cavity which can cause unacceptable thinning of the container wall. The undercut behind the handle could tend to hold the container in the tool as it opens – we will have to work out a way to release the container after moulding. The shape will also affect label appearance because there will be a witness line down both the front and back of the bottle. This will make the label stick with a raised centre section. We will need very close liaison with the mould manufacturers and we will need to investigate labelling alternatives with the suppliers.

August Meeting at Halfords

Chris Forman chaired a meeting of the design team and the manufacturers. The meeting reflected on the results from the focus groups which had been held to assess consumer reactions to the prototype concept design. Pentagram had developed two mock-up containers, in pearlescent yellow, for consumer reaction. They had tried to make the containers as realistic as possible, even filling them with salt so they felt as if they were full of oil. Consumer opinions were recorded, and it became clear that yellow was not a popular choice of colour. The consumers liked green especially, and black and silver were seen as logical choices for diesel and synthetic oils. Red was accepted, although with some reservations. All consumers liked the metallic finishes. Consumers immediately spotted the pouring advantage of the bottle and liked the shape. Flip-top caps were seen as a good idea, but there were concerns about leakage. It was evident that the appearance of the bottle was going to be important.

It was noted that a lot of time had been spent examining the technical issues in the manufacturing process. The cap manufacturer pointed out some of the difficulties associated with fitting a flip-top cap to the larger bottle, suggesting that the stress put on the top could create leak points, and pointed out that more time would be needed to develop the design further. It became clear that Halfords had a choice to either compromise on this part of the design, and to go with a more conventional screw-cap, or to extend the critical path of the project. Chris Forman was anxious about the overall project progress and reiterated the launch date he wanted to meet.

Blowmocan outlined the progress they had made:

Uniformity and positioning of the visi-stripe is a major consideration at this stage. It is achieved by extruding a clear line of molten plastic into the coloured tube already being extruded. The change of section down the container from a thick curved handle to a flat front face could lead to a visi-line that is not of uniform width, and the tube could become distorted during forming of the handle so that the visi-line is not straight. We will only finally be able to confirm this during moulding trials due to the 'open' nature of the process, but we will consult with both the toolmaker and the blowmoulding machine manufacturer as necessary. The incorporation of a finger-recess in the base of the container will require a separate base plate which moves downwards from the main mould to allow container release, and the resulting join of the two parts will cause a witness line to be formed in the container. This can be overcome by making this plate fit within the base leaving the witness lines underneath the container.

Chris Forman presented the proposals for labelling. The wording would be very clear, to identify the grade of oil and to reassure customers with a clear statement that they were getting a product comparable in quality to the major brands. Pentagram's preference was for a clear label which would allow the bottle colour to show through. Blowmocan pointed out:

The use of clear labels can give a ghosting effect due to the surface finish of the blow moulded HDPE and it may be necessary to use coloured labels.

It was agreed that a sub-group be formed to review the labelling alternatives. The meeting also noted that the plastic supplier was trying hard to match the plastic samples to the new pearlescent colours – the pearl additives were not mixing well and they were looking into this.

November: About to Cut Metal

The design team had reached a critical stage in the development process. In order to meet delivery deadlines they were going to have to make a commitment to the mould-tool manufacturer about the design of the tooling. Peter Foskett met with the Blowmocan draughtsman, technical representative Ken Mott and Chris Chick, and representatives from the tool-maker, to discuss the issues.

The purpose of the meeting was to approve the wooden models produced by the tool maker prior to the manufacture of the tool, and to consider the real detail of how the containers would appear. Peter Foskett later reflected:

This was a critical stage in the project – the time when we nail our colours to the mast, because the tool makers are wanting to start to cut metal. We discussed the handle radii and the blend between the top section and the neck platform of the container, but the key issue centred around mould split detail. The tool makers pointed out that 'vent plugs' were planned. I have to confess I didn't know what these were. I learned that for the mould cavity to be completely filled with plastic, and to achieve an acceptable surface finish, they have to allow air to escape. The problem for me was that the witness of the vent plugs then appears in the plastic …they would have looked awful and would have been all the way down both faces of the container. Customers wouldn't understand what they are for. Ken Mott proposed changing the mould design to make it in four pieces, rather than two, allowing it to vent down the joint line and therefore eliminating the vent plugs. But this would need additional work, involve additional cost and delay the tool arriving.

Peter Foskett was hoping Blowmocan and the tool-maker could make a commitment to the tool design quickly to give sufficient time for testing. Peter pointed out:

We really need to know what product characteristics we should commit ourselves to, which ones we can keep options open on and which ones to drop. That will allow us to confirm the detailed product design features to you and enable you to finalize the tool.

HALFORDS MOTOR OILS (B): TRANSLATING CONSUMER NEEDS INTO PRODUCTS

QUESTIONS

1. Identify all the consumer requirements for the Halfords containers.

2. Develop a list of the technical requirements which need to be specified at the final meeting.

3. Use quality function deployment (the House of Quality tool) to decide which product features you would deploy at this stage in the project.

4. What compromises might Halfords and Pentagram have to make?

SAINSBURY'S AND SHAW'S: REFLECTIONS ON MAKING AN ACQUISITION A REALITY

DAVID MUSKETT

This case examines the nature of the relationship between J Sainsbury plc of London, UK, a major UK grocery retailer and Shaw's supermarkets of Massachusetts, USA, since the latter's takeover. Interviews took place between September 1995 and July 1997.

The author would like to thank Sainsbury's and Shaw's for their support in developing this case. In particular he would wish to thank Mr Dino Adriano, Mr David Bremner and Mr Phil Francis for the openness with which they discussed the issues. The exchange managers, Mr Stuart Mitchell and Mr Rodney Wooliscroft (UK) and Mr Brian Pijanowski and Mr Tom Vesey (USA) were also all extremely helpful in explaining their experiences.

The case information presented and the issues raised were the result of the author's own reading of the situation and should not be attributed to any particular individual cited in this case. The individuals were chosen as representative of the overall process of integration between Sainsbury's and Shaw's.

INTRODUCTION

Phil Francis, executive president of Shaw's, the New England-based grocery chain owned by J Sainsbury plc, said when interviewed by the author in early 1996, 'Sainsbury's figured out what they bought in 1982. They had sorted out correctly what they had bought by 1992.'

Francis was discussing his role and how the relationship between Sainsbury's and Shaw's of Massachusetts, New England, had developed since Sainsbury's first acquired an interest in 1982. He implied that the relationship had been somewhat troubled in the early years of Sainsbury's ownership. Consequently, Shaw's had not delivered the expected level of profitability during the initial years of Sainsbury's ownership (*J Sainsbury Report and Accounts*, 1998, pp. 26–7).

There had been rapid expansion of the Shaw's New England grocery business during recent years and this had delivered more turnover and profitability, although increases had latterly levelled off. Views on the reasons for Shaw's patchy record of profitability under Sainsbury's ownership varied among the several senior actors involved in the process.

BRIEF HISTORY OF SHAW'S AND SAINSBURY'S

J Sainsbury plc began its acquisition of Shaw's with a 21 per cent stake bought for £13m in 1983 from the then owners of the company, the two Davis brothers. Shaw's then had 41 stores spread around central New England but specifically avoiding the Boston conurbation. According to Phil Francis, the current president, the two brothers ran virtually two separate autonomous organizations, one north and one south of Boston. They did have a new store opening programme of one new store every fifteen months. The chain could only claim market leadership in their immediate core area around Brockton Mass, and according to Alexander (1989) had established a 7 per cent market share in New England. The company has its headquarters based at East Bridgewater in the Massachusetts countryside, 30 miles to the south of Boston.

All those spoken to by the author considered that Shaw's was perceived by Sainsbury's as having key trading principles of quality, service and value for money. There was some suggestion that Sainsbury's felt at the time that Shaw's EPOS system might be in advance of their own, offering some level of potential backward synergy. Sainsbury's slowly built their shareholding and acquired the company completely in 1987. Sainsbury's placed two directors on Shaw's board and then pursued an active policy of expansion via store openings. By 1995 they had 90 stores, and by 1997 a total of 115 stores spread around Massachusetts, New Hampshire, Maine, Rhode Island, Connecticut and most recently Vermont. Of these, twelve had been acquired from Royal Ahold NV in Connecticut, an area previously thought by Shaw's as too competitive to enter. At the time of the interview, a total of eight store openings were planned, continuing the policy of expansion under Sainsbury's ownership.

Wrigley (1997) took the view that much of the comment about Sainsbury's acquisition from financial journalists in the City of London was moderately hostile and has broadly remained so, relying on the 'folk memory' of previous UK retail failures in the USA that is, Dixons, Ratner's, Gateway and Marks & Spencer. It was viewed from the City's perception that the acquisition was a non-core business element which had not delivered adequate profitability during the period of Sainsbury's ownership. This remained so up to 1997. During the mid 1990s Sainsbury's had lost their market leadership in the UK to their great rival, multiple grocer Tesco. Financial press comment tended to suggest that Sainsbury's could do better notwithstanding the tougher UK trading conditions in the grocery business. Sainsbury's diversification in the UK had continued with the acquisition of the large Texas Homecare DIY stores from Ladbroke Leisure which was added to Sainsbury's Homebase DIY operation.

Sainsbury's had chosen to give the responsibility for Shaw's to the board director responsible for Homebase. This was a result of a wider change in structure whereby the Sainsbury's chairman had wanted to improve focus inside the group and did so by creating a new board for Sainsbury's UK food business and by bringing in a new appointment to focus on DIY and the US.

In late 1994 Sainsbury's acquired 50 per cent of voting stock of Giant Food Inc., then 16.7 per cent of total equity costing $337m. In August 1996 this was increased by 3.2 per cent for a further $62m in what Bremner saw as a technical increase, not an expression of future intentions. Nonetheless it did still leave Sainsbury's in a position to take full control later, as Giant were market leaders in the Washington DC and Baltimore areas. Put together with the Shaw's operation, this potentially has Sainsbury's 'on the verge of becoming one of the top ten US food retailers', Wrigley commented in 1997. This wider perspective sets a background for Sainsbury's developing group internal relationships with Shaw's.

The Early Years

Initially Shaw's did not make a great leap forward in terms of profitability although store opening was pursued very actively with over 100 new store openings since acquisition. According to both senior executives, Sainsbury's sent out a number of senior managers for brief weekly spells and apart from that, left Shaw's pretty much to themselves. They did not offer enough 'hands on' advice and leadership to make a crucial difference. There was some suggestion from one UK respondent that those people who were sent may have been too abrasive in approach to effect change in a positive way. These operational managers could all point to strong cultural issues which needed adaptation when they crossed the Atlantic to work.

Both senior executives were concerned about how the acquisition was made in terms of auditing the business which was bought, not in strictly financial terms, but in terms of what sort of business had been acquired.

J Sainsbury had bought a family business with high standards. Shaw's trading policy was summed up as 'everyday low prices'. Sainsbury's sought to manage it like their UK operation J Sainsbury, pursuing a high quality, high margin operation. Dino Adriano's view was that it had not quite been as basic as Kwik Save, yet still a discounter. Yet there was some initial discontent, slow progress and poor profitability at Shaw's. It took, again according to Phil Francis, 'brute force, awkwardness and determination' to get Shaw's where it is today, which is more like Sainsbury's. This is illustrated by the use of a familiar slogan 'Good Food Costs Less at Shaw's'. In the meanwhile, new ideas about own-label, higher standards of tidiness in stores and better presentation were not well received by staff.

When Phil Francis joined Shaw's with experience in food retailing and in particular logistics, he asked Lord Sainsbury and the then managing director, David Quarmby, to identify the three biggest problems at Shaw's. They indicated: real estate (property), systems and own-label. Six months later, he felt these were problems two, three and four and that they had missed the key area of distributional logistics. The logistics chief appointed by J Sainsbury had not done a good job, and no-one had sought to check on his progress. Since 1991, progress had been better and relationships and profitability had all been improved up to 1997.

Shaw's Trading Policies

Shaw's trading philosophy is best summed up in their strap line 'Everyday Low Prices'. They couple this with a quality perishables offer.

Sainsbury's had long pursued a strap line 'Good Food Costs Less at Sainsbury's' which in reality did not mean a low price pointing strategy. They had a policy of wide range customer choice and quality but had never sought to be a discounter. Their net margins of between 6–8 per cent indicate clearly the Sainsbury's objective.

Dino Adriano was chairman of Shaw's between late 1992 and 1995 and took the view that what they acquired was, in effect, a discounter with a price led format 'not a Kwik Save, but nearly'. Sainsbury's set about introducing own-label (private label) which has a much lower profile in the US than the UK. They also attempted to redesign and remerchandise the stores into a format similar to Sainsbury's. Rodney Wooliscroft, who came to Shaw's from the UK to act as a district manager for one year, felt that they tended to run less tidy stores in the US than the UK with more promotional material and dump bins in aisles. Initial tidying up attempts were resisted by US customers and according to Wooliscroft, 'we had to untidy the stores slightly again to meet these customer expectations'.

The inherited marketing policy was altered in the pursuit of Sainsbury's direct equivalent and this was reflected by a change in strap line to 'Good Food Costs Less at Shaw's'. This could not match the trading reality in terms of margins. Direct comparison between US and UK margins are more difficult to make. According to Alexander (1994) US food retailing net margins average around 2–3 per cent. If a direct comparison is made with the UK margins that Sainsbury's average (that is, between 6–8 per cent) then the comparison appears invidious. However, measured in terms of return on capital invested, both countries achieve more equal returns, with the USA slightly ahead, and Bremner agreed that this was a more valid comparison than any apparent net margin difference. Nonetheless, under Francis, Shaw's had improved net margin to 2.85 per cent through careful cost control. The two trading cultures clearly had a detrimental impact on Shaw's progress. This was further enhanced by more subtle national differences in operating practices between 'Old England' and New England. Viewed from the perspective of the financial journalists from the City of London, the inevitable consequence was reduced profitability.

Staff Exchange Policies

It became clear that there was a need to integrate the systems and practices of both companies; a number of ways were sought to address this. There was some recognition of how large a problem needed to be addressed. Francis felt that the British and US styles were 'very, very different' with Sainsbury's by 1990 'large, buttoned down, autocratic, report driven, chart driven, sort of business'. According to Francis, Shaw's was by contrast in 1982, 'an entrepreneurial seat of the pants dream and by 1987, based upon the desire to retain low cost, the Sainsbury vision was not embraced'.

In order to address the Sainsbury's vision, an initial policy of short staff secondments was changed and longer term middle management exchanges were undertaken between both sides of the Atlantic.

KEY ACTORS IN THE SAINSBURY'S–SHAW'S RELATIONSHIP 1992–97

In order to understand how the relationship had worked, a number of key individuals were consulted. It is unclear whether these are all the ones involved in building these relationships or just a small sample.

The senior management involved were Dino Adriano, who was chairman of Shaw's between 1992 and 1995. He was also chairman of Homebase, the Sainsbury's DIY chain at that time. He subsequently became chairman of Sainsbury's Supermarkets Ltd and one of the J Sainsbury Group plc main board directors. He spent no extended time at Shaw's and relied on frequent short visits.

David Bremner became chairman of Homebase in August 1996 and Shaw's in April 1997, having previously served on Shaw's board. Phil Francis, president and chief executive officer of Shaw's since 1991, had worked in a number of US retail and wholesale companies prior to joining Shaw's.

Rodney Wooliscroft was a UK district manager from the Midlands who went to Shaw's to act as a district manager between early 1994 and mid 1995. Stuart Mitchell, a senior buyer at Sainsbury's head office with 13 years' experience, spent a year between 1993 and 1994 as part of the team planning a new format store to enter the competitive Connecticut market.

The two US managers interviewed were Brian Pijanowski (a vice president of Shaw's grocery buying, who went to Sainsbury's head office at Blackfriars in London between July 1994 and July 1995) and Tom Vesey (a Shaw's district manager, who did a straight swap with Rodney Wooliscroft and went to the south west as a district manager also between 1994 and 1995).

These exchanges reflected an active change in policy from short secondments of staff to longer term exchanges of staff in order to address a perceived need to integrate the systems and practices of both companies.

THE IMPACT OF NATIONAL AND COMPANY CULTURES ON THE ACQUISITION

Some common key themes emerged for the two British managers despite Wooliscroft having worked in the field in stores and Mitchell at head office as a buyer. Both noted key style differences which applied to the Shaw's operations. The themes stressed by both were people, operating cultures, training failures, resistance to change and a perceived mediocre welcome due to a poor personnel function at Shaw's.

The people issue seemed to have a number of dimensions. Wooliscroft found difficulties in getting staff to accept what he saw as constructive criticism when, for example, merchandising was not adequately completed by store staff. He felt that department and store managers had failed to take ownership of merchandising. It was 'quite difficult to get across to them – this isn't good enough. They misconstrued this as you've done a lousy job, you're a failure.' He felt that constructive criticism was more accepted by Sainsbury's staff. Mitchell saw this from a different angle. He found that meetings were inconclusive in outcome because of this tendency to fail to address difficulties with individuals in meetings. 'You too often come out of meetings wondering what has been agreed.'

Both agreed that a different aspect of the people problem was that of getting the personalities of secondees right in order to be effective to Shaw's. Both stressed that Sainsbury's must not choose over-assertive people as they would face resistance which would have a negative effect on the outcome. 'They can make things move pretty slowly', said Mitchell, 'you need people who are results driven but have a human side to them. We should have put more people in key positions earlier than we did.'

In terms of operating cultures both saw the operation in New England as more relaxed than Sainsbury's and attributed it in part to lower average sales per store. In addition, the fact that Shaw's headquarters are not based in a big city may have an impact and also to some extent that Americans have a more informal style. Language was obviously important in this. 'You have to use their terminology, their phrases, their language when you're in their country. US people won't change their language' comments Wooliscroft. Initially he began by giving instructions and wondering why they had not been complied with. He then began to realise that he had not been understood due to language, accent or terminology. In desperation he resorted to asking staff to reflect back what he was asking them to do. Both felt that any resistance to change came from the operating culture which was more consensual and informal than the Sainsbury's style which is more directive.

Neither British manager had disliked their experience in the exchange, in fact both had enjoyed their time in the USA and claimed to have learned much from their experience at Shaw's. However, both felt that they had brought much back which could be applied in the UK, although Rodney Wooliscroft did imply that the experience of more informal communications and the delivery of more positive feedback had been useful.

Us Managers' Views of Sainsbury's Operation

Both the US managers came over at the same time, July 1994 to July 1995. Brian Pijanowski, a vice-president of grocery buying went to Sainsbury's head office at Blackfriars, London, to be located in the buying function there. Tom Vesey, a district manager (in stores) at Shaw's, went to English South West in a swap with Rodney Wooliscroft. Both broadly saw the exchange as a positive experience and could identify clearly what they perceived as similarities and differences.

Pijanowski's experience seemed to be slightly less happy in terms of work, at least initially. As the plan for him had evolved, it was intended he work in four departments for three months each to maximize experience. He was actually installed with the status of senior buyer (below his Shaw's status) and moved between meat, toiletries (health and beauty) and eventually to produce for the final five-month period. He found his colleagues helpful but was not given real responsibility because of his lack of experience in the UK market. He felt some frustration at this. Eventually at produce he did have sole charge of salad vegetables helped by a senior manager who was about to retire and would more readily devolve responsibility to him.

Vesey exercised immediate equivalent responsibility once he had got used to the mechanics of living in the UK, that is, driving on the left and finding his way around. He said he found the staff who reported to him broadly supportive, 'out of 29 direct associates, 28 were with me'. With regard to the odd one out, he comments 'he was a tough one to crack. It took about six months to crack and then it was fine. There wasn't a personality thing for him, we overcame it by talking.'

In terms of general business differences, Pijanowski saw Sainsbury's as having more protocol due to a bigger hierarchy – although it was not as formal as he expected. 'You still hang your suit coat up as here' he states, and concludes that he felt senior managers were more approachable at Shaw's. Also he saw their managers enjoying more empowerment due to Shaw's smaller size. These views were shared by Vesey who added that he felt Shaw's were more open and less rule driven than Sainsbury's.

Both managers shared the language barrier problems of the differences between US and British English with the British managers. Vesey felt this was the most frustrating aspect initially.

Perhaps a surprising difference for Pijanowski was the relative lack of business regulation in the UK compared with the US. 'In the UK you negotiate what you can negotiate and being American, we always feel that America is the commerce leader… yet the rules are much more limiting in the US than the UK, it seems to be a freer market.'

Communication and Language

All the managers' views on the acquisition seem to revolve around communication in particular. Vesey felt the merger could have gone better if Sainsbury's and Shaw's had 'communicated values' more clearly and shared their differences openly. He felt that his swap with Rodney Wooliscroft was very positive in achieving this values exchange. Pijanowski shared this feeling and felt that it was really important that Shaw's and Sainsbury's 'communicate with each other and use each other as resources'. He suggested that the video conferencing link was vital to keep this process alive. Vesey added that in the beginning of the acquisition, 'there were not a lot of Sainsbury's people here'. He felt that this had been a hindrance to the development of the relationship.

All had alluded to differences in culture between the nations and the organizations having complex interactions on the development of a successful acquisition. The themes highlighted by the British managers of people, operating cultures, training failures, resistance to change and a perceived poor welcome were not completely shared. People and operating cultures clearly featured large in the US managers' analysis of similarities and differences. Informality versus formality and stark differences of driving on the left and difficulty of parking (mentioned by both) did crop up. Neither mentioned resistance to change overtly although Pijanowski's account of head office buyers being reluctant to yield real power or influence clearly implied this. Vesey's one reluctant manager got a special mention. In terms of UK help, both said personnel had helped in the first week.

The wider perspectives on the merger and its success or failure was more the concern of the senior management involved.

BUSINESS PLANNING STRUCTURES: SENIOR MANAGEMENT'S PERSPECTIVES

Dino Adriano considered how well the organizations had developed together. He felt that while informal and positive in style, the Shaw's people were 'less good at identifying failures'. He also shared the British middle managers' views that they were poor at offering immediate negative feedback. 'People (management) will go round a store and appear to condone problems because you don't actually say anything is bad there and then.' He shared Phil Francis' view that Sainsbury's at the time of purchase in 1987 may have not fully researched what they were buying. He did feel that Shaw's had good standards and were run pretty well at the time of acquisition with a high ethic and sensible financial controls.

He felt that 'the push towards own (private) label instigated by Sainsbury's was not readily received by the Shaw's' management' among a number of things. 'It is difficult for the customers if ideas are not readily received by the management.' 'We took away lots of cardboard shippers (from display) as we tend to run very tidy stores and they tend to have rather untidy stores... the customers (of Shaw's) had liked them so sales went down a bit. We didn't understand it as well as we should in an important core trading area.'

Adriano felt that it took a long time to get things moving among the Shaw's managers. Sainsbury's sent out British managers to develop and implement own-label. Eventually, 'it (own-label) has delivered and that's always the proof'. But they did send people out to try to impose a common Sainsbury's retailing standard which proved difficult, partly because of the history of Shaw's having run two semi-autonomous operations north and south of Boston and because US grocery retailing is perceived as more cluttered than British retailing. He conceded that it could be more Shaw's problem as Giant Food's standards were much higher.

In retrospect he felt that it would have been better to bring in people at a slightly lower level to help implement changes rather than sending only high level staff. 'We didn't help ourselves'. More recently, 'Wooliscroft's secondment was very successful. We'll do more.'

He felt that the hardest thing about working with the Americans was 'getting them to accept things that we think are crucial in the medium term. They all say it's different over here.'

This appears to have been influenced by Shaw's wish to go for low cost but high service at the checkouts which is seen as vital for success in the US. Giant, in contrast, was seen to have invested hugely in their stores and are committed to the delivery of skills and are training and product knowledge led.

When asked about Shaw's customers' reactions, Adriano stressed the new format at a store which Shaw's were using to enter the Connecticut market which is currently dominated by their competitor, Stop n Shop, using large stores of 60,000 sq ft. He felt that new customers to Shaw's on the whole had liked it, even though the introduction of own-label had reduced the traditional American policy of huge brand choice in supermarkets.

Adriano echoed the comments of the British middle managers with regard to Shaw's personnel function which he saw as having been 'awful, minimalist, with poor staff'. He felt that after eight years' involvement by Sainsbury's they now had a better set up.

When asked about lessons they could learn from their then minority stake in Giant Food, he stressed the usefulness of an audit of any business. He also stressed that Sainsbury's were committed to America as a long-term plan in their strategy. He felt they could put more emphasis on an exchange of ideas in both directions. 'It's crucial we do this.'

Adriano's successor but one, David Bremner, was also officially chief executive for all US operations. He saw it as vital to be in the USA one week out of four each month and offering a greater sense of strategic direction to Shaw's. He also added that 'Giant is more on the horizon than ever before'.

Bremner had had an initial involvement with Shaw's when they were first bought by Sainsbury's. He also felt that Sainsbury's had perhaps misjudged their purchase as being a quality end retailer rather than what he characterized as a 'middle of the road, blue collar food retail company'. He felt it had been detrimental to try to remake Shaw's in their own image. Nonetheless, in his view, some key competencies had been transferred from Sainsbury's to Shaw's, particularly buying and own-label. Bremner felt that US management style had a quite different cultural approach. According to him, British management tended to focus on the nature of a problem whereas the US style accepts a problem and then concentrates on a solution. He felt that this style mix created a positive tension that worked quite well. When asked about possible backwards positive transfers from the US to the UK, his view was succinct 'there were none whatsoever'.

Bremner did comment on the view expressed by Phil Francis that being owned by a retailer rather than a financial institution was an advantage to Shaw's. He agreed that retailers as owners should make better returns in the long run by the very nature of their investment. He felt that 'leveraged buyouts (that is, led by financial institutions) only occur when you've had poor management beforehand'.

BUSINESS DEVELOPMENT AND EFFECTIVE COMMUNICATIONS

Bremner expressed the clearest views in this area. In terms of shared values and culture he felt that while it was important that directors share the Sainsbury's culture, lower down it was less important. 'An element of self-identity is no bad thing in its own right.' When asked about management resistance to change, he felt that Shaw's management were more open than their British counterparts. 'I've had absolutely no resistance at all.' He did accept Stuart Mitchell's criticism of a reluctance to give and receive negative feedback. He felt that the US style of management is very 'self-congratulatory' by comparison.

Adriano merely commented that he had enjoyed working with the Americans once you 'get to grips with two nations divided by a common language'.

Bremner also pointed out that Shaw's is now three times the size it was at takeover yet remained a small company, number 32 in the list of largest US food retailers. He viewed this as very important in a market which had been fragmented regionally and yet was now consolidating fast.

He argued that in the future 10–12 super-players in grocery would be able to perform more profitably because of their sheer size. He felt this would then put more pressure on regional players like Shaw's and Giant.

When asked about management style differences, he regarded this as less important than Phil Francis' emphasis on informality. 'UK people kid themselves that just by moving to a first name basis you break down barriers... Just because you have a dress down Friday, it doesn't make the business more casual'. He felt that it was the smaller size of Shaw's that made for better informal relationships.

His views on Shaw's customers' reactions differed from his predecessor. He felt that in Shaw's core territories of Massachusetts, Rhode Island, Maine and New Hampshire, own-label was now thought of very highly. However, in their newer stores in Connecticut you get a negative customer response, 'how dare Shaw's assume they can force own-label on us to the detriment of proprietary brands... we went too far and had to pull back'. He felt you had to earn the right to sell own-brand or own-label, not assume it.

Bremner accepted that Sainsbury's had made a mistake in trying to do two things at the same time – to remake Shaw's in their own image and concurrently to grow the business very rapidly. He felt the lessons to be learned were related to the application of core competencies and getting them into any new business which has been acquired. He agreed that what they have today was a good business model for Shaw's that has taken the best of Sainsbury's minus the bad bits and applied it to US management skills. 'We've got something worth building on, we know that. A model which we can apply to Giant if that's what we choose to do.'

He then considered an analogy with Sainsbury's UK acquisition of Texas Homecare, the DIY chain. 'You have to realise that you can't overnight obliterate one way of working... The big problem with Texas was not changing the brand fast enough. We discovered quickly that the brand had negative values.'

He felt that the learning gleaned from the Shaw's experience may not have been applied fully to the Texas Homecare acquisition. He saw this as a lack of a particular core competence at Sainsbury's, that is, the transfer of learning from one part of the organization to another.

He argued that if the Sainsbury's group had ambition to become a global international retailer it must ensure that key business competencies become available to all of the group operations to ensure that 'the values of Sainsbury's get reflected in all our operating companies... We must make sure we transfer key skills and people around the business.' He added that in Shaw's case the biggest challenge was to get the right people to deliver those competencies over the next five years.

With regard to Giant he felt that 'Giant is more on the horizon than ever before'. By mid 1997 Sainsbury's still owned 20 per cent of Giant Food shares but over 50 per cent of the voting shares. Quite what the next step was about to be remained unclear. However, when asked to comment on the performance of Shaw's in terms of its currently declared profit in the 1997 results, Bremner felt they were worse than unsatisfactory. Yet the news since the 1987 acquisition of Shaw's had been far from all bad. The business had more than doubled in size and was continuing to grow successfully. It had provided a first foothold abroad for the Sainsbury's group and had offered many lessons for the company.

CONCLUSION AND THE FUTURE

Key elements identified by all the participants can be seen in that all were concerned with business planning and communication. The theme of language also emerged as an important factor as a key to reading contrasting cultures. Any business like Sainsbury's which acquires another business must acknowledge the likely barriers to development which they face. The added dimension of crossing country boundaries merely builds upon this.

How far Sainsbury's could, or would, apply those lessons for the future expansion was now up to them. The subsequent disposal of their interests in Giant Food in spring 1998 to Royal Ahold NV of the Netherlands clearly showed that Sainsbury's had reviewed their North American position in the light of their experience. It was accompanied by a statement of their future commitment to Shaw's as a key part of their continuing business.

QUESTIONS

?

1. Outline the key similarities and differences between UK and US grocery retailing that have impacted on this case. Cite specific examples which have impacted on the Sainsbury's–Shaw's relationship.

2. How might Sainsbury's have come to make the assumptions they did about Shaw's? Is there any evidence of the research they have undertaken since to address the difficulties they encountered? Is there any evidence of the organization learning from its mistakes?

3. Was the staff exchange programme part of an overall strategy for managing the people concerned? Can you identify the team leadership strategies which Sainsbury's employed? Put yourself in the place of one of the British or American exchangees, what objectives would you set for this experience?

4. What are the lessons to be learned regarding own (private) label products? Propose a research project for future private label extensions.

5. A number of cultural differences are alluded to in the case. Evaluate the nature and importance of cultural differences between Sainsbury's and Shaw's. Put yourself in Brian Pijanowski's place and assess how you would choose to manage relationships at Sainsbury's head office.

6. How far do the roles of the senior executives and the middle managers complement each other? Are there any significant differences between the two groups? In the light of the evidence of this case, should Sainsbury's have a formalized strategy for evaluating potential acquisitions?

REFERENCES

Alexander, N. (1995) 'Sainsbury's move into New England'. In McGoldrick, P. J. (ed.) *International Trends and Strategies Retailing*, Pitman: London.

Attwood, T. (1990) 'Corporate culture: for or against you?' *Management Accounting*, **68**(1): 26–9.

Gibb, A. A. (1987) 'Entrepreneurial (Intrapreneurial) vs corporist management and its implications for business schools'. *Journal of European Industrial Training*, **11**(2): 20–3.

Hofstede, G. (1980) *Cultures Consequences: Interactive Differences in Work Related Values*. Beverly Hills: Sage.

Hofstede, G. (1991) *Cultures and Organisations*. London: McGraw-Hill.

Lewin, K. (1935) *A Dynamic Theory of Personality*. New York: McGraw-Hill.

Plant, R. (1987) *Managing Change and Making it Stick*. Aldershot: Gower.

Sathe, V. (1985) 'How to decipher and change corporate culture' in Kilman, R. H. *et al.* (eds) *Gaining Control of the Corporate Culture*. San Francisco: Jossey Bass.

Siehl, C., Ledford, G., Silverman, R. and Fay, P. (1988) 'Preventing cultural clashes from botching a merger', *Mergers and Acquisitions*, **22**(5) March/April.

Trice, H. M. and Beyer, J. M. (1984) 'Studying organizational cultures through rites and ceremonies'. *Academy of Management Review*, **9**(4): 653–9.

Wrigley, N. (1997) 'British food retail capital in the USA – part 1: Sainsbury and the Shaw's experience'. *International Journal of Retail and Distribution Management*, **25**(1): 7–21.

CWS RETAIL: RESPONSIBLE PRODUCT DEVELOPMENT

JOHN TEMPERLEY AND MALCOLM KIRKUP

The authors would like to thank the Co-operative Wholesale Society for their support in developing this case study. In particular we are grateful for the contributions provided by Janette Bamber, Frank Newsham and Rebecca O'Malley.

The information in this case study has been compiled from a variety of sources. Parts of the case have also been simplified in order to focus on key learning objectives for students of management. For these reasons, while believed to be largely accurate, the material should not be regarded as a totally factual account of views, procedures or events.

INTRODUCTION

This case study is concerned with new product development at the Co-operative Wholesale Society (CWS). The case study has two parts. Part A reviews the history of the Co-operative Movement and CWS, and highlights aspects of the co-operative identity and strategy which have a bearing on new product development. In particular this part of the case focuses on the CWS commitment to openness, honesty and responsibility in trading, and provides an ideal basis for discussing ethical and environmental issues in retailing and for improving debating skills. Part B considers the process involved in developing an own-label product, providing an opportunity to examine the practical implications of responsible retailing for product development, and the benefits of formalized structured processes, planning, teamwork and co-ordination. The case draws on a series of interviews with managers from CWS Retail together with documentation provided by the company.

PART A: CO-OPERATIVES AND RESPONSIBLE RETAILING

The Co-operative Movement

The roots of retail co-operatives can be traced back to the early-1800s, and in particular to the 'Rochdale Pioneers' who established the Rochdale Equitable

Pioneers Society in 1844. This society was set up by 28 men who believed they could protect the working classes from the unfair trading practices of the time by opening a shop that was actually owned by its customers. They started by selling basic provisions (butter, sugar, flour, oatmeal and candles), but as membership and sales grew so the society expanded its product range and retail network. The society proved an efficient and effective retailer, but like many other co-operative societies inspired by the work of Robert Owen and William King, it aimed to be more than that. The society planned to build houses, put the members to work in productive enterprises, buy land to be cultivated by members, and even set up a co-operative community. During the 1800s the co-operative philosophy and benefits inspired the rapid growth of co-operative societies throughout the UK, in retailing, manufacturing, whole-saling, farming and anywhere where groups could provide a service that would challenge conventional organizations.

Co-operative societies are distinguished from other businesses by their values and principles, which are based on the original working practices and rules of the Rochdale Pioneers. The International Co-operative Alliance defines a co-operative as an autonomous association of persons united voluntarily to meet their common economic, social, and cultural needs and aspirations through a jointly owned and democratically controlled enterprise. Co-operatives are based on the values of self-help, self-responsibility, democracy, equality, equity and solidarity. In the tradition of their founders, co-operative members believe in the ethical values of honesty, openness, social responsibility and caring for others. Co-operatives also adhere to key 'principles' – including voluntary and open membership, democratic control, limited interest on capital, the sharing of surpluses with members in proportion to their purchases, concern for the community, and the provision of educational facilities. At its peak in the 1950s the co-operative movement in the UK consisted of over 1000 societies, with 12 million members. Collectively these societies accounted for 12 per cent of all retail sales (Eliot, 1994).

During the 1960s the co-operative movement suffered a significant decline in market share. The abolition of resale price maintenance brought intense price competition from the growing national multiples, and this presented problems for the Co-op's typically smaller shops. Unlike their well-financed rivals, many co-operative societies did not have access to the same sources or scale of funds necessary for major store modernization and development, and a high dividend policy also inhibited investment in some societies. The fragmented structure of the movement also meant higher costs compared to their slicker specialized nationally-controlled rivals. There was insufficient co-operation between societies, and in particular the tremendous buying power of the retail and wholesale sides was not co-ordinated into a national marketing force. The Co-op was also criticized for variability in the quality of its shops and its management, and an outdated image. All of these problems contributed to a decline in market share, and financial pressures among many of the smaller societies forced them to merge with the stronger co-operative organizations.

The co-operative movement has endeavoured to stem the decline in market share through many marketing and organizational changes, including major investment in shop-refurbishments, national branding and advertising, closures of old, small or poorly-sited shops, and investment in convenience stores and large modern superstores. The co-operative movement's share of retail sales currently stands at 4 per cent with a turnover over £7b a year. The number of Societies has fallen to 51, and 4 of these account for two-thirds of the co-operative movement's retail business. Stephenson (1996) notes the main retailing co-operative organizations as follows;

	Share of co-operative movement's trade
CWS Retail	29%
Co-operative Retail Services	20%
United Norwest	8%
Midlands	8%
Next 10 societies	25%
Remaining 37 societies	10%

The Co-operative Wholesale Society

The CWS began trading in 1864, initially as a wholesaler selling to the rapidly growing number of retail co-operatives. The business started by importing cheap foods, opening depots in order to buy direct from growers and owning their own plantations. They also became bankers and insurers to the retail societies and their members. Where they were strongest – in boot and shoe making, clothing and food production – they developed a high degree of vertical integration by starting their own manufacturing and processing facilities, leather-tanneries, cloth-making factories and farms. By the Second World War the CWS had 155 factories.

In recent years the role of the CWS has changed from being a 'seller' of goods to the retail societies to that of 'buying' on their behalf, and there has been a significant rationalization in production facilities. The CWS has also built up its own extensive retail interests, originally through acquiring retail societies but also through developing its own chains. The CWS food retailing business includes 730 stores, principally located in Scotland, the south east and north east of England, Cumbria, Northern Ireland, and the south and east Midlands. These stores trade through four different formats – 62 superstores, 176 super-markets and 428 other grocery outlets. Of the latter, 286 are extended opening c-stores trading as Late-Shop, while the remaining 142 trade under other fascias. CWS also has a non-food division that includes department stores, travel agencies, opticians and garages. CWS is now the largest Co-operative retail organization in the UK and in Europe, and the second largest Co-operative retail organization in the world. The CWS continues to have substantial interests in funeral services, milk processing and distribution, property and farming, and owns the Co-operative Bank and the Co-operative Insurance Society. It also has major stakes in the two federal co-operative chains, National Co-operative

Chemists and Shoefayre. For 1996 CWS total sales increased to £3026m, with an overall profit of £86m. CWS Retailing achieved £1054m from food operations and a profit of £37m (CWS, 1997a).

The large CWS retail base has enabled CWS 'to work more effectively for and with other Co-operative societies – in buying, marketing, distribution and the supply of Co-op brand products' (CWS, 1995a, p. 9). In 1993 CWS led the creation of the Co-operative Retail Trading Group (CRTG), linking up with other leading co-ops in a tight buying-and-marketing circle based on concentrated negotiating strength. The CRTG includes CWS and currently 35 other co-operative societies. The CWS Manchester buying team at the operation's centre negotiates for the whole of CRTG completely, enabling it to wield vast purchasing power which exceeds two-thirds of the Movement's grocery trade. At the group's retail sharp end is an army of grocery stores ranging from convenience stores to superstores.

CWS and Responsible Retailing

The CWS has in recent years been the chief architect behind concerted campaigns to enhance the positioning of the Co-op as a 'responsible' retailer. In 1993, for example, major initiatives in labelling led the industry in the development of ethical retailing practice. At the time, Chief Executive David Skinner noted that 'these and other initiatives illustrate that the CWS is not just another business – it is first and foremost a Co-operative and responds to the concerns of its members on consumer, community and environmental issues' (CWS, 1994, p. 12). The CWS believes that, more than any other retailer, the Co-op can genuinely claim that 'caring' is the basis of their trading philosophy. They believe that consumers have increasing and wide ranging ethical concerns about the products they buy, and that the Co-op can go further than any other retailer in responding to these concerns. Graham Melmoth, current CWS Chief Executive, stresses the commitment of CWS to further strengthening 'the traditional co-operative values of openness, honesty and responsibility' (CWS, 1997a).

In 1994–95 the CWS commissioned Gallup to undertake a survey of 30,000 consumers and Co-op members to examine ethical issues (CWS, 1995b). The research suggested that consumers are prepared to penalize retailers and products which fail to meet their ethical standards and reward those that do. Most respondents wanted the food industry to provide more information on the goods and services they provide, and most would pay more for goods if it met their expectations. The survey suggested that consumer concerns focused on animal welfare, care for the environment, packaging and labelling, and facilities for the disabled and elderly. Two in three respondents said retailers should ensure their cosmetics and toiletries are not tested on animals. A majority of respondents urged retailers to stop promoting products made from non-sustainable resources, and wanted product packaging kept to a minimum. Almost two-thirds of respondents wanted labelling standards improved so they can make fair choices about what to buy.

The 1995 survey prompted the CWS into specific action, including the launch of a 'Right to Know' policy. 'As an immediate priority the Co-op will take action on behalf of consumers in light of its survey findings. It will do all it can to ensure shoppers are supplied with the facts they need, so they can make informed decisions about what they buy. The Co-op is also ready to lead retailers by example' (CWS, 1995b, p. 14).

In 1995 the Co-op launched initiatives on information, animal welfare and diet and health. Information initiatives include new customer leaflets on products, issues and campaigns which may influence what consumers want to buy; telling consumers which manufacturers make Co-op brands; a Freephone number and Freepost address to facilitate enquiries; highlighting products and manufacturers which meet consumers' ethical standards (on shelf-edge cards and leaflets). Animal welfare initiatives include clear labelling on production methods for eggs; working with the RSPCA to extend the Freedom Food range and imposing an eight-hour maximum transportation time for live animals. In addition the Co-op promises that no Co-op brand household or toiletry product has been tested on animals or uses any ingredient which has been tested by the Co-op, their suppliers, or by a third party on the suppliers' behalf, since 1985. In relation to diet and health the Co-op has committed to promoting foods which move towards government nutrition targets, declaring trans fatty acids in foods, and including information about fat and calorie content per serving on the front label of all Co-op Brand products.

As a result of the survey the CWS also produced a Customer Charter (CWS, 1995c), setting out specific promises and commitments, and details of their approach in supporting them (see Figure 19.1). In November 1995 the Co-op won an award from the Caroline Walker Trust conferring national recognition on the CWS's Responsible Retailing campaign. This was followed by an award from the UK Ecolabelling Board to mark the fact that the Co-op will be the first major UK retailer to introduce ecolabelling on its own-brand products. Ecolabels are accorded only to products that have passed strict criteria laid down by the EU with a view to reducing harm to the environment.

In 1997 the CWS published a report, and launched a campaign, calling for honest labelling (CWS, 1997b). They expressed a commitment to be open and honest in labelling – using accurate photographs and descriptions, clear and prominent ingredients and legible print. They have produced a labelling code of conduct and invite customers to voice their concerns on either Co-op brand or manufacturer-brand labelling in their stores. They call for a new universal code of practice for the food manufacturing and retail sectors, and they want the new code enforced by government.

PART B: RESPONSIBLE RETAILING AND NEW PRODUCT DEVELOPMENT

In an increasingly competitive market a strong own-label can be important for retailers as a means of differentiation and enhanced profit margins. During the

1980s and 90s the image of own-label has improved considerably – from the original low-price and poor quality perceptions to a situation where the quality and perception of some own-label ranges can rival major brands.

The Co-op's Commitment to Customers and the Community

The Co-op has served Britain for over 150 years. It was founded to provide the highest quality goods and services within a framework of social responsibility. While society has changed dramatically in the intervening period our commitment to these principles remains. Now we set out eight specific promises. These are not empty aspirations – we back them with action.

■ Our promise to **serve everyone**. Our commitment: *We aim to cater for the needs of the young, the old, those with disabilities, busy families; in fact to serve the whole community.*

■ Our promise to **provide a high quality service**. Our commitment: *We seek to offer a friendly, courteous and efficient service to all our customers.*

■ Our promise to provide **accurate information and to respect your rights**. Our commitment: *We will always aim to scrupulously adhere to laws designed to protect the consumer and to describe the goods and services we offer accurately, giving as much information as we can. We will campaign to secure further legal safeguards wherever we believe that the consumer is vulnerable in order to raise the standard of protection for all.*

■ Our promise to **offer quality products and value for money**. Our commitment: *We seek to offer good quality products at fair prices and all our food products are backed by our unique double guarantee (replace product and refund).*

■ Our promise to the **community**. Our commitment: *The Co-op is part of the community and actively contributes to the well-being of the communities it serves.*

■ Our promise to **employees**. Our commitment: *Retailing is a business about people and we are committed to offering comprehensive training and fair terms and conditions for all our employees.*

■ Our promise on the **environment**. Our commitment: *We recognize that all commercial activity has an impact on the environment, but are determined to measure and minimize the adverse effect of our activities while positively contributing to environmental improvement where we can.*

■ Our promise to the **wider world**. Our commitment: *The Co-op believes it is wrong for many of the world's citizens to be condemned to a life of poverty and while recognizing the limitations of our influence we seek wherever we can to ensure that producers in developing countries get a fair reward for their efforts.*

Figure 19.1   The Co-op Customer Charter (*Our Customer Charter*, CWS Ltd, 1995b)

The CWS has its main own-label range under the Co-op brand and a value range under the 'Everyday' label. The organization has a well-established policy of own-label development. The Co-op was one of the first own-label retailers. The Co-op brand runs to 3000 products in foodstuffs and 1500 in non-foods, and own-label sales account for 23 per cent of CWS retail turnover. Each year CWS Retail introduce approximately 1000 new products (including product variations) for between 1000–1200 CWS Retail and Co-operative Retail Trading Group outlets, representing 35 societies and 60 per cent of purchases in the Co-op food sector (CWS, 1997b).

The process of product development in such a large organization is complex and involves many different managers and departments. A considerable degree of effective co-ordination and teamwork is required to successfully launch just one new product, and careful planning and procedures are needed to ensure new products reflect CWS responsible retailing objectives. The following case example describes the early stages of planning a new product for CWS Retail. The example is designed as the basis for an exercise in planning own-label development, to appreciate the complexity, activities, departments, organizations, relationships, factors and skills involved and to consider the implications of the Co-op's responsible retailing strategies. The names in the example are disguised.

A New Product Opportunity for 1995

Mary Paul is Category Marketing Manager for CWS Retail, involved in laundry detergent and fabric conditioner products. She works closely with a buyer, Jim Smith, and merchandiser, Liz Wilson, to ensure profitable growth for this particular area of the business and they keep a watchful eye out for any opportunities to introduce new products. She is constantly being reminded by her boss, the head of marketing, of the need to develop further Co-op own-label presence – whenever there is sufficient sales potential to generate increased profit for the organization. Indeed this is a corporate objective and one that the marketing group is taking a proactive stance on in all its range reviews.

In January 1995 the category team were undertaking a regular category review. Mary had produced an in-depth analysis of the whole laundry detergent and fabric conditioner sector, and the team discussed at length the possible development options for growth. The value of the market was substantial at around £1b. Powder and liquid detergents accounted for 80 per cent of market value (for example Ariel and Persil), fabric conditioners 17 per cent (for example Comfort and Lenor) and laundry aids accounted for the remainder. Mary's analysis of the fabric conditioner sector had raised some particularly interesting observations and the team felt there were some real opportunities for further development of the Co-op range.

Fabric conditioners are used to condition and soften fabrics and reduce the static of synthetics. Three quarters of all housewives use them in one form or another, with usage being up to three times a week among 50 per cent of housewives. Fabric conditioners come mainly in liquid and sheet form, although they also come as part of all-in-one washing detergents such as Bold. Liquid conditioners are the most popular format with 95 per cent of market value, sold in both standard and concentrated forms in both primary bottles and refill cartons. Mary's analysis showed that standard versions of fabric conditioner were losing share to 'concentrated' forms, resulting in a volume decline in the sector. Value growth was not projected to be strong due to continuing market price pressure and own-label development, and growth was expected only where product performance was enhanced and convenience improved. Advertising spend continued to be high at around 10 per cent of sales, which was one reason why own-label penetration wasn't far higher.

Mary's analysis suggested the market for fabric conditioners was worth around £190m, and the CWS and CRTG retailers as a group were taking about 6 per cent share of trade. The market was dominated by two major manufacturers – Proctor and Gamble and Lever Bros. Comfort and Lenor were the most popular liquid conditioners (with 70 per cent of the market between them) and Bounce and Tumble-Fresh were popular sheet brands. Own-label had a 25 per cent but growing penetration of the fabric conditioner sector. Mary noted, however, that the Co-op continued to lag behind the other major multiple retailers in terms of own-label penetration – around 20 per cent compared to 30–40 per cent at Tesco, Sainsbury and ASDA. She also noted the Co-op appeared to be under-ranged in terms of own-label options.

The category team felt the analysis confirmed there was scope to extend the CWS own-label fabric conditioner range, particularly into the luxury market segment which offered growth potential. They presented their ideas at the annual range review meeting and Mary prepared a presentation covering sector market trends and brand shares, a review of the previous year's actions and results, category strategy proposals and specific range proposals for the coming year. Her presentation was backed up with statistics and a thorough understanding of consumer requirements and competitor strategies. The presentation went well, and the meeting concluded with a clear decision to extend the current fabric conditioner range by developing a new luxury range – with standard, concentrated and refill variants. The team wanted to launch the new product by the end of the year.

Planning Considerations

Mary was asked to consider how the new product was going to be developed, what issues had to be investigated to ensure a successful launch, and how long each activity would take so that a realistic timescale could be put together. Although she was aware of the stages involved in the company's formal product development process (see Figure 19.2 for extract), she had not previously been involved in planning the launch of a new fabric conditioner. She had plenty of ideas of her own, but she knew it would be best to sit down with her colleagues to brainstorm what needed to be done and to set up some fairly quick meetings to consult with other departments she expected to be involved.

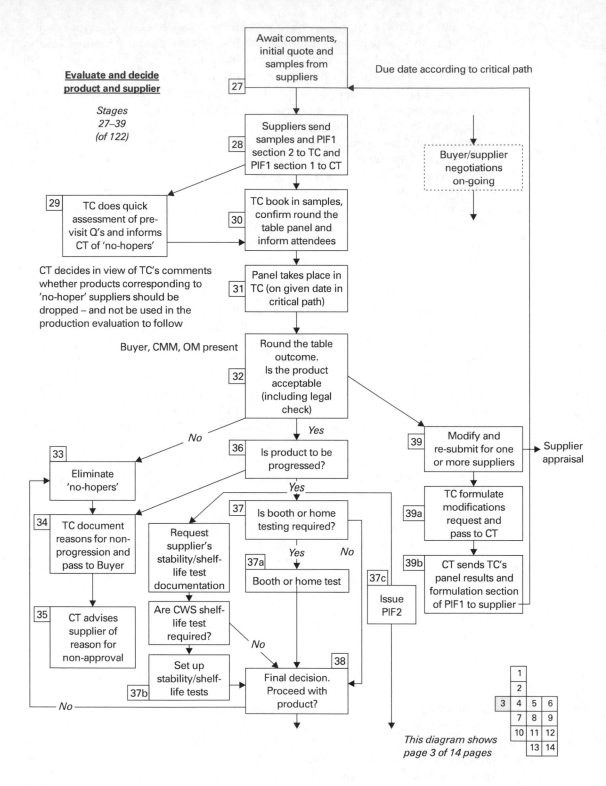

Figure 19.2   Extract from new product development process

Within a week Mary had compiled a set of notes – combining her own thoughts with comments received from other managers. Her notes are presented below. Mary's next task was to prepare a plan to see whether, and how, they could meet a target launch date before the end of the year. The plan would need to show activity milestones and ensure sufficient time to comply with the important issues. Even on a rough estimate she realized she would need around nine months development time, and she knew her discussions to date had only scratched the surface.

She also had briefs to prepare – a buying brief for Jim Smith to start talking to suppliers and a packaging concept brief for the design consultants. She needed to get to work quickly so the new product development process could swing into action.

Notes Prepared by Mary Paul, January 1995
New luxury fabric conditioner – Co-op own-brand

Packaging design will be important, and we'll need to get an external design consultancy involved. I need to make sure we achieve a strong image which has strong shelf impact, reflects the product's premium position and also has an overall gentleness which reflects the product's usage. Consumer research suggests fragrance will be crucial – it's a key consumer benefit for the target consumer group. Most conditioners are labelled with a particular fragrance – we need to come up with something with 'luxury' connotations.

Liz is worried about shelf space. She's got to fit the new ranges into all our different outlets – pack sizes and range options will affect whether she can make the new product available in the smaller stores. I reckon we'll need two pack sizes for the standard product (one- and two-litre plastic containers), two pack sizes for concentrated liquids, and two for concentrated refill cartons need to talk to Liz about this.

Bill Baines (packaging designer) suggests using pack shapes capable of taking standard labels without causing too much waste and hence cost in the printing process. Need to avoid any special colour matching required between label and container – otherwise costs are bumped up again if we need special colours. If we go for refill cartons we need to check quality of the board and lamination for colour reproduction to ensure the quality will look good. We must remember this is a 'luxury' product.

We need to allow time for a brainstorming session on fragrance names before we produce the final design concepts. I need to prepare a detailed packaging design brief for Bill – he'll want to know marketing background, objectives and how the new product fits in with the existing range.

Jim says he's got some good suppliers we can choose from for the conditioner itself. He says it's quite a complex process producing the conditioner – the supplier needs all sorts of raw materials (dialkylester ammonium methosulphate, dyes/pigments, preservative and electrolyte) from probably 12 or 13 different sources. Perfume samples will need to be sourced from fragrance houses to test fairly early on. Suppliers will be needed for the refill cartons and for the outercases. The plastic bottles could be own-blown or also sourced externally. We'll also need a company to print the labels. Container caps – again we could source externally or use own-manufacture.

I need to get a brief ready for Jim so he can get the ball rolling with suppliers on prices and samples. Jim can't move until he's got the buying brief. The brief needs to include – commercial justification, product description, pack size, case size, type of packaging, target volume, number of colours, shelf-life, target margin, date of sample submission, launch date and any anticipated claims (for example not tested on animals). The labelling standards department and CWS technical centre will need to be asked to comment on the buying brief before it's sent to suppliers. We need to allow a few weeks for suppliers to get back to us with quotes and samples.

Notes from meeting with Malcolm Gregory, CWS Technical Centre (TC)

The supplier samples will need to be sent to TC for testing – they'll have a quick look to rule out any 'no-hopers' and then arrange tests for the others. TC will do tests for 'fragrance substantivity' and 'softness'. We must ensure any claims made on the packs can be delivered in the product and match our competitors. Malcolm wants around ten products and two dozen different perfume variations to ensure good spread for testing purposes. A product assessment officer in the TC will organize the tests. A trained panel of house-wives will be used to smell the fabric conditioners – in liquid form and on towels – and rank them in order of preference and impact. I'll get a report showing fragrance and ranking – we can then evaluate and shortlist a final selection for more detailed tests. Need to allow around six weeks for tests. TC also use a housewife panel for softness tests because there's no accepted tech-nical tests which simulate softness. They use freshly-washed terry nappies dosed in fabric conditioner solutions. We also need to allow minimum of 12 weeks to undertake stability/shelf-life tests to ensure product ingredients don't separate after production.

Once tests are complete the product and supplier can be chosen. We need to then organize supplier appraisal – either whole company or just the production line if the company is already being sourced. Objective – to produce adequate defence to support due-diligence and to assess whether the company's factory is actually capable of making the product to a good enough standard. TC (and Jim) would do the supplier appraisal.

A critical path for the production process and a draft technical specification need to be drawn up in association with supplier. Commercial contract needs to be drawn up and supplier code of conduct sent off. The technical specification will be done mainly by TC and the main headings are shown in Figure 19.3. The final technical specification can't be sent off until labelling standards have confirmed copy brief.

We need to allow a major chunk of the timetable for the evaluation of first production run samples from suppliers. TC staff (and Jim?) will visit factory to check production samples against original lab samples.

CWS PACKAGED NON-FOODS SPECIFICATION

Headings only

- **Product title.**

- **Supplier** (name, address, manufacturing units).

- **Manager contacts at CWS.**

- **Product description** – product title, size, general description, odour, colour/appearance, texture/viscosity and unacceptable defects. Suppliers must avoid unacceptable defects at all costs – defects on product (for example incorrect or missing ingredients), packaging (for example absence of coding, poor print), and packs (for example insect damage, any injurious substances and so on).

- **Product composition** – ingredient declaration, formulation.

- **On-pack first aid instructions.**

- **Raw material code of conduct for suppliers** – requirements of suppliers when sourcing raw materials to ensure materials are produced in compliance with good manufacturing, horticultural or agricultural practice, and legal requirements. Guidelines on storage.

- **Identification of raw material suppliers.**

- **Product parameters** – viscosity, perfume, chemical and microbiological characteristics.

- **Product processing** – description of how product will be made, process flow chart, safety devices and filling/packing details.

- **Product packaging** – dimensions and characteristics of carton, outercase and pallets.

- **Packaging requirements** – quality and integrity of packing to make sure product is contained and protected properly for its agreed life; label alignment and adherence; sealing and print on outers; pallet loads and stability.

- **Conditions of handling, storing and delivering finished goods** – location of warehouse, delivery points and transport to be used.

- **Product coding** – coding required on pack and outers; product identification numbers; and shelf-life detail.

- **Sample requirements** – how samples are to be collected for quality assessment.

- **Conformity with legislation** – details of key legislation that the product needs to abide by.

- **General requirements** – requirement to maintain quality records, pest control and hygiene standards, training for production line staff.

- **Health and safety information for fabric conditioner** – details of composition, potential hazards (toxicologically, ecologically and so on), and measures to be taken in relation to first aid, fire fighting, accidental spillage, handling and storage, exposure, disposal and transport.

Figure 19.3   Technical specification for new product

CO-OP BRAND NON-FOOD PRODUCTS COPY BRIEF

Headings only

■ Name of category marketing manager

■ Designer

■ Supplier

■ Labelling standards officer

■ Product category

INFORMATION ON SELLING FACES

■ **Product name** *(for example Concentrated Silk Fabric Conditioner (Tropical Breeze) Refill Pack)*

■ **Weight/volume statement** *(for example 640ml e)*

■ **Minimum letter height:** *4mm*

■ **Boxes** *(for example 'Not Tested on Animals')*

INFORMATION PANELS

■ **Statement of information** *(for example description of product and benefits provided to user)*

■ **Directions for use** *(for example Do not pour directly onto clothes; how to use refill packs and so on)*

■ **Ingredients** *(for example percentage of surfactants, preservative and other ingredients)*

■ **Animal testing** *(Product and ingredients not tested on animals, by us or our suppliers, since 1985)*

■ **First aid directions** *(for example not to be taken internally; instructions if swallowed and so on)*

■ **Caution** *(for example keep out of reach of children; use with sensitive skin; and so on)*

■ **Comments? Questions?** *(Details of Freephone, address, what to do with a complaint)*

■ **Country of origin** *(for example Product of UK)*

■ **Address of CWS Ltd**

Figure 19.4   Example of copy brief content

Notes from Meeting with Jane Taylor, Labelling Standards

We've got to be really careful with the legal issues in packaging and labelling. Need to avoid direct packaging similarities with other main brands (passing off and so on). Need to bear in mind Trade Descriptions Act – any claims or product descriptions must be justifiable. The Consumer Protection Act will affect us in terms of product liability (we might need warnings on the packaging of any dangers in using the product) and price marking. The Weights and Measures Acts will affect letter heights and descriptions of product volume. EC Commission Recommendations also affect the listing of ingredients when labelling detergents. Mustn't forget to consider the various CWS policies/guidelines on labelling – legibility of text, ingredient listing, animal testing, recycling symbols if appropriate and 'Freephone' offer and so on. If we claim the product isn't tested on animals we must make sure we can prove it if required. Also need to look into corporate policy on waste in packaging.

Jane's offered her help if we've got any queries on labelling. We need to get labelling details together fairly soon – we need to be extremely precise in terms of product name, weight/volume, descriptive information, directions for use, guarantees, cautions, ingredients, and so on. We then send details to labelling standards – they'll check against legislation and produce copy brief. LS will send it to me and I can pass it to designers to work up artwork samples for labels. Example of copy brief headings are attached (Figure 19.4). When we get label samples back we need to allow three to four weeks for checking copy. We'll probably have to do two or three re-runs of artwork because of technical detail involved and making corrections. Labelling standards need to check final artwork before it goes to printers.

Other Notes

We need to apply to corporate data and information systems department to request a bar code, and allow some time for the bar code allocation to be made. Product samples eventually need to be distributed to management to help with things like planograms for shelf location, store layout and promotions and so on – we need to send samples to Exec, societies, and CRTG. We need to think about final marketing – on-shelf display materials plus in-store leaflets – and we need to talk to PR about supporting the launch.

QUESTIONS

1. What are the advantages and disadvantages for the CWS in adopting an ethical stance? Do you agree with this approach? Justify your response. Identify the practical problems involved for CWS Retail in implementing this approach in the UK retail grocery market.

2. What are the implications of (a) the co-operative values and principles and (b) the specific initiatives on 'responsible retailing', for buying and new product development? What implications are there for suppliers to the CWS?

3. Using illustrations drawn from Part B of the case study, discuss the benefits of a formal, documented system for new product development.

4. Assuming the role of Mary Paul, draw up a simplified list of the main activities to be completed by the category management team, the technical centre, labelling standards and suppliers prior to the launch of the new fabric

conditioner. Draw a timetable (Gantt) chart showing these activities and, based on estimates of how long each activity might take, try to identify what might be an appropriate launch month.

5. Assuming the role of the buyer, Jim Smith, or the merchandiser, Liz Wilson, discuss the aspects of the new product development process that you would be focusing on and the departments and organizations you would mainly be working with. Remember that not all activities for a new product launch are included in the case.

6. Assuming the role of Mary Paul, prepare an outline buying brief for Jim Smith, and/or a packaging concept brief for Bill Baines, based on the information provided plus any additional assumptions you might wish to make.

REFERENCES

CWS (1994) 'CWS announces retail-driven profits rise'. *Co-op Retail Review*, 25 May, pp. 11–12.

CWS (1995a) 'Record Year for CWS'. *Co-op Retail Review*, 5 June, p. 9.

CWS (1995b) *Responsible Retailing*. Manchester, CWS Ltd.

CWS (1995c) *Our Customer Charter*. Manchester, CWS Ltd.

CWS (1997a) *Summary Report and Financial Statement for CWS Financial Year 1996*, Scene Special, CWS Communication Group, April 1997.

CWS (1997b) *The Lie of the Label*. Manchester, CWS Ltd.

Eliot, S. (1994) 'The Co-operative difference – Asset or handicap?' In McGoldrick, P. J. (ed.) *Cases in Retailing*. London: Pitman.

Stephenson, T. (1996) *UK Co-operative Retailing: Still Seeking a Distinctive Role*. The World of Co-operative Enterprise, Plunkett Foundation.

CASE 20

BEING SMART – DEVELOPING CUSTOMER LOYALTY AT CHELMSFORD STAR CO-OPERATIVE SOCIETY

PHILIPPA WARD, HANNE GARDNER AND HELEN WRIGHT

The authors would like to thank the staff at the Chelmsford Star Co-operative Society for their help and support in developing this case study.

INTRODUCTION

This case study examines one retailer's strategy to maintain market share and gain competitive advantage. It focuses on loyalty schemes and new technology within the context of the co-operative movement. The diversity and differences within the co-operative movement are often misunderstood in that there are many independent co-operative retail societies, some of which are very small while others are multi-million pound businesses. The Co-op is not like a multiple retailer with one management structure but is more like a group of different businesses collaborating in some areas but not in others.

This case study looks at an innovative loyalty scheme using smartcard technology introduced by the Chelmsford Star Co-operative Society in 1995. Using the results of research commissioned in 1997 to assess the working of the scheme so far, students have the opportunity to use their analytical and problem solving skills, to match data and draw logical conclusions as well as developing their planning skills. Additionally, students will gain an appreciation of the unique position of the Co-op in UK retailing.

Background To The Co-operative Movement

The Co-operative movement has played a major role in the development of a number of different markets: grocery, milk, pharmacy, clothing, travel and funerals, for example. Since the beginning in the nineteenth century, all societies in the movement redistributed a proportion of the profit made as 'dividend' or 'divi' back to the co-operators – that is, the members. In essence this was a loyalty scheme which kept customers coming back to spend. The dividend was paid in cash to customers. The Co-op dominated the UK retail scene for over a century. Historically the Co-op's substantial share in retail markets can be attributed to loyal customers. And it is not hard to understand why, when some co-operative retail societies paid dividends biannually of between 25 and 30 per cent on customer purchases. Many families relied on this to pay for children's clothes and shoes and also other major expenditure, such as holidays. Such dividends were thus ploughed back into the Societies, ensuring that future dividends would be substantial, not only maintaining but often increasing the Co-op's market share.

Before the abolition of Retail Price Maintenance in 1964 the Co-op dominated the grocery market because of the payment of dividends. It is particularly important to recognize that the Co-op lost the in-built trading advantage when Retail Price Maintenance was abolished. Before then selling prices had been controlled by the manufacturers and, because the Co-op paid a dividend on purchases, the Co-op was in effect reducing the selling price to customers, something no other retailer could do (Co-operative Union Ltd, 1997).

Such payments had long been a bone of contention among manufacturers and other retailers. However, it was not until the 1970s that the multiple grocers began in earnest to increase their retail shares significantly by focusing on price competition. Faced with centralized buying and integrated distribution systems the Co-op began to lose market share and as a result some co-operative societies decided to abandon paying the dividend to their members. Not surprisingly, members became less loyal. It was such conditions that encouraged Tesco to launch its Checkout Campaign in June 1977 with the specific objective of increasing market share, while at the same time dropping Green Shield stamps, despite the fact that these had been an important loyalty builder. The timing of this campaign was due to the culmination of a number of different factors, such as high inflation and increasing competition. The savings derived from abandoning Green Shield stamps enabled Tesco to implement deep price cuts in an attempt to win customers back into its stores. Tesco boosted its share of the packaged grocery market from 8 to 12 per cent, as measured by Audits of Great Britain (AGB), in a relatively short space of time.

In 1979 the Co-op's total market share for packaged grocery was 18.9 per cent compared to Sainsbury, which held 10.7 per cent and Tesco with 13.3 per cent according to AGB. During the 1980s and 90s the Co-op's market share continued to fall. Many Co-operative Retail Societies have made considerable efforts to halt the downward trend. However, this task is not made any easier by the structure and inter-relationships between the independent societies that constitute the wider co-operative movement and the Co-operative Wholesale Society (CWS). The structure of the co-operative movement places co-operative societies in a very different trading position to that of the major multiple retailers. The democratic, independent structure of the co-operative movement has enabled smaller regionally-based societies to continue to exist. In 1998 the total Co-op market share was estimated to be 5.8 per cent compared with that of Tesco at 15.8 per cent and Sainsbury with 13 per cent (*The Grocer*, 1998).

RETAIL LOYALTY SCHEMES

The aim of retail loyalty schemes has been to attempt to establish long-term relationships between the retailer and the customer – creating a sense of belonging by making the individual customer feel that his or her custom is valued by the retailer.

This can be seen in the moves by a number of the major companies into the field of customer loyalty. Historically, the dividends paid in cash by the co-operative societies were the first loyalty scheme. Trading stamps in the UK can be traced back to 1928, although the best known was Green Shield trading stamp, which started in the late 1950s. The Green Shield Trading Company pioneered the idea of different types of non-competing retailers all using stamps that could be redeemed for a range of gift products. Tesco introduced Green Shield stamps in the early 1960s (Cynog-Jones, 1963).

Modern-day schemes – not only at individual retailer but also at consortium level – mimic the concepts that the earlier schemes embodied: rewarding customers in line with their level of spending, using new technology instead of issuing dividend numbers or stamps. This also enables retailers to develop sophisticated databases of customer spending patterns that can be used to analyse and understand their customers by providing insights into their customers' behaviour and spending patterns.

There have been strong indications that the proactive development of customer loyalty is a difficult if not impossible task and that, in fact, the concept should be inverted with the loyalty obligation residing with the retail organization to its customers and not vice versa. There are indications that loyalty schemes will achieve only limited success, especially for smaller retailers and that customer behaviour will only be modified where the loyalty scheme adds to the overall appeal of that retailer and by rewarding customers for their loyalty on the one hand, while increasing market share for the retailer on the other.

The introduction of a customer loyalty scheme brings with it a number of financial and managerial implications for retailers: the level of discount derived; the cost of the incentives used; investment, implementation and running costs; the potential of retail groups to establish a group-wide scheme without impacting unfavourably on individual retailers' images; the management of the data collected and its potential usefulness.

The Technology

The majority of the technology-facilitated customer loyalty schemes that have come into existence are card-based. These schemes use magnetic-swipe technology, which facilitates data collection at a central point. Some retailers have elected to use 'smart' technology as the basis for their loyalty programmes. These are, however, low in number. The relative costs of the two options have been cited by many retailers as the reason behind their choice of facilitating system. This may in the long-term prove to be a somewhat short-sighted move because smartcards open up a much wider range of potential opportunities.

The smartcard is a plastic card, similar to the widely-used bank cards carried by most adults in Western society. The one difference is that the smartcard has a microchip embedded within it, which can be used to store relatively large amounts of data. This storage capacity is the feature that sets smartcards apart from their magnetic-swipe and bar-coded counterparts. This provides smartcards with a much broader range of potential application formats and uses. These can be defined in terms of three basic categories:

- memory cards – used for data storage, and commonly used in commercial applications such as retail loyalty schemes, and as telephone payment cards;
- microprocessor cards – these have a very large capacity, and have been used in the development of electronic purse applications, including the Mondex initiative;
- contactless cards – these enable information to be transmitted without the use of direct contact between card and terminal, and therefore have potential applications where 'rapid turnaround' is required – for example in the collection of tolls and fares.

It appears that direct retail uses – such as the development of smartcard-based loyalty schemes and the continued proliferation of electronic purse (EP) cards – will play an increasingly important role. The use of the cards as multi-functional tools containing many banking services, such as debit and credit card facilities, cashless purses and loyalty schemes, has led to varied responses from retailers – many worrying about the potential problems, caused by a lack of smartcard standards, leading to additional costs. To try to curtail the development of such a scenario, the government has instigated the 'National Smartcard Forum' to help boost the development of the technology in the UK. The forum consists of chip manufacturers, software developers, suppliers, users, banks, regulators, government officials and consumer representatives. It will consider issues such as inter-operability, consumer protection, privacy and financial regulation.

It would seem that smartcards have the potential to provide retailers with the necessary technology finally to integrate customers into their systems. However, the development of smartcard loyalty schemes has been limited, and questions have been raised regarding the ability of any loyalty scheme to actually develop customer loyalty. The power of such schemes to develop loyalty may be limited, but there may be substantial potential benefits linked to the analysis of the data generated and stored by these card-based schemes. This analysis can be used to retain defecting customers and to steer customers to making purchases that are profitable for the retailer. These doubts have not halted the continued roll-out of customer loyalty schemes by retailers – the heavy and continued promotion of the Boots Advantage and WH Smith cards illustrating the continued interest in such programmes. Even those companies, such as Sainsbury's who were initially reticent about the potential of loyalty cards calling them 'electronic Green Shield stamps', have subsequently entered the loyalty arena.

In a competitive market, IT could have a profound effect on retailing: shifting its focus from the distribution of goods and the satisfaction of demand, to the management of processes and the ensuing relationships not only with customers but also with suppliers. The traditional pattern of IT implementation – for example, applications that aid efficiency of stock control and management – has now been augmented by the introduction of technologies that are aimed at increasing effectiveness – for instance, the introduction of data-warehousing and data-mining to boost retailers' abilities to understand and target individual customers. Alongside the application of IT for effectiveness, there has also been a shift towards the management of the demand chain. Retailers are increasingly looking towards the management of their relationships with the customer; and now this process, both at the front and back-of-house, is being conducted through the application of IT.

The development of such relationships may be favourable for a number of reasons: cost-reduction, greater customer share and better insulation against the competition – thus providing considerable competitive advantage. To exploit fully these potential sources of competitive advantage, retailers must not simply develop customer loyalty schemes but need also to analyse the information generated to establish if loyalty can be predicted from such data.

It is reported that the Sainsbury Reward card cost over £30m to set-up, and that the postage charges incurred by Tesco in the first year of the operation of its scheme totalled £10m – with Tesco claiming that it has issued over £150m in rewards to its customers within the same period. These issues mean that there can be almost insurmountable exit barriers for those retailers who have established customer loyalty schemes. The schemes may also create unrealized expectations among participants, who then become disgruntled customers and not loyal when rewards do not match expectations and loyalty does not follow. On the contrary customers may become interested in other retailers' schemes to seek 'satisfaction'. Indeed customers may become loyal to loyalty schemes *per se* and have a whole range of cards in search of the best rewards.

DEVELOPMENT OF THE CHELMSFORD STAR SCHEME

The Chelmsford Star Co-operative Society has a turnover of £30m and is ranked 25th – based on yearly turnover – in the hierarchy of 52 retail societies (Co-operative Union Ltd, 1997). It launched a customer loyalty scheme in 1995, making it one of the earliest grocery retail loyalty initiatives, as part of a wider strategy to retain customers. It was decided that this scheme would be best served by using a smartcard-based system. This decision has had obvious financial implications for the Society – the smartcard system cost the Society a great deal more to implement and develop than would a magnetic-swipe based one. The cost of the technology required a substantial financial investment by the Society. However, if this decision provides this Society with an additional means of developing competitive advantage, then the decision to invest initially in the more expensive scheme will be justified.

The loyalty programme runs throughout the Society, which offers grocery, non-food, petrol, travel and funeral services. Members are issued with a smart-card, referred to as a Starcard, which facilitates additional features, such as an electronic purse system. The collection of reward points can be transacted at any site. Members make an investment to become a scheme participant and the level of reward received is dependent upon the amount invested. The reward and investment structure of the scheme is summarized in Table 20.1.

Table 20.1 **Reward and investment structure**

Investment levels	£1	£50	£100	£150	£200	£500
Store type	*Stars issued for each £5 spent (net price)*					
Foodcentre	20	25	30	35	40	100*
Department stores	20	25	30	35	40	100
Motor services	20	25	30	35	40	100*
	(Every 1000 stars earns £5 dividend)					
	Cash dividend for each £5 spent (net price)					
Travel	5%	5.5%	6%	6.5%	7%	15%
Funeral services	5%	5.5%	6%	6.5%	7%	10%

Source: Scheme promotional material, 1997

* 5% for purchases below £50

The highest level of investment is termed the '500 Club' and there are additional benefits associated with its membership, including higher levels of interest on capital invested, the provision of funeral bonds and the availability of preferential interest-free credit. The use of membership investment as a criterion for reward-level determination provides the Society with the facility to reward those members who have invested most heavily. This is particularly important to a business which has non-food operations such as travel, furniture and electrical goods. For members of such schemes this can provide significant benefits, which are far greater than those obtained from weekly food shopping.

The Chelmsford Star Co-operative Society felt that the data generated from its loyalty scheme, although providing a means of tracking customer spending, did not generate information on the motivations and future requirements of scheme members. In 1996 the Starcard marketing and development manager commissioned research to identify what motivated members to become involved and why some were prepared to invest £500 and others opted for the minimum investment of only £1. Was it because they did not understand the potential benefits? If that was the case, was that because of unclear communications? And what could the Society do to address these issues? At that time membership of the scheme was in excess of 14,000, with more than 750 participants belonging to the 500 Club. Qualitative research was conducted by interviewing members at different levels of the scheme to help develop a broader understanding of their perceptions of the scheme and to identify potential opportunities for further scheme development.

RESEARCH RESULTS – CUSTOMER PERCEPTIONS

The following research results were presented to the development and marketing manager.

500 Club Members

The primary factor for involvement in the scheme at this level was the potential to derive discount on a range of purchases. Membership of the 500 Club provides greater rewards than scheme participation at any other level, and 500 Club members typically use a wider range of society offers on a more frequent basis.

One member of the 500 Club put it like this:

> if buying, we'll do it from here [Chelmsford Star Co-operative Society], or make certain that we check the Co-op prices. If it's competitive – maybe a few pounds extra – at least you're getting the 15 per cent off in dividend. I try to make my weekend purchases here rather than anywhere else, because I get the dividend… We get wine from here… and odd things as we need them; and the major [food] shopping is done elsewhere, I have to say. Well, over the last two years, we have bought a new lounge suite; we have bought a television set; we've bought a CD player, and various other things… We have gone out of our way on major items like that – oh, and a holiday!

> It [membership of the 500 Club] straightaway makes me think: well, if the Co-op's selling that, why not go there? You've got the card. You've got to take advantage, and use it as often as you can. Well I am… I know the price will be competitive. They've got a reasonable selection, and I get discount on it.

Although the collection of up to 15 per cent dividend acted as the primary spur for membership of the 500 Club, a number of other factors – such as the funeral plan and increased levels of interest on investment – acted as additional attractors: making the participation in this highest level of the scheme enticing.

Alongside those motivations that can be attributed directly to elements of the loyalty scheme's reward structure, there are other factors that have been cited by members of the 500 Club as important in their decision to join the programme at this level. The personal recommendations of acquaintances acted as the spur for scheme participation in some instances: with the detailing of potential benefits being the deciding factor in the decision rather than the instigator. Members of the 500 Club also appeared to act as advocates of the scheme and its potential rewards – one respondent actively drawing the attention of other family members to the benefits of the programme; and others suggesting scheme participation to their friends and colleagues as a means of deriving potential rewards for spending.

> A friend of mine had just bought a television and video, and knew that I was looking to replace my television and video; and he said why not become a member of the 500 Club?… I'd seen it, but it hadn't registered. …He said, you will immediately get this 15 per cent in dividend. So, I said, well, it can't be a bad idea: so I drew £500 out of the building society and put it in here.

There were other factors that appeared to affect the decision to invest in this level of membership in a similar manner. Several of the 500 Club members interviewed considered the level of service they received from the Chelmsford Star Co-operative to be an important factor, although not perceived directly as the motivator. The service levels described were viewed favourably in the majority of instances across the spectrum of offers presented by the Society, both in the food and non-food divisions.

The emphasis on augmenting features to the scheme extended to other factors such as price competitiveness, and in fact, at each interview, issues of price were raised. The Society was perceived as being price competitive in its non-food offer:

> all the stores are competing with each other, and, if you can come in here and say I can get exactly that washing machine here or there at £5 cheaper, they will immediately drop the price to you. They do. I'd rather buy it here: the service is much nicer.

The non-food offering was well received by the majority of 500 Club respondents. The food was perceived differently; it was seen as being less price-competitive and aimed at a convenience shopping format, but was also seen as being both less expansive than that of the major grocery multiples, such as Tesco and Sainsbury's; although a number of the respondents stated that the smaller size of the Society's food stores was prohibitive to the development of an extensive food offer.

When asked if membership of the 500 Club had increased the level of spending with the Society, the majority of participants said that it had, although the frequency of their visits had not necessarily increased. The Society is now being used as a source of a wider range of products and offers than had been the case for those respondents who had previously used the Society. Therefore, rather than generating loyalty, the scheme appears to have reinforced loyalty in these customers.

There was a smaller number of participants who had not shopped with the Society on a regular basis previously. For these respondents the motivation to join was driven by the potential rewards. In these cases, spending with the Society had increased substantially. It was interesting to note that these members appeared to have an appreciation of the potential facilities available through the Starcard: some having used the savings and electronic purse facilities. However, this knowledge was sporadic and selective – a number of the respondents were not aware that the card could be used for any purpose other than the collection of dividend, which was seen as its primary role.

Other Scheme Members

The motivations for scheme membership at the lower levels of investment bear a number of similarities to those displayed above. Some respondents had become scheme members on the recommendations of a friend or Society staff at the point-of-sale.

> one of the women at work ...she just said, well, it's [the Starcard scheme] good, it doesn't cost you nothing, and, if you're spending money all the time, it builds... So, we just thought, oh well, we used to have a divi. I used to like the divi thing then: so I thought I might as well – there's nothing to lose, and that's really why I did it.

The motivations of this group of members for joining the scheme appears to be much more 'passive' than the more self-guided motivations for members of the 500 Club – where the decision to become a member appears to be self-guided. The focus here appears to be the collection of dividend. However, in this instance, this is associated with existing spending and patronage patterns. None of the respondents stated that their spending patterns with the Society had increased due to scheme membership. They were, however, more 'aware' of the Co-operative's offer: considering making purchases from the Society, especially where larger items were concerned. This occurred for two reasons: first, many believed the Society to be price-competitive; and also because large purchases increased the amount of points collected and therefore the dividend they received.

> if you know something is going on your card, and you can get it for the same price there as other places, you would obviously go there. But, then again, I mean the Co-op here – apart from the food, even in the big stores – is very competitive, and you always tend to look there and think: oh well, you get your extra points on top of it... I always check prices, like on bigger items... I do check there and see if it's competitive: sometimes even if it's only very slightly you know you're getting your points and that.

With this category – as with that of the 500 Club – factors other than the discount derived from the Starcard appear to be of importance. There was a high degree of price sensitivity; and, again, the concept of competitiveness was viewed as an additional motivator. The issue of product range – although mentioned in relation to the food offer – was not as prominent a factor as it had been with the 500 Club. Perhaps most significant was the lack of unprompted consideration of the service levels provided by the Society, which was very much the converse in the previous group. Those in this category appeared to be much less concerned with this aspect of the offer.

In contrast to the 500 Club responses, the fundamental nature of the relationship between these members and the Society appeared to focus on the food offer – although non-food purchases were mentioned. The nature of the food-based relationship varied: one participant using the Society for her main food shopping – using the Society's larger food stores – and the remaining three tending to participate in top-up shopping at the smaller food shops. These patterns were well-established prior to participation in the scheme and membership appears to be a mechanism for generating additional benefit using existing spending. A number of comments were made which supported this proposition – the following example is typical:

> the card, …at the end of the day, it's something that is there to mount-up because you're spending the money there really. So I suppose, basically, just that little bit of saving there and there.

This was also supported by the lack of usage of the other facilities available through the Starcard, such as the electronic purse – many of the members using it purely for the collection of dividend, and not being fully aware that the card could also enable other facilities.

Retailer Trust

All respondents trusted the Society to act in an 'appropriate and responsible' manner with regard to the use of the data collected through the scheme. Many saw the collection of data as an inevitability, stating that data could be gained from a number of other sources, and therefore they did not hold undue concerns regarding the data held by the Society – many stating that they felt sure that it would be treated as confidential.

This issue of retailer trust permeated a number of the comments made by participants and is perhaps best illustrated in the following:

> any other store, if you had tied money up in it you might have a moment of doubt, but… you can remember the Co-op when you were a child, and your parents can remember it when they were children, and the thought of there not being a Co-op is the equivalent of saying there might not be a Bank of England.

DEVELOPING CUSTOMER LOYALTY AT CHELMSFORD STAR CO-OPERATIVE SOCIETY

QUESTIONS

?

The marketing and development manager of the Chelmsford Star Co-operative Society is now in the process of considering the research findings and making recommendations about the future of the Starcard to the chief executive.

1. Consider the research findings and make recommendations about a future strategy for Starcard. Your recommendations should suggest potential areas for development and consolidation.

2. Based on the experience of the society with smartcard technology, draw up a critical appraisal of its use which would demonstrate the advantages and disadvantages of the technology to a retailer considering the introduction of a loyalty scheme.

3. 'any other store... you might have a moment of doubt, but... you can remember the Co-op when you were a child, and your parents can remember it when they were children, and the thought of there not being a Co-op is the equivalent of saying 'there might not be a Bank of England!'

   Analyse what features of the Co-op's retail offering engender this type of customer response. Discuss whether you believe there are any other retailers who would provoke this response to their offer. Make recommendations as to how other retailers might develop their customer relationships so as to emulate the Co-op's experience.

4. Select a retail sector: Imagine that you are the marketing manager of a retail company in your chosen sector planning to introduce a smartcard loyalty scheme. Identify the data that could be collected by the company from the use of the smartcard and stored in a database. Draw up a three-year plan for a long-term promotional campaign by the company on the basis of the data on customers obtained from use of the smartcard.

REFERENCES

Co-operative Union Ltd (1997) *Co-operative Statistics – Information Service*. Manchester: Co-operative Union.

Cynog-Jones, T.W. (1963) 'Trading stamps: some facts and figures'. *The New Dawn: Union of Shop, Distributive and Allied Workers*, **17**(24): 738–48.

Gannaway, B (1998) 'The OFT's new stamping ground'. *The Grocer*, 8 August, pp. 26–8.

CASE

'OPERATION RETAIL': MARKETING LOCATIONS TO RETAILERS

GARY WARNABY

The author is indebted to Neil Horsley of Nottingham Development Enterprise, Stephen Hyde of Globebirch Ltd. and Tracy Croft of Nottingham City Council for their assistance and provision of information for the case study. The author also acknowledges the helpful comments of David Bennison and Dominic Medway of the Department of Retailing and Marketing, the Manchester Metropolitan University and two anonymous Retail Education Group reviewers.

INTRODUCTION

Nottingham is the major city in the East Midlands, holding a key position in the regional economy. The population of the city is currently 283,800, with 740,000 people living in the wider Nottingham conurbation. The city enjoys a diversified economic base. While long-established industrial activity remains important to the local economy, 70 per cent of the city's workforce are now employed in the service industries. A sector that has exhibited particular growth in the city has been financial services – where employment has recently grown to 23,000 (constituting 17 per cent of the city's total workforce). Major private sector employers in the city include: The Boots Company plc; GPT; Raleigh Industries Ltd; Speedo (Europe) Ltd; Royal Ordinance plc; Experian (formerly CCN Group Ltd); Imperial Tobacco Ltd and Northern Foods plc. As the administrative centre of the East Midlands, the public sector employs many of the population through both Nottingham City Council and Nottinghamshire County Council. The two universities based within Nottingham are also major employers. Current trends indicate that the City will enjoy continued population and economic growth into the new millennium.

RETAIL PROVISION

The city of Nottingham offers an extensive retail provision of 1150 outlets in total, incorporating a broad mix of retail outlet types. The total gross retail floorspace stands at 463,000 sq m. The retail attractions of Nottingham are such that, in 1989, the city was ranked seventh in a list of the UK's top shopping venues by Hillier Parker, and in 1995 the city was ranked fourth in a similar listing by Management Horizons. Over two million people (800,000 households) regularly shop in Nottingham city centre, and Nottingham has a catchment population of over three million people within one hour's drive of the city.

The retail provision in the city centre is accessible and well contained within an area of 2.5 sq km. There are four covered shopping malls: the Victoria Centre, the Broadmarsh Shopping Centre, Flying Horse Walk and the Exchange Arcade.

The Victoria Centre, situated on the northern edge of the town centre shopping area, is the largest of these covered shopping centres with over 120 shop units covering 91,000 sq m. The major anchor stores include Jessops (John Lewis Partnership), Boots, Tesco (Nottingham's main city centre supermarket) and a new House of Fraser store. Other retailers represented in the centre include River Island, Richards, Dorothy Perkins, Principles, Ciro Citterio, Early Learning Centre, H. Samuel, The Gap, Hamells, Adams, Dixons and Woolworths. Footfall within the centre is over 400,000 shoppers a week.

The second largest centre is the Broadmarsh Shopping Centre, situated on the southern edge of the city centre shopping area. The centre comprises 41,000 sq m, over 90 stores and has a customer footfall of over 330,000 shoppers a week. The major anchor stores include Allders, BHS and Boots The Chemists. Other retailers represented in the centre include C&A, Holland and Barrett, Radio Rentals, Dorothy Perkins, Superdrug, Poundstretcher, Thorntons and Birthdays.

The other two covered centres are much smaller, each with 17 units. Flying Horse Walk covers 3325 sq m, and the Exchange Arcade covers 2787 sq m. The tenant mix of these smaller centres is focused on upmarket retailers such as Mondi, Alexon and Ouiset in Flying Horse Walk; and Jacadi, Country Casuals and Oasis in the Exchange Arcade.

Outside of the covered malls, there are a number of specialist and niche retailing centres, including: Bridlesmith Gate, specializing in designer fashion; Derby Road, specializing in antiques, art and design and music shops; Hockley, which focuses on youth fashion, fashion accessories and art and design; and also Clumber Street, which focuses on sports, leisure and multiple retailers.

In addition to retail provision, Nottingham city centre also contains 250 restaurants and cafes with daytime and evening provision. The expansion of cafe bars, themed pubs and specialized clubs within the city centre has helped to develop more of a street pavement cafe culture as well as providing a more cosmopolitan night life.

Recent Initiatives

Initiatives to improve the city centre can be dated back to 1972 when a city centre plan was drawn up by the council in collaboration with retailers. The main emphasis of city centre improvement activities during the 1970s was the pedestrianization of parts of the city centre. During the 1980s increased competition led to a number of initiatives to provide a more attractive and holistic city centre experience. These included the Nottingham Safer Cities Project, whose action plan of 1989–90 aimed to make the city centre safer; implement specific actions in local areas to improve safety and reduce crime; and take action to help those groups who suffer most from crime (Oc and Tiesdell, 1997).

However, at the start of the 1990s there was greater recognition that if Nottingham's position as a major retail centre was to be maintained in the face of increasing competition – particularly out-of-town shopping centres such as Fosse Park in Leicester (opened in 1989) and the regional shopping centre at Meadowhall in Sheffield which opened in 1990 – then both public and private sector actors would have to work together even more effectively than they had to date. Although a number of specific joint ventures and partnerships between the public and private sectors had been established, none had focused primarily on retailing or had addressed the marketing, promotion and co-ordination of service provision within the city.

Recognizing the need for a co-ordinated strategy for the city centre, a City Centre Management Steering Group was set up in 1990, and met monthly through 1990–91. This steering group consisted of representatives of both public and private sector stakeholders in the city centre, namely: Nottingham City Council; Nottinghamshire County Council; Nottinghamshire Police; the Nottingham Safer Cities Project; Nottingham Development Enterprise; Boots The Chemists; Marks & Spencer; the City Centre Retailers Association; the Victoria Shopping Centre; the Broadmarsh Shopping Centre and Dusco Ltd (owners of the Victoria Shopping Centre) (Oc and Tiesdell, 1997).

The deliberations of this steering group resulted in two complementary strategic plans: a city centre review titled City 2000; and a City Centre Management Plan – a detailed business plan which focused on specific objectives that would facilitate the development of retailing and other complementary commercial activities in the city centre. The objectives of the City Centre Management Plan were as follows:

1. To improve the accessibility into and around the city centre.
2. To promote Nottingham city centre as a shopping, tourism, leisure and business centre to relevant target audiences.
3. To encourage and facilitate improvements to the physical environment of the city centre.
4. To monitor crime levels and implement a strategy to reduce crime and the fear of crime in the city centre.
5. To encourage improved business performance and customer service in the city centre by developing business skills support for city centre businesses.
6. To initiate and maintain establishment of representative organizations for city centre businesses.
7. To maintain and improve the economic development of the city centre.
8. To monitor the performance of Nottingham city centre and that of the City Centre Management Project (Ellis, 1996).

Each of these specific objectives was followed through with an action plan, translated into an operational programme or series of targeted projects (Ellis, 1996).

In 1991 a town centre manager was appointed to co-ordinate many of the activities contributing to the achievement of the objectives of the business plan. The City Centre Management Initiative was initially funded by Marks & Spencer, Boots The Chemist and the city and county councils who between them contributed £40,000, with a further £14,000 contributed by other private sector sponsors. By 1996 approximately £70,000 was committed to the funding of the Town Centre Management Initiative, with £30,000 of this coming from the private sector (URBED, 1997).

Since then a number of innovative cleaning and maintenance initiatives, involving both the public and private sectors have been established. These include the employment of a city centre 'Ranger' to effect immediate repairs to damage in the city centre and deal with graffiti and fly posting, and the development of a city centre shopfront and security/signage guide which helped to upgrade the appearance of many retail outlets. The issue of parking in the city centre was addressed by priority parking for shoppers and those visiting the town (as opposed to commuters) with rates targeted appropriately. All on-street car parking in the immediate city centre was removed and the park and ride system improved dramatically. At weekends a radio information system was introduced which provided parking and accessibility information to shoppers and visitors (URBED, 1997).

Consumer Perceptions

The effect of these improvements to the shopping environment was evident in the results of a survey into perceptions of Nottingham city centre carried out by social research associates in March 1995. This research comprised interviews with 538 people over a four-day period in the city centre and a random household survey in which 135 people were interviewed. It investigated the perceptions of both users and non-users regarding Nottingham city centre and views about how the city centre could be improved.

Over 70 per cent of respondents perceived Nottingham city centre as having improved in recent years. In particular there appeared to be widespread support for existing and further pedestrianization. Perceived improvements in paving, street furnishing and car parks were also indicated. There was also a high level of awareness that these changes had been initiated by the city council.

The main positive aspects of the city centre were perceived to be the variety and range of shops (in an unprompted question over 60 per cent of respondents classified the shopping provision as 'good'). Other features mentioned as positive aspects of the city centre were pedestrianization, the nightlife and leisure facilities, and there were many specific references to favourite shops, buildings and other features, particularly the main square and the 'Council House' (the local name for the old Town Hall).

Regarding the negative aspects of the city centre, by far the most significant related to personal safety, which incorporated a range of concerns including vandalism, begging, graffiti, the homeless, groups of young people in the street, car parks, subways and litter. Another specific problem mentioned was parking. Here, the major concern was the ability to find a parking space rather than the cost of parking. This dimension appeared to be of particular concern to people living outside the city who found it very confusing driving around trying to find a parking space, a problem which was exacerbated for many by the fact that they would only consider on-street parking, or certain familiar or convenient car parks. Other respondents were unwilling to use multi-storey car parks due to the fear of theft or attack. Traffic congestion and the resulting engine fumes were also perceived as negative aspects of the city centre environment.

THE COMPETITIVE ENVIRONMENT

Despite the success of the various initiatives undertaken by the city centre stakeholders within Nottingham to improve the environment of the city centre shopping experience in recent years, the city could not afford to be complacent in the face of increasing competition from other shopping destinations. Such competition comes from a number of quarters. For example, the regional shopping centre at Meadowhall is less than one hour's drive up the M1 motorway, making it an attractive alternative. In addition, the neighbouring city centres of Sheffield, Leicester and Derby have all benefitted from the recent completion of major city centre shopping developments, and smaller towns in the vicinity of Nottingham, such as Loughborough, Lincoln, Mansfield and Newark, are also developing their retail facilities (Oc and Tiesdell, 1997). Indeed, a number of these centres have appointed their own town centre managers.

As has been stated, the recent Management Horizons UK Shopping Index, ranked Nottingham as fourth in the country in terms of its retail provision with an index score of 239. Major competitors in the East Midlands were ranked as follows:

Leicester	192
Derby	152
Northampton	146
Lincoln	124
Mansfield	91

Other potential competitors to Nottingham were ranked as follows:

Sheffield	186
Meadowhall	147

The Management Horizons Shopping Index rates shopping destinations using a weighted scoring system which takes into account each destination's provision of non-food multiple retailers and anchor store strength. Anchor stores, such as John Lewis Partnership, Marks & Spencer and Debenhams are given higher scores (between 6–15 points) than retailers classified as variety stores (such as BHS and C&A, which are given 4 points), local anchors (such as Woolworths and Argos, which are given 3 points), destination retailers (such as Boots and Virgin, which are given two points) and other multiple retailers (such as Monsoon and Miss Selfridge, which are given one point) (Management Horizons, 1995).

While it may seem that the Meadowhall regional shopping centre on the outskirts of Sheffield scores relatively low on the Management Horizons Index, its integrated shopping and leisure offer in a controlled, purpose built environment (covering over 1.2 million sq ft of retail accommodation with the provision of 12,000 free car parking spaces and a railway station) means that it must be regarded as a significant competitor.

OPERATION RETAIL

Concerned with the increasing competition to Nottingham's retail provision, in 1996 Nottingham city council convened a meeting of relevant parties to discuss ways of enhancing the diversity and attractiveness of the city's shopping centre. Present at the meeting were representatives from the city centre management team, a number of city council departments, Nottingham Development Enterprise and various private sector organizations with an interest in retailing (including surveyors and property companies). One of the main outcomes of the initial meeting was a recognition of the need to attract more specialist retailers to the city. Over the next two meetings a 'hit list' was drawn up of over 60 retailers currently unrepresented in Nottingham which it was felt would improve the city's retail provision if they could be persuaded to locate there.

One of the issues that needed to be considered in developing any initiative to attract new retailers to the city was the current low vacancy levels of shop units within the main retail area. Indeed, local estate agents had indicated that many retailers interested in locating in Nottingham had been prevented from doing so by lack of suitable premises. This apparent contradiction between the shortage of retail units in Nottingham and the desire to undertake some form of marketing activity to encourage location of suitable retailers could be explained by a number of factors. For example, it was thought that evidence of unmet demand from retailers would help bring forward new retail developments in the city centre. Indeed, the Victoria Centre was currently in the process of being extended which would create more retail units. The main rationale behind Operation Retail was to ensure that as new retail units become available they were occupied by high quality specialist retailers. Such retailers would add to the city's diversity as opposed to more 'downmarket' retail operations that would not enhance Nottingham's shopping reputation.

It was decided that as the first step in attracting retailers on the 'hit list' (and, indeed, other appropriate retailers who had not yet been identified), some promotional material would have to be developed that could be made available to potential retail inward investors. Some initial exploratory research was undertaken to identify the type of information that would be required by retailers in making locational decisions and a checklist was drawn up. This checklist identified a range of general information requirements including data relating to population demographics and psychographics, the local economy, costs (in terms of occupancy, staffing and so on), accessibility, current retail activity in the city and so on.

Using this checklist as a basis, the various partners in the Operation Retail initiative developed a promotional factpack titled 'Nottingham – First For Retailing'. The factpack, in the form of glossy loose leaf sheets in an A4-size folder, provided information on the city's consumer profile (with the assistance of the geodemographic databases developed by Experian); the local economy; accessibility, tourism and leisure provision; and shopping provision (with separate factsheets on the two main shopping centres – the Victoria Centre and the Broadmarsh Centre). Contact names were provided for recipients of the factpack to follow up any specific information requirements.

The factpack was officially launched in May 1997 in London at the offices of city solicitors Clifford Chance. The event, which was attended by over 70 members of the trade press and development companies, was organized by Nottingham Ambassadors, an organization set up to promote the city of Nottingham using its members contacts. In addition to the official launch, over 500 agents and retailers were mailed a copy of the pack, and a postcard reply insert was placed in *Retail Week* which generated over 40 responses, each respondent being sent a copy of the pack. The pack is being sent to all leisure and retail inward investment enquiries. In addition, over 100 retailers were invited to a city familiarization tour. This event did not take place as scheduled because many retailers stated a preference for one-to-one visits rather than a collective event at which competitors may be present. About 30 retailers have subsequently expressed interest in such an event and an event is planned.

The initial stages of the Operation Retail initiative have been deemed a success. However, the members of the Operation Retail steering group realize that this is just the start, and that the initiative needs to be developed further. In particular, more extensive research needs to be undertaken into the effectiveness of Operation Retail in targeting appropriate retailers, and also gauging the reaction of retailers and their agents to the factpack and the approaches made by the Operation Retail team. The key factor that needs to be ascertained is whether this activity has in any way altered targeted retailers' perceptions of Nottingham as a retail destination: in terms of placing the city on retailers' lists of potential locations; or alternatively, moving Nottingham up their list of priority destinations.

1. From the perspective of a potential retail inward investor, what information would you require to help inform your decision as to whether to invest in a particular town or city?

2. From which sources would you seek to obtain this information and what influence do you feel proactive place marketing initiatives such as Operation Retail would have on the decision-making process?

In answering Questions 1 and 2, you should assume that the potential retail inward investor is an upmarket specialist ladies fashion retailer with a limited number of outlets (approximately 10–15), located mainly in London, Glasgow, Edinburgh, Manchester and Leeds, with smaller outlets in cities such as York and Bath, where the population profile is perceived to closely match the target customer.

3. From the perspective of the stakeholders in the Operation Retail initiative, detail the programme of activities you would undertake to evaluate success to date, indicating who would be responsible for the various activities.

4. How do you think the Operation Retail initiative can be developed further? In doing this you should indicate in general terms who would be responsible for implementing any further activities recommended and how the finance would be raised to pay for these activities.

5. There is potential for the Operation Retail initiative to link in with wider economic development activities in Nottingham. To this end the Operation Retail stakeholders have been asked to develop ideas regarding the development of a 'marketing mix' for a city when targeting retailer inward investment. Detail the factors under the control of the Operation Retail stakeholders (or which can at least be influenced by them), that could be used in isolation or in combination to attract specialist multiple retailers to the city.

REFERENCES

Ellis, J. (1996) 'Place competitive – the Nottingham response' In *Association of Town Centre Management Yearbook*. London: Association of Town Centre Management, pp. 26–7.

Management Horizons (1995) *Management Horizons Shopping Index 1995–1996*. London: Management Horizons Europe.

Oc, T. and Tiesdell, S. (1997) 'The Coventry and Nottingham experience'. In Oc, T. and Tiesdell, S. (eds) *Safer City Centres: Reviving the Public Realm*. London: Paul Chapman Publishing, pp. 198–221.

URBED (1997) *Town Centre Partnerships: A Survey of Good Practice and Report of an Action Research Project*. London: The Stationery Office.

PART 3

TEACHING NOTES

CASE 1

TEACHING NOTES
RETAILING IN TWO CURRENCIES

NICHOLAS ALEXANDER

SYNOPSIS

European Monetary Union (EMU) will have a major impact on all retailers in Europe, irrespective of their national government's decision whether or not to join the system. For many retailers, either because of their customer base, or because of their geographical position, retailing in more than one currency is already a reality. This case explores the issues around retailing in two currencies which are facing retailers in the period leading up to and during the introduction of the single currency in Europe.

The case follows the planning process within Marks & Spencer, focusing in particular on the point of sale issues the retailers will have to address. The electronic point of sale systems discussed in this case, which Marks & Spencer began testing in 1997, are commercially relevant whether the UK joins EMU or not. The case takes the reader through a process of change and evolution in thinking within Marks & Spencer, as an example of one major European retailer.

LEARNING OBJECTIVES AND CORTCO COMPETENCIES

(3)   Organizational Ability and Creative Thinking

Critical thinking and analytical consideration:
- To consider the information and identify the key issues.
- To sort the information and asses the relative importance of the material.
- To apply logical analysis and draw conclusions.
- To solve problems.

Planning and organizing:
- To identify short, medium and long-term issues and problems.
- To prioritize tasks.
- To benchmark progress.
- To review the changing nature of tasks.

CASE APPLICATIONS AND CONTEXTS

The nature of the problem under consideration is one which demands an ability to think around the problem and understand its many implications. EMU has many dimensions to it. In this case study, because of the operational nature of the cases in this collection, particular emphasis has been placed on point of sale issues. However, other issues are raised because of the interconnected nature of the changes which will occur. This is a case study which may be used to encourage students to explore the multi-dimensional nature of a problem and to understand how organizational thinking on management issues evolves. It may also be used to illustrate the need for planning and the organization of different groups and functions within a retail operation.

The case is designed to provide both teachers and students with enough information to discuss the case in class without further reading or research. However, this is a dynamic area and changes will occur within the planning environment after this case goes to press. Therefore, as time progresses, teachers may wish to ask students to read around the subject.

The case takes the reader from May 1996 through to the beginning of January 1998. It emphasizes the uncertainties faced by retailers and the manner in which retailers' understanding of EMU has evolved. The case focuses on Marks & Spencer because they have had a high profile in the national debate on this matter and because they have made specific changes in order to manage the challenges of EMU at the point of sale.

The case concludes by presenting the issues faced by Paul Smith in his new role as Euro Project Manager. This will allow students to place their thoughts on this issue within a real management context.

Question 1 places operational issues in the wider context of the company's business. The simple answer is that option C, that is, not entering the EMU in the foreseeable future, will minimize disruption. However, the operational issues should be considered in the light of channel relationships which might benefit from a common currency and international development which might be facilitated by EMU.

A company such as Marks & Spencer, which operates within countries which are members of the EMU and supplies those stores with goods produced in the UK, will be affected by the relative strength and volatility of the euro and the pound sterling if the UK remains outside the system. For managers operating stores within the Euro zone, profitability will be affected by changes in currency values. This may have an impact on a retailer's ability and willingness to increase exposure to such changes.

Question 1 also gives teachers the opportunity to explore broader economic issues associated with the EMU. The impact of interest rates may be one issue that would be particularly relevant.

Question 2 is a straightforward question which will allow students to focus on the different phases in the introduction of EMU. Unless students appreciate the timetable of EMU, they will not be able to understand the urgency for certain planning decisions.

Students should use the appendices to construct their planning chart. They should be made aware in class discussion that EMU will be in place from 1 January 1999 and that 1 January 2002 is the date at which notes and coins are introduced. This will mean that business to business trading will occur in euros from an early date and this may have a knock-on effect as far as retail customers are concerned.

Students should also be made aware of the long planning times involved with certain changes such as the introduction of new technologies. This was emphasized in the evidence given to the House of Commons Select Committee.

Question 3 provides an opportunity for the students to consider the practicalities of changing over from operating in one currency to operating in two currencies. If the UK does not enter EMU in the first wave, then there will be an opportunity to choose the best date for EMU introduction within the UK at a later date. In the UK, a February date is favourable because of the lower trading levels at that time of the year.

Retailers would favour the rapid phasing out of national currencies so that they do not have to operate with high volumes of both currencies for an extended period. Ideally, they would not want to give change in the national currency and thereby have to operate two till drawers or the equivalent.

Question 3, while of a very practical and operationally based nature, may also be used to explore the lobbying role retailers have in such matters as those raised in this case.

In working on **Question 4**, students should build on their knowledge of retail store operations to establish guidelines. The purpose of this question is to emphasize the pervasive nature of the problems associated with new currency introduction. As the question suggests, all possible aspects should be considered. Staff training will be particularly important, as will the education of customers.

Like Question 2, Question 4 encourages the student to come to terms with the day to day operational disruption that two currencies will cause. As a means of focusing discussion and to aid students in constructing their answers, teachers may wish to suggest that students begin by discussing the handling, pricing and ticketing issues. From that point they will be able to work out logically to other aspects of the store's communication with the customer.

Question 5 allows students to apply their knowledge of the latest developments to the case. As the timetable provided in the case study indicates, the period 1998–2002 will see major changes in currency matters and retailers will be expected to manage these changes at the point of sale. Therefore, there is an opportunity here for teachers to use this case study to provide focus to students' thoughts about those changes.

At the beginning of 1998, many retailers were only beginning to come to terms with the changes associated with EMU. Some of the problems envisaged by retailers, which are discussed in the case, will gain in importance while some will appear less problematic as time progresses. In this light, students may wish to monitor the emphasis placed on different issues by different types of retailer within Europe.

In conclusion, EMU provides an interesting mix of macro and micro issues. For the retailer, there are numerous operational issues to be overcome. There are also important public policy decisions which will have to be made before the introduction of the euro. The purpose of this case study is to provide students with the opportunity to consider the interplay of such issues.

TEACHING NOTES
B&Q ENFIELD: STAFFING A GREENFIELD OPERATION

JOHN AUSTIN AND MANDI PARTRIDGE

SYNOPSIS

This case has been developed to highlight the complex operational issues associated with planning and meeting the human resource requirements of a large scale, greenfield retail operation. The case focuses on the specific circumstances of the store within the context of the local labour market and competitive situation. It also reflects the wider business dynamics and the interface between local discretion and corporate direction.

B&Q operates through two formats: Supercentre and Warehouse. The Enfield store featured here is a new Warehouse store which is now trading successfully. The case follows the store opening process from the occupation of the site, through manpower planning, advertising, recruitment, selection and training to first day trading. Within B&Q all of these activities are undertaken on site while the physical construction of the store, both internal (racking, lighting, merchandising) and external (erecting the building) is underway. The case is written to illustrate the complexity of this interactive situation.

Consideration is given to budgetary requirements and locally and corporately imposed control mechanisms. The case study format is necessarily somewhat sequential to enable students to explore particular aspects of staffing a greenfield site. However, the difficulties of managing non-sequential and dependent processes are explored in order to help heighten awareness of conflicting demands and pressures. The Summary Staffing Schedule (Table TN2.1) indicates the overlaps, particularly between recruitment deadlines and ongoing development activities.

LEARNING OBJECTIVES AND CORTCO COMPETENCIES

(3) Organizational Ability and Creative Thinking

Critical thinking and analytical consideration:
- To develop an understanding of the interface between staffing and retail performance in terms of operational efficiency, customer service and competitive edge.

Planning and organization:
- To build an operational awareness of human resourcing practice.

Forward planning:
- To facilitate an awareness of the importance of forward planning and the organization of resources in a dynamic situation.

(4) Business Focus

Business awareness:
- To clarify the relationship between staffing issues and other business considerations such as finance.
- To encourage consideration of human resourcing issues within the wider context of legislative requirements and the labour market.

CASE APPLICATIONS AND CONTEXTS

The case has been designed to allow for flexibility in teaching approaches, variations in learning style and different levels of retail understanding. The case may be approached at different levels which could allow the student to simply demonstrate an awareness, critically evaluate or practically explore the issues raised, depending on their current level of experience and ability to integrate prior learning.

It will also be possible to use the case for individual and group learning scenarios. The case can be applied on a stage by stage basis. For example leading with the section on the background, a tutor might facilitate a discussion of the issues which appear pertinent before moving on to the next sections and allowing students to discover B&Q's chosen approach. Alternatively, the case could be approached as a whole with a view to critiquing B&Q's store opening processes. Clearly, determining the most appropriate approach is at the teacher's discretion. The questions and exercises offered at the end of the case are intended as a guide only.

The case itself provides examples of a diverse group working towards the accomplishment of a complex task. The difficulties and benefits experienced by the B&Q team are the focus of analysis and discussion. If the case is used for collaborative or team approaches, the development of personal effectiveness and team working skills will be enhanced. In particular, Questions 1 and 2 could be used to support this.

Question 1 requires students to carry out a critical path analysis of pre-opening recruitment activities. This exercise could be approached on an individual basis whereby the student has a clear and specific task in the role of the general manager or on a group basis whereby the group members assume different roles within the management team, for example store managers, management services team leader. An example of the critical path – summary staffing schedule employed by B&Q is included in Table TN2.1 at the end of these teaching notes for comparison and discussion.

Question 2 requires the production of draft job adverts for the local press and could be set either as an adjunct to Question 1 or treated as a stand alone. In tackling the task, students could draw on their own knowledge of B&Q advertising either in the press or on television, and they might be asked to collect appropriate sample adverts in preparation.

This question could be used as a vehicle for critiquing B&Q's public representation. For example, students might have a discussion on the topics 'What do B&Q's advertisements say about it as an employing organization?' 'How does B&Q position itself within the employment market?'

The case provides an example of planning in progress, set in the context of business constraints and real life obstacles. It gives an account of the organization required in order to adhere to plans and adapt and remodel them as required. Thus the case can be used to gain practical experience and develop awareness in these areas. If the case is worked through in a stage by stage way, students' own plans can be compared to B&Q's real life experience.

Question 3 could support this and help students develop their organizational abilities as it requires students to assume the role of the team leader management services whose responsibility it is to co-ordinate induction. They need to brainstorm information requirements, differentiating between ex-Supercentre staff and new recruits, and based on this design a programme and plan a schedule for its delivery. The Summary Staffing Schedule (Table TN2.1) provides an outline of the timescales adhered to by B&Q. The induction process should take account of promoting the particular culture of B&Q Warehouse. This question could be approached in a highly active way with students presenting their induction activities to a group of colleagues.

The case gives examples of problems arising and being dealt with against a backdrop of conflicting priorities. B&Q constantly review their own processes in order to improve. The Enfield store opening was a valuable learning experience for B&Q. Students can also use this case study to analyse and critique in a similar way. Questions 4 and 5 give students the opportunity to put their creative thinking skills to practice.

Question 4 can be pitched at different levels as it allows students to draw on previous experience and retailing knowledge to assess improvements of the greenfield staffing process and evaluation measures to assess the impact of the changes made. In this, for example estimated financial savings could be requested or more general statements about the overall approach.

Question 5 asks for a full evaluation of planned staffing ratios against actual requirements during initial training. Depending on prior knowledge, students could be encouraged to consider this from a purely local perspective or to consider shifts in corporate policy and practice.

Table TN2.1   Summary staffing schedule

Timeframe	Recruitment	Training/Development

January
Weeks –31/–28
	Appoint general manager
	Advertise for/select/recruit:
	    three store managers
	    team leader management services
		Store manager training

February Weeks –27/–24	Agree team leader recruitment process Appoint two team leaders Supercentre visit and interviews	

March
Weeks –23/–19
	One store manager starts
	Agree staff adverts
	Team leader, management services starts
	Recruitment administrator starts
	Adverts sent out
	Team leaders start
		Store manager training
		Induction training:
		    team leaders
		    recruitment administrator

April
Weeks –18/–15
	Interview and make offers to selected staff:
	    nightcrew
	    receivers
	    hardware etc.
		Team leader training
		60 day reviews:
		    team leaders
		    store managers

May
Weeks –14/–11
	Selected staff commence:
	    hardware
	    receivers
	    nightcrew etc.
	Interview and make offers to:
	    gardening
	    show room
	    front end
		Induction training: hardware
		                  receivers
		                  admin.
		                  nightcrew etc.
		Operational training for above
		90 day reviews – store managers
		                    – recruitment administrator
		60 day reviews – team leaders

June
Weeks –10/–6
	Move into store
	Selected staff commence:
	    decorative
	    building
	    gardening etc.
	Interview and make offers to:
	    front end
		Induction training: decorative
		                  building
		                  gardening etc.
		Reviews
		30 day: admin.
		           receivers
		           nightcrew
		90 day: team leaders
		General training: all departments

July
Weeks –5/–2
	Selected staff commence:
	    front end
	    cashiers
	Top up interviews
		Induction: front end and cashiers
		General training: all departments
		Reviews:
		30 day: building/showroom
		60 day: nightcrew/hardware
		90 day: receivers/admin.

August Weeks –1/+2	STORE OPENING 11/8 Top up interviews	Delivery crew training Reviews 30 day: cashiers 60 day: building/timber/showroom 90 day: building/trade etc. Sign off training

Question 6 asks for an evaluation of the extent to which B&Q's employment policies can be seen as beneficial or damaging to operational performance. Here, ethical debate can be encouraged around part-time working, B&Q's working culture and so on. A summary of the different working arrangements and pay scales is attached as Table TN2.2 to assist in this.

Table TN2.2   Distribution of hourly rate and contracts – excluding management team

	Pay						Hourly contract per week				
	3.50/ 3.99	4.00/ 4.49	4.50/ 4.99	5.00/ 5.49	5.50/ 5.59	6.00+	<10	10–15	16–20	21–38	39
Decor	2	12	4	4		2	2	8	5	10	
Gardening	2	10	2	3		1		5	2	2	10
Showroom	2	9	1	2	3	4		6	1		12
Hardware/building	4	12	5	1	2	8		8	4	3	
OPERATIONS (checkout warehouse admin. nightcrew)	10	69	18	7	2	4	22	32	20	12	24

FURTHER READING

Beardwell, I. and Holden, L. (1997) *Human Resource Management*. London: Pitman.
Taylor, S. (1998) *Employee Resourcing*. London: IPD.

CASE

3

TEACHING NOTES
STRESS IN GROCERY RETAILING

ADELINA BROADBRIDGE

SYNOPSIS

Stress has become a disease of modern working life, and the threat of litigation, as well as reduced organizational performance, has encouraged many organizations to take stress management more seriously. In comparing stress levels of different occupations, sales and retailing jobs have been classified as very stressful. This case presents a scenario of day-to-day life in a large grocery superstore. It contains many examples of the potential stressors of the job, and provides the opportunity for the student to identify and categorize these stressors, as well as reaching practical solutions for the alleviation of stress at work.

LEARNING OBJECTIVES AND CORTCO COMPETENCIES

(2)   Managing People and Working with Others

Team working and awareness:
Communication skills:
- To appreciate links between management style and stress within organizations.

(3)   Organizational Ability and Creative Thinking

Critical thinking and analytical consideration:
- To identify and categorize work related stress factors.
- To critically evaluate the impact of stress on both the individual and the organization.

Innovation and strategic thinking:
- To identify a range of individual and organizational responses to stress and to select the most appropriate approaches to stress relief.

CASE APPLICATIONS AND CONTEXTS

Question 1 requires the identification and categorization of potential stressors experienced by all store based staff. Students may group these in a variety of ways. They may simply identify the stressors and demands placed on individual characters or be encouraged to place them into the categories identified by Cooper and Marshall (1978): factors intrinsic to the job; role in the organization; relationships at work; career development; and organizational structure and climate. Some issues which may be identified are:

Factors intrinsic to the job:

- poor working conditions (for example the necessity to work fast and expend a lot of physical effort; repetitive tasks such as checkout operators)
- shift work
- long hours
- travel and relocation (may affect career-orientated managers);
- risk and danger (shrinkage and the threat of violence)
- new technology
- work overload

Role in the organization:

- role ambiguity (lack of clarity about the scope and responsibilities of the job, and inadequate information about the work role)
- role conflict (conflicting job demands, and the requirement to perform tasks disliked or outside of the job specification)

Relationships at work:

- relationships with superiors, subordinates, colleagues and customers

Career development:

- job security (short-term contracts, delayering, recession)
- retirement and reaching one's career ceiling
- job performance (evaluation and appraisal)

Organizational structure and climate:

- scope for participation and consultation
- communications between store and head office personnel

- sudden changes in the work environment
- sense of belonging

Question 2 allows students to consider the implications of having a stressful workplace both on each individual and on the organization. At an individual level, students should be encouraged to consider the aspects of work place demands on the individual's home life (and vice versa). They could be encouraged to identify the symptoms of stress in an individual (and how a manager may recognize them). Examples may be anxiety, aggression, boredom, depression, fatigue, frustration, irritability and bad temper, moodiness, low self-esteem, nervousness. The physiological effects include sweating, lump in throat, indigestion, rashes, tiredness, difficulty in breathing, increased heart rate and blood pressure. Stressed individuals may become more accident prone, resort to nervous laughter, emotional outbursts or trembling. Their speech may become impaired and their behaviour become impulsive. Drug use may become apparent and they may sleep, eat, drink or smoke to excess. Alternatively, they may lose their appetite or be unable to sleep.

The implications of the demands placed on individuals can have a direct bearing on store performance. For example, inability to make decisions and concentrate, frequent forgetfulness, hyper-sensitivity to criticism, mental blocks and so on. This may lead to high absenteeism, poor industrial relations and low productivity, high accident and labour turnover rates, poor organizational climate, antagonism at work, job dissatisfaction and low motivation.

Question 3 will lead students to appreciate that individuals can help to relieve their own stressors in a number of ways. However, in order to be effective in doing this, they need to be aware of the things which cause them stress and be prepared to take action to resolve them. Examples might include:

- clarify their own values and ensure they are running on their own track, not the fast track
- discipline themselves not to over-react
- learn how to relax
- create leisure time and switch off from work
- do breathing exercises
- exercise regularly
- adopt dietary goals (maintain weight and eat breakfast)
- avoid reliance on cigarettes, alcohol, caffeine and drugs
- practice time management skills
- go for a walk by themselves
- have a sense of humour

Question 4 asks students to evaluate potential organizational approaches towards stress alleviation. This builds on the insight that organizations can do a great deal to help to relieve the stress employees experience. The type of action required to reduce or eliminate workplace stress will vary according to the kinds of strategies operating, the coping skills of those involved and the culture of the organization. Various issues which may be raised by students include:

- setting objectives (in particular, a participative process of setting objectives should help to reduce and resolve role conflicts and uncertainties)
- building cohesive teams (junior managers and staff may feel more valued if integrated into cohesive work teams and provided with social support and feedback from their line managers)
- providing emotional support (for example collaborative conflict management techniques often build a perception of caring, empathy and trust)
- special programmes (for example counselling programmes, physical fitness facilities, well-being programmes, leadership training, group decision-making)
- selection, induction and training (by recruiting the most suitable people for the job and organization, and providing the training they need to do their jobs)
- provision of sensible working conditions (including rest facilities)
- feedback on performance (appraisals and general 'thank you's')
- career counselling
- job design to allow choice, variety and flexibility
- placement and career development in accordance with the individual's capabilities
- motivational strategies which do not place undue demands on people
- provision of a company medical officer

Question 5 leads to a critical evaluation of the links between individual management style and workplace stress. Gerry, the manager featured in the case, is a task-orientated manager. His job is very demanding but he enjoys the pace of change in the grocery sector. He thrives on that kind of environment, and doesn't tend to understand others who do not. His style of management may place demands on other workers by the example he leads. He works long hours which the more junior managers may feel they need to copy to progress their career. Discussion on how this, in turn, affects social lives may ensue, with the benefits of leading a more balanced lifestyle explored. Students may also debate the following questions. Should staff be encouraged to take their time off so that their family life doesn't suffer? Should staff be encouraged to leave work at their appropriate finishing times? Is there scope for providing more flexible hours of work for the benefit of the employee or are flexible hours only for the benefit of organizations?

Gerry does delegate tasks to his management team, but because he is concerned with running a complicated business, has he considered whether he is overloading his staff with work? His task-orientated approach may lead him to be aggressive with people in order to increase profits. There is little evidence in the case of team working and allowing groups of staff or departments to participate in decision-making. The views of general assistants do not appear to be considered. Should Gerry's management style change in order to accommodate these concerns?

REFERENCES

Cooper, C. L. and Marshall, J. (1978) *Understanding Executive Stress*. London: Macmillan.

FURTHER READING

Cooper, C. L. and Cartwright, S. (1994) 'Stress-management interventions in the workplace: stress counselling and stress audits'. *British Journal of Guidance and Counselling*, **22**(1): 65–74.

Cooper, C. L. and Marshall, J. (1976) 'Occupational sources of stress: A review of the literature relating to coronary heart disease and mental ill-health'. *Journal of Occupational Psychology*, **49**: 11–28.

Cooper, C. L. and Williams, S. (eds) (1994) *Creating Healthy Work Organizations*. Chichester: John Wiley & Sons.

Elkin, A. J. and Rosch, P. J. (1990) 'Promoting mental health at the workplace: the prevention side of stress management'. *Occupational Medicine: State of the Art Review*, **5**(4): 739–54.

TEACHING NOTES
MANAGING THE IMPACT OF NEW STORE DEVELOPMENT: TRADING POTENTIAL AT SCOTTISH POWER RETAIL

IAN CLARKE AND MIKE PRETIOUS

SYNOPSIS

The impact of new retail developments on retail outlets is at the heart of the dynamics of the retail landscape. By far the greatest impact, generally, has been brought about by the growth in scale of retail stores. In addition, the tendency for larger units to locate in out-of-town sites, either free standing (as is often the case with grocery outlets) or on retail parks containing a variety of stores from different retail sectors has also proven influential. While relatively simple to define, retail impact has very real implications for store management decisions and operations. Impact assessment is particularly important when retailers have to gauge the effect of proposed new competitors on their existing operations; it is also often implicit within the calculations of potential turnover for proposed new outlets. However, although trading impact is central to all retail sectors, little if anything has been written about the subject from the point of view of the implications for store management. Scottish Power's Retail Division – the retailing arm of one of the newly privatized regional electricity companies (or RECs) – forms a revealing example of the importance of impact, as the company operates town centre stores and out-of-town super-stores, frequently in the same catchment areas. It provides an opportunity, therefore, to examine the effects and implications of impact from the view point of intra-company as well as inter-company competition. The case study is based on insights obtained from a series of interviews with members of the company at head office and store management, coupled with supporting documents and information from the company, as well as publicly available information on the electrical retailing sector.

Importantly, the case explores the interface between strategic and operational decisions which surround the process of evaluating turnover potential for planned new stores (normally produced within a multiple head office by a site location unit or department). The recommended tasks put forward at the end of the case study, ask the reader to consider the difficulties and uncertainties of assessing trading impacts within Scottish Power, and then evaluate the effect on key areas of management decision making at the store level.

LEARNING OBJECTIVES AND CORTCO COMPETENCIES

(2) Managing people and working with others

Team leading:
Communication skills:
- To develop an appreciation of the role of specialist head office functions and the importance of their relationship with management and staff in the store.

(3) Organizational ability and creative thinking

Planning and organizing:
Forward planning:
Critical thinking and analytical consideration:
- To develop an awareness and understanding of the implications of impact for planning and management decisions.

(4) Business focus

Commercialism and business awareness:
- To develop an appreciation of the key influences on profitability at the store level.

CASE APPLICATIONS AND CONTEXTS

The case is particularly suitable to courses on retail operations as well as marketing and store location. In relation to competencies, the case study provides a significant opportunity to develop and bring together analytical problem solving skills, with those of teamwork and negotiation. Readers will be required to assimilate and analyse data, and then use this understanding as a basis for decision making. The scenario of a meeting in which store-based personnel meet with specialist head office functions to discuss and negotiate key issues relating to the impending opening of a new store is a common occurrence within retailing. The scenario provides readers with an opportunity to tease out the assumptions of the individuals and their respective roles and to help the team arrive at balanced decisions.

Using the Role-play Briefs

The role-play briefs are a starting point for participants in the New Store Opening Meeting. You are encouraged to think around the issues and insights from the case itself. It is suggested that this is a useful case to enable readers to get a feel for discussion in meetings, so that the number of attendees at the meeting (six) limits the maximum number of participants. The rest of the group can either be asked to:

(a) Observe the meeting, in order to provide feedback on the dynamics of the session; or
(b) Take part in other similar meetings with other groups.

Some of the briefs also include exhibits of new information to be introduced at the meeting by particular participants.

It is suggested that the tutor takes part in the case as the Scottish Power Managing Director, Alan Jefferson, to provide a 'surprise' element to the proceedings. To this purpose, an additional role brief is provided at the end of the teaching notes. It is up to the tutor to introduce this role into the case, although this is probably best done towards the end of the meeting: you live close to Stirling, and could use the issue of the new Currys proposal being of concern to you; you felt it useful to drop in on your way to the head office in Cumbernauld.

No attempt is made to provide 'model' answers since the richness of the discussion that is possible from the nuances, perspectives and counter-perspectives in the case and role briefs will elicit many learning points. After the discussion, a session for debriefing the group is therefore highly recommended.

Brief 7: Alan Jefferson – Managing Director, Scottish Power Retail Division

53 years old. Three years with the company after a career in Dixons Stores Group. A call from Peter Doyle alerted you to the potentially problematic issue at the new Stirling store. Trading 'knocks' themselves are inevitable in your view. Stuart Noble informed you of the new assessment with Currys trading in Stirling alongside Scottish Power at Springkerse. Even on a worst-case scenario with Currys opening half way through the first year of trading of the new store, the return on capital employed (ROCE) would only have fallen by two points to 13 per cent. However, ROCE is only one measure of profitability of an *individual* project. The true effect can, you feel, only be judged when jointly taking into account the net cost or benefit of the new store in terms of new trade it generates, minus the trade lost at other company stores. Stirling Sound & Vision had, individually, always been extremely profitable, so there was room to accept impact. The key was adding the reduced cashflows of this store to those of the new store trading at a lower level, and then bringing them all back to today's prices. On this 'discounted cashflow' (DCF) method of calculation, the net effect of the opening, even in the worst case scenario, financially speaking, was still better than 'putting the money in the bank' to earn interest. On these terms, both Stirling stores should be profitable.

You intend to drop into the New Store Opening Meeting to get this viewpoint across tomorrow morning. The immediate problem is not to let the fixation with this single measure of ROCE ruin the motivation of the store team. The store *will* be profitable.

You are also keen to propose that the 'Trowbridge New Look' concept, which you personally pioneered, should be incorporated as a late amendment to the Springkerse store. The market research report on Trowbridge suggests that one of Scottish Power's strong points is its service quality.

TEACHING NOTES
SAINSBURY'S – THE TRIFLING CASE OF THE MISSING TRIFLE: LESSONS IN STOCK LOSS

RICHARD CUTHBERTSON AND CHRISTOPHER M. MOORE

SYNOPSIS

The case explores the management of inventory in Sainsbury's, a major grocery retailer. The focus is on stock loss and considers the wide variety of areas and circumstances in which stock loss may occur – from receiving product at the retailer's distribution centre to product leaving the store. The case is written from the perspective of a graduate trainee and begins in a store where there is a discrepancy between the stock and sales figures for a particular trifle. The case illustrates the importance of detail and reflects the fact that apparently small errors can cost large sums of money over time.

The graduate trainee considers why the discrepancy in stock figures may be occurring, beginning with the graduate trainee's immediate assumption it is due to shoplifting. The case then rapidly progresses from customer theft, through staff theft, transport packaging problems, out-of-date stock, over allocation of stock, product packaging problems and mislaid stock at the store level, before considering the distribution and inventory management systems issues.

Distribution issues include incorrect labelling as well as a general appreciation of the substantial volumes of operation. This can be used to emphasize the fact that some stock loss is perhaps understandable given the scale of operations.

The inventory management issues discussed include poor sales forecasts, incorrect stock figures and incorrect delivery figures. The text includes basic information on the current Sainsbury's inventory management system and so can be used to illustrate and confirm understanding regarding such systems.

The case ends by reiterating the graduate trainee's task, namely to produce a report on potential stock loss of the particular trifle. This may be carried out as part of a group discussion or set as a written report.

LEARNING OBJECTIVES AND CORTCO COMPETENCIES

(2) Managing people and working with others

Team working and awareness:
- To illustrate the importance of the interdependence and integration of different parts of the organization and the necessary reliance of one member or part of the organization on another.

Communication skills:
- To understand the importance of the correct application of formal internal communications procedures, for example recording of product codes and wastage information, plus flagging up problems to line management.
- To gain an appreciation of the way in which the compilation of alternative views adds to the full understanding of the complexities of the multi-faceted stock loss problem.

(3) Organizational ability and creative thinking

Critical thinking and analytical consideration:
Innovation and strategic thinking:
- To facilitate study skills development by practising gathering the relevant information, identifying issues and drawing logical conclusions in order to attempt a solution to the problem.
- To integrate the material presented in the case with broader strategic frameworks.

(4) Business focus

Commercialism and business awareness:
- To evaluate the impact of stock losses on financial performance.
- To appreciate the relationship between operational decisions on, for example type of product line, packaging and so on, and stock loss.

CASE APPLICATIONS AND CONTEXTS

The case allows for discussion of many aspects of stock loss, especially in the areas of store operations, distribution centres and inventory management systems. Stock loss must be considered in relation to the overall retail business environment, both in terms of external and inherent factors. For example, a fresh cream trifle is always likely to suffer higher stock loss than a tin of baked beans. Most students can empathize with the problems surrounding store operations. After some basic grounding in the theory of inventory management students can be expected to understand the systems issues involved. However, many students have not experienced a distribution centre and so it is useful to visit such a centre. If a visit is not possible, then at least some video footage of such operations would be useful background here. It is important that discussions are not constrained to the case study. Wider strategic considerations (if only at a basic level), must be incorporated if other external or overruling issues are not to be missed. For example, the easiest way to avoid stock loss is not to purchase any stock, but that does not make a successful retail business!

Question 1 requires students to list the full range of potential causes of stock loss. These would include:

a. Theft – staff and customer, although thought unlikely.
b. Poor bulk packaging for transportation.
c. Out-of-date stock due to poor stock rotation.
d. Out-of-date stock due to excessive product allocation/delivery.
e. Poor product packaging, for example a faulty lid.
f. Carelessness in the goods-in section of the store.
g. Incorrect data, for example product codes, wrong quantities, sell-by dates.
h. Poor sales forecasts resulting in excessive stock allocation.

Students should also show an appreciation of the relative importance of these various factors.

In their explanation of the links between head office and distribution centre issues and stock loss at store level in **Question 2**, students might make use of the factors identified in Question 1 and point to the following likely relationships:

■ g and h above may result in c, d and possibly f
■ a, b, e and possibly f may result in g and h

In response to **Question 3** which focuses on stock loss reduction measures, there is a need to understand where the major stock loss is occurring before recommending any required changes. For example, is most stock loss due to particular products, particular stores and/or particular parts of the supply chain?

To answer this question in more detail, students should review each of the answers given to Question 1 and make suggestions as to how stock loss could be reduced. For example, in answer to 1b, students may suggest that buyers and product designers should be more aware of the potential impact of their decisions regarding packaging.

Question 4 asks students to identify and explain a realistic monitoring programme that could be implemented to help identify and reduce the major areas of stock loss. They may consider that education and training would need to stress the importance of stock loss and to encourage staff initiatives, with successful initiatives disseminated throughout the organization. Increased daily awareness of stock loss might be achieved via visible monitoring information, possibly linked to pay or rewards. The introduction of technology could serve to monitor stock movements and associated stock loss automatically and more accurately. Specific measures to reduce stock loss will depend on where stock loss is highest, for example, if theft is a major issue then electronic article surveillance may be considered and so on.

FURTHER READING

Jessop, D. A. (1998) *Stores and Inventory Management*. Stamford: The Chartered Institute of Purchasing and Supply.

MAPS (1998) *Technology in Retail Distribution*. London: Market Assessment Publications.

Van Maanenberg, D. (1995) *Effective Retail Security*. Oxford: Butterworth-Heinemann.

TEACHING NOTES
CONCESSIONS MANAGEMENT IN DEPARTMENT STORES: THE DEBENHAMS LUGGAGE DEPARTMENT

PAUL GAFFNEY AND MALCOLM KIRKUP

SYNOPSIS

Concessions are used by a wide variety of retail organizations and, in the case of department stores, account for a significant proportion of sales turnover. In spite of their importance, and the significant implications of trying to integrate independent businesses within a store environment, there is little case material available, particularly at the operational level. Debenhams provides a useful example of the management of concessions. They are unique in having a dedicated concessions directorate and particularly close working relationships with concessionaires. The case is based on a series of interviews and supporting documentation provided by Debenhams and Luggage Management International.

The case examines strategic and operational issues, and the case can be divided to examine each separately. The recommended tasks raise numerous discussion points on the rationale, advantages and disadvantages behind concession strategies, but the main issues relate to contractual and operational implications of the proposal to launch the new Luggage Management International concession.

LEARNING OBJECTIVES AND CORTCO COMPETENCIES

(3)   Organizational ability and creative thinking

Planning and organizing:
- To develop an awareness of the operational implications of concessions for store management – including the store managers concerns and actions in attempting to achieve a seamless join between concession and own-bought departments from the consumers' perspective, and the issues involved in managing concessions.

Critical thinking and analytical consideration:
- To develop an understanding of the nature of the retailer-concessionaire relationship, contractual arrangements, and the criteria for a successful partnership.

Innovation and strategic thinking:
- To develop knowledge of the nature of concessions, and the advantages and disadvantages of concessions as a strategy for both retailers (the host) and suppliers (the concessionaire).
- To develop an awareness of the differences between concessions and new stores from a development, planning, management and operational point of view.

(4) Business focus

Commercialism and business awareness:
- To make and justify recommendations and alternatives for the new department and for potential contractual arrangements.

CASE APPLICATIONS AND CONTEXTS

The case is ideal for courses on retail marketing, retail strategy, merchandising and store operations. The case can form the basis of a negotiation exercise, and help students develop communication skills to achieve a win-win situation for the new trial. Students can examine the main concerns, objectives and motivations of each party in the proposed project. A planning and organizing assignment can be set around launch activities, and the visual merchandising aspects offer an opportunity to be creative in presenting visual solutions.

Role of Concessions

The first questions focus on the advantages and disadvantages of concessions. Bob Falconer is naturally upbeat about the benefits of concessions – powerful brands to support marketing, benefit from concessionaires' advertising and promotion, specialist selling staff, expertise in buying and merchandising, flexibility, adding interest, pressure on concessions to perform, cost-savings, and use of excess space. The case does not reveal disadvantages from the hosts' perspective. However, students should consider whether Debenhams are typical of department stores in their approach to concessions and their relationship with Luggage Management International. Some concessionaires do not dedicate themselves to one specific host – preferring to pick and choose where they might wish to place their brands – with potential conflict with host retailers chosen. Certainly a number of texts (for example McGoldrick, 1990) suggest disadvantages for host department stores, and students can consider the circumstances under which these problems might occur. Potential problems may arise from an excessive use of concessions (on image and innovation), diversity of design formats in-store, concession failures, margin implications, control over stock, prices and staff, and relationships between store and concession staff.

The Debenhams–Luggage Management International partnership is strong and may not be typical of host–concessionaire relationships. Davis outlines advantages of a concessions strategy for Luggage Management International, although there may be other benefits for other types of supplier (for example market testing). The potential drawbacks warrant further examination, and Luggage Management International may not be typical. Disadvantages may arise from the length and nature of contracts, dependence on the host, ability of host to learn from the concessionaire, and restrictions on space/location/ranges.

Operational Implications

Students can consider the operational implications of the new concession and assume Darryl Carter's role. The new concession scenario can be compared with a new store opening – how might the store managers role be similar or different? Timescales, costs, training and responsibilities will vary. Students should consider Darryl's role in the widest possible sense, and try to resolve some of the questions and concerns he raises in the case to ensure the proposed trial is successful. Pre-launch planning should be distinguished from post-launch operations. Issues might include arrangements for contractors, health and safety procedures during fitting-out, co-ordination of recruitment, induction and training, till support and procedures, stock-holding arrangements, stock delivery and handling, catering, security arrangements, and window and promotion support. Students should consider which Debenhams and Luggage Management International personnel might be involved in the planning, preparation and launch activity and their respective roles.

Contractual Arrangements and Negotiation

The case can be used for role-playing and a negotiation exercise around terms and contractual arrangements between host and concessionaire – albeit for a trial programme. Students should consider the motivation of each party, how their individual goals might differ and where there might be common ground. The case highlights aspects where negotiation might be needed (for example commission rates and shopfit costs) and the nature of the high-value product needs to be considered.

Students can develop their own ideas of terms and conditions for contractual arrangements. For Debenhams the main issues would include commission rates, payment dates, accommodation and services to be provided (for example porterage, cash collection, cleaning, tills, catering, telephone costs), shopfit and maintenance costs, shopfit design approval, stock levels, staffing hours, adherence to company policies (ethical stance, press statements), copyright and trademarks, insurance (damages or loss), credit facilities for customers, employment and payment of staff, recruitment, staff discounts, training, supporting promotional events, approval for signage and advertisements, and termination notice arrangements.

Commercial and Visual Solutions

Students can analyse and judge whether Debenhams should proceed with the trial and/or the new concession department. Strategic issues need to be considered here, alongside operational complexities and implications. There are a number of uncertainties, including the hint of a store rebuild, and students should compare the proposal with other possible uses for the space – own-bought ranges, alternative new concessions or the extension of existing concessions.

For the new fine leather goods department students can develop the concept in terms of visual merchandising to communicate the premium offer. Headings might include detailed range plans, floor layout, methods of display, appropriate furniture and props, floor and wall materials, brand adjacencies, stock levels, graphics support and point of sale aids. There are particular challenges involved – not least the restriction on space, the physical shape and obstacles within the department and the existing store environment. A detailed layout of the ground floor and department is provided to prompt consideration of the merchandising issues.

REFERENCES

McGoldrick, P. (1990) *Retail Marketing*. London: McGraw-Hill.

FURTHER READING

Corporate Intelligence Group (1996) *Concession Retailing in the UK*.
McGoldrick, P. (1987) *Shops within Shops: Their Role in Department Store Retailing and the Reactions of Consumers*. UMIST: Manchester.
McGoldrick, P. (1990) *Retail Marketing*. London: McGraw-Hill.

TEACHING NOTES
THE LONGEST NIGHT: MANAGING A CRISIS EVENT AT MARKS & SPENCER

CATHY HART

SYNOPSIS

The case charts the escalation of events following a power failure in a small Marks & Spencer store. It follows the viewpoint of a recently appointed graduate regional store manager and focuses on the management decision making required to contain the problem. The issue of management competencies is intrinsic to the case and offers students the opportunity to analyse competence requirements at various levels. In the first phase of the scenario, the store manager has to prioritize immediate operational elements such as customer needs, managing and deploying staff, stock, systems, security and so on. As the scenario develops into the second phase, the manager moves into contingency planning mode by evacuating customers, preservation of stock, reducing the amount of loss and recovering the situation in preparation for the next day of trading.

THE CAST

Diane Webster – graduate Regional Store Manager
Lynne – Textile Supervisor
Jim Cross – Deputy Foods Supervisor
Bob Mason – Warehouse Assistant
Mike – In-store Technician
Alex Jones – Commercial Manager, Parent Store
Jenny – relief Textile Manager
Dave – relief Food Manager
Julie – Food Sales Assistant
Gerry Preston – Maintenance Manager
Pete Field – Reporter, Middletown Mercury
Anna – Textile Sales Assistant
Debbie – Textile Sales Assistant

LEARNING OBJECTIVES AND CORTCO COMPETENCIES

(1)   Personal effectiveness

- To appreciate the importance of management competencies in store operations.
- To identify the competency profile required to manage a small retail store.

(2)   Managing people and working with others

Team working and awareness:
Team leading:

- To understand the operational aspects of controlling a retail store on a daily basis and to appreciate the interaction between the different team members.
- To examine the role of the store manager.

Communication skills:

- To consider how to handle communication to staff before and after the crisis.

(3)   Organizational ability and creative thinking

Critical thinking and analytical consideration:

- To identify and evaluate the possible outcomes from different decisions and to appropriately prioritize operational elements.

Planning and organizing:

- Understand the purpose of contingency planning, following a crisis event.

(4)   Business focus

Customer focus:
Commercialism and business awareness:

- To evaluate and prioritize the typical problems to be managed in a crisis situation and their likely impact on customers and profitability.

CASE APPLICATIONS AND CONTEXTS

The case is designed to prompt analysis and discussion of a variety of topics including crisis management, contingency planning, risk management, and various aspects of store operations. Due to the general nature of the scenario it could be used either in undergraduate or post graduate teaching or for training purposes. Additionally, the case is written from the viewpoint of a graduate manager and could therefore be used to illustrate the role of the store manager.

The case provides an opportunity for students individually, or as a group, to analyse management competencies in a specific dynamic context. Through this process, students will also enhance their individual competency development.

The case may be used in a group situation such as role-play to enable students to adopt different team and leadership roles.

In answering **Question 1**, students should critically evaluate Diane's decision making and prioritizing in relation to different issues for example health and safety issues, food safety, Marks & Spencer customer service standards, local and community image and positioning.

Many of these issues come within the direct control of the regional manager for example staffing, preservation of stock (protecting assets), maximizing security. Students will also need to consider Diane's objectives and limitations for the event. Diane's chief concern as manager of the store is to ensure customer and staff safety, while maintaining the commercial and public integrity of the store. The Commercial Manager, Alex Jones, will be looking for Diane's ability to control and use resources in the situation. The problem is that Diane has only been in the store a short time and while she has been trained in disaster recovery, she does not know the management team and their capabilities.

In making recommendations, students might consider specific aspects of this incident that could be rectified to minimize future disruption – for example generator testing, more stringent lift procedures – excluding customer use.

In answering **Question 2**, students should start by comparing and contrasting the Marks & Spencer competencies with the CORTCO competencies. This will then form the basis for discussion of different crisis situations and the competencies required.

Marks & Spencer recruit to a defined set of management competencies that have been identified as being most applicable to the Marks & Spencer manager profile. They include planning and organizing, job motivation, leadership, awareness and teamwork, adaptability, assertiveness, analytical consideration, and commercial creativity. These competencies are then used as a framework for training, development and appraisal purposes. While the routine components of managerial jobs and the skills required to handle them are relatively easily identified and developed, the skills needed to 'handle the emergent, non-routine and dynamic components that characterize a large chunk of managerial work tend to get neglected' (Kanugo and Misra, 1992). In more extreme situations, managers have to be prepared to deal with a critical disaster, with little opportunity to practise these skills in a daily situation. For staff, there is a standard health and safety training and operating procedure to follow in the event of a disaster (fire, bomb and so on). However, it is less clear how to prepare the managers to control and manage the event.

It is impossible to plan or prepare for a disaster, as every disaster is different, with different availability of staff, each having a different skills base. Once the disaster has occurred and it cannot be rectified immediately, it is a case of accepting the circumstances. People are naturally frightened by emergencies, and thus need the reassurance of an operating framework to guide them. The regional manager, or duty manager's, role is then to manage the staff and customers until the objectives have been met. Marks & Spencer have adopted a generic approach to developing the competencies required to manage an emergency. All managers undertake disaster recovery training by adopting different roles in practise disaster scenarios. They are placed in a simulated, vulnerable situation to challenge them and let them manage the situation. It is however, more difficult to anticipate and thus train for how the same person will react in reality, in a high stress situation. It is thus important to develop the collective skills of the management team to ensure there is sufficient cover. It is also important to balance the responsibility and develop synergy within the management team; high levels of individual member competence do not guarantee group competence (Burgoyne, 1989). Parallels can also be drawn between demands faced by managers in an organizational context and in a personal context. (Kanugo and Misra, 1992). This offers trainers the opportunity to recognize and build on managers' existing competencies.

In answering **Question 3**, students will need to consider the impact of a power failure on store operations and how to plan for this. Some broad areas which should be considered include:

- Extent of power failure – short-term/long-term power loss? Is there a back-up generator to support essentials for example lighting, fridges/freezers?
- Health and safety – at what point does the store, its facilities and/or its products become a risk to customers, thus necessitating evacuation? How would staff cope with this?
- Staff – who is available with what experience/competence? What roles are important in handling this event?
- Communication – internal and external. Lack of phone lines, informing the senior management, keeping internal communication flowing. Public relations – minimizing the impact on the wider audience.
- Systems – how are these affected? What might be the implications for the end of day procedure in sending or receiving sales/pricing data? Impact on trading the following day?
- Security – how vulnerable are the staff, and stock? What measures are in place to contain this? Which of these measures are still operating?

Other issues to consider are possible events that might be affected by a power cut thus affecting the management of the crisis for example the power cut in the case affects the whole town centre including traffic lights, causing traffic jams delaying emergency and support services.

In answering **Question 4**, students need to review the situation from the staff viewpoint. Diane could view this as a motivational opportunity to bring the store team closer together. One approach might be to generate staff feedback on how they felt the incident could have been better managed – in terms of where they had direct control. There may have been an over-reliance on Diane for management decision making, possibly due to her short time as manager, however, it is important that there is someone who takes charge of the situation.

From a motivational viewpoint the staff coped well under the pressure of the event and any injuries were dealt with effectively. In some respects much of the decision making regarding food stock was kept away from Diane, leaving her to focus on the critical areas. Certain aspects may have been handled better- security might have been tighter, particularly from the lift viewpoint. Students should be encouraged to make any necessary assumptions regarding missing information such as level of team spirit and so on.

REFERENCES

Burgoyne, J. (1989) 'Creating the managerial portfolio: building on competency approaches to management development'. MEAD **20**(1): 56–61.

Kanugo, R. N. and Misra, S. (1992) 'Managerial resourcefulness: A reconceptualisation of management skills'. Human Relations, **45**, 1311–32.

FURTHER READING

Bartlett, R. (1997) *Business Continuity and Crisis Management in the Food and Drinks Industry*. Leatherhead Food Research Association, Randalls Road Leatherhead KT22 7RY, August (ringbinder).

Cox, S., Janes, W., Walker, D. and Wenham D. (1998) 'Emergency plans and procedures'. *Office Health and Safety Handbook*. London: Tolley, pp. 153–75.

Doeg, C. (1995) *Crisis Management in the Food and Drinks Industry: A Practical Approach*. London: Chapman & Hall.

TEACHING NOTES
EUROPEAN AND UK PACKAGING WASTE LEGISLATION: THE MARKS & SPENCER RESPONSE

CATHY HART AND JOHN FERNIE

SYNOPSIS

The case focuses on the UK Packaging Waste Regulations 1997, and the resulting implications for retailers. It examines the UK interpretation of the original EC directive compared with other EU member countries, with particular emphasis on the German approach to packaging waste collection and recycling. A central theme of the case is Marks & Spencer's response to the legislation. As an international retailer, operating in a number of European countries, the legislation posed a number of potential operational problems. Marks & Spencer's strategies for resolving these problems are briefly presented. The case concludes with a discussion of issues likely to conflict with the core objectives of the legislation, followed by the wider implications of future environmental policy and its impact on retailers and the supply chain.

LEARNING OBJECTIVES AND CORTCO COMPETENCIES

The case is designed to generate considerable debate at a number of levels depending on prior knowledge of the area and at what point it is introduced in a module. The case may be used to illustrate elements of European environmental legislation and policy, supply chain issues, retail operations strategy or to introduce aspects of environmental management. While it is applicable to both undergraduate and postgraduate level, it is recommended that students have a basic understanding of the supply chain.

(1) Personal effectiveness

Assertiveness:
Self-confidence:
Students should be prepared to challenge the legislation, to question other people's decisions and actions while also being receptive to new environmental or legislative developments.

(2)   Managing people and working with others

Team working and awareness:
Team leading:
The ability to present and explain individual environmental viewpoints, effectively argue a case while involving and including other people is necessary. Clear and concise communication of ideas, gaining others' commitment and support to the chosen argument will develop these skills.

(3)   Organizational ability and creative thinking

Critical thinking and analytical consideration:
Various issues have to be interpreted and identified, causes researched, information gathered and assimilated. Students will need to constructively evaluate the different options, legislative and environmental implications and advise a logical solution. More specifically, the following objectives are addressed, and by the end of the case students will be able to:

■ Evaluate the UK Packaging Regulations compared with other European waste policies.
■ Understand the environmental implications of packaging waste across the supply chain.
■ Appreciate the operational problems involved in implementing the legislation.
■ Develop an awareness of the data collection and specification systems required to manage packaging data.
■ Appreciate the supply chain partnerships in relation to reverse logistics.

CASE APPLICATIONS AND CONTEXTS

In answering **Question 1**, students need to consider the key differences between the UK and the German legislation. Particular aspects that may be discussed are the different types of packaging identified by the different legislation; supply and demand of packaging waste and the reprocessing capacity of each country. Despite the UK Government's late entry into the European environmental waste legislation, it has arguably developed a system that should 'pull' the packaging through the waste stream (being driven by reprocessing capacity) as opposed to the German 'push' approach which began with the waste collection which subsequently had to generate a market for its disposal or reprocessing.

In **Question 2**, a number of barriers inhibiting the legislation may be identified:

■ Consumer issues – the increasing demand for packaged convenience foods may require careful management. Interestingly, the need for convenience food (and thus more packaging) appears to be increasing on the continent.

■ Marketing issues – the use of packaging as the main form of sales promotion, particularly in own-label goods, may conflict with environmental objectives. For example eye catching attractive designs are not necessarily the most environmentally friendly. Merchandising practicalities may also conflict with recyclability for example additional packaging may enable easier stacking and display. Different strategies for educating the consumers thus need to be considered.

■ A number of internal barriers might prevent the legislation being fully implemented, for example bureaucracy, lack of adequate systems and lack of an environmental orientation. Externally, other members of the supply chain not integrating could prevent full implementation.

Question 3 urges students to consider how the responsibility for packaging waste can be widened across the supply chain. One idea from The Association of Convenience Stores, suggested that a recycling levy (0.001p) be put on to every item of packaging and raised directly from the packaging manufacturers themselves. It was proposed that the proceeds from this levy should then be distributed to the local authorities and businesses in proportion to the amount of packaging waste they recycle, as an incentive for them to mount effective recycling programmes.

Others feel there is insufficient incentive to encourage companies to reduce the quantity of waste generated. The Friends of the Earth pressure group (Thomas, 1997) is calling for:

■ The landfill tax to be increased to at least £30 a tonne and extended to cover incineration to promote reduction, reuse and recycling of resources.

■ Local authorities to be given adequate access to funds to set up recycling schemes which will meet the government's 25 per cent recycling target.

■ The government to set new tough statutory waste reduction, reuse and recycling targets for 2010.

■ 20 per cent of the landfill tax to be devoted to waste reduction, reuse and recycling programmes and be publicly controlled.

Students should be able to recognize strengths and weaknesses of other EU systems in **Question 4**. Despite obvious weaknesses in the system, the German approach had a strong emphasis on the collection and return aspects. Involving the consumer and the local authority, it engendered responsibility for returning the packaging waste directly from the end user. Compared with the continentals, the UK suffers from a lack of green orientation, yet research has shown that UK consumers would be willing participants in recycling strategies. For example the Body Shop plastic container recycling system has been well supported in the UK.

The UK system for packaging recovery notes (PRNs) involves a middleman whose role is primarily to trade in waste. This way the retailers and other generators of packaging waste may become detached from their responsibility. The German approach via the Duales System Deutschland (DSD) offers a more democratic solution, whereby no external party should profit.

Question 5 provides an opportunity for students to think creatively and laterally by suggesting future strategies to reduce the quantity of packaging generated. Different approaches can be generated and debated:

■ Develop greener packaging at the design stage of the product
■ Use larger packages – thereby saving on quantity
■ Eliminate any unnecessary layers of packaging
■ Develop more reusable consumer packaging, similar to the transit route
■ Encourage consumers to buy products 'loose' or unpackaged for example returning to weighing products in stores.

Finally, **Question 6** provides more in-depth debate on the current and future revisions to the packaging legislation. There are a number of possible directions that the legislation could take, the following points are intended as guidelines and are not definitive answers:

■ If the UK follows pressure from environmental groups and its continental peers, it may further tighten up by increasing targets and quotas.
■ Some predict that the current targets are unattainable (particularly given the current reprocessing capacity) and therefore the quotas can only remain at the same level.
■ One possible outcome is that the system cannot work without more cooperation from consumers, they will need encouragement to recycle the packaging and the systems to collect it. For example Germany put a tax on bottles to encourage return.
■ However, the reprocessing capacity is a fundamental driver and unless the market for waste is developed, the prices for PRNs will increase.
■ Another criticism is that loopholes encourage indescrimate recovery, even non-environmentally friendly packaging with no environmental gain. Perhaps a revised objective of one overall waste diversion target for each type of pack may be more appropriate.

REFERENCE

Thomas, A. (1997) *Waste Campaigner*. Friends of the Earth, 30 September. webmaster@foe.co.uk

FURTHER READING

AIM, CIAA and ERRA Secretariats (1998) *European Packaging Waste Legislation 1998: Law and Industry Initiatives*. London: Financial Times Business Ltd.
Lord, K. R. and Putrevu, S. (1998) 'Acceptance of recycling appeals: The moderating role of perceived consumer effectiveness'. *Journal of Marketing Management*, **14**: 581–90.

SHRINK BUSTERS! A DIY CASE IN FINANCIAL MANAGEMENT AND CONTROL

RUTH A. SCHMIDT, BRENDA M. OLDFIELD AND DAVID LEAVER

SYNOPSIS

The UK DIY sector is a highly competitive mass market with intense pressures on prices, and therefore a management focus on cost controls in all areas. Consequently, at store level, the tight management of stock is a key area for enhancing profitability through constant improvements in operations. A major controllable cost (at store level ranked second only to staff) which can reduce gross margins by several percentage points is shrinkage, defined as the measured amount of total avoidable money losses attributable to poor stock management. Paintworld, a leading DIY retailer, recently implemented a set of detailed guidelines and staff training concerning the core areas of booking in procedures, merchandising, stock counts, sampling, batching, theft, complaints, returns, stock transfers and store own use in order to enhance shrinkage control by establishing a wide awareness and adoption of best practice throughout the business. The twin focus of the case is the development and implementation of the Paintworld Shrink Busters initiative and an evaluation of its impact on overall business performance.

LEARNING OBJECTIVES AND CORTCO COMPETENCIES

For case application in general retail education or within a more specific retail management training context objectives can be split. Students with prior store management experience will most fully appreciate the management training objectives listed in relation to CORTCO competencies (1) and (2). The general objectives related to competencies (3) and (4) will be applicable more widely.

(1) Personal effectiveness

- To gain an understanding of the way in which management actions can inadvertently create shrinkage and to learn how to avoid this.
- To gain a thorough insight into the critical role of management in ensuring that procedures, roles and processes are adhered to properly.

(2) Managing people and working with others

■ To develop a full appreciation of the importance of the manager's role as a trainer of people.

(3) Organizational ability and creative thinking

Critical thinking and analytical consideration:
■ To develop analytical, data handling and reasoning skills.

Planning and organization:
■ To gain an appreciation of the operational implications of implementing the Shrink Busters initiative.

Innovation and strategic thinking:
■ To appreciate how shrinkage can link into other strategic and operational issues and to propose and develop novel and integrated solutions.

(4) Business focus

Customer focus:
■ To critically evaluate potential trade-offs and synergies between customer service, merchandising and shrinkage control measures from both a business and customer point of view.

Commercialism and business awareness:
■ To make visible links between in-store operational measures and aggregate company financial performance.
■ To enhance student awareness of the financial consequences of in-store staff actions.

CASE APPLICATIONS AND CONTEXTS

The case can be used to varying levels of analysis with students on the full range of undergraduate and postgraduate retail courses and will be of particular use in working with store management trainees in the context of in-house tailored retail education programmes. In both contexts the case can serve as a basis for in-class tutorial discussion, or form the basis of an assignment and/or exam preparation.

Question 1 is about case comprehension in terms of causes and controls of shrinkage. Key sources to be identified might include customers, either through theft (for example abuse of free merchandise samples or fraudulent abuse of discounts); through staff themselves (for example careless and unrecorded staff use of products; errors in administrative procedures; and ignorance of correct processes. Other sources could include: a raid from professional thieves; poor security throughout the chain of distribution; and supplier errors.

Students might identify that from the above, the greatest weighting is on customers and staff, with customers more prone to theft and staff more inclined towards administrative errors and carelessness.

Students could classify control measures as either focused on staff or on investment in information-gathering equipment. A staff focus might include: increased expenditure on in-store guards and detectives; increased training in administrative procedures; introducing a shrinkage control bonus; and forming in-store Shrink Busters teams. Looking to an equipment and information gathering focus, this could include: putting in CCTV in all the stores; investing in new technology (for example intelligent text); and profiling the stores on their shrinkage history.

Staff measures are potentially harder to monitor as they are 'softer' in focus and will need to be updated and reviewed on a regular basis to remain effective. Possibly much of the real control depends on staff motivation and, therefore, communication. In this the introduction and maintenance of HQ communication initiatives, such as Shrink Line, Shrink Rap and so on should provide a vital link.

Question 2 looks at the financial implications of the control measures identified, both in terms of costs and benefits and the impact on profit and loss account and balance sheet. As explained in the case proper, the cost of shrinkage, as measured by Paintworld, has a direct impact on cost of goods sold and therefore, depresses gross margin. All the control measures suggested have an impact on the profit and loss account via additional expenses. They will therefore result in somewhat decreased net margin, unless outweighed by a relatively higher saving through lower shrinkage figures.

With the staff focused measures much of the cost is of a variable nature and therefore more easily adjustable in the light of changing circumstances. These measures are also more easily evaluated in cost/benefit terms as they largely impact on expenses in the profit and loss account rather than on the balance sheet. By contrast, investment in equipment means fixed capital costs and a commitment for some time, with a certain need to update the fixed assets purchased at a future date. The impact is both on the profit and loss account (as depreciation under expenses) and on the balance sheet, where an increase in fixed assets will result. An increase in fixed assets which is not balanced by a growth in turnover tends to decrease overall performance as measured by the return on capital employed ratio – however, this could be outweighed by substantially enhanced net margins due to falling shrinkage figures on the profit and loss side.

It is intended that **Question 3** should serve to integrate different aspects of the students' studies, such as services marketing, merchandising and finance with the information provided in the case study. An analysis of Paintworld's overall marketing strategy and positioning within DIY retailing could form the starting point. Students might identify the trade-offs and complementarities between the three areas under considerations. Within a mass market, a climate of price wars and escalating raw materials prices, cost-effectiveness is likely to be a key criterion. This will include the cost of stock holding, as well as shrinkage, plus the cost of space, staffing and any extra schemes proposed. In the area of stock management, the policy of keeping a tight check on the display of high value items creates a good degree of synergy between shrinkage control and the management of space costs. Where extra staffing for security purposes is proposed, there must be substantial associated cost savings (for example through tighter control of free samples by that additional member of staff) or good synergies with perceived customer services, (for example additional guards doubling-up as friendly in-store 'meeters and greeters').

Questions 4 and 5 move away from individual analytical work and encourage a team approach to innovation, as well planning and organizing the implementation of new ideas for shrinkage control and communication between stores and HQ.

FURTHER READING

Bank, J. (1992) *The Essence of Total Quality Management*. London: Prentice Hall.

Key Note (1995) *UK DIY & Home Improvements*. 1995 Market Review. London: Keynote.

Leaver, D. (1993) 'Legal and social changes affecting UK retailers response to consumer theft'. *The International Journal of Retail and Distribution Management*, **21**(8): 29–33.

Lin, B. Hastings, D. A. and Martin, C. (1994) 'Shoplifting in retail clothing outlets'. *The International Journal of Retail and Distribution Management*, **22**(7): 24–9.

Pretious, M., Stewart, R., and Logan, D. (1995) 'Retail security: a survey of methods and management in Dundee'. *The International Journal of Retail and Distribution Management*, **23**(9): 28 35.

Schmidt, R. A. and Wright, H. (1996) *Financial Aspects of Marketing*. Basingstoke: Macmillan.

UK Retail Crime Statistics (1997) http://www.emnet.co.uk/retailresearch

Verdict (1997) *Verdict on DIY Retailers*. Verdict Executive Retail Summary, July. London: Verdict.

CASE 10

TEACHING NOTES
BUYING OPERATIONS AT BOOTS THE CHEMIST: THE CASE OF A PRODUCT RANGE UPDATE

ROSEMARY VARLEY

SYNOPSIS

The case explores the merchandise and marketing operations of the retail division of The Boots Company. The focus is on an under-performing product range in the food area, and a scenario of a product manager constructing a proposal in response to the situation of poor sales is presented. The case begins with a brief introduction to the complex nature of product management in retailing, and then moves on to give company and departmental background, including personnel roles, to build an understanding of the context. The reader is given detailed information about the product, its place within Boots' lunchtime and snack offer, and within the general product market. Some market research findings are included to offer some additional customer insight. The case ends with the presentation of a situation in which a senior member of the merchandise and marketing department voices concerns about the under-performing 'Light' range (a small group of reduced fat and low sugar confectionery products) and gives the product manager for sweet snacks the task of reconsidering the Light range and reporting back with recommendations.

LEARNING OBJECTIVES AND CORTCO COMPETENCIES

(2) Managing people and working with others

Team working and awareness:
- To develop an understanding of the structure of a retail buying organization, and the roles played by personnel within the organization.

(3) Organizational ability and creative thinking

Planning and organizing:
- To explore the relationship between product development and other aspects of retail marketing (pricing, point of sale communications, advertising, public relations, positioning within the store and so on) within the planning process.

Critical thinking and analytical consideration:
- To explore the concept of positioning of a product range within a retail offer.
- To develop an understanding of the product monitoring and evaluation process in retailing and, using critical analysis, to consider the response that a retailer might make to an under-performing range.
- To gain an appreciation of the various criteria which need to be considered when developing a new product range, and how decisions about product features may be constrained (for example by legal requirements, technical limitations, competition and so on).

(4)   Business focus

Customer focus:
- To understand the notion of positioning being the customer's viewpoint of a product among alternative competing products, and to appreciate the need for a retailer such as Boots to offer choice to a diverse customer base.

Commercial and business awareness:
- To develop an understanding of the role of the supplier in the product development process, and the factors upon which suppliers are assessed.

CASE APPLICATIONS AND CONTEXTS

Questions 1, 2 and 3 would be appropriate for discussion in tutorial or seminar situations, whereas **Questions 4, 5 and 6** are more involved and task orientated and therefore would be useful for assignment work (group or individual).

To answer **Question 1**, students will need to analyse the data presented in the case (for example the market research findings and the sales data). This information may be supplemented with market data from other published sources such as Mintel reports (see further reading section).

Question 2 will draw upon the analytical and problem solving skills of students by asking them to use the case information to identify relevant issues. Product crieria that should be considered include: physical properties – size, shape, ingredients, taste, packaging (design and materials); quality; price – relative to other products in range, and in the market generally; branding.

Supplier selection criteria would include issues such as: ability to supply – quality, technology, capacity; service – delivery, reliability, sampling; price – cost implications and terms. Supplier relationship development is a theme that could be introduced here. The case highlights some of the selection criteria, and indicates some of the issues involved, but students may need to be directed towards generic lists of criteria which they can then adapt (see Cash *et al.*, 1995, for product criteria and McGoldrick, 1990, for product and supplier selection criteria). This question will develop analytical judgement skills and an appreciation of the implications of choice among alternatives.

In **Question 3**, an application of the traditional decision making unit roles (for example Webster and Wind, 1972) may help to understand the levels of decision making. Asking the students to use organization charts and diagrams will help develop the skill of the using appropriate presentation methods. Students who are not familiar with organizational charts may wish to consult for example, the US department store buying office structure shown in Retailing Management (Levy and Weitz, 1998) and adapt it to the Boots structure.

Question 4 would develop a student's ability to plan and organize, prioritize decision making, establish an appropriate course of action and consider resource implications. The product proposal should include the following: the range that will be offered (number of items and product assortment); pricing of the various products in the range; packaging and branding; in-store marketing support (space allocation, point of sale materials, demonstations and trials); out-of-store promotional activity (media advertising, PR, direct communications to loyalty card holders). Students should justify their recommendations, and consider the likely available resources. Published sources (as in Question 1) may provide background data and information to help develop a credible proposal.

For **Questions 5**, students need to refer to case data, and market data (for example Mintel reports) to establish the customer profile. They could then refer to an introductory marketing text (such as Brassington and Pettitt, 1997, Chapter 16) which gives a framework for working through the stages of formulating an advertising message, considering alternative advertising media, and developing a campaign.

Question 6 asks students to communicate clearly and effectively, using written and graphical information and consideration of the audience (for example a design agency) is important. Students would need to consider the inadequacies of the existing packaging, shown in the case. They would then need to explore issues such as product range branding versus individual product branding, brand positioning and the labelling information needed on the product. Background reading in an introductory marketing text will give the theoretical framework for branding and packaging issues, for example Brassington and Pettitt (1997).

The case can be used in a number of ways to develop communication and influencing skills. Role-play could be introduced, for example Linda Kingston and her assistant could report back to Stephen Panns and Rowena Smith with the reconsidered product range proposal. The students taking the role of Linda and assistant would need to use clear communication directed at the appropriate level; they might need to sell their ideas, argue their case and deal with conflict. The students in the role of Stephen and Rowena would practice listening skills, and the use of empathy and sensitivity, as well as arguing a case and dealing with conflict.

REFERENCES

Brassington, F. and Pettitt, S. (1997) *Principles of Marketing*. London: Pitman.

Cash, R. P., Wingate, J. W. and Friedlander, J. S. (1995) *Management of Retail Buying*, 3rd edn. New York: Wiley.

Levy, M. and Weitz, B. A. (1998) *Retail Management*. Chicago: Irwin.

McGoldrick, P. J. (1990) *Retail Marketing*. Maidenhead: McGraw-Hill.

Webster, F. E. and Wind, Y. (1972) 'A general model for understanding organisational buying behaviour'. *Journal of Marketing*, *36*, April: 12.

FURTHER READING

Collier, R. A. (1995) *Profitable Product Management*. Oxford: Butterworth Heinemann.

Davies, G. (1993) *Trade Marketing Strategy*. London: Paul Chapman.

Levy, M. and Weitz, B. A. (1996) *Essentials of Retailing*. Chicago: Irwin.

McDonald, M. and Tideman, C. (1993) *Retail Marketing Plans*. Oxford: Butterworth Heinemann.

McGoldrick, P. J. (1990) *Retail Marketing*. Maidenhead: McGraw-Hill.

CASE 11

TEACHING NOTES
THE ROAD TO EMPOWERMENT AT SAINSBURY'S

ANGELA M. ARNOLD, MORAG M. MCLEAN AND
CHRISTOPHER J. DUTTON

SYNOPSIS

This case study was developed in the comparatively early stages of a strategic change process in Sainsbury's. By concentrating on issues related to the empowerment of staff at all levels of the organization within the changing strategic context, the case invites readers to consider the inter-relationships and complexities inherent in such change processes.

LEARNING OBJECTIVES AND CORTCO COMPETENCIES

(3) Organizational ability and creative thinking

Critical thinking and analytical consideration:
- To gain an in-depth understanding of the factors underlying the conceptualization and implementation of empowerment activities and subsequent staff responses from a multiple stakeholder perspective.

Planning and organization, forward planning:
- To appreciate and be able to anticipate and plan the operational implications of empowerment for day-to-day staff activities.

Innovation and strategic thinking:
- To analyse the links between strategic vision, innovation and culture change.

(4) Business focus

Customer focus:
- To understand the strategic links between empowerment, store positioning and customer service.

Commercialism and business awareness
- To evaluate the impact of empowerment measures on a range of both hard and soft business performance measures.

CASE APPLICATIONS AND CONTEXTS

This case can be developed at different levels depending on the capability and academic background of students. All students should be able to appreciate the implications of empowering staff through exploration of the concept within the context of UK retailing, and also understand the balanced scorecard approach to performance management. It is of particular relevance to students undertaking modules in organizational behaviour, human resource management and change management. It can be used at either a descriptive or analytical level, or at a level that seeks to critically appraise management control and managerial ideology.

Question 1 seeks to explore the potential role of empowerment as a strategic lever encouraging students to consider the role of people as a significant source of differentiation in an industry where production and consumption of service are simultaneous and consumer expectations are increasing. Customer service excellence requires all first-line employees to be customer orientated, competent to manage 'moments of truth'.

Tasks will be contingent upon circumstances within companies but may include examples of empowerment (that is, decisions without reference to a superior) such as: instant mark downs or refunds; dealing with customer complaints; ordering stock and equipment; changing displays, allocating tasks within a team; setting targets, and so forth.

Difficulties may include: the loss of (corporate) store image, variations in product and service offering, reduction in economies of scale, and possible increased HR costs. Openness regarding confidential companies' information may be risky in such a highly competitive industry. Also front-line staff, generally low paid and least respected, may resent the additional responsibility without increased compensation/grading.

Benefits of empowerment may include: clearer accountability for performance, increased staff contribution to business, improved communication, improved competitiveness through better service, higher customer satisfaction and retention, increased productivity and financial performance. Individuals may experience higher intrinsic rewards, a reduction in role conflict, ambiguity and stress and being more involved in decisions.

Question 2 is about store positioning. Positioning, in terms of customer and competitors, is based on a number of factors and levers which may include: products stocked (range, quality), items in stock (availability), pricing strategy, store atmospherics and environment, location, quality of customer service offered, communication strategy (customers), employee responsiveness (HRM strategy).

Question 3 seeks to explore how Sainsbury's has effected change – that is, the process of empowerment. The approach is classic, in that it starts with the vision which provides clear direction and a framework for the company's mission and strategy. Students could explore the reasons behind the introduction of empowerment, levels and forms of empowerment. The 'culture' must be appropriate. The company structure and management style must fit the new mode of operation. Students should explore why. Practices must change so that decentralization of decision-making can occur. All 'elements' must focus on improved performance (Figure TN11.1).

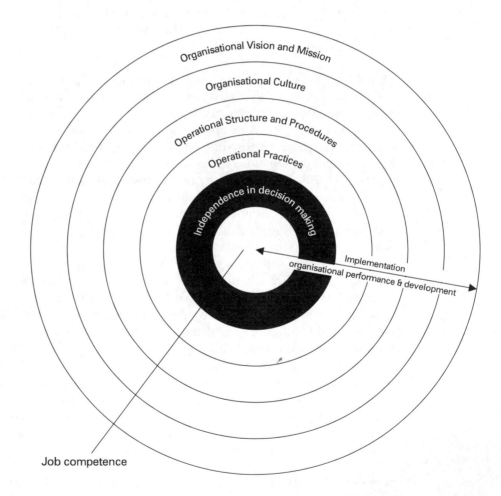

Figure TN11.1 Model of contextual empowerment (McLean and Maxwell, 1994)

The communication of change is very demanding on organizational resources. Students should explore the general difficulties retailers have in communicating to staff. Students could be encouraged to develop alternative strategies to the communication of change at Sainsbury's and consider the difficulties and benefits that might arise.

Question 4 seeks to deepen the students' understanding of the potential difficulties of full empowerment and thus moves thinking from evangelism to pragmatism. Empowerment may not be financially viable or feasible. The industry is labour intensive. It typically has difficulty recruiting high calibre staff, has disproportionately high numbers of part-time and temporary staff accompanied by low staff retention. Jobs in retailing are often routine and mundane, requiring low skills and with extended trading hours; the costs of training and time required to involve all staff may be prohibitive.

The type and level of customer service offered by a retailer is contingent upon the customer or market segment the company is trying to attract and retain. A high degree of centralization may create tensions in the implementation of empowerment. Empowerment occurs more easily in organizations with a relatively flat operational structure and usually involves teamworking, functional flexibility and a more participatory style of management, facilitating improved communication and decision-making.

In addressing issues around the concept of a balanced scorecard, **Question 5** challenges students to consider the longer-term strategic position of the organization from a multiple stakeholder perspective. It is through the integration of strategic objectives and individual accountabilities that organizations seek to fully utilize the potential of their intangible assets towards strategic transformation. Retailers traditionally have built their performance management systems around financial, short-term measures and targets, and are unable to link actions based on these with their long-term strategy. Kaplan and Norton (1996, p. 75) recommend that 'companies track financial results while simultaneously monitoring progress in building capabilities and acquiring intangible assets they would need for future growth'. Students should explore whether retailers can in reality balance all stakeholder perspectives through this approach.

For the sales assistant who can help at the checkouts, hard measures (typically tangible, financially focused and short term) might be: sales turnover, profitability, sales per sq ft, value per transaction, accident rate, customer complaints, absence levels, and so forth. Soft measures are less tangible indicators of performance. Ultimately they are calculable but could involve (significant) costs for example customer satisfaction and retention, employee satisfaction, employee competence.

Question 6 challenges students to consider the cultural barriers to implementing change. From an ideological perspective, the notions of unitarism and pluralism could serve as an interesting platform for such an exploration. Students are expected to recognize that culture is shaped by four factors: the alignment of staff values and expectations with the company vision, how work is organized, how people are developed, and how performance is managed.

Question 7 addresses the issue of the changing role of line managers, for example role clarity and changing development needs. With the job enlargement of line managers there has been a fundamental change in the role of the store personnel department – this also could be explored. Line managers are now expected to balance task with people activities, and their personal management agenda (performance objectives) reflect this.

REFERENCES

Kaplan, R. S. and Norton, D. P. (1996) 'Using the balanced scorecard as a strategic management system'. *Harvard Business Review*, **74**(1): 75–85.

McLean, M. and Maxwell, G. (1994) 'The Impact of Empowerment on Store Performance in UK Retailing'. Paper presented at 1st European and Canadian Institute for Retailing and Services Science Conference on Recent Advances in Retailing and Services Science, Banff, Canada, May 1994.

FURTHER READING

Bowen, D. E. and Lawler, E. E. (1995) 'Empowering service employees'. *Sloan Management Review*, **36**(4): 73–85.

Cunningham, I., Hyman, J. and Baldry, C. (1996) 'Empowerment: The power to do what?' *Industrial Relations Journal*, **27**(2): 143–55.

Ford, R. C. and Fottler M D (1995) 'Empowerment: A matter of degree'. *The Academy of Management Executive*, **9**(3): 21–32.

Kaplan, R. S. and Norton, D. P. (1992) 'The balanced scorecard – measures that drive performance'. *Harvard Business Review*, **70**(1): 71–9.

Kaplan, R. S. and Norton, D. P. (1993) 'Putting the balanced scorecard to work'. *Harvard Business Review*, **71**(5): 134–42.

Randolph, W. A. (1995) 'Navigating the journey to empowerment'. *Organisational Dynamics*, **23**(4): 19–33.

Ripley, R. E. and Ripley, M. J. (1992) 'Empowerment, the cornerstone of quality'. *Management Decision*, **30**(4): 20–43.

Spreitzer, G. M. (1996) 'Social structural characteristics of psychological empowerment'. *Academy of Management Journal*, **39**(2): 483–505.

TEACHING NOTES
STORE MERCHANDISING AND EFFECTIVE USE OF SPACE: THE SAFEWAY EXPERIENCE OF IN-STORE PHARMACIES

GRETE BIRTWISTLE

SYNOPSIS

The case study is developed to highlight the complex nature of incorporating an in-store pharmacy into a large supermarket. This is one of the key additional services the food retailers may select to offer their customers. Safeway first introduced a chemist in 1981 into one of their Scottish stores. Since then, all dispensing chemist facilities at Safeway have been developed, licensed and managed by the company. The majority of in-store pharmacies at Tesco, Sainsbury and Asda were introduced as concessions but today these retailers are moving towards company managed units.

The case gives the reader an overview of trends in food retailing with a focus towards service provision. This is followed by a description of the development of in-store pharmacies at Safeway and examines the management of space and merchandising within this area. The financial results are based on the financial year of 1996 which are quoted in the most recent Mintel reports published in 1997. Students should use the most recent data available to them. In the recent 1997 year end results Safeway has slipped into fourth position with a market share of 7.8 per cent. The suggested case tasks are centred on daily and seasonal stock management routines, the factors influencing lines stocked and examine the use of space within the pharmacy manager's responsibility. Furthermore, the case allows for discussion of the benefits to the customer, the community and the company of having an in-store dispensing chemist.

LEARNING OBJECTIVES AND CORTCO COMPETENCIES

(3)   Organizational ability and creative thinking

Planning and organizing; forward planning:
- To practice proactive planning of merchandising.

Critical thinking and analytical consideration:
- To develop an understanding of pharmacy management with particular regard to stock management and merchandising.
- To be able to identify factors influencing stock ordering and stock holding such as seasonal trends and local considerations.

Innovation and strategic thinking:
- To evaluate the strategic impact of having an in-store pharmacy.

(4) Business focus

Commercialism and business awareness:
- To develop an understanding of the way space can be used within categories and within the store to optimize profitability and to demonstrate awareness of the commercial impact of proposed changes.

Customer focus:
- To analyse the advantages to customers and the local community of having a dispensing chemist in a superstore and furthermore, to evaluate the contribution of an in-store pharmacy to the retailer.

CASE APPLICATIONS AND CONTEXTS

The case is suitable for the operational, tactical and strategic levels of retail management programmes, but could also be used on general business studies or marketing courses with retail options. By applying previous learning and integrating experience, students should be able to demonstrate commercial skills by planning stock management routines and analyse the utilization of space. Furthermore, the case can be utilized to identify and evaluate customer service provisions in food retailing as well as examining the wider contribution to the community.

Questions 1 and 2 investigate the ability of students to integrate their experience of seasonal sales within a pharmacy. For example, visual merchandising, leaflets and advice are focused on patients suffering from asthma, hay fever and the prevention of sunburn during the spring and summer. The questions allow for proactive planning of merchandising; that is the organization of requiring additional shelving; ordering additional stock to fit planograms; managing to remerchandise during the quiet times in the store to minimize disturbance; and printing of shelf edge labels.

Question 3 allows students to demonstrate their commercial abilities. For example, the factors students may take into consideration are high margin on own-label lines; stock turnover; local requirements such as homeopathic ranges; or local requests such as veterinary ranges.

Question 4 can be included in Question 3 or taken separately. Herbal medicines, homeopathic products and aromatherapy oils are impulse purchases. Customer information needs to be available from staff or by leaflets for these products to be displayed effectively.

In **Question 5** it has been suggested that the pharmacy may not be as profitable as originally planned and students are required to discuss ways of optimizing profitability for the store. This could mean proposing a new layout for the store when a new shopfit takes place. For example, many new stores now place the pharmacy within the main aisles as this would avoid doubling up on stock for three gondolas. These gondolas could then be used for more profitable categories and would enable the pharmacy to lower stock levels.

For the second part of this question, students would be expected to discuss factors such as sales per sq ft per department, profit contribution, sales turnover and general trends. Pharmacies are often more profitable per sq ft than the rest of the store (pharmacy profitability is about 15 to 18 per cent with over the counter (OTC) lines averaging about 30 per cent profit margin).

Question 6 could be discussed at a tactical or strategic level. Do food retailers gain additional sales by having an in-store pharmacy? Where a pharmacy has been located in a store after a refit, or when space has been found and the licence granted, the store turnover has increased. Safeway is aiming for a one stop shopping environment by providing as many ancillary facilities as possible to make the shopping environments more comfortable. Customers may come in to the store to use the pharmacy and decide to buy other products or vice versa.

How do the longer opening hours contribute towards consumers using the facilities? Pharmacy managers find that there is an increasing trend towards having to provide advice to customers about medication. How does that affect customer perception of retailing? Why should food retailers invest in having their own in-store dispensing chemist rather than using the facility of a concession?

A number of issues could be developed further through directed reading:

Does increased consumer advice available from in-store dispensing chemists help the local community and ease the burden on the NHS?

What are the food retailers' plans for maximizing OTC sales? Could the link-up with petrol suppliers lead to petrol forecourt retailing in providing OTC and maybe even prescription medicines 24 hours a day and thereby increase their share of this market?

The retail price maintenance (RPM) legislation is being reviewed by the Restrictive Practices Court with a final verdict expected in 1998. How will the ease of restrictions on price change the sales of OTC medicines? Who will benefit and who will lose out? The issues mentioned above are just some of the few that can be discussed with students.

FURTHER READING

Campbell, M. (1997) 'In the know (category management in the retail industry)'. *The Grocer*, 6 September: 41–2.

Dapiran, P. (1997) 'Shifting category management relationships in the food distribution channels in the UK and Australia'. *Management Decision*, **35**(3/4): 310–19.

Denning, J. and Freathy, P. (1996) 'Retail strategies for the petrol forecourt: the example of Road Chef Forecourts Ltd.' *The International Review of Retail, Distribution and Consumer Research*, **6**(1): 97–112.

Dove, B. and Hickman, C. (1997) 'More can mean less (business strategy of category management)'. *The Grocer*, 11 October, 34–5.

Hart, C. and Davies, M. (1996) 'The location and merchandising of non-food in supermarkets'. *International Journal of Retail and Distribution Management*, **24**(3): 17–25.

Main, A. (1994) 'Multiples choose their paths for pharmacies'. *The Grocer*, 25 June, 40.

TEACHING NOTES
'MAINE NEW ENGLAND' AT DEBENHAMS: DEVELOPING A NEW RANGE

GAYNOR LEA-GREENWOOD, CHRISTOPHER M. MOORE AND BRENDA M. OLDFIELD

SYNOPSIS

The case concerns the development of a premium own-brand by Debenhams. Based on consumer demand for casual wear, 'Maine New England' was developed as a range of lifestyle products in close co-operation with a dedicated supplier. The case facilitates student understanding of the key features of fashion labels and fashion brands and asks them to critically evaluate the processes of a retailer's fashion own-brand development, from creation over launch and trial to evaluation and eventual market penetration. While the case comes from a perspective of strategic innovation, the detailed focus is on operational issues.

LEARNING OBJECTIVES AND CORTCO COMPETENCIES

(2) Managing people and working with others

Team working and awareness; communication skills:
- To identify and communicate the roles and responsibilities of a successful brand manager.

(3) Organizational Ability and Creative Thinking

Critical thinking and analytical consideration:
- To understand the concepts of fashion label, fashion own-brand and brand extension.
- To critically evaluate alternative sourcing methods to be deployed in the creation of a successful fashion own-brand.

Planning and organizing:
Forward planning:
- To devise and plan the appropriate marketing mix, creation, launch and evaluation strategy for a new fashion own-brand.

(4) Business focus

Customer focus:
■ To appreciate the way in which brands become meaningful to consumers.

Commercialism and business awareness:
■ To evaluate the success of a fashion own-brand by selecting and using a range of appropriate business indicators.

CASE APPLICATIONS AND CONTEXTS

Question 1 gets students to think about the purpose and function of a fashion own-brand, both from the perspective of the fashion retailer, as well as from that of the fashion consumer. In response to this question it is important that a clear distinction is made between a fashion label and a fashion brand. By a label, we typically mean a naming device, that which denotes the origin or ownership of the product, but little else. The notion of a fashion brand refers to its ability to have representational value and meaning. Therefore a fashion brand will have associations with, perhaps, a given set of lifestyle values and images.

As to the features of the successful fashion own-brand, these must:

■ at a functional level, satisfy the requirements of the target customer grouping – utilitarian requirements will include those related to quality, fit, durability and so on;
■ have an identity (personality) which consumers recognize and wish to be associated with. This identity is typically based upon the mass communications strategy adopted by the company and is also dependent upon the image of the retailer, the ways in which the product is merchandised, as well as other marketing mix decisions which have an impact upon the positioning of the brand within the marketplace;
■ enjoy significant and continuous resource investment in relation to product development, quality management, advertising and promotion.

As the case study highlights, brand extension is a commonly used strategy in fashion retail marketing. Consideration should to be given to the conditions which ought to be satisfied before an own-brand can be successfully extended into other product categories. Typically, these conditions will relate to:

■ the success of the brand within the original and other product categories;
■ the nature of these product categories;
■ the extent to which the identity of the brand is recognizable and attractive to the target customer group;
■ whether the brand, with all of its values and imagery, can be appropriately transferred to the proposed new product categories;

- whether the brand is currently over-extended; for example, is it the case that customers are sceptical of the brand due to over-use? Does the brand now appear to be nothing more than a device used by the retailer to exploit success in other, non-related areas?

Question 2 asks students to evaluate whether 'Maine New England' can be considered to be a successful fashion own-brand, and in many respects it could be argued that 'Maine New England' exists somewhere in the middle, between being a retailer own-label and a retailer own-brand. From the perspective of Debenhams, it could be argued that, in the case, they did not really treat 'Maine New England' in the manner we would typically expect a manufacturer to care for one of its brands. For example, there was no advertising support, the company did not develop a brand planning strategy. On the other hand the Debenhams customer clearly saw this as a brand in its own right, even distinct from the Debenhams business. The key points which could be raised from this are:

- that an own-brand may be developed on the basis of customer experience;
- that the reputation of the retailer can have a positive impact upon brand adoption by consumers;
- that brand success in fashion is dependent upon some association with a lifestyle imagery, identity or connection;
- that many own-brands are developed on a me-too basis.

The four tests for a viable own-brand which Davies (1992) presented may be applied equally well to that of the fashion own-brand and are applicable for consideration in the context of both Questions 1 and 2.

In response to **Question 3**, the main stages of fashion own-brand creation and development can be delineated as follows:

- analysing markets
- generating ideas
- briefing one or more suppliers
- reviewing concepts
- selecting suppliers and products and ranges
- working with suppliers to refine, modify or enhance product concepts
- continuous sampling, either in house or involving targeted customer groups
- evaluating performance, including laboratory tests, wearer tests, user trials
- agreeing the details of the specification, including price
- agreeing the design of promotional material, packaging and directional or customer care labelling
- detailing initial order quantities from product and raw materials suppliers (for example, colour, size, length, style, pack size rations)
- confirming selling price
- setting up factory trials and pre-production runs

- launching and trialling on a limited basis
- evaluating
- feeding back results, which may lead to a programme of market penetration, modification and then extension to more outlets or elimination.

In the context of the case study, this activity was undertaken by an independent supplier on behalf of Debenhams. Students ought to consider why this is one way in which retailers can avoid the risks and problems associated with own-brand development, but emphasis should be placed upon the need to have a third party supplier that is capable, trustworthy, and reliable.

Question 4 requires consideration of the advantages and disadvantages of the sourcing method adopted. The process of fashion own-brand development is complex and far from risk-free and what may appear to be an advantage could also cause problems for the retailer.

Table TN13.1   Advantages and disadvantages of own-brand development

The expertise of a third party can be exploited	The retailer is dependent upon the skill and expertise of the third party supplier
The contacts of the third party can used, particularly in relation to the identification of raw materials suppliers, manufacturers and so on	The retailer is totally dependent upon the stability of the third party for the success or otherwise of their own-brand
The risk associated with the development is not confined to the 'shoulders' of the retailer alone	The third party may be involved in development work with rival companies and so on
The operational monitoring of the situation can be passed on to the third party and away from the buying team	The third party may become complacent as the relationship develops

With regard to **Question 5**, observations that could be made concerning the appointment of the brand manager could include such things as the fact that the appointment came rather late in the development process and that this could be the beginnings of some form of 'category management' with the buyers working around a key brand 'custodian'.

Indicative job description:
To be responsible for:

- the sales and profitability performance of 'Maine New England' branded products
- management of all functions supporting the Maine brand
- future developments of the category
- quality monitoring

- management of the implementation of all in-store merchandising and promotional activities relating to Maine
- PR liaison – the 'human face of the brand'; representative for the brand at corporate/functional level.

Question 6 focuses on the key features of a successful brand extension strategy. In terms of the key characteristics of successful brand management, it is imperative that the brand has a clearly defined identity and image which is attractive to the consumer, but which is not 'bound-in' with any particular product category. The visual identifiers of the brand must be strong, such as in relation to the branding images, the labelling, packaging and so on. The brand values must be accessible to the consumer – and these values ought to be capable of replication within a variety of product situations. The key dynamic, then, is that the brand have some form of personality and reputation which is capable of transportation.

Question 7 asks students to identify the issues which may arise in the future with regards to the management of the 'Maine New England' brand portfolio and to suggest ways in which these issues could be 'successfully managed'.

The key problems that the Maine brand may face in Debenhams are those of:

- over-extension – whereby the brand is added to inappropriate product types and/or the customer becomes sceptical or tired of the brand's values
- quality – too many products may lead to inconsistencies in the brand in terms of quality performance and standards
- design/innovations dry-up
- the Maine brand itself may become the focus of competitor action
- an over-emphasis on 'Maine New England' may mean that Debenhams could be vulnerable to changes in consumer taste, particularly if Maine goes out of favour.

In order to protect the long-term future of the 'Maine New England' brand, Debenhams may have to ensure that a coherent strategy be developed for the future management of the brand and that on-going commitment to quality, fashionability and value for money continues to be the basis for the management of the brand. It is likewise important that the brand stays 'bright and interesting' through product innovations, advertising, in-store merchandising initiatives; that future extensions of the brand are carefully controlled and managed; competitor activity is carefully monitored; and other new brand ideas be developed in order to ensure some form of succession for 'Maine New England'.

REFERENCE

Davies, G. (1992) 'The two ways in which a retailer can be a brand'. *International Journal of Retailing and Distribution Management*, **20**(2): 24–34.

CASE 14

TEACHING NOTES
SUPERDRUG: THE ROUTE TO BECOMING MORE INNOVATIVE

HELENE HILL

SYNOPSIS

This case study represents an insight into the processes, procedures and issues faced by a large multiple retailer attempting to develop a more innovative culture. Superdrug designed the strategic *Living the Mission* programme to develop a mission and vision for the future of the company to ensure a competitive edge by facilitating a more innovative and customer focused culture. Key issues facing Superdrug in the process included how to design the programme, how to achieve consistent roll-out across all levels of the company, and finally how to measure, evaluate and disseminate outcomes across the company.

This case study offers a practical insight to students on how an organization may instigate the development of a more innovative culture, and the key issues involved in this process. The programme is explored from the multiple perspectives of strategic managers, regional and store staff. The focus is upon the way in which the strategic objectives and implementation process were devised, and the major factors which had to be managed in turning the vision into practical reality. The far reaching implications of this case study lead it to be ideal for taking a number of approaches, whether broad, or more specific. The programme investigated in this case encompasses the complete design and implementation process, and concludes as the organization has implemented the programme and faces its first series of assessments of progress to date.

LEARNING OBJECTIVES AND CORTCO COMPETENCIES

(1) **Personal effectiveness**

(2) **Managing people and working with others**

- Within the case tasks, to implicitly analyse the extent to which the CORTCO core competencies are incorporated into the design, implementation and outcome of the *Living The Mission* programme. These involve self-confidence and personal strength; assertiveness, decisiveness, flexibility, judgement, initiative, stress tolerance; leadership and teamwork; planning and organization; analytical and problem solving; human relations and influencing.

(3)   Organizational ability and creative thinking

Critical thinking and analytical consideration:
Planning and organizing:

■   To develop an understanding of the process of managing strategic change within an organization: its fit with corporate objectives; the specific aims of the change programme; developing a programme outline that specifies the roll-out strategy; the role staff commitment plays within such a programme; designing a programme which is tailored to all levels of an organization; and the complexities of evaluating and measuring these programmes as they progress.

Innovation and strategic thinking:

■   To develop an understanding of the role of innovation within corporate strategy, and how a more innovative culture can be encouraged at an operational level: the role and strategy of changing a company's culture to embrace innovation, how to facilitate the involvement of all personnel in the generation and application of new ideas, the importance of developing a system which ensures effective assessment of all potential ideas, the role of personnel awareness and training, the importance of communication and feedback in this process, and the ability to ensure consistency of new products/services developed across a large number of branded distribution outlets.

(4)   Business focus

Customer focus:
Commercialism and business awareness:

■   To develop an understanding of the above issues in a retail management and marketing context: the pivotal role of the consumer, the increasing importance of services marketing issues – customer satisfaction, the service encounter, the role of branding, the strengths and weaknesses of extensive use of part-time workers, and the central issue of the cost driven nature of the retail environment and its implications on the above issues.

CASE APPLICATIONS AND CONTEXTS

Due to the extensive number of issues this case raises, it is feasible to approach this case from a number of perspectives: either a general business or retail specific perspective; and from either a management of change or developing an innovative culture viewpoint.

At a basic level the case would be suited for the exploration of how a more consumer focused approach to management can improve the competitive standing of a company in the market. It could also be used for exploring the issue of managing strategic change. On a more detailed level, specific consideration may be given to the role of an innovative culture within service organizations at the operational level, the design and implementation of this process at the operational level, and the format and process of measuring this process.

In approaching **Question 1** students should consider the role of staff involvement and commitment, the measurement of achievement of programme objectives, the need to align the programme with overall corporate objectives and strategy.

Issues raised in response to **Question 2** must reflect the fit between programme design and the operational aspects of the organization, for example retailing, service industry, brand and retail outlet consistency. Students can be asked to rank the difficulties and suggest the significance of each difficulty within the overall programme.

Question 3 can be approached from either an academic or practical perspective. For the academic option students need to have a deeper understanding of the academic literature pertaining to innovation management and the role of culture. Such models and frameworks can then be tested against this specific programme taken from the chosen literature articles from the reading list. For the practical exercise students need to reflect on the key lessons learnt from this case in terms of the programme's outcomes – do they think this programme has facilitated the organizational culture becoming more innovative? In what way? Is this consistent across all levels of the organization? What insights can they gain from the programme so far to use as indicators of potential successful modifications for the future of the programme? What are the key issues they must tackle, in what order of priority, and how?

For **Question 4** students are required to summarize the key learning points and then to see the extent to which the issues indicated are relevant to other industries. Which industries can these points be applied to and why?

Question 5 asks students to specifically consider the service/retail context of the case. Again this task can be approached from a practical application of experience, or an academic perspective. Students could be asked to consider the differences between product marketing and services marketing, and their answers used as a basis to answer this question. Alternatively, they could be presented with the key issues from the academic literature on services marketing: the distinguishing factors (intangibility, heterogeneity, perishability, inseparability), the extended marketing mix, the service delivery system, the service encounter, service quality. These issues could then be applied, asking for the implications of these on the design, implementation and measurement of this programme? How does this vary from a product?

In **Question 6** students need to think of how this programme needs to be further developed to add to its future success. Key issues involve measurement of this programme, staff commitment over time when new staff are appointed in-store, ensuring that all staff 'live the mission' and signal to staff lower in the organization its importance, how the successes to date are being communicated and learned from. Students could be asked to pull out these key issues and asked for suggestions on how these could be achieved.

Issues to be included with regard to **Question 7** are how to train and involve staff while still meeting the overall store goals; how to have an effective strategy without imposing your own views and experience as store manager; the issue of continual new store staff joining the team; the impact of limited team time, and general time constraints which make it difficult for all staff to step beyond their immediate task. This question raises some fundamental questions specific to the core competencies - human relations, influencing skills, leadership, teamwork.

FURTHER READING

Carnall, C. (1999) *Managing Change In Organisations*. Europe: Prentice-Hall.

Easingwood, C. (1986) 'New product development for service companies'. *Journal of Product Innovation Management*, **4**: 264–75.

Galbraith, J. (1982) 'Designing the innovating organisation'. *Organisational Dynamics*, **10**(3): 5–25.

Kaplan, R. and Norton, D. (1992) 'The balanced scorecard – measures that drive performance'. *Harvard Business Review*. January/February: 71–9.

Lovelock, C. (1996) *Services Marketing* (rev edn). New Jersey: Prentice Hall.

Normann, R. (1984) *Service Management*. Chichester: John Wiley & Sons.

Pedler, M., Burgoyne, J. and Boydell, T. (1991) *The Learning Company*. Maidenhead: McGraw-Hill.

TEACHING NOTES
THE ROLE OF CATEGORY MANAGEMENT IN HAIR COLOURANTS: BRISTOL-MYERS

SANDRA HOGARTH-SCOTT AND IAN WALTERS

SYNOPSIS

This case examines the role of category management in the haircare category. This is a growth market and the general trade marketing manager of Bristol-Myers Squibb is reviewing his strategy for the next twelve months. In particular he is assessing current consumer research in the context of category management relationships in his three separate trade channels: independent pharmacists; the multiple grocers; and the drivers of the category, Boots and Superdrug. This is set in the context of market share leadership in the hair colourant subcategory, and a growing presence in the overall haircare category. Consumer information and retailer–supplier relationships are central to category management and are the focus of this case.

LEARNING OBJECTIVES AND CORTCO COMPETENCIES

(3) Organizational ability and creative thinking

Critical thinking and analytical consideration:
■ To understand the function of category management and its role in retailer–manufacturer relationships.
■ To understand how different market segments require separate relationship marketing strategies.

(4) Business focus

Customer focus:
■ To understand the role and importance of relationships in trade marketing
■ To understand the role of category management in
   – building manufacturer market share
   – providing a consumer-focused shopping experience
   – providing a major plank in retailer–supplier relationships

CASE APPLICATIONS AND CONTEXTS

This case is suitable for courses in retail operations, channels, trade marketing, supply chain management, and retail marketing. It could also be of use in an introductory marketing course to illustrate the importance of segmentation in business-to-business marketing.

There are two major challenges facing the company which provide the focus for students' analysis of the case, and a thorough exploration of these two issues will test all the management competencies. First students will need to assess what the market for haircare is really like, and more problematically, where it is going, in order to decide where Bristol-Myers should put their money. The rest of the analysis and discussion will hinge on this. The consumer data is also relevant here. If the young are driving the market, the question needs to be addressed whether they shop in Boots or in Tesco, regardless of the figures. Issues of critical mass need to be evaluated. Second, a thorough evaluation is required of whether Bristol-Myers are in a position to make the jump to preferred supplier status in the total haircare category. Students should also consider that the Bristol-Myers team's perceptions and ambitions might be unrealistic and unduly influenced by Ian's ambition and Nestlé background. However, if on reflection aspiring to preferred supplier status is deemed realistic, the question needs to be addressed with which retailer(s) key partnership(s) should be developed.

The case is rich in data and the first task for students is to sort the material, decide which are major concerns and which are minor, and how to use the material to answer the questions. There is considerable raw data, some conflicting. Students will have to decide which to go for, which will aid the development of analytical and problem solving skills. One advantage of the case is that all the students will be familiar with most of the retailers and be users of the category of products. Analysis might start with a standard SWOT – of total market, then of health and beauty retailers and of four major players. There is enough information in the case to provide detail on Bristol-Myers' strengths and weaknesses. There is substantial consumer information and students will need to come to grips with this to reach strong conclusions. This could be followed by competitor analysis. In this context the more precise issues of category management could be addressed.

Category management is an evolving process. It involves the management of individual consumer markets as businesses in their own right and aims for increased total category profitability due to a mutually agreed (between retailer and supplier) consumer focused strategy. As a result retailers and suppliers jointly develop strategic category plans. The process aims to develop strong, collaborative retailer-manufacturer relationships and provides integrated responsibility for buying and merchandising decisions (IGD, 1995)

Category management has partly been driven by the high concentration of the retail food market, with the top four retailers, namely Tesco, Sainsbury, Asda and Safeway, in competition in a relatively static marketplace. These retailers are committed to high investment in sites and store design, they face restrictions in planning permissions for expansion outside urban areas, and are committed to increasing customer service, in the presence of consumer demand for everyday good value. Added to this there has been the entry of discounters. In consequence the retailers have applied downward pressure on costs in order to increase the bottom line of individual categories. Category management aims to decrease costs, enhance retailer and supplier information and technologies, optimize ranges, improve return from existing assets, increase the focus on the consumer, and expand profitable categories (IGD, 1995) This same trend is evident in the leading health and beauty retailers, such as Boots and Superdrug. Retailers are seeking to sweat assets harder.

The case is not really about the fine detail of category management that is, what goes where, but about how Bristol-Myers might grow market share and gain competitive advantage in the current marketplace, taking into account their own competencies, the retailers and the consumers. The focal point of the key issues covered in the case is Bristol-Myers' relationship building with retailers. As there are three separate market segments, this means that there are also potentially three different types of relationships. The case facilitates the exploration of the role of category management in brand management, relationship building and selling more to the ultimate end-consumer. It also highlights the impact of a category management approach on profitability for Bristol-Myers and their retail partners. The case illustrates how a manufacturer may use dominance in a sub-category to move towards increased share in the total category. It shows ways in which a manufacturer can build on the foundations for preferred supplier status. It demonstrates how Bristol-Myers make use of shopper research and category management to optimize their sales in the hair-care category.

One way that the relationship management issues might be tackled in a learning situation is to have three teams: Bristol-Myers (that is, Ian Walters and team); the health and beauty retailers – Superdrug and Boots; and a team for one of the major grocers. Each team would be asked to put forward proposals for the next year, concentrating on relationship management and joint team objectives and strategies. This would be an excellent way to exercise leadership and teamwork skills.

REFERENCE

IGD (1995) *The Category Management Revolution*. Watford: IGD Business Publications.

FURTHER READING

IGD (1999) *Category Management In Action*. April. Watford: IGD Business Publications.

HALFORDS MOTOR OILS (A): A CASE OF SUCCESS BY DESIGN

MALCOLM KIRKUP, PAUL WALLEY AND JOHN TEMPERLEY

SYNOPSIS

This case study is one of two developed by the authors on the relaunch and repositioning of Halfords Motor Oils in 1996. Case (B) focuses on the technical challenges involved in designing and manufacturing the oil containers. This case examines the commercial objectives behind the product relaunch, the characteristics of the oil market and consumer requirements, and the process of research and design deployed by Halfords. The suggested case tasks are focused on developing launch strategies, but the case raises numerous discussion points on aspects of new product development and marketing. The case intentionally finishes prior to the development of the launch strategy, presenting a clear focus for student assignments. The case helps develop an understanding of the role and importance of effective research, planning, management, teamwork and co-ordination to the success of a product, particularly when a complex process and large numbers of managers and organizations are involved. The case permits detailed analysis and problem-solving in the context of a real business situation and an appreciation of the importance of communication.

LEARNING OBJECTIVES AND CORTCO COMPETENCIES

(2) Managing people and working with others

- To understand the role of project managers in new product development, the nature of linkages with other managers internally and the importance of a team approach.
- To appreciate the complexity of the supplier and agency network involved in a new product launch, and aspects of buyer–supplier relationships.

(3) **Organizational ability and creative thinking**

Critical thinking and analytical consideration:

- To develop an understanding of the process of new product development; the role and importance of planning, project management and effective co-ordination.
- To develop innovative and creative solutions in the context of marketing strategies.

(4) **Business focus**

Customer focus:

Commercialism and business awareness:

- To develop an understanding of key aspects of retail marketing, for example: the importance of research, competitive positioning, range segmentation, the concept of added value, branding, and the role of design and packaging.
- To develop an understanding of the importance of effective communication – internally within the retail business and externally with customers.

CASE APPLICATIONS AND CONTEXTS

The detail provided in the case allows for discussion of many issues associated with the new product development process and retail marketing. For example,

- Own-label versus proprietary brands debate (rationale for own-label, mix decisions and so on).
- New product development (NPD) process – how the emphasis, stages, tasks, and durations may differ in this case relative to other textbook frameworks.
- The role and importance of planning, project management and effective teamwork and co-ordination – particularly given the number of external suppliers involved.
- The need for effective partnerships with suppliers.

Question 1 is designed to help students appreciate the complexity and duration involved in new product development, and the role of the buyer. Answers should include a summary of tasks already completed, and tasks still remaining – for example, bottle tooling, producing bottle samples, producing the final bottles, bottle filling, cap production, carton/packaging cutting, distribution to stores, plus numerous other tasks. Students can develop a bar chart to establish when each task might need to be completed in order to ensure a launch in, say, May 1996.

Question 2 focuses on the primary task evident from the case, which is for students to develop a launch strategy for Halfords. Given the considerable detail presented in the case, and the scope available in such a task, it is perhaps best suited to a written assignment. Students can be asked to assume the role of Chris Forman or a member of the marketing team and to prepare a marketing strategy. Students can refer to the marketing objectives laid down by Halfords and consider how they would approach each element of the marketing mix. Each element will require careful consideration and students must be encouraged to take into account market characteristics, consumer requirements (and findings from the focus groups), along with the commercial objectives.

In developing a launch strategy students should consider prioritizing the key issues, and thereby derive a firm basis for subsequent strategy recommendations. In developing a pricing strategy students should give special consideration to the implications of the promotional tactics of the leading brands for Halfords' pricing.

Discussions on an appropriate in-store merchandising strategy should cover the following issues. Should Halfords use the existing display plinths or attempt to bring yet more innovation through in novel displays? How can graphics be used to communicate the key messages to consumers? How might the merchandising strategy vary between smaller high street stores and larger superstores?

In devising a communications strategy students should explore the following areas. Should Halfords deploy advertising and PR or rely on POS? What media will be deployed? How will the nature of the Halfords customer affect the type of media chosen? When will (any) external communications be introduced and why? What key messages would Halfords wish to communicate in their campaigns? A creative element can be introduced to help students appreciate the challenges of communicating through different media – for example billboard posters versus specialist magazine advert versus advertorials.

The final part of Question 2 homes in on internal communications. Internal marketing is crucial in the context of a product relaunch and repositioning. Store managers and staff need to be fully briefed on the new range, its characteristics, the key selling messages and the type of information/service required by customers. It is the stores that will make or break a new product launch and it will be vital to get them on board, fully informed and motivated. How would students suggest this can be achieved? A staff video is suggested – but is this feasible? What form might a launch-document take – and what messages should be communicated? How can staff be trained and who would train them? How will sales staff be trained to encourage customers to change their usual brand of oil and trade-up? As a creative element for internal marketing, students could be asked to develop a storyboard for a staff-video, encouraging students to identify key messages to be communicated and to consider how to effectively pass these on to store management and selling staff.

Question 3 focuses the attention on the customer. The case notes the use of focus groups to test reactions to the concept design and in-store interviews to examine labelling. Students could be asked to comment on the advantages and limitations of these techniques and the particular approach used, and to suggest alternative or additional research.

Question 4 is concerned with forecasting and forward planning. It is important to consider the implications of the visual merchandising and communications strategy adopted for the planning of stock requirements. Stores also vary in size, from high street to superstores. Students could also be asked to consider the advantages and disadvantages of a 'national launch' compared to a test marketing approach.

FURTHER READING

Kotler, P., Armstrong, G., Saunders, J. and Wong, V. (1996) *Principles of Marketing* (European edn). Hemel Hempstead: Prentice Hall.

McDonald, M. and Tideman, C. (1993) *Retail Marketing Plans*. Oxford: Butterworth-Heinemann.

TEACHING NOTES
HALFORDS MOTOR OILS (B): TRANSLATING CONSUMER NEEDS INTO PRODUCTS

PAUL WALLEY, MALCOLM KIRKUP AND JOHN TEMPERLEY

SYNOPSIS

This case takes a detailed look at one particular aspect of the product development programme developed in the Halfords Motor Oils (A) case and focuses on the technical issues involved in manufacturing the oil containers. It introduces some of the complexities and challenges involved in translating a unique design into a manufacturable container, and explores the collaboration between the company and development people from the suppliers who worked in conjunction with Halfords and Halfords' appointed designers and consultants. The initial part of the case contains some detail of market characteristics and customer requirements, but much of the case details the technical issues which the manufacturers would have to address in order to achieve a successful outcome to the project. The designers used a simplified form of the quality function deployment (QFD) tool, to analyse which features could be 'deployed' in the design, and the case provides sufficient information to allow students to do this for themselves. Certain details have been omitted from the case to allow tutors to set the design project as the first exercise in class.

LEARNING OBJECTIVES AND CORTCO COMPETENCIES

(3) Organizational ability and creative thinking

Critical thinking and analytical consideration:
- To develop an understanding of the need for a 'design chain' of people to take the concept from idea into production.
- To identify the types of constraints placed upon product design by manufacturing and logistics considerations.
- To provide a detailed example of the use of quality function deployment.

(4) Business focus

Customer focus:

■ To develop an awareness of the influence of consumer preferences on product design.

Commercialism and business awareness:

■ To highlight the impact of good product design upon market performance.

CASE APPLICATIONS AND CONTEXTS

Tutors have a choice about how to use this case. It can be used as a stand-alone case about new product development, or an exercise which concentrates on the specific tool of QFD.

Using the Case as an Example of New Product Development:

If the case is used as a stand-alone design case, the authors recommend that Halfords (A) is not distributed in advance and students are required to come up with their own designs in class. Creativity of ideas should be encouraged. If time allows, students could be encouraged to produce cardboard mock-ups of their ideas. This especially works well during modular courses where evening work on tasks of this nature can be scheduled.

Students should provide a good list of factors which the designers should have considered when initially designing the product. These could include:

Shape. Students should be able to identify both the aesthetic and the functional importance of the shape of the product. Special emphasis should be given to the shape of the packaging as the oil itself is very much a standard commodity item, with little or no means of differentiation. Students should be encouraged to debate how adventurous the new shape could be, and consider issues such as whether the shape should be 'themed' in some way. For example, by developing concepts such as a 'car wheel' shape (see an example in case (A)).

Colour. The importance of the colour of the package needs to be discussed during the case debrief. The colour choice is influenced by a number of factors: the colour can be used as an identifier emphasizing the difference between grades of oil; the colour needs to encourage in-store sales; there is a simple aesthetic value to colour choice. During the case dénouement, it can be commented that the bold colours and clear colour distinction between grades made the product identifiable for less-informed customers.

Pouring performance. The role of pouring performance needs to be discussed in detail. The shape required for good pouring performance was a particular challenge to the detail engineering designers. Where possible, students should be encouraged to identify the technical limitations of the key manufacturing processes, especially that of the blow moulding process.

Students should identify a series of constraints within manufacturing and logistics. Apart from production costs, these would include dimensional limitations, transportability and so on. There are a number of other factors mentioned in the case, including the visi-strip, the flip-top lid, the dual use as a spent oil container and so on, all of which can be cited to provoke discussion.

Using the Case as an Illustration of Quality Function Deployment

The product requirements from the earlier part of the case analysis can be used to develop a 'house of quality' diagram, which highlights the most important features which might be developed in the new product. The QFD analysis can be taught either as a continuation of the earlier exercise or by itself. If this case is used in conjunction with case (A) then the outcome would be more an exercise in the use of QFD.

The main outcome of the case is a top level QFD chart, which should recommend the deployment of attributes such as pourability, shape and features such as the visi-strip. The main point of this exercise is to illustrate that some market-driven ideas have to be rejected on the grounds of practicability, but there is a poorly defined dividing line between stretching engineers to innovate beyond existing practice and forcing them to take too big a developmental leap. An ideal example to quote here is the idea of a flip-top lid, which could not be fully developed on the large can and was subsequently withdrawn from use on the small can after poor performance in the marketplace. The authors find the QFD tool very useful to bridge the gap between marketing and technical perspectives. Finally, the concluding remarks to the case could be used to illustrate the impact of the bold design features upon performance in terms of margins, market share and profitability.

REFERENCE

Evans, J. R. and Lindsay, W. M. (1993) *The Management and Control of Quality*. St Paul, MN: West Publishing.

FURTHER READING

Other suggested books and articles, which cover the operations aspects of new product development, or the QFD tool include:

Akao, Y. (ed.) (1990) *Quality Function Deployment*, Cambridge, MA: Productivity Press.

King, R. (1987) 'Listening to the voice of the customer'. *National Productivity Review*, **6**(3): 277–81.

Sullivan, L. (1986) 'Quality function deployment', *Quality Progress*, June: 39–50.

Wheelwright, S. C. and Clark, K. B. (1992) *Revolutionising Product Development*, New York: Free Press.

TEACHING NOTES
SAINSBURY'S AND SHAW'S: REFLECTIONS ON MAKING AN ACQUISITION A REALITY

DAVID MUSKETT

SYNOPSIS

The case is fundamentally an analysis of how Sainsbury's managed the take-over of Shaw's of New England viewed from the perspective of some of the key actors involved. It is based upon key informant interviews undertaken between September 1995 and July 1997 and includes not only the views of senior managers on both sides of the Atlantic but also of the four mid-range executives who changed companies across the Atlantic to obtain experience of each other's operating practices.

Having acquired their first stake in Shaw's in 1983, Sainsbury's had been relatively 'hands-off' in their management of the business in the early years. After full acquisition in 1987 this style persisted for a time with only board level supervision by the British chairman. Gradually greater involvement by Sainsbury's began, and more UK based Sainsbury's people joined Shaw's organization. The middle management staff exchange policy discussed in this case operated between 1993 and 1995 bringing Shaw's managers to the UK and Sainsbury's managers to New England.

The individual mid-ranking managers were interviewed between late 1995 and mid 1996 on their views of the differences between Shaw's and Sainsbury's and were asked for their assessment of the effectiveness of the merger. All the actors concerned seemed proud of the achievements of the acquisition. Equally all were critical of how long it was taking to make a complete success of it and concerned about what they considered wasted opportunities.

The overt focus of this case is on cultural differences between the UK and US in terms of both business practice and linguistic nuances which can cause confusion, and this is explored in the dialogue. Many organizations suffer a sense of corporate myopia and 'not invented here'. There is some suggestion that it might have been this which led Sainsbury's to misapprehend the nature of the business that they had acquired in Shaw's and then to devote resources to that misapprehension in the changes that they imposed on Shaw's business.

The case closes with Sainsbury's being in a position to expand their holding in Giant Food. (Sainsbury's sold their interests in Giant Food to Royal Aholt NV of the Netherlands in spring 1998 for £375m leaving Shaw's as their only US interest.) This can be used to ask students to evaluate whether the lessons learned in Shaw's can be applied more quickly to Giant. Thus, while this case is not primarily about the potential acquisition of Giant Food, it does set a background context for future expectations of further US development by the Sainsbury's group at the time of writing.

LEARNING OBJECTIVES AND CORTCO COMPETENCIES

(1) Personal effectiveness

Emotional resilience:
Assertiveness:
Self-confidence:
Task management:
Flexibility/adaptability:
Self-development:

- To explore the full range of interpersonal management skills required both at senior and mid-management level in interacting with colleagues and subordinates who come from a different business and national culture.
- To assess the extent to which the nature of the exchanges and job definitions supported or hindered personal effectiveness, flexibility, adaptability and self-development in this case.
- To investigate ways in which personal learning can be translated into organizational learning and to appraise the extent to which this has taken place within Sainsbury's as a result of the Shaw's acquisition.

(2) Managing people and working with others

Team working and awareness:
Team leading:

- To further students' appreciation of the critical necessity of team leading in retail management with regard to adapting behaviour to meet business objectives.
- To evaluate the role of team leadership in the integration of two corporate cultures following a merger.

Communication skills:

- To demonstrate the need to adopt an appropriate style for the different cultural expectations that are faced, and the use of appropriate language.

(3) Organizational ability and creative thinking

Critical thinking and analytical consideration:

- To appreciate how fresh thinking can be applied to the buying and negotiation for products.

- To contrast and compare the responsibilities required of middle managers in a centralized bureaucratic organization as opposed to those within a more devolved, 'looser' business structure.

Forward planning:
- To crystallize key learning points from the Sainsbury's/Shaw's merger and formulate a strategy and implementation plan for applying them to the next proposed merger with the aim of facilitating smoother and more effective cultural integration.

(4) Business focus

Commercialism and business awareness:
- To assess the impact of merger activity on business performance with special emphasis on a critical evaluation of the hidden costs of the acculturation process.

CASE APPLICATIONS AND CONTEXTS

The case has important lessons for any business related course dealing with companies or organizations which are involved in mergers or takeovers. It is therefore widely applicable. Focusing on the impact of corporate culture in transnational merger situations, it can be used in teaching international retailing, retail strategy, and human resource strategy and management, as well as in any module dealing with business and national cultures.

Different approaches might be used to customize the application of the case to different levels of student achievement. Thus, in the earlier years of undergraduate programmes the impact of cultural differences and interpersonal management styles at operational store level might be explored in detail, whereas for final year or postgraduate students the emphasis may be on the broader strategic aspects and overall organizational learning.

Question 1 requires analysis based upon information given throughout the case on US versus UK grocery retailing. It could be set as an assignment in its own right requiring further secondary research to support or contest the picture drawn in the case.

To address **Question 2**, the student will have to analyse the different business cultures and operating styles which are described by the interviewees in the case. They should be able to spot the inherent contradictions between general aims and specific objectives for the staff exchange programme. Success factors as well as 'wasted opportunities' and their underlying causal factors should be explored by the students in some detail.

To address **Question 3**, the student will need to assess critically the original decision to acquire and debate the extent to which Sainsbury's were fully informed and open minded in their decision. Classroom discussion might explore the contributing role of Sainsbury's own corporate culture and the implicit critique of this culture's inability to see clearly or evaluate objectively things which are outside its experience. A range of theory could apply for background reading particularly Attwood (1990) and Hofstede (1980, 1991).

This question can be developed further by encouraging students to examine possible parallels with the later acquisition of Texas Homecare. While there were no national barriers in this latter case, Sainsbury's have struggled to integrate Texas Homecare into their Homebase DIY operation since its acquisition, due to a whole range of incompatibilities of operating systems plus company style and culture. It appears from evidence of some of the respondents in this case who shared an interest in the Homebase/Texas operation, that many of the lessons learned 'the hard way' from Shaw's merger were never effectively transferred back across the Atlantic and had to be relearned. The lack of continuity of staff involved in developments across businesses seems to offer long-term inefficiency in some crucial cases as learning is not easily passed on. The history of the business can be lost along the way and with it much learning.

Question 4 requires students to analyse relevant points of product policy within the marketing mix as it might apply to the case. The apparent hostility of US customers to own/private label needs to be examined for its impact on post take-over decisions at Shaw's. Plant's (1987) force field analysis could be applied to analyse the impulse towards change despite difficulties encountered.

Question 5 specifically requires team working and team teaching to be addressed within cultural context. Gibb's (1987) analysis of corporist versus entrepreneurial management styles could be applied respectively to Sainsbury's and Shaw's here as a paradigm.

Question 6 addresses a core theme of middle versus senior management decisions. It requires students to compare and contrast the stances of both groups of managers and to draw out tensions which become apparent.

REFERENCES

Attwood, T. (1990) 'Corporate culture: for or against you'? *Management Accounting,* **68**(1): 26–9.

Gibb, A. A. (1987) 'Entrepreneurial (intrapreneurial) vs corporist management and its implications for business schools'. *Journal of European Industrial Training,* **11**(2):20–3.

Hofstede, G. (1980) *Cultures Consequences: Interactive Differences in Work Related Values.* Beverley Hills, CA: Sage.

Hofstede, G. (1991) *Cultures and Organisations.* Hemel Hempstead: McGraw-Hill.

Plant, R. (1987) *Managing Change and Making it Stick.* Aldershot: Gower.

TEACHING NOTES
CWS RETAIL: RESPONSIBLE PRODUCT DEVELOPMENT

JOHN TEMPERLEY AND MALCOLM KIRKUP

SYNOPSIS

This case study considers new product development at the Co-operative Wholesale Society (CWS). The case study has two parts. The first part briefly reviews the history of the co-operative movement and CWS, and highlights aspects of the co-operative identity and strategy which have a bearing on new product development. In particular the case provides an insight into how the co-operative movement differs fundamentally from other types of retail organization in terms of its philosophy, values and principles. The company's commitment to 'responsible' trading is highlighted and the case shows how this has translated into a set of detailed promises including a customer charter. The second part of the case study considers the specific processes involved in the development of a CWS own-label product, allowing students the opportunity to consider how a commitment to responsible retailing affects new product development.

LEARNING OBJECTIVES AND CORTCO COMPETENCIES

(2)   Managing people and working with others

Team working and awareness:
■ To develop an understanding of the impact of an ethical stance on the management team and new product development – particularly in relation to commitments on labelling and animal testing – and to understand how these concerns are operationalized.
■ To develop listening and oral communication skills, and sensitivity to the views of others in the discussion of ethical and environmental issues in retailing.

(3)   Organizational ability and creative thinking

Planning and organizing:
■ To develop an understanding of the process of new product development in a retail own-brand context; the role and importance of planning, project

management and effective co-ordination in the new product development process; the role of marketing in new product development; the nature of linkages with other managers internally and hence the importance of a team approach and a co-ordinated approach.

Critical thinking and analytical consideration:
Innovation and strategic thinking:
- To understand the rationale for a formal new product development process.
- To develop an understanding of how the values and principles of an organization can affect strategy and impact the operational decisions of the management team and new product development.

(4) Business focus

Commercialism and business awareness:
- To enable students to problem-solve, and demonstrate commercial awareness, in the context of developing own-label products – based on information similar to that available to managers involved in a real-life project.

CASE APPLICATIONS AND CONTEXTS

The case lends itself ideally to courses on retail marketing, product development, and buying and merchandising, depending on the depth of detail the tutor wishes to explore. The detail provided in the case allows for discussion of many issues associated with Co-operative retail strategies, business ethics, and the new product development process.

Part A

The primary issues to address in Part A of the case study relate to the implications of the Co-op's overall strategy. The ethical stance sets the Co-op apart from competitors (with marketing advantages in terms of differentiation and added value), but there are also dangers. A failure to adhere to stated policies or promises might attract significant criticism, and there may be cost implications to ensure rigorous internal procedures. Other companies might have equal claims to being a responsible retailer but they may not choose to promote it quite so prominently – students can consider the advantages and disadvantages of each approach, and justify their own particular views. Students could be asked to consider the practical problems involved for CWS Retail in implementing their ethical approach in the competitive retail environment.

Students should consider the implications of co-operative principles, values and history for both strategy and new product development in particular. The commercial versus ethical considerations are worth drawing out – the organization is a co-operative society and hence a mutual society owned by its members, as opposed to a plc quoted on the stock exchange and answerable to shareholders via the stock market. The specific implications of the ethical stance for new product development are worth examining – whether it places constraints on product ranges offered. Should the Co-op be involved in developing new products in areas such as cigarettes and alco-pops? Is the new product development process, development time, or responsiveness to market changes affected at all by the need to be very rigorous in supplier evaluation and labelling standards? The possible ways that the Co-op values and ethics are built into the day to day operations of the business are a consideration. In addition to the customer charter, tutors should note there is also a CWS code of business conduct for all employees, including a contact system both inside and outside the organization which any employee can use to express their concerns. In support of this there are also specific codes of practice relating to dealings with manufacturers, and students should consider the practical implications of the CWS ethical stance for existing and new suppliers.

Part B

The second part of the case has been constructed using only selected information provided by the CWS. This was done deliberately in order to encourage students to think through the detailed process of new product development. The case provides a flavour of the rigorous and procedural nature of new product development and the 'responsible retailing' approach of the company is reflected in certain of the activities described. The Co-op has developed formal processes for new product development, and the students can be asked to consider the merits and disadvantages of such structure. The process is subject to a series of formal stages with reviews at each stage, and although the actual process varies dependent on the type of product variation involved, in the case of the fabric conditioner the main stages are as follows.

The process begins with the rationale for the proposed launch presented and assessed at an annual range review. The category marketing manager examines the critical path and considers tasks and dates. A buying brief is prepared (in association with the technical centre and labelling standards) and a packaging concept brief is prepared for design consultants. Quotes and samples are requested from suppliers and then formal evaluation and testing of products takes place to choose suppliers. The chosen supplier(s) are then appraised (company and production line). Draft technical specifications are developed in conjunction with suppliers and a copy brief is developed in tandem by labelling standards. Packaging concepts, product information, the labelling copy brief and supplier code of conduct are brought together in the final technical specification to be issued to the supplier. Label artwork is then developed and proofed. Production runs and evaluations are organized. Samples are distributed to Co-operative Retail Trading Group, individual societies and the executive managers. Finally, consumer communications are developed to support the launch and PR activity is organized by CWS's press office. Three months later there is a post-launch review of results, and feedback.

Students can also be asked to examine the role/activities of different members of the category management team during the project period. This is a useful activity to separate out the main negotiating activities for the buyer, the marketing activities, and the role of the merchandiser, but also to appreciate the inter-relationships of the roles. Students could also be asked to map out the entire organizational framework and network of departments/suppliers involved – particularly to understand the complexities involved and the critical need for effective communication and co-ordination. Not ALL activities in the new product development process are specifically referred to in the case, and so students will need to consider other requirements behind the development/production/launch/distribution process.

A list of activities to be completed prior to the launch can be drawn up, in the form of a gantt chart. Based on estimates of how long each activity might take, a launch date can be predicted and students can consider which activities would be particularly 'critical' to ensure a timely launch. Students could also be asked to identify how the success of the launch would be evaluated – what parameters would be used to judge success and over what time period.

As a creative element for an assignment students can be asked to assume the role of Mary Paul and prepare an outline buying brief for Jim Smith, and/or a packaging concept brief for Bill Baines. The packaging design brief will need to present the marketing background, objectives of the launch and demonstrate how the new product fits in with the existing range. Creative concepts can be drawn up to show pack illustrations, shapes and the nature of the copy required. The detail required for the buying brief is outlined in Mary's notes, and students will need to make (justified) assumptions to present a complete picture. Students can be encouraged to visit retail stores to develop creative concept ideas.

FURTHER READING

Birchall, J. (1994) *Co-op: The People's Business*. Manchester: Manchester University Press.

Corstjens, J. and Corstjens, M. (1995) *Store Wars: The Battle for Mindspace and Shelfspace*. Chichester: John Wiley & Sons.

Crawford C. Merle (1996) *New Product Management* (5th edn). USA.: Irwin.

Eliot, S. (1994) 'The Co-operative difference – asset or handicap?' In McGoldrick, P. (ed.) *Cases in Retailing*. London: Pitman, pp. 8–15.

Gordon, W. (1994) 'Retailer brands – the value equation for success in the '90s'. *The Journal of the Market Research Society*. **36**(3): 165–88.

Kotler, P. (1997) *Marketing Management – Analysis, Planning, Implementation and Control*, (9th edn). New Jersey: Prentice Hall.

TEACHING NOTES
BEING SMART – DEVELOPING CUSTOMER LOYALTY AT CHELMSFORD STAR CO-OPERATIVE SOCIETY

PHILIPPA WARD, HANNE GARDNER AND HELEN WRIGHT

SYNOPSIS

This case focuses on the customer loyalty scheme run by The Chelmsford Star Co-operative Society. Whereas the majority of loyalty schemes run by the major retailers are based on magnetic-swipe technology, this co-operative society decided to use a smartcard-based system unlike the cards developed by other co-operative societies.

The first part of the case gives background on the co-operative movement's developments in this area, from paying dividends to members, loyalty schemes in general and loyalty schemes in particular, and finally describing the more sophisticated Chelmsford Starcard. Details of the rewards currently available to the members of the Chelmsford scheme are provided.

Different levels of membership are available, with those investing at the highest level becoming members of the 500 Club. After two years of operation, the marketing and development manager of the Chelmsford Star Co-operative Society commissioned research to assess the current state of the scheme. In particular, the manager wanted to find whether those who were members of the 500 Club had different characteristics and spending patterns from those who were more 'limitedly' loyal having joined at a lower membership level.

Results from this research, based on interviews, form the second part of the case study. The study ends at the point where the marketing and development manager has to decide on the future development of the scheme and its wider implications for the co-operative movement.

LEARNING OBJECTIVES AND CORTCO COMPETENCIES

(3)   Organizational ability and creative thinking

Critical thinking and analytical consideration:

■   To develop awareness of the application of smartcard technology in customer loyalty schemes.

Innovation and strategic thinking:
Planning and organization:

■ To demonstrate how innovative technology can be exploited to generate competitive advantage.

(4) Business focus

Customer focus:

■ To provide an insight into how a loyalty scheme can be developed and implemented beyond its initial aim.

Commercialism and business awareness:

■ To give an understanding of the uniqueness and difference of the co-operative retail offering in the retail market where multiple retailers dominate today.

CASE APPLICATIONS AND CONTEXTS

The case has three different strands that are of particular interest to students of retail marketing: customer loyalty schemes, smartcard technology and the co-operative movement. In analysing the data collected for the marketing manager, students will not only be able to develop their analytical and problem-solving skills but also their ability to identify relevant data and draw logical conclusions. Planning skills are needed to develop a future strategy for the Starcard. Students could be encouraged to refer to articles related to the case in order to build up both their wider knowledge of the retail environment in which the co-operative movement operates and the use of information technology in customer loyalty schemes.

Question 1 looks at the future strategy for Starcard in general, this question is designed to get students thinking about the commercial use that can be made of all the data that is or could be collected through a smartcard. This gives the student the opportunity first to decide what data are appropriate to collect, given the capability of the smartcard technology, and second how the data generated by a smartcard loyalty scheme can be used to promote long-term relationships with individual members. Demographics, dates, time, size of spend and items purchased are obvious data, but turning these into a viable promotional planning campaign requires commercial awareness and judgement.

After students have studied the research results they should be encouraged to construct a matrix to show the differences in opinion between the 500 Club members and those who are more 'limitedly' loyal. As the results of the research indicate marked differences among the different tiers of membership, it is important for any strategy to address these differences. It may be useful to build up a profile of a 500 Club member. Points to consider are:

- how to retain existing members,
- how to encourage 'limitedly' loyal members to move up to the 500 Club,
- how to recruit new scheme members,
- whether to introduce additional features such as a newsletter, catalogues, in-store kiosks, tailored discounts and so on.
- whether to encourage other societies to introduce a similar loyalty scheme.

In this, students will need to show commercial awareness of the marketplace in which the co-operative movement operates and consider the impact (for better or for worse) which other multiple retailers' schemes could have on the Chelmsford Star Co-operative Society's business.

Question 2 gives students the opportunity to consider in detail the benefits offered by a smartcard as opposed to a magnetic-stripe card. They should show which features of a smartcard have been utilized by the Starcard scheme. Students should discuss whether the extra costs involved with the introduction of a smartcard system are worth the additional benefits accrued. They may wish to consider whether there are any uses of the smartcard that other retailers have experimented with that have not yet been taken up by the Co-op, for example, the use by dispensing pharmacies to keep details of past prescriptions.

Question 3 facilitates an evaluation of the impact of the long-term history of the co-operative movement on customer perceptions, values and behaviour. The co-operative movement is over a hundred years old and has been in the customer loyalty 'business' a long time. Students may have been unaware of this and believe that customer loyalty schemes are a recent phenomenon. The additional references provided give further background to the co-operative Movement and their dividend schemes.

Students should analyse the data given in the case and use the references to identify the particular features that give rise to strong customer loyalty. They may then wish to consider other major multiple retailers or independent local retailers of whom they have knowledge and make recommendations as to how these retailers could proceed to engender greater loyalty. Longevity, financial soundness, range of offering and mutual trust would be important issues to discuss.

Question 4 allows the students to transfer the knowledge and skills gained to a different retail sector and to practice their planning and organizational skills.

FURTHER READING

Birchall, J. (1994) *Co-op: The People's Business*. Manchester: Manchester University Press.

Blackwell, D. (1998) 'CWS heads back to roots with divi scheme'. *Financial Times*, 2 February.

Preston, C. (1997) 'The smart card as a component in a disseminated retail system'. *Journal of Retailing and Consumer Services*, **4**(1): 36–57.

CASE 21

TEACHING NOTES
'OPERATION RETAIL': MARKETING LOCATIONS TO RETAILERS

GARY WARNABY

SYNOPSIS

This case describes the efforts made by a particular retail location, the city of Nottingham, to market itself proactively to specific types of retail organizations currently perceived as under-represented in the city. Responding to the threat of competing shopping destinations, the city of Nottingham has implemented a number of projects to improve its retail offer, including most recently the development of new promotional initiatives designed to attract more upmarket specialist retailers to the city, in order to further improve the shopping offer.

The case details the Operation Retail initiative, whereby a factpack of general information relevant to retail locational decision makers was produced and disseminated. Operation Retail is currently at a crossroads – the initial activity has apparently been successful; but how is the project to be fully evaluated and taken forward? The case enables students to comprehend the full complexity of place marketing activities and allows them to explore both a retailer and place marketer perspective, in order to understand the relationship between the two.

LEARNING OBJECTIVES AND CORTCO COMPETENCIES

(3)   Organizational ability and creative thinking

Critical thinking and analytical consideration:

- To identify types and sources of information used in retail location decision making.
- To critically evaluate the utility of this information to the place marketer and retailer.
- To identify measures by which retailers can be attracted to a specific place.

Planning and organizing:
Forward planning:

- To assess the relative importance of the different types of information in benchmarking and in planning locational marketing decisions.

■ To assess the relative importance of the various elements of the marketing mix for a place product.

■ To ensure information is identified and evaluated in an appropriate timescale.

■ To develop an action plan for completing the task.

(4)   Business focus

Customer focus:
Commercialism and business awareness:

■ To identify evaluative criteria for the Operation Retail initiative.

CASE APPLICATIONS AND CONTEXTS

This case can be used in two separate, yet complementary, ways:

1. To consider the decision-making processes involved in retail location planning.
2. To investigate the utility of the approach taken by the Operation Retail initiative in proactively marketing a destination as a shopping venue worthy of consideration for retail inward investors.

The case, therefore, addresses issues of retail location from the perspectives of both the retailer and the shopping venue. Accommodating both perspectives is crucial if an effective retail offer is to be presented to consumers within a locality.

Thus, the rationale behind the Operation Retail initiative begins to be revealed. The Operation Retail steering group identified a perceived weakness in the shopping offer of the city of Nottingham – namely a lack of upmarket specialist shops – and have taken measures to address this deficiency through the development of promotional materials aimed at such retailers. From the perspective of a potential retail inward investor, such a proactive approach may influence the locational decision-making process in terms of identifying a potential location that may not have been considered, or streamlining the process of gathering information regarding the location, thus facilitating the location decision.

Thus, in using the case for class discussion the students could be split into two groups and charged with the case tasks from the contrasting perspectives of retailer and place marketer. These roles reflect the reality of many retail managers' lives. Location issues will obviously be the province of retail managers at all levels working in location or site assessment departments of multiple retail businesses. However, it is also conceivable that retail managers will also have experience of such issues from the perspective of the place marketer, given the fact that many steering groups (such as that for Operation Retail) have representatives from retail companies within the locality. In addition, secondees from retail organizations are common in economic development/inward investment organizations and also in town centre management schemes.

Some issues relating to these perspectives are addressed below.

Retailer perspective

Location decisions have to be made within a wider strategic context. Ghosh (1994) emphasizes the importance for retail firms to have a 'locational policy':

> It translates the firm's marketing strategy into a concrete policy that is sensitive to the spatial pattern of demand and the availability of desirable sites, and targets the firm's investments towards specific locations and market areas. (1994: 249)

Jones and Simmons (1990) identify a 'hierarchy' of retail location decision structures which places specific locational analysis into a strategic context, stating that in contrast to corporate and marketing strategy, location strategy deals with decisions relating to the number of outlets, threshold market, market profile and location criteria. With specific reference to this case, students could be directed towards developing a checklist of factors which would inform the decision as to whether or not to locate in Nottingham. (Most general retail texts describe the main locational decision-making techniques in outline terms, for example McGoldrick, 1990; Ghosh, 1994.)

Place marketer perspective

Cities and towns exist in an increasingly competitive environment, and, as a result, have had to become more entrepreneurial in their outlook, and the application of marketing concepts and techniques to urban places is a manifestation of this (see Gold and Ward, 1994, for more detail). Ashworth and Voogd (1990, p. 8) define city marketing as:

> a process whereby urban activities are as closely as possible related to the demands of targeted customers so as to maximize efficient social and economic functioning of the area concerned in accordance with whatever goals have been established.

The role of retailing in such activity is often neglected, if not totally ignored by many economic development agencies (who are often charged with responsibility for the marketing of urban places). This arguably underestimates the importance of retailing to many urban economies. Thus, as part of a class discussion on the case the role of retail as a motivating influence for visiting specific urban centres, and its interactions with other elements of the urban place product can be discussed.

There are obviously a number of specific factors that could be used in combination to enhance the attractiveness of an urban place product. Ashworth and Voogd (1990) describe the concept of a 'geographical marketing mix' comprising a combination of at least the following sets of instruments:

1. *Spatial-functional measures*
   Considers the interaction of land uses in the urban area (for example cultural and leisure venues and activities, the historical character of the urban place and so on) and its effect on perceptions of the city as a whole and, more specifically the quality of the retail provision therein (for more details see Jansen-Verbeke, 1986; Warnaby and Davies, 1997).

2. *Promotional measures*
   Considers the methods used to promote the urban place and the main messages projected, with particular reference to the economic advantages inherent in a specific location and the quality of life within that location.

3. *Organizational measures*
   Considers responsibility for the promotion of an urban place, which may be fragmented across many different agencies from both the public and private sectors, each agency possibly having a different remit and a different jurisdictional area.

4. *Financial measures*
   The financial aspects of place marketing cannot be ignored as the resources allocated to this activity are often very limited and may be drawn from a variety of sources. The financial feasibility of place marketing measures must be constantly monitored.

Consideration needs to be given to all these dimensions of the geographical marketing mix if an appropriate perception of the vitality and viability of a city centre in retailing terms is to be achieved. Indeed, many retailers will only locate in those towns and cities that they perceive to have a bright future. The adoption of an effective marketing orientation by urban places will help to ensure the co-ordination of activities among all public and private sector stakeholders within the urban area in order to optimize its attractiveness to retailers, and indeed, any other inward investors.

In terms of specifically promoting an urban place as a shopping destination a number of issues can be raised (see Warnaby, 1998, for more detail). More specific measures could be developed to attract retailers, perhaps in terms of favourable leasing terms and/or other start-up help for embryonic specialist retailers. Also, the dynamics of the relationships between the various urban stakeholders, particularly in terms of potentially conflicting objectives, may need to be addressed. For example, efforts to promote the attractiveness of an urban place to potential retail inward investors may be resented by existing retailers who may face increased competition as a result of competitors opening new outlets in the vicinity. Likewise, some multiple retailers may not want to 'push' a particular urban place for fear of cannibalizing sales from their stores in neighbouring shopping destinations. The question of the interests and objectives of each of the main stakeholders in terms of their complementarity and in terms of their potential for conflict is an area that could be explored in more detail.

REFERENCES

Ashworth, G. J. and Voogd, H. (1990) *Selling The City*. London: Belhaven.

Ghosh, A. (1994) *Retail Management* (2nd edn). Fort Worth: The Dryden Press.

Gold, J. R. and Ward, S. V. (1994) *Place Promotion: The Use of Publicity and Marketing to Sell Towns and Regions*. Chichester: John Wiley & Sons.

Jansen-Verbeke, M. (1986) 'Inner-city tourism: Resources, tourists and promoters'. *Annals of Tourism Research*, **13**, 79–100.

Jones, K. and Simmons, J. (1990) *The Retail Environment*. London: Routledge.

McGoldrick, P. J. (1990) *Retail Marketing*. London: McGraw-Hill.

Warnaby, G. (1998) 'Marketing UK cities as shopping destinations: problems and prospects'. *Journal of Retailing and Consumer Services*, **5**(1): 55–8.

Warnaby, G. and Davies, B. J. (1997) 'Cities as service factories?: Using the servuction system for marketing cities as shopping destinations'. *The International Journal of Retail and Distribution Management*, **25**(6): 204–10.

APPENDIX
CORTCO COMPETENCIES, 1998

(1) PERSONAL EFFECTIVENESS

Personal presence: having a positive impact
Setting high standards for your own work and expecting to succeed through tenacity, drive and commitment.

Emotional resilience: bouncing back quickly from setbacks
Learning from experience including mistakes, is prepared to be proactive, coping under pressure.

Assertiveness: acting and communicating with others in a confident manner
Expressing opinions, which are influenced by personal convictions, and defending them when challenged. Demonstrating independence.

Self-confidence: having belief in one's own ability and judgement
Behaving in an open and honest way, a self-starter, who is able to admit to mistakes, take as well as give criticism and actively influence events.

Task management: completes tasks in the most effective and efficient way
Getting the job done is important. Does not give up easily, tries to solve problems rather than postpone them and recognizes the importance of deadlines and timescales.

Flexibility/adaptability: responds promptly and effectively to changes
Coping with planned or unexpected change and developments, modifying behaviour if necessary in order to achieve a goal.

Self-development: seeks to improve own performance
Takes responsibility for own performance, reviewing experiences and seeking new activities to learn from. Positively encourages feedback.

(2) MANAGING PEOPLE AND WORKING WITH OTHERS (INTERPERSONAL SKILLS AND PEOPLE MANAGEMENT)

Team working and awareness: willing and able to participate as a full member of the team
Encouraging contributions, actively listening to others, and participating even when the subject or task will not deliver personal gain. Taking actions that indi-

cate, recognition of one's own impact, and take account of the feelings and needs of others in order to build a working relationship.

Team leading: *showing the ability to guide, direct and motivate individuals or groups to task accomplishment*
Offering support; taking ownership quickly; prepared to accept responsibility on issues and be judged on them, not 'passing the buck'. Shaping the outcome of the group's output

Communication skills*: adopting an appropriate style, tone and language to inform and influence*
Delivering all communication clearly and accurately with an appreciation of the need to always check the receiver's understanding. An awareness of the range of skills and techniques involved with both written and spoken communication, including non-verbal indicators.

Managing and coaching for performance*: demonstrating the ability to improve the skills and performance of others*
Giving and finding opportunities for others to develop. Explaining clearly the objectives which are being set, checking that what is required and why are appreciated. Delegating, giving feedback and support, mentoring and managing expectations are important elements.

(3) ORGANIZATIONAL ABILITY AND CREATIVE THINKING

Planning and organizing*: establishing a course of action for oneself and/or others to accomplish a specific goal*
Involving both the short and long term; requires an ability to prioritize; the monitoring of progress and benchmarking to check progress. Reviewing the completed task to gain insights for next planning cycle.

Forward planning*: developing clear and logical step-by-step plans for self and others*
Setting out what needs to happen, how and when, and with what.

Critical thinking and analytical consideration*: knowing the problem, getting facts/data before applying judgement*
Gathering relevant information, identifying issues, sifting and sorting complex information, effectively analysing data and situations; and then applying logic to draw conclusions and solve the problem.

Decisiveness*: readiness to make decisions, act or commit oneself*

Innovation and strategic thinking*: is enquiring and has the ability to grasp new concepts quickly*
Demonstrating an ability to think laterally and 'outside the box', producing innovative and creative solutions.

(4) **BUSINESS FOCUS (attributes possessed by successful retail managers)**

Customer focus: understanding and anticipating the needs of the customer
Seeking to encourage customer loyalty, an awareness of customer trends.

Commercialism and business awareness: understands the retail business environment
Seeing how new events and situations will affect the organization, understanding the nature and effects of competition and what is important to the bottom line.

Job motivation: enjoys and is motivated by the buzz of retail
Retail/managerial activities and responsibilities provide and maintain interest and deliver job satisfaction.

INDEX

Retailers and other firms are shown in *italic*